W9-BBH-341

ALSO BY ALEXANDER STILLE

Benevolence and Betrayal:
Five Italian Jewish Families Under Fascism

Excellent Cadavers:
The Mafia and the Death of the First Italian Republic

The Future of the Past

The Sack of Rome:
How a Beautiful European Country with a Fabled History and
a Storied Culture Was Taken Over by a Man Named Silvio Berlusconi

The Force of Things:
A Marriage in War and Peace

THE SULLIVANIANS

The Sullivanians

SEX,
PSYCHOTHERAPY,
AND
THE WILD LIFE OF AN
AMERICAN COMMUNE

ALEXANDER STILLE

Farrar, Straus and Giroux
New York

The Westport Library
Westport, Connecticut
203-291-4840

Farrar, Straus and Giroux
120 Broadway, New York 10271

Copyright © 2023 by Alexander Stille
All rights reserved
Printed in the United States of America
First edition, 2023

Title-page and part-opener background by Shutterstock / AnzhelikaP.

Library of Congress Control Number: 2023007080
ISBN: 978-0-374-60039-6

Designed by Patrice Sheridan

Our books may be purchased in bulk for promotional, educational, or business use. Please contact your local bookseller or the Macmillan Corporate and Premium Sales Department at 1-800-221-7945, extension 5442, or by email at MacmillanSpecialMarkets@macmillan.com.

www.fsgbooks.com
www.twitter.com/fsgbooks · www.facebook.com/fsgbooks

1 3 5 7 9 10 8 6 4 2

34015073026823

For Erika

Contents

Author's Note

In researching this book, I interviewed more than sixty former patients of the Sullivan Institute and their family members. My interview subjects were exceptionally kind, generous, and open in sharing with me some of the most personal, delicate, and sometimes painful chapters of their lives. Many of them agreed to be interviewed "on the record," identifying themselves with their first and last names. Others had varying concerns about maintaining their privacy, and as a result, it was important to be flexible in the way I identified them. Some agreed to let me use their first name and the first initial of their last name. Others preferred that I use their initials. In a few instances I agreed to change people's names. All these interviews were recorded and transcribed to guarantee their accuracy.

I was also able to make use of the voluminous documentation generated by a series of lawsuits that involved members of the group. These included depositions of individual members, letters, financial information, pretrial interviews, and court testimony as well as promotional material of the Fourth Wall Repertory Company, the political theater the group operated from 1975 until 1991. Individual members were kind enough to share some of their personal papers, diaries, membership lists, and correspondence between their friends in the group.

There is no universally accepted term for the group that grew out of the Sullivan Institute. People who were patients in the 1950s and

'60s often use the term "Sullivanian" to refer to their therapists, themselves, their fellow patients, and the life they led together. After the group formed the Fourth Wall Repertory Company in 1975, patients of this later period, particularly those who stayed to the end, often refer to themselves as having been in the Fourth Wall—preferring to identify with the political theater rather than with their therapy. Although the main characters of this book joined in the late 1960s or early '70s—spanning both periods—I have decided to use the term "Sullivanian" because therapy at the Sullivan Institute was the common thread that ties together the experience of all the group's phases.

THE SULLIVANIANS

1

A Parallel World

Chris Pearce grew up in the loud silence of his own mysterious origins. Born in 1974, he lived in a handsome five-story town house on West Seventy-Seventh Street in New York, raised by Jane Pearce, an older woman already in her sixties when he was an infant. She had white hair and, after a bout with skin cancer, was missing part of her nose. He knew that Jane was not his biological mother, but no one explained how he had ended up with her or who his birth parents were.

Playing alone in his upstairs room, he filled the silence and his lack of knowledge with his own imagination. "Ever since I was little, I believed . . . I was raised by wolves, born from the earth, from the mist or the foam of the ocean like the Greek gods," he later wrote in an animated film he made about his childhood.

In his teens, he learned that Jane was a well-known psychiatrist and cofounder of something called the Sullivan Institute for Research in Psychoanalysis and that the town house where he lived had been the institute's headquarters for many years. In 1963, more than a decade before his birth, she and her then husband, Saul Newton, had published a book called *The Conditions of Human Growth* and had pioneered a maverick form of psychotherapy. Pearce and Newton believed that the nuclear family caused most psychological problems and that mothers inevitably squelched their children's vitality. They founded a community of a few hundred people on the Upper West Side of Manhattan in which their patients lived together in large group apartments.

Jane had been a student of Harry Stack Sullivan, one of the pioneers of American neo-Freudian psychoanalysis, although Sullivan was no longer alive when she founded the institute in his name. Sullivan believed that people grew from their relationships with others—even in adulthood—and he treated people with schizophrenia by having them live together in a group setting. Jane Pearce took these ideas much further. She and Newton encouraged their patients to live in same-sex group apartments and to have multiple sexual partners so that they would continue to grow and not form and stagnate in stable couples and traditional families. Even patients who were married would live in separate apartments so that they would not remain trapped in exclusive relationships. The community she created was known in New York psychoanalytic circles as the Sullivanians, notorious for their unorthodox approach to analysis and the distinctive lifestyle that grew out of it. Along with believing that traditional families were bad for children, they also believed that a child's biological inheritance was unimportant and that environment was everything. And so they encouraged patients to entrust the care of their children to babysitters, boarding schools, or other adults in the community. Chris eventually learned that his birth mother—one of Newton's patients who had felt (or had been deemed) incapable of raising him—had agreed to hand him over to Jane. "This made me feel like I was an experimental subject raised by the core theorist of the group," he said, wondering whether people never spoke about his origins because it might throw off the experiment as they watched to see how he would turn out. But the silence left him, as he put it, "a man without a story."

Until he was about five, Chris went every day to play in a big house on West Ninety-First Street, where Newton, who had by then divorced Jane Pearce, lived with his new family and about twenty other people in a building that also served as the new headquarters of the Sullivan Institute. Unlike the rest of the members, the leaders were allowed to live with their spouses and children, albeit communally and polygamously. The building was a former school building that had been converted into a multifamily residence, with offices on the ground floor for the therapists. Chris recalls the house as a kind of magical children's playground. Three or four families lived there, including at least a dozen children, with babysitters, dogs, cats, hamsters, and sometimes even a chicken. The families occupied separate floors, but there were no locks or doors separating them, and the children and pets raced upstairs and down in search of playmates and new games to play. There were clusters of kids around the same age, and Chris was part of a little band of four or five boys who were as close to one another as brothers. To him it seemed like a utopia for children. He would realize much later that it was in fact designed that way. Along with Newton, his adoptive mother had stressed the importance of "chumship"—children developing close bonds with other children. Their book stressed that children needed to be free from the overweening presence of their parents and that they needed other adults in their lives who could be their "alternate validators." Sullivanian children spent more time with and were usually closer to their babysitters than to their parents. At the same time, Jane Pearce was a caring parental presence in Chris's life; they generally saw each other every evening at dinnertime.

Then something happened. One day Chris was told that he would no longer be going to the house on Ninety-First Street. Overnight, he would no longer see the friends he had come to regard as siblings. He didn't know what had forced such a radical change in his life, and no explanation was offered. It was for him a paradise lost, his banishment as mysterious as his own origin. "It was absolutely traumatic," he said. "I lost all of my best friends, my whole family."

As best as he can recollect, at Christmastime in 1979, a group of Sullivanian patients arrived at Jane Pearce's town house and rang the bell loudly, carrying gifts for him. But Jane Pearce didn't open the door—she was afraid, Chris believes, that they were there to take him away. When they wouldn't leave and kept ringing the bell, she called the police. One of his memories of Christmas 1979 was of two police officers bringing an armful of gifts into the house.

Evidently something had gone wrong with the experiment, but no one explained to Chris what had happened. It would be many years before he learned the actual story of his origins and saw that it was intimately connected with many other stories in a much larger psychological experiment that stretched back many years.

*   *   *

Forty years later, in 2019, Michael Cohen—a sixty-nine-year-old psychologist in Brooklyn—got a phone call from a woman he hadn't heard from in decades. They had both been therapists at the Sullivan Institute, though Cohen had left the group in 1985, a departure that was seen by those who stayed behind as a major betrayal, and so the two had lost touch. Now the woman needed his help: her two children, both adults in their thirties, were desperate to find out who their biological father was, and Cohen was a possible candidate.

The Sullivan Institute had encouraged women who wanted to have children to involve several men in the process of getting pregnant— part of the strategy to prevent people from forming stable, monogamous couples and nuclear families, as no one would know who the father was. Many Sullivanian children were conceived and raised collectively and taught that their genetic inheritance was of no importance. But now that they were adults—and there were inexpensive DNA tests available—many of them wanted to solve the mystery of their paternity as a way of coming to terms with a complicated past.

All this was deeply confusing and difficult for Mike Cohen and his family. He had spent much of the previous thirty-four years putting that chapter of his life behind him. At the same time, like almost all former Sullivanians, it remained a central part of his life. His wife, Amy Siskind, was also a former group member—twice over—having grown up as the child of a Sullivanian patient in the 1960s, as well as being a child patient herself and then becoming a patient again as an adult in the 1970s and '80s. Mike and Amy had left the group because they wanted to marry and have a family together—something their therapists tried to prevent. Amy had then written a Ph.D. dissertation about the group, which was published as a book.

Despite all they knew and had experienced of life in the group, it had frankly never occurred to either of them that some of the kids running around the Sullivanian apartments all those decades earlier might be Cohen's. It was distressing to their grown daughter, who was not keen to learn whether she had older siblings somewhere. But Cohen felt that as a matter of decency, he should consent to provide a DNA sample.

What was happening with Cohen was happening throughout the Sullivanian community. Dozens of kids who were born in the group banded together to share their genetic data in order to solve the puzzle of their parentage. They were forcing their parents into frank conversations about the past that they had been avoiding for many years. Many former members had not even told their children that they'd been part of a polygamous group. Some children who grew up without a father now found one, as well as an extended family. Others made the disconcerting discovery that the person they considered their father was not in fact their biological parent and that some relative stranger was. When all the tests were in, it was as if the threads of a complex tapestry were tied together completing the story begun by Pearce and Newton long ago. The flurry of DNA revelations and the search for missing relations carried out by the children of the Sullivan Institute provided a strange and ironic ending to the story of a group that had set out to dismantle the nuclear family.

For the Sullivanian children, the genetic search was part of a deeper attempt to make sense of their lives and to figure out what their parents were doing and thinking back in the 1970s. "I think for me it's been about, first of all, try and understand what the hell that was. You know, what is that thing I was raised in?" says Pam Newton, one of the ten children of the movement's cofounder, Saul Newton.

It was also a moment of reckoning for one of the most radical social experiments of our times: a thirty-five-year attempt to reengineer family, sexual, and social life in what may have been the largest urban commune in the United States.

*　　*　　*

I learned about the Sullivan Institute by chance in the 2010s and was stunned to realize that, although I had been living on the Upper West Side for decades, I was entirely unaware of what was, in effect, an alternate society in our midst, hidden in plain sight.

The group, which operated from the mid-1950s until it dissolved in 1991, was extremely secretive during its life and remained so for many years. But as its former members have reached their sixties and seventies, they have begun to speak more openly about their experiences. As a result, it is now possible to put together a narrative history of this little-known and singular chapter of the American counterculture.

They created a parallel world, living by precise rules and precepts almost entirely at odds with those of mainstream society. Under the direction of their therapists, the Sullivanians were trying to create a utopian world based on the principles of free love, collective living, self-actualization, and a commitment to socialism. In one sense, the group partook of the counterculture of the 1960s, the decade of sexual liberation and communal living. Yet most of the era's communes—an estimated three thousand in the 1960s and '70s—lived in isolation in such places as rural Oregon and Vermont. This group was composed almost entirely of high-performing urban professionals—doctors, lawyers, computer programmers, successful artists and writers, professors—who went to normal jobs by day but returned in the evening to a very different and highly secretive world built around fellowship, polygamous sex, radical politics, and political theater.

A key event in the group's demise occurred four blocks from where I was living in 1986. A member of the group had kidnapped her own child in front of the building on West 100th Street where she lived at the time. She had been in Sullivanian therapy for fifteen years, and when she had finally had a child, the senior therapists of the group had prevented her from seeing her infant daughter for several months. After consulting a lawyer, she hired two bodyguards, took the child, and went into hiding. This was the first of several legal battles that helped lead to the group's dissolution in 1991. How could all this have happened in my own neighborhood without my having any idea?

The Sullivan Institute came into being during the 1950s, when the idea of traditional marriage and family was at the height of its power and authority in American life—the decade of *The Adventures of Ozzie and Harriet* (1952–66) and *Father Knows Best* (1954–60). Being settled in a well-adjusted, monogamous marriage was the goal of most psychoanalysis, the gold standard of mental health. At the same time, under the surface, various forms of dissatisfaction and rebellion were rumbling, as evidenced in such works as the James Dean film *Rebel Without a Cause* (1955), Allen Ginsberg's *Howl* (1956), and Jack Kerouac's *On the Road* (1957). The Kinsey Reports (1948 and 1953) revealed that Americans' sex lives were far messier and more complicated than the conventional model everyone paid lip service to. People yearned for more, but society condemned them for it. Betty Friedan's *Feminine Mystique* (published in 1963, the same year as Jane Pearce and Saul Newton's *Conditions of Human Growth*) revealed the intense dissatisfaction of women straitjacketed by the life of wife and mother.

Why should therapy simply try to help patients "adjust" to what was essentially a bad deal? What if therapy could expand people's lives, open their opportunities for growth, and free them from the crushing weight of conformity and societal expectations? The family seemed, to some, like the primary instrument with which society forced a deadening conformity on its members.

Jane Pearce and Saul Newton believed that the family had trained children to suppress their own deepest desires, their spontaneity, and their need for warmth and empathy. Children were trapped under the weight of expectations of parents who pushed them to conform and felt threatened by any attempt on the part of the child to break free and act on their instincts and desires. Pearce and Newton were not the only maverick therapists to feel this way. R. D. Laing, David Cooper, and Paul Goodman came to similar conclusions in the same period. "The child, in fact, is taught primarily not how to survive in society, but how to submit to it," Cooper wrote in his book *The Death of the Family* (1971).

"From the moment of birth," Laing wrote in *The Politics of Experience* (1967), "the baby is subjected to these forces of violence, called love, as its mother and father have been, and their parents and their parents before them. These forces are mainly concerned with destroying most of its potentialities. This enterprise is on the whole successful."

What if therapy taught people to trust and follow their own deepest desires and instincts rather than suppress them in order to adapt to the expectations of parents and society? Pearce and Newton—and like-minded radicals—believed that the "underground" of instinctual life remained alive but buried inside people, and that the therapist could be the ally of the "guerrilla fighter" that lived within each of us, yearning for real growth and real experience. Political radicals—who viewed with sympathy guerrilla movements and revolutions in such places as Cuba and China—believed that individual liberation was essential to social justice. "Successful analysis involves becoming accustomed to revolution," they wrote.

The Sullivan Institute was founded in 1957, the year that the birth control pill was submitted to the Food and Drug Administration for approval. And, in a sense, the life of the group spanned and was a cultural expression of the window of time between the introduction of the pill and the AIDS crisis of the 1980s, a brief slice of history during which it seemed possible to rethink sex, love, marriage, intimacy, and family—institutions that had been, until then, limited by biology and procreation, along with the possessive ethos of monogamy designed to guarantee a father's paternity. This seemed an opportunity to rearrange human relations, to go beyond the limiting nuclear family, and to create a larger community with a different set of values built around the ideals of fellowship, political commitment, and sex without guilt, jealousy, or possessiveness.

Sexual revolution was central to the idea of achieving a fuller, more authentic, and spontaneous emotional life. "Making love is good in itself, and the more it happens in any way possible or conceivable between as many people as possible, the better," Cooper wrote in *The Death of the Family*. But it wasn't just about sex. Cooper also advocated for the development of communal arrangements that broke down the walls of the family prison house. "Children should have totally free access to adults beyond their biological parental couple," he wrote.

While therapists like Cooper and Laing described the family as a kind of trap for shackling our desires and creative potential, Jane Pearce and Saul Newton actually tried to carry out their radical program of getting rid of the family on a large scale. They tried it—to an extent—in their own lives and on their own families as well as in those of their patients, creating a community of several hundred people whom they encouraged or pushed to rigorously carry out their program. Members of the group were strictly forbidden (even if legally married) from having exclusive sexual relationships. Even if not having sex, therapists encouraged them to sleep with other group members— whether of the same or the other sex—in order to create bonding and fellowship. They were forbidden from spending too much time with their own children—that is, if their therapists allowed them to have children.

It is not coincidental that the Sullivanian experiment began in an era when psychoanalysis was at the height of its prestige. Psychologists felt emboldened to try out their theories in ways that would never pass muster today with any academic ethics board. The Robbers Cave experiment (1954) pitted groups of boys into opposing camps that resulted in a kind of *Lord of the Flies* degree of group hostility. Stanley Milgram's famous obedience experiments (1963) encouraged participants to inflict pain on others—to see how far they would go in obeying authority. In the Stanford Prison Experiment (1971), a psychology professor created a simulated prison in which students were asked to be either prisoners or guards, leading to disturbing levels of cruel and sadistic behavior. These experiments lasted a short time, but their meaning and value—as well as the potential harm they caused—are still widely debated.

The Sullivan Institute was an enormous natural experiment to test a specific idea of human nature: that nature was nothing and nurture was everything. It was carried out on several hundred—perhaps even a few thousand—people over a thirty-five-year period. Yet, ironically, the group was finally done in by the thing it had set out to destroy: the family. Couples who were tired of being kept apart and parents who rebelled against being separated from their children eventually caused the group's disintegration. "They thought biology was nothing," said one child who grew up in the Sullivanian community, was allowed to see her mother only one day a week, and was kept in the dark about her biological father. "Well, it's not everything, but it's not nothing."

During its different phases the Sullivan Institute encapsulated many of the major themes—and pitfalls—of twentieth-century counterculture.

In its first ten or fifteen years, this novel form of treatment, which encouraged patients to experiment sexually, trust their impulses, and break free of family dependency relationships, appealed to many artists and creative individuals. The famous art critic Clement Greenberg was an early patient, as was the artist Jackson Pollock, both of whom entered Sullivanian therapy two years before the formal creation of the institute. A Who's Who of abstract expressionists followed, as did a host of other exceptionally creative people, including the dancer and choreographer Lucinda Childs (who became famous for her choreography of *Einstein on the Beach*, which premiered in 1976), the novelists Richard Elman and Richard Price, and two members of the music group Sha Na Na, and many others. There were lots of patients who were not famous artists: men trapped in dull jobs or suffering from loneliness; frustrated wives, whose therapists encouraged them to leave their husbands, have affairs, and hand over the care of their children to others so that they could explore their own creative potential.

In the 1960s, Pearce and Newton began to give therapeutic application to Sullivan's belief in the importance of same-sex friendships, encouraging their patients to live together in single-sex apartments. This approach fit a zeitgeist in which communal living and sexual freedom thrived. Gradually, a Sullivanian community emerged that became increasingly codified: patients had datebooks that they filled up with appointments, not just for sexual encounters but also for study dates, friendship dates, men's and women's groups, painting classes, writing groups, dates to play music together. Along with having multiple sexual partners, patients were encouraged to have "sleepover" dates, often with same-sex friends, to get closer to one another. Every weekend there were Sullivanian parties, which invariably ended with everyone pairing off and going to bed with someone else. To do otherwise was seen as a refusal to grow. In the summertime they all rented shares in houses out in Amagansett on Long Island, near where the lead therapists owned houses.

When Richard Price, as a young graduate student working on his first novel, stumbled onto this community, welcomed by women happy to sleep with him and men eager to become his friends, he felt as if he had been admitted to a kind of elite secret society that had devised a superior way of life. "It was like instant community, instant sex. It felt like somebody had opened the gates of heaven," he said.

But with time, life in the group became increasingly regimented and controlled. What began as a loose community of like-minded souls morphed into a more formal group with the creation of a political theater company—the Fourth Wall Repertory Company, which put on plays and performed music in a large theater they acquired in the East Village. There were monthly dues and membership lists, and members—all Sullivanian patients—were expected to work a certain number of hours each week. Jane Pearce, the chief theorist and cofounder of the Sullivan Institute, was forced out, her place taken by two younger and more attractive women in Saul Newton's life who became his fifth and sixth wives as well as lead supervising therapists for the institute. As the years passed, Newton created a personality cult around himself and adopted an increasingly autocratic leadership style.

A group led by self-described communists with egalitarian ideas ended up becoming extremely hierarchical, with the leadership enjoying rights they denied to other members of the group. A number of former members cited George Orwell's *Animal Farm*, in which the original proposition "All animals are equal" is later modified to add "but some animals are more equal than others." In that sense, the story of the Sullivan Institute encapsulates one of the great themes of the twentieth century: the tendency of utopian projects of social liberation to take a totalitarian turn.

In the 1970s, the group took on aspects that most people would associate with cults. This was the decade of cults of alternative therapies. Indian gurus such as Bhagwan Shree Rajneesh and the Maharishi Mahesh Yogi gained an international following and established communities in the United States. Werner Erhard founded EST in 1971, combining elements of Zen Buddhism with self-help precepts straight out of Dale Carnegie. Arthur Janov developed "primal scream" therapy, in which patients were encouraged to dig up their deepest traumas by screaming their lungs out.

The AIDS epidemic of the 1980s created a challenge for a group practicing polygamous sexual experimentation—as well as an opportunity for leaders to exercise stricter control. Members were no longer allowed to have sex with people outside the group. Although some AIDS restrictions were quite reasonable—no sex without condoms—others, such as no eating in restaurants or no eating food not prepared by another group member, seemed designed more to isolate the membership from the outside world and increase leaders' power over their members.

The Sullivanian community is interesting to consider in light of the #MeToo movement, adding a chapter to the history of sexual abuse. Some women enjoyed—even celebrated—being encouraged to take the initiative in sex, but others felt pressured by their therapists to have sex with people they weren't attracted to. "Shut your mouth and open your legs," one therapist told a female patient, insisting that she stop "withholding" her emotions. Their stories expose the vein of misogyny that was prevalent on the countercultural left of the 1960s and '70s, in which there was often a presumption that a woman refusing sex was repressed and bourgeois. On top of this, psychotherapy, like Hollywood and academe, was rich terrain for the abuse of power. The

Sullivan Institute was started when the boundaries between therapist and patients were routinely crossed. The American Psychiatric Association did not categorically forbid sex with patients until 1973. Some Sullivanian analysts slept with their patients or with former patients, and all of them had sex with other patients of the institute for whom they were figures of great authority. Saul Newton frequently demanded that his female patients perform oral sex on him during their sessions and then expected them to pay him for his time.

The story of the Sullivan Institute is also a story about the power of groups, the degree to which people will do things in groups that they would almost certainly not do outside them. Many former members—almost universally people on the political left—said that they experienced the rise of more recent authoritarian movements, from Putin's Russia to Trump's America, quite differently than many of their fellow citizens, knowing that they themselves were held in the thrall of a leader with strong authoritarian tendencies.

Many of the former members remain in close touch with one another and have a wider and more tightly knit community of good friends than most Americans. "How many cults have reunions?" said Eric Grunin, one of the most enthusiastic defenders of the group and its unofficial archivist. At the same time, other former members consider it the most traumatic experience of their lives, choosing to have little or nothing to do with other former members.

Some former Sullivanians continue to feel that they participated in a noble if failed utopian experiment. "You can find many other cases in history where a group of people have said, 'Why can't we be like Adam and Eve before the Fall?'" Grunin said. The first known example of a prelapsarian group was an early Christian sect known as the Adamites, which began in the second century A.D.; its members performed their religious rituals in the nude and called their church Paradise, like the Garden of Eden before the Fall. "We didn't do anything like that, but the idea that you can reboot your culture from scratch is very appealing," Grunin added. The Oneida Community in upstate New York in the mid-nineteenth century was closer to the Sullivanians: they lived communally and practiced what they called "complex marriage," meaning that couples were not allowed to maintain exclusive, monogamous ties. "I guess the thing which made us stand out to people was that we renounced blood as the primal tie," Grunin said.

If anything, Grunin feels, the group was simply ahead of its time. The recent resurgence of interest in polyamory, plural marriage, socialism, and alternative family arrangements shows that the Fourth Wall was onto something. Those who were active in the group during the 1980s generally prefer to think of themselves as members of the political theater rather than as patients of the Sullivan Institute— although they were both.

The group went beyond polyamory or "complex marriage." Many ex-members use the term "group marriage" when talking about their time in the Fourth Wall. "I was, in effect, married to 250 people," one of them explained.

Others were also drawn to the group's politics. "It was an attempt to put the human into Marx," said Michael Cohen. Looking back, he feels that the group tried to address very real issues—the absence of community, the need for belonging, the desire for sexual freedom and more authentic relationships, the failings of capitalism—but ended up constructing an increasingly regimented, totalitarian world. "We asked all the right questions and got all the wrong answers," he said. "But the questions were legitimate, and we're still asking them."

PART I

PRECURSORS

2

Origins

We live in a dangerous world.

—Jane Pearce and Saul Newton,
The Conditions of Human Growth

Saul Newton was in many ways a classic American type: a self-invented figure whose shadowy biography is a blend of myth and fact, a kind of Jay Gatsby of psychotherapy. In keeping with the tradition of personal self-fashioning, he was not, in fact, an American, nor was his name really Newton. He was born in 1906 in New Brunswick, Canada, with the name Saul Bernard Cohen. His parents were Russian Jewish immigrants. His father, Samuel Cohen, was originally named Aronoff, but American immigration officials changed his name when he arrived in New York before settling in Canada. Saul was a thin, wiry young man with dark, soulful eyes, but he projected an air of toughness and aggression. His childhood nickname was supposedly Jack Johnson, after the famous Black heavyweight champion. He learned boxing from his older brother George, who was an amateur fighter; Saul purportedly served as his sparring partner. "I never backed away from a belligerent situation," Saul said in an unfinished memoir that he dictated toward the end of his life. The threat of violence and a willingness to act on that threat were a central part of Saul Newton's persona.

Reading his account of his early life, it is not hard to see in it the origins of and justification for the central tenet of his therapeutic philosophy: the total repudiation of family. His Russian grandfather, a Hasidic rabbi, stunted his mother's personal growth by forcing her to quit school and work as a seamstress. "She hated [her father] all her life for this evil deed," Saul wrote. Emigrating to Canada, she spoke imperfect, Yiddish-accented English but insisted on filling the house with books in English that she would never be able to read. The books were partly for show—to appear cultured before her friends, Saul said—but she also asked her children to read aloud from them, which may have only deepened her sense of regret about her limited education. "A frequent phrase out of her mouth during my growing up was 'If I only knew how to read and write English, what I couldn't do!'" Saul recounted.

Despite (or because of) her anger over being prevented from pursuing her education, Saul's mother turned around and inflicted the same punishment on her own child, forcing her eldest son, George, to quit school after eighth grade and go to work, even though the family was prosperous at that point. "She visited the same fate on her children, in Saul's view because of her bitterness about her own lack of education," Esther Newton, Saul's stepdaughter, whom he legally adopted, wrote in an essay to which she gave the pugilistic title "A Hard Left Fist."

In Saul's case, he insisted, his mother went further, trying to kill him. When he cut his finger as a child, she put his bleeding finger into a bowl of flour, and Saul was convinced that this could have given him blood poisoning. In fact, flour is a common home remedy for stopping a cut from bleeding and is used to this day without known ill effect. At another point he blamed her for an accident in which she appears to have played no part. "When as a small child," Esther Newton wrote, "he sneaks away from the house and hops on a raft and almost drowns, he blames his mother, sure that she wants him dead. What an egotist he was! His mother was always, he imagined, thinking about him."

Saul's imputation of homicidal motives to parents would become a standard feature of Sullivanian therapy: therapists would always see dark, violent, and murderous intent behind their patients' parents' seemingly innocuous actions.

In Saul's account, his family story is laced with conflict and hatred, a kind of daisy chain of murderous enmity passing from generation to generation. Saul describes his father as hating his siblings for cheating him out of an inheritance. And he describes his father as alternately charming and violent, with an explosive temper, much like Saul himself. Samuel Cohen was especially cruel and bullying to George, to the point where, one day (in Saul's telling), George decided to defecate into one of his father's boots so his father would step in it the next morning.

Eventually, Saul literally came to blows with his father. When Saul was about to finish high school, Samuel Cohen came up with the harebrained idea of selling his clothing factory in Montreal and buying a dairy farm in upstate New York. Saul was forced, along with George, to abandon everything and follow his father on this misbegotten venture. Cohen, who knew nothing about farming, decided to buy a thousand chickens, only to watch many of the birds come down with a disease that threatened the entire population. The infected chicks had to be killed, and the task of killing them fell to Saul.

"I sat there for a long time, picking up one after the other of the infected chicks, taking its body in my right hand"—Saul was lefthanded—"and putting my forefinger and middle finger of the left hand onto the neck of the chick, and, with one twist, beheading it, tossing the corpse to the designated spot," he recounted. "It was not a pleasant experience, ripping off the heads of baby chicks."

Finally, Saul rebelled against the tyranny of a father who had derailed his education and subjected him to a life of peonage on a farm he had come to hate: "My father was standing, musing, in the farmyard. I walked up to him. I struck a rather hard left fist smack in the middle of his chest. He was so violently—as I expected—outraged that a Jewish son could even conceive of striking his father, let alone carry it out, that he ran around looking for the largest stone he could locate that would crush my skull with one blow." Saul fled in the family car and drove to the local train station, where he bought a ticket for New York City.

There is something deeply primal—biblical or mythic—about this scene. Cain and Abel, Jacob and Esau, Abraham and Isaac, and, of course, Oedipus, who kills his father and becomes king. In the therapy Newton would help develop, he would push his patients to do something very much like this: violently expel their parents from their lives.

After moving to New York, Saul worked at various jobs to save money for college and was preparing to go to the University of Wisconsin. He later told the story that, after managing to save some six hundred dollars—a considerable sum for the 1920s, about half the annual income of an average civil servant—he went to see his mother, who by then had moved to Brooklyn. Somehow she managed to persuade him to give her his college money, so he went off to school with almost nothing. Saul, the master manipulator, had met his match.

Saul's father ended up spending his last years in a mental hospital. Esther's cousins—the children of Saul's two brothers—suspect that Samuel Cohen suffered from bipolar disorder. But Saul was convinced that he was driven mad by his impossible wife. "[Saul] thought the fighting with his mother drove his father insane and ultimately killed him," Esther Newton wrote. Fending off his overbearing mother, Saul said, had prepared him for lethal combat. "She was good training for surviving two wars," he wrote in his memoir. At another point he answered a question that clearly many people had asked him: Did he really have to lose his temper so often? To which he replied, "Yes, for my health."

Saul did attend the University of Wisconsin, then moved to Chicago and pursued a degree in social work. He joined the American Communist Party after finishing college and was tasked with organizing workers in the city's shoe factories. He married twice during the 1930s but soon found time to take up with Virginia Bash, who would eventually become his third wife and Esther Newton's mother. Registration records at the University of Chicago showed him taking courses intermittently in its school of social work between 1932 and the fall of 1936.

He and Virginia moved in circles of radical politics at the University of Chicago. Virginia (born in 1913) was young, pretty, and full of political courage. She edited a student magazine, *The Upsurge*, that protested the lack of opportunities for Black students at the university and was arrested in a demonstration on behalf of the League of Struggle for Negro Rights, decades before civil rights became a national issue. The University of Chicago initiated an investigation of communist ties in its midst, and Virginia Bash testified in defense of another student activist who was the secretary of the Young Communist League. The 1935 case attracted the attention of the *Chicago Tribune*, the city's ultraconservative newspaper, because Virginia's father was General Louis Hermann Bash, quartermaster general of the U.S. Army. Twenty-two-year-old Virginia (referred to by the *Tribune* as the "red co-ed") appears as a spunky and self-confident young woman, coming to court dressed in a mink coat and answering hostile questions with a defiant air. "I'm not a Communist and I will sue your paper for libel if you call me one," she said, adding provocatively, "Of course there is Communism at the university but it is all informal." When asked what her father would say when he learned of her views, she replied, "I am not responsible for anything my father says."

Saul was evidently quite taken by this fiery young radical, finding her (according to Esther) "full of life." They shared an interest in communism and racial discrimination. The Communist Party was virtually the only major political force seriously taking up the cause of Black civil rights, and its Chicago branch was an especially interesting one, attracting such figures as the young Black writer Richard Wright. Saul and Virginia began a torrid affair, which she broke off when she learned that he had "forgotten" to tell her he was married.

At some point during his time in Chicago, Saul Newton met another woman who was to play an important role in his life: Jane Pearce, a smart and serious young Texan who was attending medical school at the University of Chicago. One evening (according to their son Paul Newton, the third child Jane and Saul would eventually have together), a friend who lived downstairs from Pearce invited her over to make a fourth in bridge. Her partner that evening was the communist labor organizer Saul Newton. Jane suspected that she was being set up on a date, and Paul Newton believes that they began some kind of relationship after that. And so, while still married to his second wife, Newton appears to have started relationships with the two women who would go on to become his third and fourth wives.

In 1937, Saul decided to travel to Spain to join the Abraham Lincoln Brigade, a unit of mostly communist volunteers who wanted to combat the fascist revolt against Spain's republican government. There is a four-year gap in his presence at the University of Chicago between late 1936 and 1940, nearly two years of which he appears to have spent in Spain.

Saul's participation in the Spanish Civil War became a big part of his identity. It was the ultimate left-wing political credential, and he talked about it frequently many decades after the fact. It was easy to be an anti-fascist during World War II, when the U.S. government was at war with Hitler and Mussolini, but only a select and courageous few— 2,800 Americans—had gone off to fight fascism in Spain, disobeying their government and risking their lives for a noble though doomed cause.

"I remember Saul wearing these moccasins on his feet and wriggling his toes, talking about how cold his toes had gotten crossing the Pyrenees," Nathan Stockhamer, one of the psychiatrists who helped form the Sullivan Institute in 1957, told me in a telephone interview. Stockhamer ended up leaving the institute after about a year, in part because of Newton's excessive interest in power. "He kind of acted like a commissar," Stockhamer said, referring to the Soviet political functionaries who wielded power and executed dissidents during the Stalin era, including during the Spanish conflict.

Decades later, Saul got into a heated argument at a family wedding over whether he had fought in Spain because he was a communist or because he was a Jew. He insisted that he had joined for political reasons having nothing to do with his religion; the other guest disagreed. The two men nearly ruined the wedding as they began shouting back and forth: "Communist!" "Jew!" "Communist!" "Jew!" Saul liked to show people the scar he received from a bullet he had taken while in Spain, a wound that left him with a slight limp. The conflict in Spain was racked by an internal war among the anti-fascists—the Russian-backed communists on one side and the anarchists and anti-Stalinist fighters on the Republican side. "Saul would brag about all the anarchists and Trotskyites he had killed," Michael Cohen recalled.

Because Saul was something of a fabulist, some question whether he actually went to Spain. Others say that he was nothing but a munitions clerk there and never actually saw battle. But the archives of the Lincoln Brigade do have a record of Saul Bernard Cohen arriving in Spain on May 30, 1937, and returning to the United States on February 18, 1939. They list his rank as artillery sergeant and record that he served in the Mackenzie-Papineau Battalion, which was manned mainly by Canadians and saw a good deal of action in the war.

The 1940 Census lists him as living in New York City with the second of his six wives, Constance Kyle Newton. He was thirty-four, five foot eight, 135 pounds, with "brown eyes and brown hair and a dark complexion." But he returned to Chicago in the fall of 1940, where the University of Chicago's school of social work has him registered as full-time for the 1940–41 academic year. It appears that the U.S. entry into World War II prevented him from finishing. He claimed (under oath) to have completed the requirements for his master's degree in social work from the University of Chicago right before joining the U.S. Army. "Various events occurred which eventually landed me in the City of New York," he testified, saying that in his haste to depart, he sent his only copy of his thesis to his adviser, but evidently it got lost in the mail—a story that has the air of a tall tale.

In New York, he evidently rekindled his flame with Virginia Bash. How Esther became Saul Newton's daughter says a lot about the tumultuous private world of radical bohemians of the 1930s and '40s. It is the story, as Esther puts it, of her "three fathers."

"My parents, all of them, by which I mean my mother and my three fathers, were all in the Communist Party," she said. In New York,

Virginia Bash had taken up with a much older man, a Hungarian refugee who was also a communist. "He was also Jewish—she only liked Jewish men, never WASPs like herself," Esther said. After they'd been married a couple of years, he had a heart attack and died. "A few years later, my mother met another guy through the party, also Jewish, a lawyer, and they had an affair; she became pregnant." Virginia wanted him to marry her, but he refused, apparently because she was not Jewish, but she decided to have the baby. "Because of a huge stigma of illegitimacy at that time, she put down on my birth certificate that her [dead] first husband was my father, and I guess they didn't ask about it at the hospital. So technically I was legitimate."

Saul and Virginia apparently corresponded while he was serving in Europe during World War II. And when he came back from the war, they took up again, and Saul very much assumed the role of Esther's father—her third, and the only one she ever knew.

Esther, who was born in 1940, became a formidable person in her own right, a distinguished anthropologist and a pioneer in the field of queer and lesbian studies, having written some of the first anthropological studies of gay life in the United States when it was hardly advantageous professionally to do so. She was about five years old in 1945, when Saul reappeared in her mother's life, and she has vivid memories of him from that time.

"When I first met him," she recalled, "he had this glamorous army uniform on and he had brought back a gun from the war and you knew he was somebody. I knew that, even at that age . . . He was scary, even though he was a relatively small man . . . He just exuded power, certainty. I guess sex appeal, because he had so many women. He just took up a lot of space and I was afraid of him, because he was violent at times."

Esther describes him as charismatic, often charming, but frightening, with a temper that could explode at any time. She recalled two summer trips to Maine in a car that Saul had bought. He was as aggressive behind the wheel as he was in the rest of his life. "He was a really scary driver," Esther said. "One day we were out on the highway and some guy cut in front of him, and Saul started screaming and he was furious, and he got up behind the car and managed to rip off the guy's fender with our car. My mother was screaming. It was clear he had this side of him." At the same time, he took young Esther on his lap when he drove and let her steer the car. "I was thrilled! It was so exciting. That he had this confidence in me, you know? It was just wonderful. He wanted me to be very, very capable and stoical."

Saul taught Esther how to ride a bicycle but expected her to pick herself up without complaint if she fell. They went to Central Park with a bike without training wheels—which didn't exist at the time—and Saul ran with the bike for several steps and then let go, watching Esther pedal for a while and then crash. He urged her to get back on the bike. This tough-love approach worked with the bike lesson, but if Esther disappointed him by acting like a child, he often lost his temper.

"He hated anybody whining, and the instances I remember where he was violent toward me had to do with whining," she said. At one point he and Esther and Virginia went for a long walk. When Esther complained that she was tired and needed to stop, he made her walk a few steps ahead of them, and he picked up a stick. "You walk this distance in front of me, and if you whine one more time, I'm going to hit you with this stick," and he did, a couple of times. In another instance Saul lashed out at Esther when she failed in her chore of preparing their cats' waste box. There was no commercial kitty litter at the time, and the family ripped up old newspaper instead. "I couldn't figure out how to do it," Esther remembers. Saul arrived home to find Esther in a fit of frustration over the task, and he started kicking her. "My memory of it is my mother was standing there and screaming, 'Don't do that! Don't hurt her! Don't do that!'" Saul continued the abuse until his temper abated.

During Saul's marriage to Virginia Bash, he was introduced to the world of psychotherapy.

*   *   *

In the middle of the twentieth century, psychoanalysis reached the high point of its prestige, popularity, and authority, nowhere more so than in the United States, which had always had a special relationship with the new field. Freud delivered his first set of prominent lectures in 1909 at Clark University in Worcester, Massachusetts—an event that helped put psychoanalysis on the map internationally and introduce it to American psychologists.

By midcentury, psychoanalysis had fully penetrated mainstream American life. *Time* magazine put Freud on its cover three times between 1924 and 1956. Kindly and wise psychoanalysts began popping up in Hollywood movies: even the dancer Fred Astaire did a turn as a tap-dancing shrink in the film *Carefree* (1938). Such phrases as "Freudian slip" and "defense mechanism" peppered the American vocabulary. "[Freud's] ideas . . . flared out to all compartments of 20th century life—religion, morals, philosophy, the arts, even commerce and industry, and the assembling of armies," *Time* reported in 1956, some eighteen years after Freud's death.

New York City had the largest concentration of psychoanalysts in the United States, twice as many (reportedly) as in all of Great Britain. It was the largest city, the country's intellectual and cultural capital as well as the city with the largest Jewish population. Freud and his principal disciples were mainly Jews, many of whom had sought refuge from Nazism in the United States. More than one-quarter of New York's nearly eight million people were Jewish, and, although psychoanalysis tried to avoid being seen as the "Jewish science," Jews were disproportionately represented among both practitioners and patients.

Between 1945 and 1948, Saul Newton and Virginia Bash both worked for the William Alanson White Institute, one of New York's leading psychoanalytic institutes. The White Institute occupied a specific place in the world of American psychoanalysis: a dissident group that had a complicated relationship with the starchy Freudian orthodoxy that dominated the field. "The William Alanson White Institute was founded in 1943 as a revolutionary alternative to mainstream, orthodox Freudian psychoanalysis in the United States," according to the institute's official history.

Harry Stack Sullivan and Clara Thompson, who were among the

founders of the White Institute, were pioneering figures in the American neo-Freudian school of psychiatry. Named after one of Sullivan's mentors, White (as it is generally called by those in the field) became the center of what is known as "interpersonal psychotherapy." If Freud concentrated on the internal drama within the individual patient—the Oedipus complex, the friction between the competing drives of what he called the id, ego, and superego—Sullivan and Thompson insisted that it was important to understand a patient in relation to the other people in their life (and not just the "family romance" with their parents). "No great progress in this field of study can be made until it is realized that the field of observation is what people do with each other, what they can communicate to each other about what they do with each other," Sullivan stated in one of his training lectures. "When that is done, no such thing as the durable, unique, individual personality is ever clearly justified. For all I know every human being has as many personalities as he has interpersonal relations."

Sullivan, born in 1892, grew up in a remote part of upstate New York, the child of Irish immigrants. He had a rather isolated childhood, causing him to place great importance on the problem of loneliness— something Freud had largely ignored—and the value of peer friendships, which Sullivan called "chumship." He had a psychological crisis as an adolescent and was subjected to electroshock therapy after confessing to having homosexual inclinations. When he went on to medical school, specializing in psychiatry, his own experience of hospitalization appears to have made him an especially compassionate doctor, willing to take on the more difficult patients whom the medical field mostly ignored.

He had achieved surprising success early in his career, treating schizophrenic patients. Freud considered it useless to try to work with people with schizophrenia, and they were generally treated by American psychiatrists with such blunt and ineffective tools as electroshock, physical restraints, and drugs. Sullivan approached these patients with the premise that the difference between supposedly sane and insane people was a question of degree and circumstance—not that they were a fundamentally different species. "In most general terms," he wrote, "we are all much more human than otherwise, be we happy and successful, contented and detached, miserable and mentally disordered, or whatever."

Sullivan created a special ward in his hospital for male patients with schizophrenia. He hired male attendants who were somewhat vulnerable individuals and thus better able to identify with their troubled patients. The fellowship that grew among patients and staff led to remarkable and unexpected improvements. Rather than believing that one's personality was formed completely in the first years of life, Sullivan thought that people passed through different phases of development and that a person could recoup experiences they had missed out on in earlier phases of their life.

Sullivan and his colleagues at the White Institute also departed from the strict Freudians in the way they practiced therapy. Freud believed that therapists should maintain an attitude of formal detachment and reveal as little as possible about themselves, holding up a kind of "blank mirror" to the patient, intervening with the occasional question. Sándor Ferenczi—perhaps Freud's most brilliant disciple—came to believe that maintaining this omniscient mask was a serious impediment to a patient's growth, infantilizing the patient under the crushing weight of the therapist's authority. A patient's growth, Ferenczi believed, required a caring, affectionate relationship of greater reciprocity between analyst and patient. (Freud dismissed Ferenczi's approach as a "kissing cure" after hearing reports that Ferenczi and his patients were physically affectionate with each other.) Sullivan heard Ferenczi lecture in New York in the 1920s and advised Clara Thompson to undergo analysis with Ferenczi so they could better understand his approach. Patients of strict Freudians complained that the only words they heard from their therapist were "Uh-huh, tell me more." The "interpersonal psychoanalysis" developed at White involved much more interaction between analyst and patient—and examining that relationship was part of the healing process. "The study of how people influence and respond to one another remains a central focus of the interpersonal treatment model," the White Institute official history states. "The interpersonal approach underscores the human qualities of the psychoanalyst as a factor in therapeutic change."

Sullivan and the other neo-Freudians also gave more weight to a patient's social and cultural context. Sullivan forged many collaborations with the University of Chicago's sociology department and pushed the field of psychiatry to see itself as a social science. For example, he worked with the pioneering Black sociologist Charles S. Johnson, who authored, among other things, *Growing Up in the Black Belt* (1941), an important work on Black people in the Deep South. It was obvious to Sullivan that being raised in a racial caste system might have a greater impact on a person's psychological makeup than an unresolved Oedipus complex. "Personality can never be isolated from the complex interpersonal relationships in which [a] person lives," he wrote.

Freud—based on the experience of his wealthy Viennese clientele—believed that psychoanalysis would only work with well-educated patients. Sullivan and Thompson disagreed. "Neither subscribed to Freud's dictum that treatment for 'those patients who do not possess a reasonable degree of education and a fairly reliable character should be refused,'" one of Sullivan's biographers wrote. Acting on this philosophy, the White Institute started one of the first programs for low-cost therapy in 1948.

Among the other founding members of the White Institute were Erich Fromm and his ex-wife, Frieda Fromm-Reichmann, both Jews who had escaped Nazi Germany. Fromm-Reichmann, independent of Sullivan, had also done innovative work with schizophrenic patients back in Germany. Erich Fromm had written eloquently in the field of social psychology, publishing the book *Escape from Freedom* (1941), an analysis of the psychology of ordinary Germans who had thrown off German democracy in favor of Nazism.

The background of some of the White Institute founders distinguished them in a field that was dominated by the medical establishment: the American Psychoanalytic Association voted in 1938 to limit its membership to medical doctors who had subsequent training in psychoanalysis. Sullivan and the White Institute broke with the orthodoxy by admitting so-called lay analysts: people like Fromm, who had a Ph.D. in psychology but did not have a medical degree. Fromm was also a democratic socialist who was interested in elaborating a humanistic interpretation of Marx—something that would have placed the White Institute outside the mainstream of American psychiatry but also made it more congenial to a communist veteran of the Spanish Civil War such as Saul Newton.

In short, the White Institute (begun in 1943 but only formally incorporated in 1946) brought together a wealth of talent and exciting new ideas that were transforming American psychotherapy. Within the landscape of American psychoanalysis, White was fairly radical. "Its internationally renowned founders . . . united by a passionate spirit of dissent," the institute's official history states, "saw the need to challenge the parochial sectarianism and growing rigidity of American psychoanalysis." This was where Saul Newton had his first serious exposure to the field and where he formed the idea of becoming an analyst.

How did Newton come to the White Institute? How long did he work there? And what, if any, training did he receive? This is one of the fuzziest passages of his biography. The early records of the White Institute (which is still a leading center of psychoanalytic training and therapy) were destroyed in a flood in 2016, although the institute did confirm that Saul worked in the bursar's office, a fairly mundane clerical position, in the mid to late 1940s. His third wife, Virginia Bash, worked as the secretary to Clara Thompson, the institute's director. Saul attended lectures and had some exposure to Harry Stack Sullivan, who gave frequent talks at the institute and whom Newton always listed as one of his great heroes. In 1989, Newton told a journalist for *New York* magazine that he had studied with both Sullivan and Erich Fromm. "Harry Stack Sullivan was the American counterpart to Freud," he said. "I was his patient when I was young . . . I loved the man." That exposure would have been limited, however, since Sullivan died in 1949. Saul also told people he was in therapy with Frieda Fromm-Reichmann before he started out as a therapist himself. He told the story that one day during a session, Fromm-Reichmann pointed to a photograph in her office (we don't know of whom) and asked Saul how he was like the man in the picture. Saul said he didn't know, to which she replied, "Well, you're both fanatics."

Did Saul come to the White Institute through his wife's job, or did she come there because he was working there? Or, as seems more likely, did they both get their jobs at the White Institute because of the presence of Jane Pearce, the woman Saul Newton had met at a bridge game in Chicago? Pearce had finished her M.D. and gone to the White Institute to do her psychoanalytic training with Sullivan and his colleagues. She and Saul may have reconnected as early as 1943. What is certain is that at some point in the late 1940s, Saul Newton began (or rekindled) a romantic relationship with Pearce, who was a rising star among the younger generation of therapists at White.

*   *   *

Jane Pearce was a Texan. Her two grandfathers fought in the American Civil War on the Confederate side. Family lore has it that Daniel Dopplemayer (Pearce's mother's father) trudged back from the war with a gold piece in the sole of his shoe and invested it in a dry goods store that evolved into a thriving string of successful department stores, though newspaper records appear to indicate that he already had a store before the war. His daughter (Jane's mother), Belinda Dopplemayer, was apparently a formidable figure: a librarian, an intellectual, and quite wealthy. At the same time, as a member of the town's small Jewish community, she was something of an outsider in Marshall, Texas.

Jane's father, James Edwin Pearce, was a figure of some renown in the field of archaeology and beyond. A teacher and later the principal of Austin High School, he schooled himself in the nascent field of archaeology by taking time off to study at the University of Chicago and the École d'Anthropologie in Paris. He was hired to teach at the University of Texas, headed up its first anthropology department, and pioneered archaeological fieldwork in Texas. He helped set up the archaeology and history museum at the University of Texas and published a well-regarded book, *Tales That Dead Men Tell* (1935), about the things we can learn about the past from the archaeological record. He was clearly one of Austin's most distinguished citizens: the University of Texas named a building after him, and the house where Jane grew up is listed in the city's registry of historically important buildings. A junior high school still bears his name. His wedding to Belinda Dopplemayer was described in the society pages. At the same time, according to one of his grandchildren, they were not admitted to Austin's top country club because of Belinda's Jewish background. Marrying a Jew made James Pearce something of a rebel in Texas society, although it doesn't appear to have hurt him professionally. He was clearly an intellectually serious and high-minded person, delivering lectures with such titles as "Science and Religion" and "Man's Sense of the Beautiful, Its Origins and Early Forms." He became a champion of prison reform, noting that Texas's punitive penitentiary system did little to rehabilitate prisoners: twenty percent returned to prison within a few years, as opposed to the Minnesota prison system, which had a recidivism rate of only five percent.

Jane inherited her parents' strong intellectual interests and independent-mindedness. Like her father, she pursued graduate studies at the University of Chicago, training to become a medical doctor at a time when only five percent of doctors were women. She was far more politically radical than her father, and she was apparently also a skilled poker player and a hard drinker. (She later bragged that she could drink most men under the table.) As a young woman, Jane was not beautiful, but was attractive; she had a roundish face, with shoulder-length blond hair; an engaging, open, and friendly manner; and piercing light blue eyes that reflected an extremely lively mind.

While Saul Newton was off serving in World War II, Jane Pearce moved to New York to do her psychoanalytic training at the White Institute, where she was reportedly in analysis with Frieda Fromm-Reichmann. After Newton returned to civilian life, and he and his wife

Virginia found their way to the White Institute, he and Jane began or resumed their sexual liaison. Saul would have been in his early forties, and Jane (who was born in 1914) in her early to midthirties. At the start of her career she was already a trained analyst with an M.D. She had what Saul Newton decided he wanted.

There are traces of Saul and Jane's early relationship in a manuscript of poems that Jane wrote, poems she clearly considered important, as she brought them together in a booklike manuscript with the title "A Love Story. . . . of sorts," which seems to document the phases of her relationship with Newton.

The first poems are dated September 1943, the year the White Institute formed. At this point Saul Newton was still married to his second wife, Constance Kyle Newton, and had yet to marry his third wife, Virginia Bash, meaning that Jane Pearce, his fourth wife, would have to wait her turn for a good while. This would suggest that (as their son Paul Newton believed) they had started a relationship when they met back in Chicago.

These early poems have numerous suggestions of a love that Jane had to hide, perhaps because her feelings were, at the moment, unrequited:

> the most that I can do is run away
> Lest you should learn from me how much I care.

By 1948, her love had emerged from the shadows, and the poetry (briefly) assumes a triumphant, exultant air:

> Now I know what ecstasy is . . .

While conducting his affair with Jane, Saul Newton took the step of legally adopting Virginia Bash's daughter, Esther. "I think that's the shabbiest thing he ever did," Esther said. "[My mother] thought that meant he was going to stay with her. Instead, it meant he was leaving her." In effect, Newton tricked Virginia into making Esther his legal child when he already had one foot out the door. Despite his intensely negative views of the nuclear family, Saul very much wanted to be a father. Even though he would never again live with Esther, he took his obligations toward her seriously, paying her mother alimony and financing Esther's education. He was a distant father, but he remained an important figure in her life, providing crucial financial and moral support at important moments in her career. He helped put her through college and graduate school, gave her a graduation trip to Europe, and bought her her first automobile. He would pay to have her visit him every day during vacations, and he took a genuine interest in her career. "Along with his terrible temper and disregard of others' feelings," Esther wrote, "Saul had irresistible charm and, improbably, a quality of sly sweetness, which appeared suddenly at some of the most unexpected moments." Saul treated his adoptive daughter with greater regard than many of the nine children he had afterward. Esther describes Saul's relationship with his children as complex, distant, yet involved: they were "greatly desired but rarely embraced." The fact that Saul, as Esther's legal father, continued to see her was a constant thorn in Virginia's side. "Something that turned out really good for me, was devastating for [my mother]." After their split, Virginia Bash, as far as Esther knows, never had a relationship with another man.

Late in Bash's life, decades after the divorce, Esther was surprised to find an old photograph of Saul in her mother's address book. It was a highly romantic photo of Saul's face, posing in a three-quarters angle, his brooding eyes looking not at the camera, but off to the side with burning intensity, hooded by dark, thick eyebrows—shot with rather dramatic lighting: half in light, half in shadow. "He had a dark, sexy energy that bowled my gentile mother over," Esther wrote. She dates the picture from 1940, when they were both living in New York but Saul was still married to his second wife. Asked why she kept near to hand this picture of a man who had not treated her well, her mother replied, "He was the love of my life, you know."

"My mother was just a secretary, and Jane Pearce had a Ph.D. and she had a medical degree," Esther said. Jane was obviously highly intelligent and deeply immersed in the world Saul had decided he wanted to be his world as well. "She was in her late thirties and really wanted children . . . She put a lot of pressure on him and I think gave him an ultimatum. So that's why my parents divorced," Esther said, reflecting her mother's interpretation of events. That he decided to divorce Esther's mother and marry Jane Pearce had little do with wanting a new sexual partner: "He cheated on every wife he ever had, so he had no problem with that," Esther said. It represented a life and a career choice. "He really wanted her, Jane Pearce . . . She represented the future."

Whether Saul Newton consciously saw his marriage to Jane Pearce as a strategic career move, as Esther Newton suggests, there is no doubt that their relationship was the pivotal point of his career, catapulting him from the bursar's office at the White Institute to his position as cofounder of his own therapeutic and training institute, the Sullivan Institute for Research in Psychoanalysis.

Saul and Jane got together in 1948 and had their first child, Sarah, in 1950, followed by Robert in 1952 and Paul in 1954. As a medical doctor and practicing psychiatrist, Jane could afford an upper-middle-class lifestyle. In 1950, the couple acquired a handsome town house at 332 West Seventy-Seventh Street, where they had a housekeeper who cooked and cleaned, as well as babysitters to help look after the children. This house—with fifty-five hundred square feet of space—would become the first headquarters of the Sullivan Institute, which officially opened for business in 1957 although they had been trying out their own therapeutic approach for several years before this.

In the early 1950s the couple also built a house together in Amagansett, a Long Island town on the beautiful white sand beach that stretched west from Montauk to the fashionable Hamptons. This became the summer enclave of the Sullivanian world.

The fact that Pearce and Newton moved from the Upper East Side of Manhattan to the Upper West Side has its own significance. The Upper East Side, where the White Institute was based, is known as the Silk Stocking District, containing some of the wealthiest zip codes in the United States, a bastion of the city's old WASP elite. The fancy apartment buildings along Fifth and Park Avenues routinely excluded Jews, as well as people in such disreputable fields as the entertainment industry. The Upper West Side in the 1950s had an edgier, more bohemian character. The Black jazz great Miles Davis lived just down the block from Jane and Saul's town house. The presence of Carnegie Hall, the Juilliard School of Music, the Metropolitan Opera, *The New York Times*, and the theater district of Times Square brought large numbers of musicians, actors, journalists, and writers to the less expensive and less exclusive Upper West Side. It was a curious mix of rich and poor. There were superluxurious buildings like the Dakota (at Central Park West and Seventy-Second Street) and elegant brownstones, along with slumlike tenements and blocks with high levels of drugs and crime. It attracted such people as the philosopher Hannah Arendt and the novelists Isaac Bashevis Singer, Norman Mailer (before he moved to Brooklyn), and Philip Roth. The area was dense with intellectuals and psychiatrists: a common joke was that if you dropped something out of a window on the Upper West Side, you were likely to hit a shrink.

One significant fact about Pearce that undoubtedly shaped her ideas regarding psychology and human development was that she suffered from debilitating bouts of postpartum depression. One of her children reported that after the birth of her third child, Pearce barely got out of bed for a year. In the book that she and Saul Newton coauthored, *The Conditions of Human Growth*, they refer not to postpartum depression, but to "postpartum psychosis." Moreover, rather than seeing this as one of many different responses to childbirth (one in five mothers suffers from postpartum depression, and only one in five hundred experience postpartum psychosis), Pearce and Newton conflate the two and paint motherhood in the darkest possible terms. In their account, the mother is overwhelmed by the demands of a helpless, screaming infant. Her anxiety and frustration over her inability to satisfy the child's needs turn to resentment and then to rage. The child, who is completely dependent on the mother, senses her anxiety and gradually learns to suppress the entirely legitimate needs that provoke anxiety in the mother.

"The baby creates in the mother a remarkable degree of anxiety, which militates against the empathic responsiveness that the baby needs," they wrote. "The prevalence of postpartum psychosis is one index of this anxiety . . . If the mother cannot experience tenderness in response to an appeal for tenderness, she misperceives the original need in the child as hostile, and the child also experiences his need for tenderness as a hostile move. This happens every day in any home with very small children."

Pearce and Newton picked up on the phenomenon—decades before it became an accepted topic—of what is commonly referred to as "Mom rage," women experiencing intense moments of anger as they cope with the demands of child-rearing. But in Pearce and Newton's formulation, this perverse mother-child dynamic was seen as a defining and universal feature of motherhood.

Pearce and Newton also believed that any effort by the child to explore beyond the prescribed limits of the parents' world is met with hostility, and so children learn to censor and limit themselves, deadening their most adventurous, spirited parts. Rather than presenting parenthood as a mixed bag in which feelings of joy and tenderness might alternate with moments of exhaustion and frustration, the Sullivanians saw it as an unmitigated nightmare. The adjectives Pearce and Newton chose to describe the everyday life of mother and child are "phobic," "psychotic," and "miserable"; common nouns in the text are "anger," "jealousy," and "blackmail"; their favorite verbs are "handicap," "paralyze," "destroy," and "atrophy."

Although the two had different biographies—Newton a Jew from Canada, Pearce a half-Jew/half-WASP from Texas—they concurred that parenthood was a kind of death trap from which both parent and child needed to be liberated.

It was hardly coincidental that Pearce and Newton would begin developing their radical new theories about the pernicious effects of family life during the mid-1950s, which was, in effect, the apex of traditional family life in the United States. People who had been hesitant to start families during the Great Depression and World War II were now marrying younger and having more children. The average age of marriage dropped to twenty for women and twenty-two for men. The fertility rate rose to a level not seen in decades, with the average American family having 3.5 children. Moreover, it was the decade of a relatively new and different kind of family in which the husband was the sole breadwinner, a luxury that most families of previous decades could not afford. During the postwar boom it became a point of pride and status for a family to live on a husband's salary while the woman raised the children and took care of the home, helped out by a dazzling new array of domestic appliances and gadgets. Even though more women were attending college, many hoped and expected to be engaged before they graduated. The president of Smith College—one of the country's leading educational institutions for women—explained that his school's aim was "to turn out women who can apply a trained intelligence to the problem of daily living and whose intellectual resources can enrich their lives and those of their children."

At the same time, on the periphery of the idealized picture there were rumblings of change and even rebellion. The novel (1955) and movie (1956) *The Man in the Gray Flannel Suit* expressed a private angst and dissatisfaction with corporate conformity and middle-class aspirations. And the actor James Dean shouted "You're tearing me apart!" to his conformist parents in the movie *Rebel Without a Cause* (1955). There were signs of quiet desperation among American women as well—what the feminist author Betty Friedan called "the problem that has no name," the feeling of emptiness and angst among housewives whose restricted lives sometimes felt blank and lonely.

The civil rights movement was picking up steam. The Montgomery bus boycott had forced the Alabama city to end its policy of segregated seating on public transportation, which the U.S. Supreme Court then ruled to be unconstitutional. Fidel Castro and his small band of rebels scored their first victory by sacking an army outpost in rural Cuba. Allen Ginsberg published *Howl* (1956), Jack Kerouac published *On the Road* (1957), and the word "beatnik" entered the American vocabulary.

On January 6, 1957, Elvis Presley appeared on *The Ed Sullivan*

Show—America's favorite Sunday-night family entertainment—and performed "Don't Be Cruel," but he was filmed only from the waist up to conceal his gyrating hips and suggestive dance moves. It was a Janus moment, like the two-faced Roman god of doorways who looked forward and backward, simultaneously respecting the dictates of a traditional repressive culture but also anticipating the sexual and rock-and-roll revolutions that would dominate the 1960s. Later that year, the birth control pill was submitted for authorization to the Federal Drug Administration, and the Sullivan Institute for Psychoanalytic Research officially opened its doors.

The changing times, Pearce and Newton came to believe, called for a radical new approach to psychoanalysis, which in their view had become a pillar of the establishment that needed toppling. Harry Stack Sullivan and Clara Thompson had gotten their training in the first quarter of the twentieth century, when the fledgling field of psychoanalysis was trying to gain acceptance in the American medical establishment. Pearce and Newton named their own institute after Sullivan, believing that they were following in his footsteps but embracing the radical implications of Sullivan's ideas that Sullivan himself had not pursued. Sullivan described the "self-system" as a kind of defensive fortress that each of us creates, built of our parents' fears and society's admonitions and expectations. But Sullivan and those who came after him at the White Institute had been reluctant to attack and destroy the fortress. Pearce and Newton came to see the nuclear family as the basic unit of capitalist production, the means by which the system perpetuated itself to the detriment of individual growth. Parents tamed and squelched their children's most vital needs in order to turn them into obedient and productive citizens.

Psychoanalysis offered the potential of human liberation by putting us in touch with our deepest needs and wants, but so far, by Pearce and Newton's reckoning, it was working only to perpetuate the status quo. Freud had a fundamentally tragic view of human nature: that people were born with powerful drives—aggression and sex—but had to learn to repress and sublimate them as part of the process of socialization.

People would tear one another apart if they acted on all their aggressive impulses and slept with whomever they wanted. Sublimation was the price of civilization—hence the title of Freud's famous book *Civilization and Its Discontents* (1930).

To win over Middle America, the American medical establishment had worked to present a somewhat sanitized version of psychoanalysis, playing down the importance of the unruly, anarchic sex drive. William Menninger, the cofounder of the Menninger Clinic in Topeka, Kansas, and the U.S. Army's chief of psychiatry during World War II, reassured the public that, far from promoting interest in sex, the job of the psychoanalyst was often "to point out how the patient's preoccupation with sex is interfering with a mature relationship with people and with constructive work." In 1952, in the *Diagnostic and Statistical Manual of Mental Disorders* (DSM), the American Psychiatric Association classified homosexuality as a disease, listing it as a "sociopathic personality disturbance." Many psychiatrists claimed to be able to cure patients of this disease.

Pearce and Newton offered a more exciting and hedonic variation on traditional psychoanalysis. Their goal was to be the champion of all the repressed desires that had been disassociated—the impulses toward growth that had been shunted aside during childhood. As they put it in *The Conditions of Human Growth*, "The child learns to repress all of its deepest desires and needs in order to avoid displeasing his or her parents." And the child develops an elaborate set of defense mechanisms to keep it that way—Sullivan's "self-system," a mechanism for fending off troublesome impulses. "Thus the self-system incorporates a security apparatus," Pearce and Newton wrote, "like a moat around a castle, that supports and perpetuates its own limitations."

Rather than seeing this operation of intense repression and sublimation as Freud did—as tragically inevitable, even necessary—Pearce and Newton insisted that there was a way out: "No matter how apparently victorious the repressive forces, certain conditions indicate that the undefeated underground, the guerrilla fighter for growth of the personality is never totally defeated."

It is not hard to see that this theory of gr̲ radical politics: the metaphors of the "und "the guerrilla fighter" were taken from the a during World War II, but perhaps more pertinently fr Revolution (1949), in which irregular forces defeated the mu funded and equipped army of Chiang Kai-shek and his American an The 1950s, when the Newtons' ideas crystallized, was also the decade of the Cuban and Algerian revolutions, both wars of independence won by poor but determined popular movements. The therapist was to be the ally of their patient's internal "guerrilla fighter for growth," helping them gain liberation from the forces of parental and societal repression. "Successful analysis involves becoming accustomed to revolution," they wrote.

Pearce and Newton believed that there was a part of the self—which they called the "integral personality"—that remained open to growth and experience: "The integral personality is a true system, logically and subtly organized, and directed unreservedly toward its own expansion and satisfaction . . . It hungers after the infinities of growth. It operates from earliest childhood, and its fuel is experience . . . It cares little for the conventionalities of that ominous audience to whom the self-system so dutifully recites its lessons."

Sullivan had shown that we are prisoners of the repressive "self-system," and that the path out of the prison house was interaction with other people. He pioneered "interpersonal" analysis, the concept that one grew through contact with others. To Pearce and Newton, this meant that patients should break out of the trap of the nuclear family and monogamous marriage—something Sullivan stopped short of doing. Championing the idea of chumship, Sullivan had his most troubled patients live in all-male group housing. Pearce and Newton would expand on this idea by encouraging all their patients to live in group apartments. They felt that after Sullivan's death, in 1949, the White Institute did not have the courage to explore the full implications of his ideas. "Sullivan died suddenly," Newton told the journalist Phoebe Hoban. "A lot of his followers got frightened and returned to more orthodox Freudian analysis."

"The White Institute was still quite conservative," said Barbara ᴋane, a psychotherapist who did her training in the 1960s but was married for many years to one of the therapists, Tony Gabriele, who admired Jane Pearce and left the White Institute to join the original Sullivan Institute. "Marriage was not just an institution; it was the goal of therapy, the standard of a healthy, well-adjusted life," Kane said. Why should therapy simply try to help patients make the best of a bad situation? What therapy was to expand people's lives, open their opportunities for growth, free them from the crushing weight of conformity and societal expectations? Sullivan had treated patients with schizophrenia by encouraging them to live together in a community. Why not give all patients the same opportunity? Sullivan had theorized that people go through specific developmental stages, such as parallel play and chumship—close same-sex preadolescent friendships. But many people suffered by missing out on these stages. "They thought they could develop a therapy that was more oriented toward helping people make up these deficits," Kane said. The Sullivanians "encouraged people to develop same-sex friendships, which is why they had people living in same-sex apartments. You could get to know people of your own gender. It was a serious, exciting project."

Pearce and Newton believed that they had an approach that aimed at nothing less than revolution. Communism in the Soviet Union had remained incomplete because it had left the traditional family intact. Pearce and Newton believed that therapy could carry out a personal revolution in each person by offering a patient the opportunity to reach for the "infinities of growth."

Along with having a compelling set of ideas, there were also practical and personal reasons for Jane Pearce and Saul Newton to break with the White Institute and found their own institute. They were in a financial position to do it: Jane was a successful analyst, with clients and the ability to earn a living on her own. She also had developed a following among a group of younger therapists. Moreover, she had inherited money from her father's estate, allowing her to buy a large five-story town house, with room for both their home and offices for the headquarters of her new Sullivan Institute. They had enough money left over to build the second home in Amagansett that would soon serve as the group's summer retreat. Saul, with no formal training in psychology, had no future at the White Institute. After Sullivan's death, White began requiring its therapists to have medical degrees as well as formal training in psychoanalysis, blocking any path to advancement for Newton. He was stuck in the bursar's office cutting checks for therapists he considered to be his intellectual inferiors.

With their own institute, Newton leapfrogged from a clerical job, becoming not only a psychoanalyst but also the director of his own organization. While Jane Pearce was listed above Saul Newton as principal author of *The Conditions of Human Growth*, their authors' bios list Saul as director of the Sullivan Institute and Jane as associate director. Despite all the complicated rules that psychoanalytic institutes had enacted in establishing who could and couldn't be admitted to their organization, anyone was free to hang out a shingle and call themselves a psychoanalyst. Credentials were required only if patients wanted to be reimbursed by an insurance company, but there was nothing to stop a therapist from charging for therapy if someone was willing to pay him to listen. Jane's credentials—an M.D. and formal training in psychoanalysis—and her growing reputation provided the credibility the new institute needed to attract both patients and young therapists who wanted to train with them. But Saul, as the more forceful and dominant personality, became the institute's driving force.

The year after Jane and Saul broke with the White Institute and went on their own, Clara Thompson, their former boss, published a paper about the climate of factionalism among psychoanalytic institutes, with their tendency, like Protestant churches, to break off into schismatic groups, each new group believing that it had found the one real truth. What other profession, she asked, calls itself "a movement," a term with a decidedly religious aura? And in a passage that may have been alluding to Newton, Thompson warned about the perils of unsupervised therapists operating in a field where there were almost no legal or professional safeguards: "Thus, there is the danger that alleged psychoanalysis can be practiced by anyone who has the nerve to announce that he is a psychoanalyst; and psychoanalysis has become a profitable business . . . More than any other specialty, psychoanalysis is meat for the charlatan. All one needs is an office, perhaps a couch, and the ability to sit still and listen a certain number of hours a day."

3

The Sullivan Institute and the World of Abstract Expressionism

In May 1955, Clement Greenberg, perhaps the preeminent art critic of the New York avant-garde, had a nervous breakdown. His girlfriend, the beautiful, young, and talented painter Helen Frankenthaler, had decided to end their relationship.

In the cultural scene of the 1940s, '50s, and '60s, Greenberg was a kind of pope whose pronouncements were taken as gospel that could make or break an artist's career. He had declared Jackson Pollock "the most powerful painter in contemporary America," and soon after, in 1949, *Life* magazine ran a major feature story with the title "Jackson Pollock: Is He the Greatest Living Painter in the United States?"

Greenberg was far more than an art critic; he played an active role in promoting and shaping the work of the artists he championed. He had met Pollock when Pollock was virtually unknown and didn't have enough money to heat his own studio. Greenberg and Pollock's wife, the painter Lee Krasner, had, through concerted effort, propelled him to the top of the art world.

Early in Greenberg's relationship with Frankenthaler, which began in 1950 when she was only twenty-one, he took her to see Jackson Pollock in his studio. Frankenthaler took inspiration from Pollock's method—working with a large canvas laid out on the floor, allowing him to move freely around the edges. But instead of building up layers of paint on the surface like Pollock, Frankenthaler decided to leave her canvas unprimed, thinning her paint so that it was absorbed directly into the canvas and spread out like a stain of color. Her technique is credited with giving birth to color field painting. After she broke things off with Greenberg, he was in bad enough shape that he was staggering about listlessly in a sleepwalking state that alarmed his friends. They urged him to see an analyst, who referred him to a younger therapist named Ralph Klein. Greenberg saw Klein for the first time on June 14, 1955.

Thus began a long relationship that Greenberg credited with changing his life. "I was like reborn," he later said. "It was the most important event in my life . . . Ralph Klein turned my life around." Reeling from the end of an all-consuming relationship, Greenberg was receptive to a therapy that urged patients to avoid "dependency" and not focus on one person at any time. Moreover, Greenberg, although forty-six and an intellectual star, was still dependent (financially and emotionally) on his overbearing businessman father, who had little appreciation of his son's very different career.

Clem Greenberg and Ralph Klein were an odd couple. Greenberg was a tall, gangly, balding middle-aged man with a famously ugly face; he had awkward posture and tended to hunch his back and shoulders, making him look shorter, but he bent his head forward intently, dominating whatever conversation he chose to enter. Klein was a handsome young Austrian Jew who, at age thirty, was still training for his psychoanalytic license when he began treating the much older Greenberg. But Klein, who had fled Europe as a teenager and worked for U.S. Army Intelligence during the war, was worldly, sophisticated. With his rugged good looks and perfect English with the slight hint of an Austrian accent, he cut a rather dashing, cosmopolitan figure.

Klein, who had been drawn into the orbit of Jane Pearce and Saul Newton, was one of the founding figures of the Sullivan Institute and would remain among its mainstays until its dissolution in 1991. Already in 1955, two years before the formal opening of the institute, Klein was operating under the aegis of Pearce and Newton. According to Greenberg's biographer Florence Rubenfeld, "Pearce's credentials gave the group its legitimacy, but Newton's ideas, far more radical than anything Sullivan taught, shaped its approach to psychotherapy. For that reason, Clem referred to the group not as Sullivanians, but as Newtonians . . . Their basic ideas were in place by the time Clem saw Ralph Klein that first time."

Greenberg's influence on the New York art scene is legendary; far less well-known is the influence that therapy had on his life—and on the art world. "The impact of Newtonian therapy on Clem's private as well as his public life cannot be overestimated," Rubenfeld writes. "It would not overstretch the facts to say that after the late fifties, Clem's comportment in the art world can only be understood in this context." He advised painters on what to show and what direction to take their work, when a painting was finished and when it needed more work. It would be equally true to say that Greenberg was a major force in shaping the early history of the Sullivan Institute. Over a period of about fifteen years, he funneled dozens of other patients to the institute, including some of America's leading artists—from Jackson Pollock and Kenneth Noland to Jules Olitski and Larry Poons. The flow of so many brilliant and creative people to the Sullivan Institute gave it an air of legitimacy and intellectual seriousness, with a decidedly unconventional, avant-garde flair.

New York was a place creative people flocked to, often needing to get away from the strictures of the smaller towns or immigrant enclaves where they grew up and the expectations of families who frequently opposed their becoming artists.

"Everyone I knew was seeing an analyst," said Barbara Rose, an art historian who married the artist Frank Stella and knew the New York art world inside and out. "There's a chapter in my memoir, it's called 'Shrink, Shrank, Shrunk.'"

Even those who came from New York had to adjust. Greenberg, for example, had to make the leap from the Jewish neighborhood in the

Bronx where his father had run a candy store to the sophisticated world of Manhattan artists and intellectuals. His parents, like Saul Newton's, were Eastern European Jews who understandably were focused on earning a living, getting ahead, and fitting into their new country. But theirs was, for Greenberg, a suffocating environment from which he needed to flee. Like Newton, Greenberg claimed to hate his father and had a violent temper. His father was a hard-driving self-made man focused on money and material success, and he had little patience for his son's intellectual and artistic interests. A famous family story was that when Greenberg was a small boy, he had beaten a goose to death with a shovel. When the art critic Karen Wilkin asked him about it, he replied, "You need to understand: the goose reminded me of my father."

Psychotherapy and art in the 1950s were a good fit. It was natural for artists to turn to therapy as part of a process of contending with—or throwing off—their past and remaking themselves into the people they wanted to become. These were people who, after all, were questioning virtually every assumption in art: Does art have to represent something? Do I need to paint on an easel? Do I need to paint with a brush? Do I need paint at all? And so it seemed quite natural for them to question the traditional assumptions of mainstream American life: What is marriage? What is family? Is sexual fidelity necessary? Psychotherapy appeared to offer the prospect of tapping into the world of the unconscious and freeing the repressed forces and desires that lay buried there. Isn't that what artists needed to do in order to unlock the full extent of their talent? It was easy to believe that a man (in those days, artists were usually men) who timidly obeyed middle-class convention in his personal life might also limit himself and fail to realize his potential in his artistic life.

The art world was fertile ground for a therapy that was rebellious and anti-conformist. "There are no rules," as Helen Frankenthaler (not herself a Sullivanian patient) put it. "That is how art is born, how breakthroughs happen. Go against the rules or ignore the rules. That is what invention is about." Sullivanian therapy, in particular, which urged its patients to follow their creative desires and throw off the weighty obligations and expectations of society, marriage, and family, was particularly appealing to people in this milieu. "[Before that] I could never take my feelings seriously; my impulses," Greenberg said. "I was always looking to the world to get my bearings."

During Greenberg's first months of therapy, in the summer of 1955, Ralph Klein moved out to stay with Jane Pearce and Saul Newton at their summer home at Barnes Landing in Amagansett. Greenberg, unable to accept a lengthy separation from the therapist he had begun to see every day, began inviting himself to stay with friends on Long Island, in particular Pollock and Krasner, who lived in Springs, only a few miles from Klein, Newton, and Pearce.

Pollock was in a period of deep crisis, one that Greenberg himself had helped create. A lifelong alcoholic, Pollock, with Krasner's help, had managed to remain sober between 1947 and 1951, one of his periods of greatest productivity. But in 1954 he decided to take his art in a new direction, moving away from the drip paintings that made him famous.

Greenberg was unimpressed, describing Pollock's 1954 show at the Janis Gallery as "forced, pumped, dressed up." His review seemed to imply that Pollock had lost his way: Pollock "found himself straddled between the easel picture and something else hard to define, and in the last two or three years he has pulled back." In the same essay, Greenberg seemed to place the crown of America's preeminent painter on the head of Clyfford Still, calling him "one of the most important and original painters of our time."

"So, Clem, who created the myth of Pollock—'this is the greatest living American painter'—goes out there and says, 'You've lost it, Jackson,'" said Barbara Rose, who was a close friend of Krasner's. "'You don't have it anymore. You're no good' . . . So Pollock, who has had the assurance and confidence and backing of both Clem and Lee, has a nervous breakdown, and he starts drinking again."

In the midst of this crisis, Greenberg became the constant weekend guest of Pollock and Krasner so that he could continue seeing his therapist, Ralph Klein. Their house was a war zone, with a drunk, angry, and highly abusive Pollock tearing into Krasner all the time. "Jackson was in a rage at her from morning till night," Greenberg recalled.

The situation was untenable. Feeling that this violent and ugly fighting would end up killing his friends, Greenberg insisted that Krasner see an analyst immediately, and he contacted Jane Pearce, hostess and mentor to his own therapist. Greenberg, Krasner, and Pollock—one of the most famous troikas of modern American art—drove over together to Pearce's house. Pollock's biographers Steven Naifeh and Gregory Smith interviewed Jane Pearce about the encounter (the only interview of any kind Pearce is known to have given). "Clem pushed her to do this because he saw that Jackson was killing her," Pearce told them. "Or allowing her to kill herself. It was a moment of absolute crisis." Pearce recommended that Krasner begin therapy right away. Although Pollock vehemently opposed Krasner's seeing a therapist, he agreed to begin therapy as well. "Jackson couldn't stand the idea of Lee and me in therapy without him," Greenberg recalled. "He didn't want to be left out." Pollock, too, would begin seeing Ralph Klein. When September rolled around and the analysts all returned to Manhattan, Greenberg resumed his regular sessions with Klein while Pollock made a weekly pilgrimage into the city for therapy.

Among other things, the Sullivanians were convinced that alcohol was an effective means of relieving anxiety and promoting creativity—a message both Greenberg and Pollock were happy to hear. Harry Stack Sullivan was a heavy drinker, and Pearce was a serious alcoholic for most of her life. Greenberg was a lifelong alcoholic, albeit a high-functioning one, at least in the first decades of his career. He worked hard but generally began drinking in the afternoon and continued into the night, which may have made his brilliant career less brilliant, fueled his violent outbursts, and brought his more unpleasant and belligerent qualities to the fore.

It is hard to overstate how important alcohol was to the postwar New York art scene. In Greenwich Village, the heart of bohemian New York, there were boozy parties, lots of flirting and sexual promiscuity, long arguments about art and politics, interpersonal feuds, shouting matches, and the occasional fistfight.

Greenberg's relationship with Frankenthaler had begun—and ended—as many things in that period did: with large quantities of alcohol. When the twenty-one-year-old Frankenthaler wanted to lure the famed critic to a show of Bennington College artists she had organized back in 1950, Greenberg told her he would come only if they served drinks. "It just so happens," Frankenthaler replied, "that we have enough money to have a lot of liquor, and we're not only going to have drinks but we're having both martinis and Manhattans." Five years later, their relationship ended in a drunken brawl.

The denouement occurred on October 4, 1955, at a party in Greenwich Village celebrating an opening by Paul Feeley, a leading abstract painter and former teacher of Frankenthaler's at Bennington. The jazz of Miles Davis and Charlie Parker mingled with cigarette smoke in the dimly lit apartment. "The room is filling up . . . people swooning with booze strain toward each other, confiding . . . secrets and lies and withholding secrets and truths," wrote Janice Van Horne, who observed the scene as a long-legged Bennington undergraduate. To her surprise, an older man sat down next to her, and they began chatting amiably. After he left, one of her friends came over to her and said, "Do you know who that was? That was Clement Greenberg, the most famous, the most important art critic in the world!" Frankenthaler, who was twenty-six, herself already famous and months beyond her breakup with Greenberg, appeared at the party with a new beau, a much younger and handsomer man. The next thing Van Horne knew, a fracas broke out in the kitchen, where Greenberg had knocked over someone who needled him about Frankenthaler's new boyfriend. Greenberg then sought out Frankenthaler and slapped her across the face. Her date and Greenberg started fighting.

Far from being deterred, the young Van Horne sat and watched, mesmerized. "This was drama, like something that happened in the movies," she later wrote in a memoir about her life with Clem Greenberg.

Before she left the party, she went over to Greenberg and asked him if he wanted her phone number.

Greenberg began seeing Van Horne, who was twenty-one years old and a virgin. When they got married the following year, he told her that their marriage would be nonmonogamous, an idea that was certainly reinforced by his Sullivanian therapy. He would act on that premise, and so would she.

Jackson Pollock also continued with his Sullivanian therapy, coming into New York every week for a session with Klein followed by an evening out on the town, drinking heavily. On Tuesdays, Pollock took the train into the city accompanied by a friend, Patsy Southgate, who was tasked with making sure he didn't detour into the bar at Pennsylvania Station on his way to Klein's office on West Eighty-Sixth Street. "On the train he kept talking about how much he loved Ralph Klein," Southgate told Pollock's biographers. "He thought Klein was the only person who understood him."

Pollock may have loved Klein because the message Klein conveyed was very much what Pollock wanted to hear. The Sullivanian view in a nutshell was that a person's creative energy and drive for growth are suppressed early in life by controlling parents, and that the answer is removing repression.

"We believe that what is dissociated in most people, infants and adults, is their energy," Jane Pearce told Pollock's biographers. "Their spontaneity, their creativity, their capacity for tenderness gets repressed, and this frustration leads to a certain amount of hostility." Therapy meant removing the levers of repression. For Pollock this meant a license to drink and carry on as much as he pleased. "He would say: 'What the fuck: everybody should always do what they want to do,'" Pollock told a friend in that period. "'And if I want to dump Lee home and sit with the guys down at the bar, so what?'"

Pollock's Tuesday evenings were usually spent at the Cedar Tavern, the downtown artists' favorite hangout, where Pollock, raging drunk, would put on a wild performance that the bar's regulars came to anticipate. "Jackson would come in as though he were an outlaw brandishing two pistols," recalled the artist Mercedes Matter. "You fucking whores, you think you're painters, do you?" he once shouted. He would knock glasses off the table, turn over people's plates of food, and insult friends and strangers. Pollock's weekly appearances came to be known as the "Tuesday-night shoot-out at the Cedar saloon.'"

The evening often reached a crescendo, with Pollock smashing up the place and creating a scene of morose self-destruction. "More than once, after breaking a tableful of glasses and plates, Pollock would sit conspicuously in a corner booth and play with the sharp fragments, casually making designs as his fingers dripped blood onto the table-top," reported one Cedar Tavern regular. This seems like a macabre self-parody of Pollock's famous drip paintings at a time when he was virtually unable to do any real work.

When Klein complained to Pearce privately about Pollock showing up drunk for their therapy sessions, Pearce advised that there was little he could do other than "pray and hope that Jackson will come to ther-apy and deal with his anxieties in a better way." Klein never discussed the possibility of Pollock's needing outside help with his drinking, such as Alcoholics Anonymous, or advised him against driving drunk. Pol-lock's friends, alarmed by his continued deterioration, convinced the artist to ask Klein about his drinking, to which Klein is said to have replied, "That's your problem," meaning that it was a mere symptom for Pollock to clear up, not a fit topic for their therapy. One of Pollock's con-cerned friends called Klein to explain that the artist was drinking so much that he hardly ate, but Klein reportedly responded that it wasn't a problem: "Look at the stuff that's in beer, the grain and so forth."

Klein instead appears to have focused—in line with what would become Sullivanian orthodoxy—on the pernicious effect of the ma-levolent mother. Pollock began to refer to his mother, Stella, as "that old womb with a built-in tomb." Klein told Pollock that his problem was that he hadn't really allowed himself to live. (Pollock supposedly told Klein that he and his wife hadn't had sex in three years.) Klein advised

Pollock "to stop repressing his feelings and 'act out his sexual impulses,' to get back in touch with his creative energy," Naifeh and Smith write. "In other words, he needed a woman."

Pollock began making passes at numerous women during his evenings of New York barhopping. Most were not interested in a self-destructive, angry drunk, but he found a receptive target in a young, extremely attractive twenty-six-year-old woman named Ruth Kligman, who harbored the fantasy of leading the bohemian life as an artist and the consort of a famous artist.

"[The Sullivanians] gave you permission to indulge yourself in anything that made you feel good," Barbara Rose said. "You drive and drink, don't worry about it. Lee was very angry, and she didn't want him to see [the Sullivanians], but Pollock was very happy. And then they said, do you like young girls? And they're beautiful and your wife is old and she's ugly. Go after the young girl. They gave him permission and he was completely out of his mind in anything he wanted to do."

Pollock began inviting Kligman out to Long Island and conducting a public affair with her. Krasner asked him to break it off and to see a different kind of therapist. To escape the situation and give Pollock the space to regroup, she took a trip to Europe. Pollock showed signs that he wanted to reconcile with her—he sent two dozen roses to her hotel in Paris and took out a passport, says Rose—but he continued to drink and see Kligman.

On the afternoon of August 11, 1956, Ruth Kligman took the train out to Amagansett, bringing along a young friend, Edith Metzger, partly to act as a buffer between herself and Pollock and partly to show off her famous romantic conquest. On the ride out, she filled her friend's head with a vision of the romantic artist's life that Pollock led among other artists, but when they arrived, Pollock was already drinking and the kitchen was full of dirty dishes and empty bottles. Rather than taking the two young women to the beach—they had brought their bathing suits—Pollock took them to a dimly lit local bar where the women spent the afternoon watching the taciturn Pollock drink. The high point of the day was supposed to be a concert at a friend's house. Pollock was so drunk that he drove his Oldsmobile convertible at a crawl, and he was stopped by a concerned police officer who let them go when Pollock assured him that he was fine. But he began to feel sick as they approached the concert, and he stopped the car and decided to return home. Edith did not think Pollock should be driving and insisted that they call a cab. Ruth coaxed her back into the car. To defy and frighten his nervous passenger, Pollock began to gun the engine, prompting Edith to scream, "Stop the car! Let me get out!" Pollock floored the accelerator, and as he took a curve on Fireplace Road, less than a mile from his house, the big car skidded off the road and flipped over, crushing and killing Pollock and Metzger. Kligman was thrown from the car, but she survived. After Pollock's death, she kept up her role as artist's muse, taking up with the painter Willem de Kooning in a relationship that lasted several years. He even did a painting called *Ruth's Zowie*.

Despite Pollock's tragic self-destruction while under Ralph Klein's care, Greenberg remained devoted to his therapist and Sullivanian therapy, continuing to refer many of his favorite artists to the institute throughout the 1960s.

4

The 1960s—Time of Transition

On a spring day in 1966 in Vermont, the painter Jules Olitski—near the peak of his professional success—locked himself in his studio at Bennington College and threatened to kill himself.

"He had something of a breakdown," remembered Susan Crile, who was then a promising twenty-three-year-old painter who had studied with Olitski at Bennington and had become his girlfriend. In the bohemian environment of the artsy progressive women's college, Crile had become an accepted part of the Olitski household. "His wife, myself, and other people were outside trying to get him not to [harm himself] . . . He was in very bad shape."

At some point they called Clement Greenberg, and eventually they were able to coax Olitski out of his suicide attempt and convince him to see a therapist at the Sullivan Institute.

Olitski was one of four American artists chosen to present his work at the Venice Biennale that year and would soon be one of the first living artists to have a one-man show at the Metropolitan Museum of Art in New York. But he had his private demons. He had been born Jevel Demikovsky in 1922 in Snovsk, Ukraine, which was then part of the Soviet Union. His father was a Jewish Bolshevik who became a Soviet commissar but was executed by the regime shortly before his son was born. His mother emigrated to Brooklyn, where Jevel became Jules. His mother married a man named Olitski, who gave Jules his last name but apparently not much else. Jules Olitski loathed his stepfather, who had two older sons. Olitski described his place in the household as "Cinderella in an all-male cast." To escape his life, he would read all night in the bathroom when others had gone to sleep.

His dead father seems to have never been far from his mind. In 1965, the year before the breakdown that sent him into Sullivanian therapy, he painted a large, seemingly abstract picture called *Commissar Demikovsky*, the bulk of which was dominated by subtly shaded red paint, with dark greens bleeding in at the edges.

By 1966, Olitski was forty-four, with a wife and two children, the elder of whom was born during his first marriage. "Jules was very charismatic," Susan Crile recalled. "He had a broad, round face, intense blue eyes, and he had an amazing twinkle in his eyes and a wonderful smile and a slight wryness to him."

Crile continued, "What made Jules attractive was an intensity and energy he brought to the things he cared about. He would get involved in something and be totally focused." Olitski was a hard worker and a heavy drinker: he would often work all night and sleep until two in the afternoon, but he frequently drank with the same abandon. "I'm an addictive personality," he said many years later, speaking about his working method. "It's like when I drank. Enough was never enough."

After his breakdown in Bennington, Olitski moved to New York and began regular therapy. His wife and two daughters followed, as did Crile. Soon all five were in Sullivanian therapy.

Olitski was only one of many prominent artists whom Greenberg steered into Sullivanian therapy during the 1960s, creating a strange symmetry between abstract expressionism and the renegade psychoanalytic institute.

Bennington, in particular, became a power base for Greenberg and a feeder institution for the Sullivan Institute. Greenberg had gotten to know Bennington through Helen Frankenthaler, who graduated from the college in 1949. He had organized a major Jackson Pollock exhibition there in 1952, and he began lecturing there regularly, bringing many of the leading artists of the day for exhibitions, talks, or teaching positions, transforming an already strong art faculty into a veritable powerhouse. "Whenever Clem was around, he was the focal point. Everyone would hang on his every word," Crile recalled.

Greenberg had begun championing Olitski's work in the late 1950s and helped him get his job at Bennington. Kenneth Noland, another artist featured (along with Frankenthaler and Olitski) in Greenberg's *Post-Painterly Abstraction* exhibition of 1964, lived nearby and came to campus often as a guest artist. The British sculptor Anthony Caro (considered by many the greatest British sculptor after Henry Moore) was the head of the sculpture department. He entered into a fruitful collaboration with Olitski and Noland to create a series of painted sculptures that are still considered groundbreaking work. (Soon Noland, his wife, and one of his daughters were in Sullivanian therapy, too.)

At the same time, Greenberg was a conduit to the New York art scene, where reputations and money were made. You couldn't quite be a full member of the club if you were not in therapy. "There was pressure, but it was almost like, in a strange way, a perk you got from knowing certain people," the sculptor James Wolfe, who taught at Bennington in the late 1960s, told Florence Rubenfeld. "If you were accepted, you were let in on this wonderful thing you could do. You had access. We all tried it." At the same time, however, "It became difficult to be part of the [Greenberg] group if the Newtonians weren't comfortable for you. People tended to think something was wrong with you."

There was a strange parallelism between Clem Greenberg and Saul Newton. Both were second-generation Jews who rejected their families and were avid womanizers, bullies who enjoyed making people squirm or using violence, but above all men who enjoyed power, created their own private clans or fiefdoms, and ruled them with an iron fist. (Among other things, the two men seem also to have shared a murderous history with fowl: Newton strangled chickens; Greenberg bludgeoned a goose.)

One might have thought that coexistence between two absolute rulers would be difficult or impossible, but for a significant period—about fifteen years—their two clans overlapped and reinforced one another to a considerable degree. By referring "his" artists to the Sullivan Institute for therapy and even into group apartments, Greenberg did not delegate or lose power; he seemed to gain it.

As Rubenfeld writes, "Within the Greenberg group, some of the power the [Sullivanian] therapists exerted over their patients was transferred to him. He replaced Saul Newton as the spider at the center of the web. Peter Stroud [an abstract artist] recalled: 'They broke off all of their dependency relationships and went to live in the Sullivanian houses . . . and then something strange occurred. I mean it was like G for "God" and G for "Greenberg." I don't know how it happened, but it seemed to be a reinforcing situation. The therapy transference seems to have been put not on the therapist but on Clement Greenberg.'"

At the same time, he and the prestigious clients he brought with him gave the Sullivanian Institute intellectual credibility and a certain downtown bohemian cool.

In 1963, Pearce and Newton published *The Conditions of Human Growth*, their one and only book, which became the bible of the Sullivan Institute. Patients were virtually required to read it and join study groups to discuss it. Although not widely read beyond the institute, *Conditions* received a respectful hearing from some reviewers, including a strongly positive review in *Commentary* (a magazine Greenberg had been an editor of for several years). The review noted the book's dense and turgid prose but insisted that it masked an important message: "Pearce and Newton have something important to say to anyone interested in how people become or fail to become as human as they can . . . There isn't a phony word in it."

The author of the review, Edgar Z. Friedenberg, even quoted T. S. Eliot to illustrate Pearce and Newton's concept of the "self-system," the defense system made up of all of parents' and society's "dos and don'ts":

> *They don't mean to do harm, but*
> *the harm does not interest*
> *them;*

Or they do not see it, or they
justify it,
Because they are absorbed in the
endless struggle
To think well of themselves.

*   *   *

The Sullivanian approach focused almost entirely on the individual patient's need for personal and creative growth, on the repressed hungering "after the infinities of growth." In some cases, this meant encouraging women who were rebelling against their traditional wifely duties to pursue their own careers. By the 1960s, the institute had begun to encourage some of its patients to live with one another in single-sex apartments. This often meant that they could pool resources, hire babysitters to look after their children, and, when they were old enough, send them to boarding school.

Consequently, Sullivanian therapy may have been better for Jules Olitski than for the rest of his family. "I think [the Sullivanians] told him he was the most important being on the planet, and he should be paying all his attention to his creative process," said Lauren Olitski Poster, his younger daughter. "They told him he could sleep with as many women as he wanted and didn't have to focus on being a parent. I'm sure he thought that was great." Living instinctually was something Olitski wanted to do in his work and his life. He compared making a work of art to making love: "Do you pause in the middle of it and say, 'What does it mean?'"

The central feature of Sullivanian therapy was the systematic dismantling of the nuclear family, which, in the case of the Olitskis, they accomplished with almost surgical precision. Within about a year, all four members of the family—Olitski; his wife, Andrea; and the two children, Eve (who was eighteen) and Lauren (who was ten)—each had their own therapist and would all be living apart from one another. Jules Olitski had a studio downtown while his wife and older daughter lived in separate Sullivanian apartments. Their therapists convinced Olitski and his wife to send Lauren away to boarding school, despite her young age. Sullivanian therapy had worked like a kind of nuclear fission, splitting the atom of the nuclear family and scattering its pieces.

"The Sullivanians told my parents that the worst thing a person can do is raise their own children," Lauren said. "I remember my mother actually telling me that I'd be better off if I wasn't being exposed to her neurosis that had been passed down to her by her parents." Given Olitski's tragic and painful childhood (executed father and cruel stepfather), the Sullivanian paradigm of the toxic family would have made a lot of sense to him. "They thought it would be better for me not to have their bad influences inflicted on me. Not sure they really believed that, or if the life they were living at that time made having a young child around inconvenient. Whatever the reason, the Sullivanian dogma fit in quite nicely with what they already wanted to hear. At least for my dad. My mother may have been more torn but had been convinced by Jane Pearce that she was harming me and I'd be better off in boarding school."

Olitski continued to see his Bennington girlfriend, the painter Susan Crile, but since they were both in Sullivanian therapy, they were encouraged to date other people as well.

A couple of years later, at the age of twelve, Lauren decided to quit therapy but was forced to continue during her vacations from the North Country School, near Lake Placid and the Canadian border. Her therapist, Dominick (Dom) Antonelli, was frequently on the phone during their sessions. "I told my mother I thought it was ridiculous to be paying a guy to sit on the phone for fifty minutes while I sat there on the other side of his desk being ignored," Lauren said. "She said she agreed and I stopped going."

For Olitski's wife and older daughter, Eve, it became something more than therapy. Both lived in group apartments with other female patients for many years. Although there was nothing like a formal group, there was enough of an "us" versus "them" group feeling that

Eve stopped talking to her half sister, Lauren, when Lauren dropped out of therapy. The estrangement continued for most of their lives.

While Olitski had a separate life from the group, he also had a place in the community that had formed around the institute. On Sunday mornings, he would get together for a life drawing class with three Sullivanian therapists—Dom Antonelli, John Cates, and Art Liebeskind—all of whom were avid amateur painters. They hired a live model. It is remarkable to think of Olitski, an almost exclusively abstract artist who normally dripped and sprayed paint onto canvases, drawing from life with a model—let alone doing so with three Sullivanian analysts. Afterward, Olitski and the three therapists would have brunch.

Susan Crile, who had followed Olitski from Bennington to New York, initially found the adjustment to Sullivanian therapy and forced promiscuity difficult. "I was very much in love with Jules Olitski, and I was not happy with all of this sort of indiscriminate sex," she said. "He was always going off with people, and I was going off with people. I wasn't a happy camper to begin with." The therapists stressed that you cannot get everything you need from one person, whether it is a parent or a sexual partner. "That was a not un-useful idea, but they took it too far," she said.

"There were several things that were absolutely invaluable about the Sullivanians," said Crile, who in 2020 was living on the Upper West Side, a few blocks from the old Sullivanian headquarters. "One was that they valued creativity and they valued work and they were very, very supportive of that." A second was that they were also supportive of the professional aspirations of women. "Coming out of middle-class America in the fifties, where everything was about finding a good husband, getting married, that was very important," Crile said. Her mother had died when she was twenty and still in college. Her father had remarried and was deeply opposed to her decision to become an artist, leading to a rupture between them. "So, obviously, I got into the Sullivanians at a point at which I wanted a family, and I think that's why it was the perfect place and time for me to be sucked up into it." A third good thing in her view was the emphasis on peer friendships.

One day as Crile sat in the waiting room of her first therapist, Julie Schneider, she ran into the singer Judy Collins, who had been in Sullivanian therapy since the early 1960s. Crile and Collins struck up a friendship, discovered that they both loved the work of Henri Matisse, and decided to make a trip together to Paris to see a major Matisse exhibition.

Collins never lived in a Sullivanian apartment, but she followed many of the group's dictates. "I sure got a lot of mileage out of the Sullivanian belief that alcohol was good for anxiety and that having multiple sex partners was a political statement and a healthy lifestyle," she wrote.

Stephen Stills, the musician of Crosby, Stills & Nash fame, who was very much in love with Collins, felt that her therapy made their relationship impossible. He wrote about it in several biting passages of the iconic song he wrote about their breakup, "Suite: Judy Blue Eyes" (1969).

Tuesday morning,
Please be gone, I'm tired of you
What have you got to lose?

Collins heard the recorded version of the song performed by Crosby, Stills & Nash for the first time in a New York City taxi ride in 1969, asking the cabbie to turn up the volume on the car radio and then staggering out of the cab afterward.

"I knew after I heard it that first time," she wrote in her memoir *Sweet Judy Blue Eyes* (2011), "I would have a hard time getting over it— the affair, the breakup, what the song meant about my addiction to the therapists who told me it was not in my best interests to commit to anyone. I am not blaming them; I was the one who threw the dice and then backed away from the table. Stephen knew exactly what he was doing; he was that smart and that gifted. In a way it was his revenge, served hot, and it was magnificent."

Yet looking back on her years with the Sullivanians, Collins places it in the context of the times: "Certain revolutionary ideas Saul Newton and Jane Pearce practiced were attractive to an already liberal girl working her way into a career in the arena of music and social justice. At the time, everyone in my peer group was espousing free love. Communal living, group parenting, and sharing the wealth were sixties ideas . . . Only later, after I had left them, did I realize I had fallen under the spell of a cult." Collins remained in Sullivanian therapy for about fifteen years.

Collins, like Olitski, Kenneth Noland, Larry Poons, Lucinda Childs, and other famous creative people who were drawn to Sullivanian therapy in the 1960s, generally did not live in Sullivanian group apartments. But Crile, who was in therapy from 1966 until about 1972, delved deeper into the life of the group and watched it become more rigid and codified.

Like other Sullivanian patients, Crile quickly filled her time with frequent dates of all kinds: not just sexual dates, but study dates, dinner dates, sleepover dates that might, in fact, not involve sex. Friends of either sex would arrange to spend the evening together and then sleep in the same bed. "You just had dinner and drank and then went to bed and slept," Crile said. "It was about bonding."

Crile—perhaps typical for this period of transition in the life of the Sullivanian community—had one foot in the group and one foot outside. She had a big, airy studio apartment on Riverside Drive that served as work and living space. At a certain point she moved into a group apartment with other female Sullivanian patients but kept her old apartment as her painting studio. But living in a group apartment, there was suddenly a sense that she had to fall in line with all the group's precepts. "There was a feeling of pressure that was really unpleasant, of having to conform in a certain way to unconformity," she said. They wanted their patients to socialize with each other, to like one another. "It almost felt like you weren't allowed to not want to have a date with someone because you didn't happen to like that person. There was some weird sense of a low-key pressure to be extremely egalitarian in a way that's not really quite natural."

In the 1960s, there was a push in the group toward communal living, especially patients living together. Not only did the patients socialize with one another, but therapists also socialized with patients and sometimes lived in the group apartments. And that's where life got very complicated for Crile.

Saul Newton and Jane Pearce's marriage had begun to come apart by the mid-1960s. Paul Newton, their third and youngest child, born in 1954, recalls his parents fighting frequently. "My bedroom was right above theirs, and I can recall waking up in the middle of the night to them fighting. My mother was a depressive alcoholic, and my father was an irascible person, prone to anger." In 1964, while still married to Jane Pearce, Newton had fathered a child with one of his patients, a former soap opera actress named Joan Harvey, who had then trained to become a therapist. In 1969, Newton and Harvey had a second child together. Around the same time, Newton took up with another patient, a pretty, young aspiring therapist named Helen Moses. By about 1970, Newton's two mistresses were living together at opposite ends of a large apartment in the Belnord, a rather grand Upper West Side apartment building at the corner of Eighty-Sixth Street and Broadway. "Joan had her area, and at the other end Helen had her area, and they were at war," Crile said. "Joan had the baby with him, and Helen wanted to be number one." Crile got to be friendly with both Joan Harvey and Helen Moses, but then she caught the eye of Saul Newton. He groomed the beautiful young painter as his latest bedmate, buying one of her paintings, which hung in the apartment where Joan Harvey and Helen Moses lived. "I think I was brought in to smooth out the rough edges of that triangle," she said.

Just to make her situation that much more complicated, Crile had changed therapists from Julie Schneider to Jane Pearce, who had, after her split with Newton, moved into a group apartment with other women. In other words, Crile was in therapy with Newton's fourth wife while carrying on an affair with Newton, which took place in an apartment occupied by Newton's two principal mistresses, future wives number five and six. On top of all that, Pearce drank vodka steadily throughout their sessions at eleven in the morning—and sometimes offered Crile a drink as well. "She had a baby bottle, so she could measure the number of ounces of vodka she could have," Crile said. It would be hard to invent a more wildly unprofessional therapeutic situation.

Looking back at the eight or nine years she was in Sullivanian therapy, Crile was astonished by the changes, even in the therapy itself. "I remember going to my first session with Julie. She lived in an apartment on the Upper West Side, which was her apartment where she lived with her daughter. It seemed perfectly normal . . . She wore skirts and stockings and high-heeled dress shoes. She looked the way you might think a therapist would look . . . By the end of the time I was there, it had devolved into communes, everybody living together, therapy sessions in the bedroom of the therapist because there was no other space to have it . . . And I was in therapy with Jane Pearce, who was drinking vodka all the way through her therapy sessions. This was quite a devolution."

What Crile experienced as a "devolution" was part of Pearce and Newton's attempt to put their theories into practice in their everyday lives. By moving out of her town house and into a group apartment with several other women, Pearce was following through on what she saw as one of the main insights of Sullivanian psychology: the need to recoup the crucial phase of chumship that Sullivan said many people missed out on. At the same time, the house on West Seventy-Seventh Street, where Pearce and Newton had lived with their children, was now a kind of male residence where Saul Newton lived with Ralph Klein and other male therapists. Along with this immersion in chumship, Newton was also exploring the other pillar of Sullivanian theory: sexual freedom.

While *The Conditions of Human Growth* described the suffocating nature of traditional family life, it stopped short of openly advocating for sexual freedom. In 1970, Pearce and Newton spelled things out much more clearly in an unpublished paper they coauthored, "Establishment Psychiatry—And a Radical Alternative," which circulated at the Sullivan Institute: "The concept of sexual fidelity or even serial monogamy, which is central to the nuclear family, is also central to the restriction of spontaneous interpersonal interaction. What goes on between two persons together involves only each other, and does not really involve a third party."

Pearce and Newton quoted the Black Panther leader Bobby Seale in arguing that sexual freedom is inextricably linked to political revolution: "Bobby Seale has said that the goal of the Revolution is that a man and a woman can get together on the basis of natural attraction."

But they took Seale's idea a step further, arguing that people freely pursuing relationships should not be limited to sexual relationships. "He understated his case," Pearce and Newton wrote. "The goal is for one person and another person to be able to get together on the basis of natural attraction regardless of sex, and whether or not physical contact is involved. This is not only the goal but part of the impelling force towards revolution." In their formulation, creating a world apart from the family, based on the "intimacy of peers," meant not just sexual freedom but also communal living, as well as the nonsexual Sullivanian sleepover dates they were urging on their patients. Because people were fundamentally "social animals," all growth, they believed, took place in contact with other people.

This laid out the theoretical foundation for what Pearce and Newton were doing in their lives and urging their patients to do: living with peers, rather than in families, while pursuing sexual freedom. Although this represented their official position about what constituted healthy behavior, Saul Newton's moving on and starting a new family with the actress Joan Harvey was clearly devastating to Pearce, as she made clear in poetry she wrote in private. On March 3, 1964, two days before Joan Harvey gave birth to the first of two children she had with

Saul Newton, Jane Pearce wrote, parodying a lyric from *My Fair Lady* (1956):

> *The pain*
> *in Jane*
> *is mainly*
> *in the brain*

While Pearce may have been made uneasy, this new radical reformulation of their theory gave Saul Newton cover for his own choice to flout traditional norms of therapeutic behavior: sleeping with his own patients, his wife's patients, and the female therapists he supervised. This was hardly unknown in psychoanalytic circles: it was not until 1973 that the American Psychiatric Association adopted the unequivocal policy that "sexual activity with a patient is unethical." Nonetheless, when the American Psychological Association conducted a survey of 703 therapists in 1979, it found that 10.9 percent admitted to engaging in erotic contact with their patients. The real number may well have been higher, as some may have been reluctant to admit it even in a survey.

At one point, Esther Newton, Saul's eldest child, sent one of her closest friends—who was going through a period of crisis—to her father for a consultation. "She was an attractive woman, and he asked her for a blow job," Esther said. "That was the first time I ever stood up to him. We went to our favorite Chinese restaurant, and I said, 'I can't believe you did that,' and he didn't deny it. He was like, 'Well, what's the problem?' And I said, 'If you ever, ever do that again, I will never speak to you again.' And his response was so typical. He said, 'Well, I think you're being very bourgeois, but if that's what you want, then okay.'"

The devolution that Susan Crile described also represented a significant power shift within the Sullivanian movement: Jane Pearce had been eclipsed in Saul Newton's life—as well as within the institute she founded—by two younger women. In 1972, Pearce was fifty-eight but seemed much older. Years of heavy drinking had taken their toll: she had white hair and was overweight. She had begun a long battle with melanoma, and doctors had been forced to remove part of her nose. She wore a Band-Aid on her nose but refused any cosmetic surgery, as if to show her unconcern for appearances. People who met her in those years recall that she was always seated, a drink in one hand and a cigarette in the other. Joan Harvey and Helen Moses, by contrast, were still young, sexually attractive, and extremely ambitious, eager to take Pearce's place in Saul Newton's life as well as in the institute she had founded in 1957. Harvey and Moses were friends, strategic allies but also fierce rivals.

Paul Newton, Saul and Jane's youngest child, recalls visiting his (now divorced) parents in that period out in Amagansett. His mother was at the margins of what had become a larger, younger group. "She was isolated, didn't have a lot of friends hanging out with her. She was sloppy drunk and sometimes a little weepy."

*   *   *

One day in 1968 the novelist Richard Elman entered his wife's apartment on the Upper West Side and found a naked Jules Olitski alone in his wife's bed. Olitski was terrified that Elman—towering over Olitski at six foot five and ten years younger—might attack him in a fit of jealous rage. But Elman had separated from his wife. He didn't have a place to store his stuff, so he had simply stopped by to get a suit he needed. Elman offered to make Olitski breakfast, and they became friends.

It turned out that Elman and Olitski, as they discovered, had quite a lot in common, aside from Elman's wife, Emily. They had both grown up in Brooklyn in Jewish families from Eastern Europe and had both taught at Bennington. Elman was, like Olitski, one of the intellectual figures who lent a certain glamour to the Sullivan Institute in the late 1960s. He had moved from Bennington to New York when his marriage was on the rocks, thinking that a therapy stressing independence and individual growth was a possible recipe for an amicable divorce. He moved into a group apartment and started teaching in the Columbia University master of fine arts program. Elman, like Olitski, was in therapy with Ralph Klein, therapist to the stars (Jackson Pollock, Clem Greenberg, Judy Collins). Like Olitski, Elman had a girlfriend, Janie P., a young student painter he'd met at Bennington. She had followed him to New York and entered Sullivanian therapy, much as Susan Crile had followed Olitski. Although Elman had not minded when Olitski slept with his soon-to-be ex-wife, he was not happy when Olitski—in the constant sexual merry-go-round of Sullivanian life— began dating Janie.

Richard Elman, who died in 1997, spent only about four years in Sullivanian therapy, but the period was a hugely important chapter in his life and one that haunted him for the rest of his days. His last book, *Namedropping* (1998), includes a series of portraits of the people he encountered during his years in Sullivania (as he called it), including Saul Newton and Jules Olitski. Although Elman ended his time in therapy with a deeply negative view of the group, he had been a big proponent of Sullivanian therapy for a while. He dedicated his 1971 novel, *An Education in Blood*, to Ralph Klein. In the fall of 1971, when the young Richard Price entered Elman's fiction writing class up at Columbia, Elman was living on West Seventy-Seventh Street, just down the street from Saul and Jane's town house, with a group of Sullivanian therapists. Elman, as Price recalled, was clever and charismatic, "a tall, gobbly guy with a Lenny Brucian schtick," a fast-talking Brooklyn Jewish patter laced with humor and profanity that reminded Price of the comedian (who kept getting arrested for obscenity). Elman, at the time, was working on an autobiographical book, *Fredi & Shirl & the Kids* (1972), that combined urban Jewish humor with Sullivanian therapy; it is a bitter-funny attack on his parents, containing such lines as "It's easy to be an anti-Semite when you grow up with a father like that."

It's not hard to see the influence of his Sullivanian therapy in the depiction of his parents as terrifying and murderous. Elman was living in the town house belonging to John Cates, with Sullivanian therapists Dom Antonelli and Art Liebeskind, all three of them fathers trying to raise their children outside a traditional family. Elman moved in with his daughter, Margaret, custody of whom he shared with his ex-wife, Emily. After entering therapy, Emily had decided she did not want to be the primary caregiver. "I took on the mothering role," Elman later wrote. The group was experimenting with alternative gender and parenting arrangements. For a time, this seemed like a nice, matey arrangement—four single men, each with children. The kids stayed on an upper floor outfitted with bunk beds. Elman's therapist, Ralph Klein, who lived on the same street in Jane Pearce and Saul Newton's town house, was also raising two children on his own.

Elman even taught a writing class for people in the Sullivanian community. Art Liebeskind, who lived upstairs from him, remembered the friendly camaraderie between them: "I started writing stories and short pieces, and I would go downstairs and show him something, he'd make corrections and then show me something he was working on: 'What do you think of this?'"

Clearly, this all-male alternate family living arrangement was another attempt at developing close same-sex friendships in the spirit of Sullivanian chumship. In fact, Elman's novel includes a chapter called "Chums." His parents, Elman wrote, had no real friends and ridiculed his own efforts at forming friendships with other boys.

But at some point Elman's experience turned very sour.

During the summer of 1972 he went out to Amagansett with a Sullivanian therapist he had been dating, whom he calls Blanche. It was she who had found him his room in the house on Seventy-Seventh Street where one of her former shrinks lived. "Oddly, I wasn't jealous when they sometimes slept together," he wrote.

Elman wrote a memorable if scathing portrait of Saul Newton holding court at dinner during that visit, surrounded by adoring acolytes and served at table by his own private chef, a Corsican anarchist who'd prepared grilled bluefish and an ice-cream bombe. "I love Saul," the guest next to Elman, another therapist, crooned to him. Elman was meeting Newton for the first time. "Unmitred, his head was . . . large, his lips coarse as chicken gizzards, a mean, petulant, interesting face," Elman wrote. They engaged in a certain amount of testy, competitive banter. "I know your wife," Newton told him. Elman asked whether that meant he "knew" her in the biblical sense. "Know-it-alls and wise guys," Newton replied. At a certain point Newton asked Elman if he had any heroes; Elman shrugged and replied that he wasn't sure. "To be weak is miserable," Newton replied. "Personally, my two heroes are Chairman Mao and Harry Stack Sullivan." Then he said, "I've always hated Jewish intellectuals like you, Elman. Though maybe you're different. We'll find out if you really want friends."

Evidently, the aggressive thrust-and-parry between them made a favorable impression on Newton. "Saul really was taken with you," Blanche told him.

Clearly, something of a cult of personality had begun to form around Newton by this point. Esther Newton recalled an incident from the late 1960s that drove this point home: "My father had always smoked four packs of cigarettes a day—everyone smoked, but he was worse." He was now in his sixties, and his doctors had ordered him to quit. "So he rented a yacht and—to give you an idea of how big a pedestal he was on—all the others went on the ship, and every single one of them had to quit, and they did quit."

Elman provides some clues as to how Newton may have exercised power over the artists who moved in his orbit, mastering them like a lion tamer with a whip: "You're all a bunch of desperate fakers, liars, and scam artists," Elman quotes him telling a group of artists. "And you know it, which is why we talk." At another point Elman writes, "I can remember watching a celebrated modern painter, with a big six-figure income and galleries showing his work around the world, cower before a withering summary of his character and then try to appease the old devil with a gift of a painting allegedly worth thousands of dollars." Elman is referring to the practice of Sullivanian therapists giving their patients "summaries," or analyses of their personality, which often felt like character assassinations. Kenneth Noland, whose paintings still sell in the seven figures, gave Saul Newton a major painting.

Newton was not trained as a therapist, but he had a shrewd intelligence for spotting and exploiting people's points of vulnerability, especially "impostor syndrome," a particular insecurity of artists who—based on a single review—could rocket from obscurity to fame or back again.

While dismissing his artist-patients as "scam artists," Newton, in one of his more candid moments, seems to have held a similar view of his own profession. He told a colleague about attending a party full of artists and being asked if he, too, was an artist. "Yeah, a bullshit artist," Saul said. The next day, apparently, the man called Newton to get into therapy.

Elman, a sometimes ornery, cantankerous individual, began to find the groupthink and groupspeak of the Sullivanian community annoying. "When you had sex with a Sullivanian, first came the pleasure, then came your summary. All your faults were enumerated. It didn't help to answer tit for tat. You were guilty of 'romantic focus' or a 'distancing maneuver.' They actually made celibacy feel good."

Two things seem to have driven Elman over the edge shortly after his trip out to Amagansett. The first regarded Elman's daughter, Margaret, who had been four years old when her parents entered therapy and was now eight. Elman began to feel that his ex-wife, encouraged by her therapist, had been making more and more difficult demands on him: "Large sums of money were extorted from me to pay for her therapy, for art school tuitions, for housekeepers." And when he raised the possibility of moving away with their daughter, he was threatened that he would lose all custody.

At the same time, his relationship with his therapist girlfriend, Blanche, was coming to a head. Blanche was a patient of Saul Newton's, and as she approached age thirty-five, Newton told her she ought to have a child, suggesting that Elman should be the father. Elman, already feeling overwhelmed managing a messy divorce and the care of one child, refused. "I understand," Blanche said, "but Saul won't like it."

Blanche then asked Elman to at least help her get pregnant. "It's a matter of playing out all the probabilities," she told him. "We'll surely increase the likelihood of conception by increasing my sperm pool input." Elman said he didn't want to "swim in the sperm pool."

Newton got involved and tried to force Elman into fathering the child. When Elman objected and pointed out that Blanche didn't want to have a child and that it was Newton's idea, Saul flew into a rage. "'Goddamn psychopath,' he shouted. The veins were popping in his forehead like a coaxial cable, his little grey goat beard oscillating against his chin. 'You have a heart the size of a pea.'"

Clearly, this arrangement of several men helping a woman have a child on her own was part of the Sullivanians' idea of alternatives to the traditional family, but Elman's experience of being bullied into fathering a child led to his leaving, or being asked to leave, his Sullivanian apartment.

Elman wandered around the Upper West Side in a daze during what may have been a genuine psychological breakdown. (He would later be diagnosed as bipolar and spend time in the psych ward at Bellevue Hospital, his second wife and widow, Alice Goode-Elman, told me.) He ran into his old student Richard Price and one of Price's Sullivanian roommates. "He looked bugged-eyed and crazy," Price recalled. "He looked like the prophet from Revelations, John of Patmos. He said he had been thrown out of his apartment, and we took him to our apartment like you would take in a big lost dog." He slept that night on Price's couch, but by the time they woke in the morning, he was gone. They never saw each other again.

In some ways, this began the hardest part for Elman. When he tried to see his daughter, Margaret, he was denied access. "A Sullivanian babysitter told me I wasn't feeling well enough and it would be best for my daughter if we had no contact at present," he later wrote.

Elman's ex-wife, on the advice of her therapist, sent their eight-year-old daughter away to a boarding school in upstate New York near the Canadian border—the same school Lauren Olitski had attended a few years earlier. Elman's former roommates, John Cates, Art Liebeskind, and Dom Antonelli, were all sending their kids away, too. Margaret Elman was miserable at boarding school and looking forward to seeing her mother over the Christmas break. After the six-hour bus ride from Lake Placid to New York City, she was met at the station not by her mother, but by one of her mother's friends from the group. The woman explained that Margaret could not see her mother but would be spending the holiday at a children's camp in Connecticut. When they arrived the next day, it turned out that there were no other children there. The only people around were an older couple, the caretakers of the facility, who lived in a house on the grounds. Margaret spent the first days alone in the empty children's dormitory, after which the caretaker couple took pity on her and brought her into their home, where she spent the rest of the holiday. Picking up on the fact that she was crazy about horses, the couple bought her a few Breyer horses, rather expensive plastic horse models, so that she would have something to open on Christmas.

It was the beginning of a long, painful nightmare for Elman, his ex-wife, and their daughter. In the period before his death, in 1997, Elman planned to write a book about his experience and about the Sullivan Institute. He left behind an outline and proposal called "Leaving Sullivania."

He had clearly been traumatized. As he wrote at the end of his unpublished book proposal: "The costs to me, my former wife, and our child were large and deeply debilitating. It's a wonder any of us have survived well enough to do work of any sort, or concentrate, or take up our lives again. It was some years before I would consider writing anything about the experience, and then I had problems concentrating on any sort of serious writing, aside from short pieces and reviews . . . This book will cause me great pain to write, but before I die it's probably something I need to do."

PART II

THE GROUP GATHERS

5

Transference

Before Deedee Agee started therapy in early 1971, she woke up most mornings crying. She was only twenty-four, had married at twenty-one a man she had known since she was fifteen. She had a little boy who was almost two. Her proper name was Julia Theresa Agee, but one of her grandmothers had called her Chickadee, which the young Julia had pronounced "Deedee," and the nickname stuck. Her father, the writer James Agee, had died when Deedee was only eight. Her husband, Bill Bollinger, a sculptor who was several years older, had filled the void her father left. Bollinger was a leading figure during the 1960s in the avant-garde art world, pioneering the field of minimalist sculpture with such people as Richard Serra, Eva Hesse, and Bruce Nauman. He made sculpture out of chain-link fence and hardware store materials like metal pipes, rope, hoses, and wooden sawhorses. According to a *New York Times* article that appeared in 2012 when a posthumous retrospective of his work was mounted, "Between 1965 and 1970 he was at the center of avant-gardist action in New York and Europe."

Deedee had artistic aspirations of her own but had put them aside to be a wife and mother. Bollinger decided he wanted to get away from what he called the "bullshit" New York art scene, and they moved up to a summer house her family owned in Hillsdale, New York, two hours north of the city. The house had no heat or electricity, and Deedee was alone a great deal of the time, taking care of a year-old baby almost by herself, boiling diapers on the gas stove and washing clothes by hand. Her husband was teaching in New York half the time, he drank a great deal, and their marriage was badly strained. During one of his absences Deedee decided to go into New York, staying at her family's house when she knew her mother was away. She got a family friend to look after the baby for a few hours while she walked around Greenwich Village. She felt as if people didn't see her as she walked along, and she became convinced that she was literally invisible. She called her sister, Andrea, who was training to become an analyst. Her sister referred her to Jane Pearce.

Later that day, Deedee arrived at the Sullivan Institute at Seventy-Seventh Street, finding Pearce in an office crammed with books, African art, abstract paintings, and no conventional Freudian couch. Pearce offered Deedee a drink and prepared herself a cocktail. Pearce's extreme informality seemed like a refreshing change from the strict Freudian therapist Deedee had briefly consulted when she was a teenager. She poured herself a hefty glass of Scotch and sat down.

"What can I do for you?" Jane asked, as Deedee recounted in an unpublished piece about her first years in therapy.

Deedee talked about how unhappy she was, how isolated and lonely she was in the country. She told Jane that she wanted to have another child, but one conceived with passion, and that she and her husband rarely had sex anymore. Repeating something a therapist had told her when she was fifteen, Deedee wondered whether she was "too focused on sex, too promiscuous, a fatherless girl looking for love anywhere I could find it."

"How old are you again?" Jane asked.

"Twenty-four."

"And how long have you been together?"

"Nine years."

Jane took a drag on her cigarette, exhaled. "Nine years," she said. "Seems to me your problem is you're not promiscuous enough."

"This simple truth was like an explosion of light," Deedee wrote. "I never again thought I was invisible."

* * *

After Michael Cohen graduated from college in upstate New York in the spring of 1972, he moved to New York City, with nowhere to stay and very little money. He crashed on the couch of an ex-girlfriend who had answered a "roommate wanted" ad placed by two women who were training to be therapists at the Sullivan Institute. The couch was in a large, shockingly grand apartment on the Upper West Side, in the Apthorp—a magnificent building occupying an entire city block, built in the style of an Italian Renaissance palace. With a soaring entryway leading to a huge interior courtyard with fountains, it was built by William Waldorf Astor in 1906, when the developers of the Upper West Side were trying to attract a wealthy clientele with buildings modeled on Medicean Florence. The apartments are vast, with high ceilings, elaborate architectural details, six or seven generously sized rooms, formal dining rooms, and, of course, a maid's room. The surrounding neighborhood was very mixed—drug and crime blocks alternating with handsome prewar apartment buildings that, because of white flight and rent control, had become ridiculously cheap, inhabited by less affluent folks like members of the Sullivanian training program. One of the women living in this apartment was Deedee Agee's younger sister, Andrea, a young training analyst.

Cohen's new Sullivanian friends welcomed him into their lives and their beds and helped him find a permanent place to live in another Sullivan apartment with a group of men. Everyone encouraged him to go into therapy, and he was immediately receptive to the idea. His father had died when he was four, leaving a huge hole in his life, and his mother died when he was in college, a loss he was still trying to fathom. His sister, to whom he was very close, had moved to Israel. He was twenty-two, alone, broke, and adrift.

The Sullivan Institute seemed a perfect fit for him. He liked the combination of psychotherapy and radical politics. He had studied English literature and film in college and participated in the anti-war protests that were sweeping American campuses in the late 1960s and early '70s. As he understood it, the Sullivan Institute provided what seemed to be missing in most left-wing politics. "This was an attempt to put the—the human into Marx," he said. "What's missing from Marxism is the human component . . . to have an authentic life and to really express oneself and have support from one's peers was very compelling as an idea."

Every Saturday evening, someone in the group would throw a big party. A typical Sullivanian party in this period included a garbage pail filled with inexpensive wine, or punch spiked heavily with gin or vodka. The record player might have been playing Santana's "Black Magic Woman" (1970) or the Rolling Stones' new *Sticky Fingers* (1971) album. New arrivals would be drawn in by the music and the body heat of dozens of people dancing or talking and flirting in corners, the windows frosted over with people's breath. If they wandered into one of the back bedrooms, they might come upon people smoking a joint or having sex. The people in these Sullivanian apartments appeared to be onto something extremely cool and exciting. And young people could afford to live in New York on the cheap, with already modest rents split five or six ways.

The Sullivanians introduced Cohen—a newcomer to Manhattan who knew only a handful of people—to a whole community of young people much like himself. At the same time, the social life was unlike anything he had ever seen. Everyone was friends with everyone else—dozens of young people in a handful of nearby buildings—in and out of one another's apartments, playing music, having parties. "And everyone was sleeping with each other in this community. And it was very natural . . . As a Jewish kid from three blocks north of the Bronx, the social part of it was extraordinary, and I was drawn into it." And all this fun was part of a larger political project: "It was a humanist revolution . . . To really have socialism, you have to transform the individual. And there was sex and communal living, and I was alone."

Richard Price began therapy around the same time, in 1972, through Richard Elman, his favorite teacher in the creative writing program at Columbia. After four years away at college, Price was back at home with his parents in a dull middle-class housing complex in the Bronx, sleeping in his childhood bedroom, lonely, unhappy, and trying to start a novel. One day after class, as he and Elman walked down Broadway talking, Elman suggested that Price get into therapy. Elman put him in touch with Dom Antonellli, one of the three Sullivan Institute therapists with whom Elman was living at the time. In that first session, Antonelli told Price that he didn't have to waste his time remaining at home squabbling with his parents. "This man is a genius," Price thought. When his therapist suggested that he go to one of the group's parties, Price decided to try it. He was a relatively short, slightly built, almost frail young man, with a baby face that made him look five years younger than his twenty-two years and a withered right arm from a childhood bout with polio that made him self-conscious. But he was smart, funny, and highly verbal, with a wicked ear for dialogue and an eye for the folkways of street life he had observed growing up in the Bronx, which would fill the novels and screenplays he wrote during his career.

Price found himself at an apartment filled with young people his own age or a little older who all seemed easy with one another and friendly toward him, a newcomer and outsider. Compared with living with his parents in the Bronx, this looked like paradise to him. The guys all had their own rooms, and women were coming and going.

A girl came up to Price and asked him if he had a date. He was initially confused. "It was eleven o'clock at night. Wasn't a date when you arranged to go to the movies?" he wondered. She suggested that they go home together that evening. "All of a sudden, you're sleeping with some woman and you're twenty-two and God just hit you with a lucky God stone." And it wasn't just the sex. The men were friendly, too. One of them would suggest that they have dinner, take out his datebook, and write it down. "Everybody had datebooks," he recalled. Price had fantasized as a kid about belonging to a kind of clubhouse with other boys, and now it was actually happening. "It felt to me like this is just: add water and it's instant friends. And you know, girls are going in and out . . . It's instant sex life. You don't have to get engaged to get laid. That's crazy. The world doesn't work that way, you know? You feel drugged with—with hopefulness. All of a sudden . . . it's like somebody opened the gates of heaven."

One of the people he recalled meeting was Michael Cohen, a slender young man with sandy-colored hair and glasses. Like Price, Cohen was bookish and highly verbal, a funny and lively talker. They were both twenty-two and native New Yorkers. Both were steeped in the tradition of Jewish humor and had the gift of gab. They decided to form a writers' group, where they read and discussed the early chapters of Price's first novel, *The Wanderers* (1974).

Some of the big-name artists who were in therapy in the 1960s were still around in the early '70s, giving the community a certain intellectual cachet and a decidedly hip vibe. Abstract expressionists like Kenneth Noland could still be found as dinner guests at Saul Newton's Amagansett house on summer weekends. Richard Elman had his writing course until he dropped out in 1972. The dancer Lucinda Childs was still giving a dance class for Sullivanian patients. Clement Greenberg's therapy had ended; the art world had changed, favoring pop art and minimalism rather than the abstract expressionism he'd championed. His influence had begun to wane, and he no longer funneled streams of artists into therapy, though he remained convinced that it had turned his life around by pushing him to break with his overbearing father. That generation of patients was beginning to drop out, but they left behind clouds of glory that helped draw in a large influx of young people, mostly in their early twenties. The town house where Price went for therapy was filled with paintings by Noland and Jules Olitski, pieces that might hang in museums, as well as paintings by the Sullivanian therapists themselves, many of whom were serious amateur artists.

New, younger creative people were coming along: there were two guys from the band Sha Na Na, a funny and talented group of Columbia student musicians who dressed up as 1950s greasers in gold lamé suits and leather jackets, with slicked-back hair or pompadour and ducktail haircuts, and did a spirited and funny repertoire of doo-wop classics. The group caught the attention of the rock star Jimi Hendrix, who invited them to perform at Woodstock in 1969. Another new member was the guitarist Elliott Randall, who had just recorded the hit song "Reelin' in the Years" for the band Steely Dan; Elliott's guitar solo in the song has been rated among the fifty greatest guitar solos in rock history. Michael Cohen became friends with a young sculptor, Roger Williams, who took him downtown to Max's Kansas City, the bar where Andy Warhol and his crowd used to hang out and where members of the musical and artistic avant-garde such as Lou Reed and Patti Smith played and congregated. Therapy had become a portal to a world that was unimaginably exciting.

When Cohen's first therapist proposed that he might want to join the therapist training program, he was flattered and interested. He hadn't really thought of being a therapist. He was enrolled in a master's program in library science as preparation to be an assistant curator at the Museum of Modern Art. But he agreed to join the Sullivan Institute's training program, and in doing that, he had to switch therapists and be analyzed by one of the institute's senior therapists, Joan Harvey. With this began a relationship that would dominate his life for the next decade.

Harvey, who had starred in the soap opera *The Edge of Night* (1956–84) and had roles in a couple of low-budget B movies, was a child of Hollywood. Her father had worked in the movie business, and her first husband, Harve Bennett, was a successful television and film producer. (He produced most of the *Star Trek* movies.) Born Joan Harris, she used Harvey, a variation of her husband's first name, as her stage and legal name. In *The Edge of Night*, she acted alongside Larry Hagman (later famous for his roles in the TV shows *I Dream of Jeannie* and *Dallas*). She was in a movie about the gangster "Pretty Boy" Floyd and a weird horror film called *The Hands of a Stranger* (1962), seemingly always cast in roles that called for high drama, strong emotion, and a lot of screaming. After starting therapy—and getting involved with Saul Newton—she decided to become a therapist and earned a Ph.D. in psychology. When she became Michael Cohen's therapist, Harvey was in her midforties, highly attractive, with raven-dark hair and a dramatic, charismatic personality. She exuded a compelling air of certainty and confidence as well as a deeply seductive charm. Her friends describe her as "brilliant and empathic," while granting that she had a mercurial and often volatile temper. For the young Mike Cohen, who had lost both parents, here was a sympathetic older person who took a deep interest in him. Cohen experienced a violent emotional attachment to her that shook him to the core. "I became dependent on her in a way that's very hard to describe," he said. "I felt that I could totally trust her; that she could be motivated by nothing but my best interests."

By 1972, when Cohen got into the group, Joan Harvey had become Saul Newton's fifth wife. Looking back, Cohen sees that in Joan and Saul he found the parents he no longer had: "Joan Harvey's maiden name was Harris, which was also my mother's maiden name. Saul Newton's real name was Saul Cohen, my last name. And so, you might say that underneath all this fancy talk and ideology, this was a family and I was really lonely."

*   *   *

Michael Bray entered therapy in early 1973. He had grown up in a fairly strict Catholic household in western Iowa. After a year of college in Nebraska, he moved to Chicago and entered a Dominican seminary with the intention of becoming a priest. He liked the communal life of the seminary but realized he didn't believe in God or in the Catholic Church, and he wasn't cut out for celibacy. He had witnessed the violence at the 1968 Democratic Party convention and sympathized with the anti-war protesters who were beaten by the police. He glimpsed the emerging counterculture, but he was a twenty-three-year-old virgin with a degree from the Aquinas Institute of Philosophy. He married a young woman at a Catholic college and decided to become a psychologist. The one graduate school that accepted him was Fordham University in New York City, so he and his new wife drove there with all their belongings and found an apartment in the Bronx, where the university was located.

Bray began his graduate work and also had a job at the Veterans Administration hospital, but he soon began to feel that his life was seriously adrift. Neither he nor his wife had ever been in a relationship before, had never had sex, and didn't really know how to do either. Undoing the inhibitions developed in preparing for a life of celibacy was not easy. By 1972, they were two years into their marriage and couldn't quite figure out how to make it work. "When I got married," Bray said years later, "I was a virgin, and we weren't even quite consummating. We were trying."

When he wasn't at work, Bray found himself spending time in the middle of the day drinking alone and watching game shows on television. He needed to do some therapy for his psychology degree, and a colleague at work named Roger suggested that he see his therapist, Art Liebeskind. When Bray showed up for his first appointment, he found himself in the office of a man in his late thirties who was very short—not much over five feet—and had a ponytail. The coffee table in his office was missing a leg and was propped up by a stack of *National Geographics*. "Well, this is different," Bray thought. But as soon as Art, the therapist, asked him why he was there, Bray burst into tears, began weeping uncontrollably, and managed to get out the words "Because I am afraid to be alive." And that, Bray said nearly fifty years after the fact, "started my part of the journey . . . I was basically saying, 'Help me, save my life.' I spilled out everything that I could possibly think of. Anything he asked of me or suggested, I was ready to try."

That moment of placing yourself in a therapist's hands, of seeing him or her as a kind of savior or genius, is one of the best-documented phenomena in psychotherapy, something Freud called "transference."

Patients enter therapy almost always in a state of some emotional distress. Unburdening themselves of their troubles to a sympathetic listener, they begin to feel better and then experience a wave of gratitude and admiration for the miracle worker who has relieved their suffering. The therapist becomes idealized in the mind of the patient in the way his or her parents were in childhood, becoming the good parent the patient may never have had. But sound psychoanalytic practice dictates that the analyst must work against this process, which may infantilize patients and throw them back into the position of dependence they experienced with their parents.

Transference often has an erotic undercurrent, which sometimes surfaces as sexual attraction. The singer Judy Collins writes of her early months of therapy with Ralph Klein: "I experienced the classic symptoms of transference with Ralph, having visions of him throwing me across the couch and having his way with me. Although he invited me out to his house in Amagansett that winter, I found myself sleeping alone in his guestroom."

Sándor Ferenczi, the great Hungarian pupil of Freud's, wrote with great perceptiveness about the need to counteract this process. Parents and therapists, he wrote, need to understand that "behind the submissiveness or even the adoration, just as behind the transference of love . . . there lies hidden an ardent desire to get rid of this oppressive love. If we can help the child, the patient or the pupil to give up the reaction of identification, and to ward off the over-burdening transference, then we may be said to have reached the goal of raising the personality to a higher level."

Sullivanian therapists did just the opposite, routinely telling their patients that they would be at risk of suicide or insanity if they were to leave therapy. "What is wrong with people being dependent on each other?" Joan Harvey, one of the group's newer leaders, told her training therapists. "You are their link to life and, you know, that dependency can go on forever." Michael Cohen recalled Harvey telling him repeatedly that if he were not in therapy with her, or ever left the group, he would wind up in a mental hospital, dead, or in prison. "And I absolutely believed it."

The Sullivanians adopted an unusually "directive" form of therapy—

literally telling patients what they should do. In classic Freudian therapy, the analyst is meant to serve as a blank mirror, revealing little or nothing of their own life and feelings, allowing patients to free-associate and follow their thoughts, helping them, by way of careful listening and sharp questioning, to discover their own deeper feelings and desires. Sullivanian therapists offered not just advice but also an alternative life, becoming the chief authorities in a patient's life, the person on whom the patient depended for guidance. They encouraged patients to socialize with one another and attend parties where therapists sometimes socialized with patients. Convinced that growth could occur only through interaction with others, they offered therapy that was, of necessity, social—not only a way of life, but an actual life. The therapist could not only stand in for the patient's parents but also offer a community that could become the patient's new extended family, replacing spouse, siblings, and the entire constellation of connections that made up the patient's previous life. It was common for a Sullivanian therapist to have a bulletin board on which patients left notices advertising a summer house share, a room for rent, or the forming of a writers' group or pottery class.

Something similar happened to Michael Bray. After he finished weeping and pouring out his soul in his first session, his therapist suggested that he needed to explore sex outside his marriage. "You're very scared of girls and you're scared of sex," Liebeskind told him. "When I got married," Bray said years later, "I was a virgin, and we weren't even quite consummating. We were trying."

Then Bray and his colleague Roger, a fellow patient, flew to Montreal to attend the annual conference of the American Psychological Association and ended up having a wild weekend of drugs, alcohol, and sex. They watched a session illustrating a therapy designed to help people overcome their greatest fears and fulfill their fantasies. "They did a group demonstration," Bray said, "where they had somebody taking a bath with the girl next door that he had a crush on. So somebody plays the bathtub, and they have somebody hold up his feet and his arms, and the two people take off their clothes and sit on this guy's chest [the person playing the bathtub], and they act out being in the bath together." Radical experimentation in psychotherapy was in the air.

Meanwhile, Mike and Roger took peyote, smoked marijuana, drank, and, like the people in the psychodrama exhibition, shed their inhibitions and acted out their own fantasies. "Here I was up in Canada, out of the country," Bray said. "I'm taking drugs for the first time, and drinking, and I have sex with about three different women that we met at this thing."

The out-of-town conference, however, seemed like a one-shot, exceptional event. How could he explore his interest in women in the course of his everyday life? His therapist, Liebeskind, said, "You know, you might want to look around and see if there's somebody." Bray asked, "How the hell am I going to do that?" A lot of the Sullivan Institute patients already lived in group apartments, and they were always having parties. Roger said, "Let's go to one of these Sullivanian parties." Bray wasn't sure about that, and with great trepidation he asked his wife if he could go. "My wife was actually kind of glad to get me out of the house, and I said I was going out for an evening with Roger . . . So we went to one of their parties, and a girl named Leslie picks me up and takes me home to her apartment, and I'm drunk. We have sex. And it's like, okay, so this is what it's all about." Leslie's bed was a mattress on the floor, and as they were having sex, she reached over and killed a cockroach that was crawling up the wall. That was the Upper West Side in the 1970s.

For a young man who, a short while ago, had been living in a Dominican seminary preparing for a celibate life as a priest, this was quite a transformation. Bray was no longer spending his days watching *Hollywood Squares* and drinking alone on his couch and failing to have sex with his wife. The therapy had given him permission to act on his desires and to imagine and pursue a new life. He began to let his hair and beard grow longer, and within a few months he had a big, bushy beard and looked like a roadie for the Grateful Dead. He started a love affair with a coworker at his job in a Brooklyn hospital. "She really became kind of my girlfriend, but then, at my therapist's suggestion,

I also joined a men's group. So I met some guys. We would go bowling. We would go running." Bray appreciated the therapy's emphasis on the importance of peers or chums—something he had missed out on in his youth. The Sullivanian belief that people got into marriages that closed off other kinds of relationships and limited growth corresponded to his own experience.

After the trip to Montreal, Bray confessed his sins to his wife, Jeanner, and she was, understandably, upset. His therapist said, "Well, you know she's in the same boat you are. She's as scared as you are, so why don't you get her a consultation with one of the therapists." Her therapist urged her to join a women's group, introducing her to the wider circle of Sullivanian patients. As the summer of 1974 approached, Bray's therapist suggested that he might want to join a group house out in Amagansett that summer. For several years, patients would band together and go in on a summer share, sometimes ten or fifteen people to a house. By now, virtually all the therapists had bought or rented places near Barnes Landing, where Saul Newton and Jane Pearce had their place.

Bray was worried that Jeanner, a devout Catholic girl from Wisconsin, wouldn't go for the idea, as they would not be together—men and women shared separate summer places, as they did in the New York group apartments. "You might be surprised," his therapist replied. When he raised the idea of his joining a group house with other men in Amagansett, his wife was upset. But when she raised it with her therapist, he encouraged the idea. "Why don't you try it. Nobody's going to die from this . . . You can just drop out. It's not like anyone's holding you prisoner. Since he wants to do this, you might find it interesting to get to know some other women." And so Jeanner joined a women's house, and Bray joined a men's house, and he ended up having the time of his life. "It was thrilling," he recalled. "I was kind of like the sailboat guy." Although from landlocked Iowa, Bray was an accomplished sailor. His parents had a summer house near a lake, and he had always sailed during the summers—a part of his early life he had loved and was happy to have back. "We'd go out and anchor the boat, jump off into the water, and God knows what. I went to these parties, and I was dating all these girls and just jumping into the whole thing."

*   *   *

For many of the men who entered Sullivanian therapy, the immediate draw was easy, uncomplicated sex, helping them break out of a pattern of inhibition and isolation, although they often found that they came to appreciate equally the focus on male bonding and group living. For women, the experience varied quite a bit. Some enjoyed being empowered to initiate sex rather than waiting shyly for someone to notice them. Others experienced a sense of pressure and the feeling that they couldn't say no. For Deedee Agee, therapy and group living meant something different: independence and freedom.

After her initial session with Jane Pearce, Deedee never returned to her husband, and she credited therapy with turning her life around. She went through a brutal stretch after ending her marriage, picking up odd jobs and moving ten times in that first year, including living out of her car for a time with her small son in tow. After their consultation, Jane Pearce referred Deedee to another therapist, Millie Antonelli. Therapy helped her stabilize her life, and she moved into a group apartment with other women who also had small children. They pooled their resources and hired an au pair to help with the kids. Deedee felt that she regained control of her life and also found a supportive community that opened a whole new range of possibilities for her.

Deedee seemed to be a perfect candidate for Sullivanian therapy, a person who appeared to be trapped in a tragic family pattern that kept reproducing itself.

Her father, James Agee, while extremely successful professionally, was an alcoholic, with serious health problems caused by heavy drinking and smoking. When he died of a heart attack at age forty-five, Deedee's mother, Mia Agee, had difficulty coping and fell into a deep depression. The eight-year-old Deedee, as the oldest child, assumed many parental duties, particularly in taking care of her younger brother. She was married when twenty-one and had a child at twenty-two. The marriage was rocky.

A talented writer (and later a visual artist) in her own right, Deedee labored under the crushing weight of her famous father and her difficult and sometimes abusive husband. One glimpses her talent and her inner struggles in an unpublished memoir she worked on and shared with various friends over the years.

James Agee had been shaped by his own father's sudden death when James was six years old, an experience he described beautifully in his most famous book, *A Death in the Family*, published posthumously in 1957. With terrible, tragic irony, Agee's own death would mark and haunt his daughter's life. She wrote:

> My father's death was a great turning point in my life, but it was his fame and legendary status—both seemingly dependent on his having died—that further complicated my growing up. His absence and legend became a smothering presence, the myth of him mingling with memory and longing, the line between truth and myth a fulcrum on which I tried to balance, see-sawing up and down.

Agee had died in a New York City taxicab on the way to visit his doctor, leaving his family in dire economic straits, with no insurance or savings to speak of. Then a kind of miracle occurred. An editor pieced together his unfinished novel, which became *A Death in the Family*, and James Agee became the first author to win the Pulitzer Prize for fiction after his own death. The book pulled him out of relative obscurity, stimulating the publication of his letters and film criticism and the republication of work that had gone out of print. As Deedee Agee wrote:

> A kind of literary cult evolved around my father as I grew up. He so fit the romantic mold of the American tragic artist-hero: hard-drinking, hard-loving, candle-burning-at-both-ends, talent-

squandered-on-bread-and-butter-work, self-destructive, dead-before-his-time genius. People bemoaned his untimely death, the spell-binding all-night talk sessions at which he seemed to acquire new energy the more he drank and the later the hour, the waste of his talents working for Henry Luce at *Time* and *Fortune* or writing scripts for television and movies. What might he have accomplished, they said, had he lived a more temperate life, had he been free from the need to earn a living, to support a family?

The creation of this literary cult—and of a mythic James Agee—represented an extra burden for a child who had already lost her father.

The glamorized image of my father as tragic hero, the legend of him, was intermingled with my own memories of a longed-for father who came and went unpredictably, whose warmth and charisma were extraordinary, who was never there for long, never long enough, and whose presence was so unforgettable. It was hard to hang on to the man who had been, who was still, my father, to build on my understanding of who he was; harder still to hang onto, discover and grow into myself.

Deedee got involved with Bill Bollinger when she was only fifteen, sleepwalking her way into a relationship that had much in common with her parents' marriage: being the support and domestic partner to a great artist. In an essay she wrote years later for a retrospective of Bollinger's work, Deedee recalled the evenings in which the male artists and their female companions congregated at some hip downtown bar, but then—even though this was the 1960s—segregated by gender, as if they were in a nineteenth-century parlor where the men smoked cigars and drank brandy while the women gathered in another room.

The men talked about art as object vs. art as idea, form as meaning, the reactionary nature of representational art, the irrelevance of beauty, the beauty of industrial forms . . . and then the women were freed up, and we'd congregate at one end of the table and swap cooking-for-a-crowd type recipes or tips on loft living: where to buy mosquito net cheap, how best to rig it up around a bed . . . how to stay warm at night and on weekends when the factories were closed and the heat was turned off, the virtues of wall mounted vs. floor model gas heaters. Our bond was our unspoken understanding that we were called to be the women behind extraordinary men, that this was a hallowed responsibility, and that the men would be hopelessly lost without our practical support and love, our unflagging belief in them, in the future greatness of their work . . . And if some of us had our own artistic aspirations, those would of course be put off until the men had their work-booted feet solidly planted in the luminary circle, no longer dependent on the light we shed. I wonder that we never thought to question what shoes would be waiting, polished and tidy by the doorstep, for us to slip into.

Bollinger, like James Agee, had a serious drinking problem, and Deedee married him despite the fact that he beat her up severely after she told him she had fallen in love with another man during a period of separation. He, in turn, carried on an affair with one of his students during and after Deedee's pregnancy with their son. After his birth, he refused to help take care of the child.

A constant theme of Sullivanian therapy was that you were always in danger of becoming just like your parents. And in Deedee's case, she appeared, without knowing it, to have replicated a family pattern that repeated itself in three generations. Her grandfather (her father's father) had died in a car crash while visiting his own father; his sudden death and her grandmother's inability to cope had cast a long shadow over James Agee's childhood. James, with his own premature, self-destructive end, had replicated this family tragedy almost to a T, dying in a car and leaving Deedee and her family in grief and financial distress. By making an early and ill-advised marriage to another talented artist with a serious drinking problem, Deedee seemed on her way to repeating the pattern again. The therapy, with its insistence on the rupture with family, seemed to offer a way of breaking that pattern.

Leaving her husband, cutting herself off from her mother, Deedee felt she was, for the first time, truly free from defining herself in relation to the men in her life—her father, her husband. She had traded the narrow world of family for something larger, a like-minded tribe of people who were involved in what seemed to be real revolution, as she later wrote:

> We felt we were bearers of the torch of the upheavals of the sixties. We'd grown up with the Civil Rights Movement, the sit-ins and marches . . . Many of us had been protesting the Vietnam War a third of our lifetimes . . . There were women's consciousness raising groups all over the city—and that really was a revolution, women talking freely to each other about everything, men, sex, birth control and abortion (which was still illegal), free love, postponing having children, living without a man, living in new ways, communally, collectively, not in nuclear families . . . We'd identify each other by long hair, peasant skirts, beads.

Breaking with Family

A few blocks from the Apthorp apartment where Michael Cohen had landed was a second Sullivanian apartment, at 465 West End Avenue, where his ex-girlfriend Sheila lived with another group of women, most of them therapists in training.

Among them was Carol Q., a young Black woman. Carol was a troubled seventeen-year-old in 1967 when she first entered Jane Pearce's office in the town house on Seventy-Seventh Street where the Sullivan Institute had its headquarters. She had grown up in a small town in rural North Carolina before winning a scholarship to the Putney School, a famous progressive boarding school in Vermont. Moving from a segregated Southern town and the conservative values of a religious Black Southern family to a virtually all-white New England boarding school in the "anything goes" 1960s was a dizzying, disorienting change. "It was like going to a foreign country," she recalled. Her parents had driven her up from North Carolina, mindful of the hotels and restaurants Black customers could safely patronize. Her father, who was a medical doctor, wore a dark suit, and her mother was dressed formally, as if for Sunday church service, her face carefully powdered. They looked out of place at Putney. "Kids wearing blue jeans, calling teachers by their first names, lots of studying and no television," Carol recalled. She was also the only Black student in her class. Her poorly funded segregated school in North Carolina hadn't prepared her for the workload or the social life at Putney. Carol developed a close relationship with and became the roommate of a girl named Penelope Barrett (not her real name). The two would dance around their dorm room performing numbers from the girl groups of the early 1960s—such as the Shirelles' "Will You Still Love Me Tomorrow?" and "Baby, It's You." But as graduation approached, the prospect of going out into the world seemed too much for her. "I had a near-psychotic break, couldn't function, I became suicidal," she said. She went to see a psychologist in nearby Bennington, who referred her to Jane Pearce in New York. (Thanks to the influence of Clement Greenberg, Bennington remained a pipeline to the Sullivan Institute.)

Carol's traditional-minded father wanted her to return to the South and attend a conservative Black women's college, but this seemed like a step backward to Carol, and home held little appeal for her at that moment. Her parents were fighting constantly—they were on the verge of breaking up—over her father's frequent infidelities. Remaining in the North seemed the more exciting option: she decided to go with her friend and roommate Penelope to Barnard College, the sister school of Columbia University, which was still all-male. Nineteen sixty-seven was the Summer of Love and the year of the Detroit riots, the reverberations of which could be felt on the neighboring New York City campuses. The Black Power movement arrived at Barnard in the form of a new organization called BOSS—the Barnard Organization of Soul Sisters. "I was a Black hippie," Carol recalled. "Blue jeans, T-shirt, and the hair," by which she meant a big Afro.

Jane Pearce became an anchor for Carol's life in New York. "She was very helpful and encouraging," she recalled. Carol, however, continued to struggle, falling behind in her schoolwork. Pearce set her up with a place to work at the Sullivan Institute and hired a typist to help her get an important paper in on time. "I wrote, and she typed until the wee hours of the morning so that I could get it done," Carol recalled. "Jane was very insightful and very understanding, and I felt that the psychologist at Bennington had referred me to the right person."

Pearce was not just her therapist but also an authority figure who appeared to be riding the social and political wave that was sweeping the country. One day in Pearce's waiting room, Carol met the Reverend Ralph Abernathy—one of Martin Luther King Jr.'s closest aides and the man who succeeded King as head of the Southern Christian Leadership Conference after King was assassinated in 1968. At another point Pearce showed her some plans she had drawn up. "It was a proposal for basically an urban commune," Carol recalled. "They [would] have a building and everybody would live there—much like . . . the communes coming up . . . all over the country. This would be an urban commune in New York City, and it would be headed up by these psychologists from the Sullivan Institute. She was very excited about that."

Carol, one of the few Black people who passed through the Sullivanian universe, explained that one of the models Pearce and Newton had in mind, in fact, was the Black Panther Party, which had started in Oakland, California, in 1966. "Jane and Saul, and I'm pretty sure some of the others too, were very interested in the Panthers," Carol said. "I remember going to a session, and Jane was all dressed up, and she told me she was going to a fundraiser dinner party for the Panthers and that they were going to donate five thousand dollars to the Panthers . . . The Sullivanians were attracted to the ideals and philosophy of community that the Panthers presented."

After several months of therapy, Pearce began to make clear that for Carol to really flourish and grow, she would need to sever her ties with her family. In their frequent sessions, her past and family life were discussed in an almost uniformly negative way. Then one day Pearce convinced Carol to write—and helped her draft—a letter to her parents making it clear that she wanted no more contact with them, ever. Carol showed the letter to Pearce, who watched her put it in an envelope and place a stamp on it and sent her out to mail it right then and there. "She could see the mailbox from her window, and she watched me as I put the letter in the mailbox. I remember looking up at her, and you know, we waved to each other."

Having committed what seemed an irrevocable act—cutting her family off forever—Carol felt dizzy with anguish and an overwhelming sense of solitude. When she went to her next session, Pearce asked her how she felt. "I said, I feel utterly alone. I feel deserted. She said, 'Well, *you* deserted *them*.' I said, I know, but I feel utterly alone. And I did."

Although it may not have been planned as such, Pearce had just carried out a brilliant if devastating two-step therapeutic judo move on her young patient. She pushed Carol to break her ties with her family and then, essentially, blamed her for deserting them. It added guilt and self-doubt to the searing pain of loss, leaving Carol doubly vulnerable and needy for the solace from the one parental figure left in her life: her therapist. This would not have worked had Pearce not also established herself as a genuinely helpful, empathic parental figure, someone who, in fact, went beyond the bounds of the usual therapist, helping her with her schoolwork, hosting her at home, and taking a special interest in her life.

Although Pearce's idea of creating a revolutionary community was partly inspired by the Black Panthers, Carol was surprised by the negative reaction she received when she tried to explain the Sullivanians' philosophy to a group of Black students at Columbia. "One man got really pissed. He was irate, saying, 'They're trying to destroy Black culture by breaking up the nuclear family.' It kind of blew me away. It was pretty clear that the Sullivanians and the Panthers were never going to mesh."

Carol had more luck promoting Sullivanian therapy with some of her white friends. Penelope Barrett recalled sitting around with Carol and poring over a copy of *The Conditions of Human Growth*, the two trying to diagnose themselves. "Did we have the psychopathic mother? The narcissistic mother? The depressed mother?" Penelope recalled. "It was always some kind of bad mother."

To Carol, Penelope's parents did not seem bad at all. "They were very kind to me," she recalled. In fact, when Carol dropped out of Barnard, she lived with Penelope and her family in their brownstone in Brooklyn for several months. She found Penelope's parents to be smart, dynamic, attractive, charming people. The mother was teaching in a program for men who had recently been released from prison, and the father was something of a mover and shaker in New York politics. Penelope's younger brothers—still teenagers—were both handsome and talented: they would go on to become professional musicians and cut a record together. The family seemed almost ideal, but as Carol pointed out, "I was not their offspring."

To Penelope and her older sister, Ellen (not her real name), home life seemed far from ideal. "My parents always pulled the wool over my friends' eyes," Penelope said. "They were amazing people—very cool—but they really sucked as parents." They were smart and sexy and had good taste in books and music. Her father was a passionate supporter of the labor movement, had a really good voice, and liked to sing union songs. Her mother was a gifted mimic, with a talent for making and keeping friends. The Barretts had met as teenagers in college, eloped after a week, and started having kids in their early twenties, producing five children in ten years. Having spent their twenties having one child after another, they were keen to get on with their own interesting lives: politics, parties, drinking, extramarital love affairs. And while they got a kick out of their kids—especially when they performed or were funny—they couldn't be bothered with the mundane day-to-day part of child-care, which they delegated to their two oldest girls, Penelope and Ellen.

By the time Penelope and Ellen were eight or nine, they were carrying around their younger siblings, changing their diapers, and bathing and feeding them. Penelope recalled her mother reading her the entirety of Shakespeare's *Macbeth* so effectively that Penelope, although only about ten, listened in rapt attention. But her mother wasn't interested in chores like dinner or checking homework. Penelope's younger siblings had found their mother passed out drunk. When they lived on a farm outside Albany before moving to Brooklyn, the Barrett parents thought nothing of going away overnight, leaving Ellen and Penelope—still in their early teens—in charge of three small children. Penelope and her siblings felt scared at night. She and Ellen were especially close and would crawl into each other's beds for comfort. "I know they loved us, but sometimes it was hard to tell," Penelope said. And though they were often disengaged, they could, on some matters, become rigid and uncompromising. Penelope had desperately wanted to go to the Rhode Island School of Design for college and had been admitted, but her father told her he would not pay for art school and insisted that she go to Barnard instead. To a Sullivanian therapist, this would have seemed like a classic case of a jealous parent squelching his daughter's creative impulses and forcing her to pursue a more conventional life.

Penelope began having panic attacks, which worsened when she got to college, exacerbated, she said, "by life in a big city, lack of parental support, and the constant upheaval on campus." She felt unmoored and a little crazy moving from the structured world of boarding school to the wild, freewheeling world of New York City in 1967. "One day I came across a naked woman lying on a bench right in the middle of Broadway, with a paper plate over her crotch and two Dixie cups on her breasts—that was New York," she recalled. She would look in the mirror and imagine she saw someone behind her, or she'd hug to the wall of the subway station for fear that she might hurl herself in front of a train. After a painful breakup with her first real boyfriend, she sought a consultation with Jane Pearce, finding her friend's therapist to be intelligent, sympathetic, and refreshingly different. As Penelope told Pearce about her ex-boyfriend—a young man who was everything a person could wish for: a brilliant Harvard student who was handsome, popular, and musically talented—Pearce said, "Poor baby." She appeared to be saying that this young man who seemed perfect in every way might be suffering from terrible pressure to be so perfect. "It was like she was onto all the bullshit that all the other adults I knew were pushing on me," Penelope recalled.

When Penelope's older sister was struggling with an unhappy marriage, she, too, went to a Sullivanian therapist. "I don't want to be married," Ellen said early in their first session. She had married while still in her teens but was already deeply unhappy; both her husband and her parents were vehemently opposed to divorce, making her feel trapped. "Your husband is an intelligent, grown-up man," her therapist replied. "He can fend for himself. You are not going to ruin his life." This simple observation was life-changing. "That may not seem like a profound big deal, but for me it instantly saved my life," Ellen recalled.

The therapist was Helen Moses, herself an attractive, well-put-together woman of twenty-eight, already a Sullivanian therapist on the rise. Although only six years older than Ellen, Moses seemed, because of her professional self-assurance, much older.

Toward the end of their first session, Moses asked Ellen about her dreams. She replied that she couldn't remember them, and Moses said, "I bet you'll have a dream soon." That night Ellen had a dream in which a composite character who looked like the actress Annette Funicello of *The Mickey Mouse Club* and Helen Moses appeared as a cheerleader at a football game. Ellen now attributes the dream to "the power of suggestion," but at the time it made her therapist appear like a seer and a prophet. "I guess I just felt like she was there for me, that she was helping me really wonderfully . . . I remember thinking, I want to place my life in someone's hands." This relationship would dominate and shape her life for the next twenty-two years.

Ellen and her sister Penelope both broke with their charming but unreliable parents, much as their friend Carol had with hers. When Penelope phoned her parents from jail in Washington, D.C., after getting arrested at an anti-war demonstration at the Pentagon, they started laughing. They found the whole thing very funny—she suspected they were well into their evening cocktails—and were of no help. She then called her boyfriend's parents, who immediately took steps to get her out of jail. After insisting that she go to Barnard, Penelope's parents almost never paid her tuition on time. "Every single semester, when it was time for final exams, I would get notification that I wasn't going to be allowed to take the exams because my tuition hadn't been paid," she said.

And so, at some point during her second year, Penelope's therapist, Sue H., came up with a brilliant solution: she found a scholarship program that Penelope was eligible for. It required, however, that she have no financial ties with her family. As a counteroffer, her father called her and said he had found a way to get her a monthly allowance, but he needed her Social Security number. Penelope figured out that, through his political connections, he had gotten her a "no-show" city job in which she would be paid for doing nothing. It was dishonest—and possibly illegal. This seemed to her therapist to call for a much more radical break. In the middle of a therapy session, Sue called up the Sullivan Institute's counsel, Marshall Perlin, a left-wing lawyer who had represented Julius and Ethel Rosenberg, the couple executed in 1953 after being convicted of spying for the Soviet Union. "Perlin dictated a letter to me," Penelope said, "basically saying to my parents, 'I want nothing to do with you. You are a liability to me in every way.' I had to write this letter and sign it, put it in an envelope, and put a stamp on it." The combined authority of this well-known lawyer and her therapist terrified Penelope. Her therapist then said, "When you leave, I'm going to watch you put that letter in the mailbox." Penelope recalled, "I was shaking. It was horrifying to me. But I was scared of everyone."

Sue H. had repeated, exactly, the tactic Jane Pearce used on Carol Q. Sue H., who was in her early thirties at this point, was a student of Pearce's; clearly, this was a technique Pearce and Newton taught their acolytes at the Sullivan Institute.

This seems like harsh medicine to be doling out, but by all accounts Pearce was not a cruel person. Quite the contrary; many, including Carol Q., describe her as highly empathetic. But according to her adopted son Chris Pearce, she had a strong belief that because her theories were scientifically true they needed to be applied with rigor and a firm hand. This fit with her and Newton's Marxist orientation: If you knew the direction history was supposed to go in, why wouldn't you urge others to follow? Pearce and Newton were certain that the family was the instrument through which society maintained the status quo. Keeping the patient in the family orbit guaranteed that he or she would develop as the parents and society wished, becoming younger carbon copies of their parents.

The anti-family ideas the Sullivanians developed during the 1950s were gaining wider currency by the late 1960s. R. D. Laing, the antiestablishment psychiatrist, became a bestselling author, offering an equally harsh view of the family and advocating for a radical break. Laing described the family as "a protection racket" in which parents offered security and protection in exchange for obedience and conformity. In his popular 1967 book, *The Politics of Experience*, Laing wrote:

> The family's function is to repress Eros: to induce a false conscious-ness of security; to deny death by avoiding life . . . to promote re-spect, conformity, obedience; to con children out of play; to induce a fear of failure; to promote respect for work; to promote a respect for "respectability."
>
> The family is, in the first place, the usual instrument for what is called socialization, that is, getting each new recruit to the human race to behave and experience in substantially the same way as those who have already got here.

In the same year, the German American psychoanalyst Bruno Bet-telheim published to great acclaim *The Empty Fortress: Infantile Autism and the Birth of the Self*, in which he popularized the (now discredited) idea of "the refrigerator mother" as the principal cause of autism—her cold detachment forcing the child to retreat into its own private world. He compared the experience to his own time in the concentration camps of Dachau and Buchenwald and compared mothers of autistic children to Nazi prison guards—metaphors that some Sullivanian therapists adopted in their own practices.

To break such a powerful cycle required force on the part of the therapist. According to Chris Pearce, Jane felt authorized to adopt a tough-love approach with her patients (and with Chris himself), like a mother pushing her chicks out of the nest in order to teach them to fly. In Chris's view, Jane was trying to help her patients achieve an almost Zen-like detachment that would grant them the ability to become truly free, but she may have underestimated the violence that this some-times entailed.

"Successful analysis involves becoming accustomed to revolution," Jane had written in *The Conditions of Human Growth*, and revolution could not be carried out without a certain amount of pain and violence.

To Jane Pearce, "the letter" would have seemed like a declaration of independence. She didn't consider, in the case of Carol Q., that forcing a young Black girl attending an almost all-white college alone in New York to break with her family might be extremely destabilizing. Whatever their faults, Carol's relatives, who had endured and prospered under the near-impossible conditions of the Jim Crow South, were also a source of great strength.

Yet the three women, Carol, Penelope, and Ellen, all cut ties with their families and remained in therapy. Ellen, after leaving her marriage, moved into an apartment with Carol and Penelope near Columbia University at 118th Street and Morningside Drive.

It was a time of extreme turmoil. The area around Columbia was like "a war zone," Penelope recalled. There were constant demonstrations, and every spring many of the university buildings were occupied. Their apartment was dirt cheap but quite dangerous. "It was on the ground floor, and one day this drug dealer crawled through the window and right into the apartment. I was sitting at the dining table. I knew him slightly because he had dated someone we knew. I greeted him as if it were totally normal to crawl through the window into someone's apartment. He asked me for some money. I gave him something like ten dollars, and as he left, he asked me if he should go out the window or the door. I think it's best to go out the door, I said. That was how crazy things were up there."

At the same time, Penelope began dating a Columbia student whom she had met in an acting class—John Fair "Jocko" Marcellino, a former football player (hence his nickname) who played drums in Sha Na Na. Penelope attended most of Jocko's gigs and asked to go with him to an outdoor concert taking place on a farm near New Paltz, New York. It turned out that she couldn't accompany him, because the band was going to be flown in by helicopter. Ellen announced that she was going; she felt that this was going to be a historic event. Penelope, who had thought of it as just another concert, decided to go after all, and she hitchhiked up to the concert grounds, carrying a black garbage bag to use as a sleeping bag. She had imagined she would be able to walk up near the stage and hear the performances, but when half a million people turned up—the largest rock concert yet—she was stuck out on the periphery unable to see or hear. "I think I just stood around and smoked joints people passed to me and slept in the garbage bag in the mud," she recalled. "I don't think I heard a note of music. That was my Woodstock experience!"

Ellen, by contrast, had a blast at Woodstock, a signal moment in what she recalled as perhaps the happiest period of her life. She loved her classes at Columbia, had a fun social and dating life, and participated in the active political life of the campus, which was still animated by anti-war protests. She developed a bit of a crush on another Sha Na Na member—the singer Scott Powell, who did killer renditions of Elvis Presley songs. Ellen would follow him around campus just to hear him sing.

The three young women were still living together in 1971 when Ellen and Carol were asked to join a training program the Sullivan Institute was starting. The group—even if it was not strictly speaking a group at this point—was expanding rapidly in the late 1960s and early '70s, fed by many students from Columbia and Barnard. As the Vietnam War raged on, the Sullivan Institute served a growing number of young patients, helping them avoid the draft, as therapists wrote letters to the draft board declaring them to be psychologically unfit. (A group of some forty patients rented a bus to attend an anti-war march in Washington.) This proved to be a good recruiting tool for new patients. Carol Q. brought a Columbia student she was dating to see Jane Pearce for a draft deferment. He thought the Sullivanians were crazy but was happy to get his deferment.

To accommodate the growing number of patients—and further spread their ideas—Saul Newton and Jane Pearce had come up with the ingenious idea of creating a training program for "lay analysts"— generally young people, often patients, who might have no previous training in psychology but would begin treating patients after about a year under the supervision of senior therapists. This would allow the institute to offer inexpensive therapy to young people and even students—sometimes for as little as five or ten dollars an hour, as opposed to the hundred dollars an hour that Newton charged. This idea of lightly trained therapists had something in common with the Chinese Communist program of "barefoot doctors" who were sent out into the countryside to serve peasants. Newton was a great admirer of Mao, but the plan was also in line with Harry Stack Sullivan's commitment to low-cost therapy.

It served a series of other needs, too. These young therapists—especially the ones without any prior training—were essentially empty vessels into which the leaders could pour their knowledge and wisdom without the trainees having to "unlearn" what they'd been taught elsewhere. All they would know was the Sullivanian approach. It would more than double the number of therapists, from about fifteen to twenty-five or thirty, meaning that if each therapist saw an average of twenty patients, the institute could serve at least five or six hundred people. Having therapists without Ph.D.s or M.D.s also served to devalue traditional training, something that sat well with Newton, who had no degree and no formal training in psychology. Although Pearce may not have realized this, it also placed a great deal of power in Newton's hands. As the director of the Sullivan Institute, he could assign or reassign patients as he saw fit, giving him control of therapists' income.

The senior therapists at the institute seemed to go out of their way to recruit people who not only had no training in psychology but in many cases had not even earned their undergraduate degree. For example, Pearce nominated her patient Carol Q., who had dropped out of Barnard after less than a year and had worked in a series of clerical jobs since leaving school; Carol had also developed a serious drinking problem.

Ellen Barrett had also dropped out of college and was only now, at twenty-three, working toward her bachelor's degree at Columbia's School of General Studies. Helen Moses explained that her lack of a degree would not be a problem; in fact, she told Ellen she should drop out of Columbia to focus on the training program.

For the three women, it was a big change: their lives would revolve much more closely around the Sullivan Institute, which was only a few blocks from their new apartment. From a real estate point of view, Ellen Barrett was also moving up: into the glamorous group apartment at the Apthorp. Penelope and Carol moved into a spacious apartment a few blocks away at 465 West End in another handsome prewar building. But Penelope felt like something of a third wheel. Ellen and Carol took classes and attended lectures at the institute, did therapy, conducted therapy with patients, received supervision of their own patients, and lived with a group of women who all did the same. For Penelope it was a somewhat painful transition: her sister and best friend had been placed above her and were completely absorbed by their new work, making her feel somehow less worthy. In compensation, pieces of their life at Columbia followed them into the group. Penelope's boyfriend Jocko entered Sullivanian therapy and moved into a group apartment, as did his bandmate Scott Powell a bit later.

In a world in which therapists were kings, being chosen to be among the next generation of royalty was a matter of considerable prestige.

When Michael Cohen showed up in New York in the summer of 1972, the Apthorp apartment where he first stayed was the same one in which Ellen Barrett was now living. Cohen's ex-girlfriend Sheila was living nearby, in the apartment into which Carol Q. and Penelope now moved. The women trainees were surprised at how quickly Cohen, who had barely begun therapy, was enrolled in the training program. "He was like the golden boy," Carol Q. recalled. "He was nice and smart and funny."

*　*　*

The early months of Sullivanian therapy consisted of taking the patient's history, a key step in breaking with the past. Since Cohen had lost both his parents, Joan Harvey had an easier time separating him from family. She was attacking an unmanned fortress. Although this kind of rereading of personal history was carried out by all Sullivanian therapists, Harvey, the former actress, conducted the assault with a degree of vehemence and flair that was particular to her.

Harvey portrayed Cohen as a mama's boy in the thrall of a stereotypical smothering, possessive Jewish mother. Early in Cohen's training, Harvey, who was herself Jewish, told him he would have to get rid of his "Jew boy yarmulke" if he was going to be a Sullivanian therapist. "She would always tell me, 'You're such a mama's boy that if your mother weren't dead, you'd never be in this group, because you wouldn't have the balls to separate from your mother.' And she was right: if I had had to cut off my mother, I probably wouldn't have done it. But this was seen as a negative. That I was a coward." She urged him to stop visiting and caring for his parents' graves up in Westchester, calling it a "ghoulish" practice. He soon gave it up.

His early life, which Cohen recalled as reasonably happy despite his father's untimely death, was suddenly reinterpreted for him by Harvey as a cemetery dominated by his mother's grief for her dead husband, which she used to wrap the family's life in a shroud of depression. His sister's decision to move to Israel was seen as an act of violent aggression designed to send their mother to a premature grave.

Fairly early in Cohen's therapy, Harvey pushed him to break off ties with his sister, the only surviving member of his immediate family. Although there was a ten-year age difference between them, she had become like a second parent to Michael after their father died. To soothe him, she had read poems to him, sparking a lifelong passion for poetry. But in a therapy dedicated to destroying the nuclear family, she became the target of constant attack.

Cohen was asked to bring in photographs of his family, and Harvey ridiculed them as "fat, ugly, stupid Jews"; the fact that his sister was overweight was seen as proof positive that she was severely depressed. His sister's desire to maintain a close bond with her brother was seen not as an expression of love but as an attempt to drag him down and drown him in her own depression. At a certain point, Harvey told Cohen that every time he opened one of his sister's letters, he was taking a year off his own life. Since his father suffered a heart attack in his early thirties and died in his late forties, this played on Cohen's greatest fear: dying young of a heart attack. Suddenly Harvey had put him in the impossible position of having to decide between his two greatest fears: early death or remaining without family. Of the two, death seemed worse. Cohen wrote his sister a nasty letter telling her he didn't want anything more to do with her. "I was instructed to tell her to 'fuck off,' that she was a 'fascist Zionist pig.'" When she called, he would hang up the phone, and he refused to speak any more to his nieces and nephews, with whom he had been quite close.

Since Cohen had almost no memories of his father, Harvey began offering an alternative history. She asked Cohen to bring in some photographs, and he brought a treasured family photograph of his father with the comedian Sid Caesar. His father and Caesar had grown up together, his father running the family delicatessen and Sid Caesar's family having an inn with a restaurant on the same block in Yonkers. The photo was taken on a Florida beach when the two were both adults: Mike Cohen's father, a diminutive five foot one, is dressed in a Hawaiian shirt, and Sid Caesar is in a bathing suit. They have their arms around each other's shoulders. Harvey insisted that the picture was not what it appeared. "Look at their body language. It's obvious from this photograph that they didn't know one another," she told him. In her interpretation it was clear that Mike's father had been walking along, spotted Caesar on the beach, and strong-armed him into posing for a picture, the way fans often do with celebrities. The story of this fabled friendship—and the photograph Mike had grown up with as a beloved family souvenir, one of the few things he had from his father—was nothing more than a bald-faced lie, a con. Memory by memory, Cohen's history was rewritten, his brain effectively rewired, the key moments of his life now strung together along a thread of malevolence.

To get patients to break with their families, it was necessary to convince them that their parents were not simply overbearing, difficult, or problematic figures (like most people), but positively malicious and dangerous. Michael Bray recalled a particular moment in his own therapy when he told his therapist of an incident in which his mother had made him some bacon and eggs and put the plate in the oven—"My mother was a big believer in hot food," Bray said—and she offered him the plate while holding it with an oven mitt, not realizing how hot it had become. Bray scalded his fingers and dropped the plate. His mother had apologized profusely, but in hearing about this, Bray's therapist, instead of seeing it as a simple mistake by a caring mother, interpreted it as a lethal, homicidal act of violence. It was the expression of an unconscious desire (shared by virtually all mothers) to kill one's child—a pillar of Sullivanian thinking and therapy. This was how Saul Newton had viewed his own mother's attempt to stanch his bleeding cut by putting it in a bowl of flour: attempted murder. What made this plausible, Bray said, is that he considered much of the rest of his analysis on the mark. In discussing his childhood, he realized how lonely and isolated his family life had been. He couldn't remember his parents ever entertaining or simply having friends over. His therapist—and others—had described Bray as a "sad sack," a shy, recessive, and depressed person, and it seemed perfectly apt to seek the origins of this in his family home. The therapy began with something real and then took it to another level by injecting an element of malice into the family gloom.

If his parents had been merely lonely and emotionally repressed, it might be possible to maintain a loving and even compassionate relationship with them while building a new and different life for himself in New York. But there was only one way to handle parents who were psychopathic and homicidal: cut them out of your life like a cancer.

After several months of analysis, Mike Bray's therapist convinced him to send a letter to his parents telling them that he would no longer be in contact with them. He cut off his older sister, too, although they had been quite close. His mother, hurt and perplexed, wrote back wondering what she had done wrong. Bray stopped answering her letters.

For some, breaking with family was relatively easy and nontraumatic. Deedee Agee had lost her father when she was eight, and his death had placed a great strain on the rest of the family. "As the eldest, I became a surrogate parent, and in so doing, I too lost my mother," Deedee later wrote. After Deedee had been in therapy for a while, she had a nightmare about monstrous people with hooks for hands who had torn her parents to shreds even though her parents were unaware of it. "Suddenly I understood who they were: they were me, my sister and brother. We were the ones who'd torn my parents to shreds." She told her therapist, Millie Antonelli, about the dream. The therapist told Deedee that even if it wasn't true, the dream "was a true representation of how our parents felt." It was very much a Sullivanian dream: parents and children as mortal enemies.

Her sister, Andrea, was already in the group. So for Deedee, trading her unhappy marriage—and her fraught relationship with her mother—for the vibrant communal life she had entered seemed like an easy choice. It wasn't just choosing friends over family; Deedee felt like she was embarking on something bigger and more important: "There was a palpable sense of the counterculture, the feeling of instant community among young people that so overshadowed the community of our families, the hope in the air that pushed us to go forth and try something new, forget the rules—they haven't worked out so well anyway—reinvent a saner way to live."

Others also experienced the break with family as a welcome relief. "I don't think I could have changed my life if I had my mother's voice in my head saying, 'No, you can't do that,'" Rachel (I've changed her name at her request) said. "Being able to say to my mother, 'Stop calling me. I'm not going to talk to you,' was totally liberating." Fortunately for Rachel, her mother was still alive after the seventeen years Rachel spent in the group. They resumed contact after the group broke up in 1991, and Rachel was able to care for her mother in the final stages of her life.

Janie P., who was part of the contingent of Bennington artists who joined the group in the late 1960s, was not so lucky. "The most tragic thing that happened to me in the group was that not too long after I got into it, my mother died, and they wouldn't let me go see her," she said. "I mean I could have, but they brainwashed me. She didn't die suddenly. I had cut myself off from my parents as I was instructed to do. And then my father called to say my mother had cancer and I needed to come home. He wanted me to come see her." Her therapist, Marc Rice, told her that if she went, she would get sucked back into the family and that she needed to separate from them entirely. "And then my brother called, and he and my father were hysterical. I was instructed to hang up the phone on them, and then she died and I wasn't there. And that's just been a huge traumatic thing in my life."

Some managed to use Sullivanian therapy as a temporary tool. Mike Cohen recalled a friend, an extremely talented dancer from a traditional Chinese American family that was pressuring him to become an engineer. He stayed in the group about three years, became a lead dancer in a major modern dance company, and then left therapy. Having established himself in his chosen profession, he was able to reconnect with his family. "He did what you should do: use therapy to help you with your life and then move on," Cohen said. This took a lot of clarity and self-possession.

In Sullivanian therapy, there was no provision for the termination of treatment. According to the theory, a person is either growing or deteriorating. Growth, in the Sullivanians' view, could only occur in a social context, so withdrawing from the Sullivanian community or refusing to follow through on therapeutic directives was testament that the patient was not committed to growth. Remove a person from therapy, and they begin to deteriorate, to slowly die. If you wanted to live, to grow, you stayed. It was a forever therapy. It was a life.

*   *   *

In leaving your own family behind, you were welcomed into a new, larger family that was, for most people, a lot more fun. An important part of that experience were the summers in Amagansett. Most ex-members who got involved in the early 1970s—even those who later left in bitterness and anger—remember those summers with fondness and nostalgia. Several of the senior therapists had built, bought, or rented homes near the house at Barnes Landing that Saul Newton and Jane Pearce had built back in the early 1950s. Patients banded together and rented houses nearby.

Steve Meshnick, a medical doctor and researcher, was a Columbia graduate student with a good academic career but a poor social life when he entered therapy in late 1973. He had been the smart, nerdy, obnoxious kid that other kids in high school didn't like, but his therapy offered a quick way out. One day in his therapist's waiting room, a young woman named Evie W. invited him back to her apartment. "She said she wanted to have a sleepover date, and then the next day one of her roommates asked if I wanted to have a sleepover date . . . And I was hooked."

That summer he joined a group of perhaps twenty men who went in on a house share. "It was some giant millionaire's house," said Meshnick, later a professor and researcher at the University of North Carolina. It was a huge mansion with seven bedrooms, in which they managed to squeeze thirty-four men. Six of the bedrooms were used as "date rooms" (the Sullivanian term for a place reserved for sex), and the enormous seventh bedroom became a kind of dormitory in which people actually slept. "It was probably one of the most enjoyable summers I've ever had. We had songwriting classes, art classes, yoga classes. There were parties. We'd go on outings to the beach or hike. Eat out at nice restaurants. You'd have dates. I met men I got to be friends with." That fall he moved into a group apartment.

Many in the group arranged to take a specific train on Friday evening out of Penn Station and congregate in the last carriage, breaking out booze and playing music. "There would be like fifty of us," Bob Putz, a mathematician, recalled. "The other people would move out. It became like a party car. There'd be a softball game on Saturday, a party at night. It was wonderful."

Ellie Bernstein remembers those first summers in Amagansett as funny and playful times of female friendship and sexual discovery. Laughing, she recalled how one year someone in her group house bought a vibrator—none of them had ever seen or used one—and it became so popular they had to create a sign-up sheet to use it. After having grown up in a household where her parents never touched each other (at least in front of others), this had a liberating, even celebratory quality. For the most part, the patients spread out among different houses saw one another at the beach and at parties, but from time to time they also saw the therapists, at nearby Barnes Landing. "Girls in the dunes," was how Ellen Barrett remembered those golden Amagansett days.

The summers of 1973 and '74 were also the summers of the pacifiers. A number of people in the summer houses would walk around sucking on baby pacifiers or carrying stuffed animals, trying to recoup stages of development they felt they had missed in childhood. Living in single-sex apartments and summer shares theoretically allowed them to experience the kind of intense friendship with people of the same sex that precedes adolescence, which Harry Stack Sullivan had termed "chumship." And so in Amagansett, men and women in their twenties would be hanging out at a pool party, drinking vodka martinis out of a baby bottle. Michael Bray—and others—considered it faddish and silly. "I felt some contempt for that," Bray said. "I thought it was taking to an extreme something that was an accurate portrayal of what my life was about. There were gaps—developmental steps that I missed out on. I was an altar boy. I went to all Catholic schools, was raised in a pretty strict family, and was a virgin until my twenties, so there was some accuracy to my being behind where I thought somebody my age would be."

Pacifiers notwithstanding, Bray's experience that first summer in Amagansett was idyllic; it seemed only natural for him, the former seminarian, to move into a group apartment with other patients in the fall. His wife, Jeanner, moved into a women's apartment. They were still married but clearly going their separate ways. Living apart, according to Sullivanian doctrine, they would continue to change and grow.

All this seemed less unusual in the context of New York in the early 1970s than might be the case today. Communes were booming. It was the decade of alternative therapies. There was "rebirthing," in which patients were encouraged to "reexperience" their own birth in order to rid themselves of trauma. (The founder of the rebirthing movement, Leonard Orr, believed he had tried to commit suicide in the womb by wrapping the umbilical cord around his neck because he knew his mother didn't want him.) Transcendental Meditation—a technique of the Indian guru Maharishi Mahesh Yogi—arrived in the United States early in the decade. Werner Erhard started his movement est (part Zen Buddhism, part Dale Carnegie) in 1971, the same year Arthur Janov published his book on the "primal scream." Primal scream therapy, in which patients were encouraged to scream out their early life traumas, attracted such counterculture figures as the former Beatle John Lennon and his wife, Yoko Ono, who lived just a few blocks from the Sullivan Institute.

"The Upper West Side of Manhattan was an island of insanity," Mike Bray said. A few doors down the block from the building where Bray lived with several other Sullivanians was something called the Psychodrama Institute, and on the street level of their own building was something called the Psycho-Karate Institute, run by a psycho-therapist who was also the owner of the building. "His office was on the ground floor, and we were living on the upper three floors," Bray recalled. "One day I had to call down because the heat had gone out or something, and I heard a patient yelling 'Fuck you! Fuck you!' It was evidently part of the therapy."

The availability of cheap therapy and the stock of large, inexpensive apartments on the Upper West Side in this period led to a rapid expansion of the community of Sullivanian patients living together in group apartments. New York City was in crisis, hemorrhaging jobs and tax revenues, its government on the edge of bankruptcy, its services in decline, crime on the rise. It lost nearly a million inhabitants in the 1970s alone, driven by a huge demographic change, massive white flight. Manhattan was particularly hard hit: its population fell by more than half a million between 1950 and 1980—a quarter of its population. This exodus from the city left hundreds of large, cavernous apartments—beautiful if a bit run-down—renting for prices even a student (or five or six students) could afford. Many of the buildings were constructed between 1900 and 1940, when the apartment building was a new idea and builders were looking to entice families out of single-family brownstones. They were elegant, well-built buildings with thick walls, high ceilings, handsome architectural details, multiple generously proportioned bedrooms, formal dining rooms, maid's rooms, and lots of amenities. Knock down a wall between two apartments and you had a mini commune. As nice as the architecture was, Penelope Barrett recalled, Sullivanian apartments always had the spartan air of a military barracks. "It was as if the Bolsheviks camped out in the Winter Palace," she said. By this point the Sullivanian community had swelled to include somewhere between four hundred and six hundred patients. Sometimes people happened into Sullivanian apartments because they were looking for a room to rent or chanced to attend a party.

People who entered into the Sullivanian community in this period—its time of greatest expansion—felt part of a special world, a kind of secret society with a superior way of life.

John M. was a young graphic designer, in his first job out of college, living in New York, where he hardly knew a soul. He would go home from work at night, roll a couple of joints of marijuana, smoke them, and go to sleep. There was a woman at his job, the office manager, who dressed in "hippieish" clothing and seemed to have an amazing social life. "Every day some interesting person would show up to lunch with her," John recalled. "I watched this for a couple of months, and finally, after everyone left the office one day, I went over . . . and said to her, 'I think you know something I don't know. You've got a ton of friends, and I am getting high to go to sleep.'" She explained that she was in this therapy and that, if he was interested, he could go too.

John M. had no interest in therapy, but he wanted the life it might bring him. He was so nervous before his first appointment that his colleague and one of her friends had to practically carry him up the subway stairs. His knees were shaking. "Then I went to my first party, and a beautiful young woman asked me if I wanted to go with her," he recalled. "Hard to say no. I had no interest in saying no. And that was my introduction." His therapist suggested that he join a summer share with a group of other patients. He found it a bit terrifying to move in with a bunch of guys, but he tried it. When it proved to be a lot of fun, it was natural to move into a group apartment on the Upper West Side, where he would remain, on the whole happily, until the group's dissolution in 1991.

Another person who got into therapy in the early 1970s, Alice Graves (originally Alice Gadeloff), recalled taking a breather during a lively group party, standing by an open window and noticing a man down on the street looking up to see where the noise—and the fun— was coming from. She thought to herself, "How pathetic." As she surveyed the city below, she felt a mix of pity and contempt for the poor souls in the outside world going to and from their dull jobs and their boring marriages. "They are living boring, empty lives because they are not part of the group," she wrote in *Don't Tell Anyone: A Cult Memoir*, which she self-published in 2019. By contrast, Graves said that she felt part of a special elite. "I am part of this amazing scene. I am allowed in. I am welcomed. I feel privileged. The people on the outside live their depressed lives with one spouse and a friend or two. All of these people are potential friends to me. I have left my old family behind, with its dysfunction and abuse, and now this is my family."

Graves describes an evening when she and a group of girlfriends from the group went out dancing at a small club in Amagansett. They didn't have much money, and they ordered Cokes, secretly filling them with rum they had snuck into the club. They then took over the dance floor, forming a circle and somewhat aggressively pushing aside the other customers, who had probably paid full price for their drinks. She said that in this period she felt superior to the ordinary people outside the group. "But we don't care; we know their world of nuclear families and serial monogamy is going to come tumbling down all around them," she wrote. "Leave them to their cluelessness. We are the vanguard of the revolution. Watch us own the world."

Life in the group was, for the most part, free and easy. Not everyone in a group apartment was in therapy, and people often had friends who were not Sullivanians. Some people insist that in this period there was no group. But from time to time things happened that would make people aware that there was indeed a group, and that it had a leader. When one of Deedee Agee's roommates, Judy Putz, died in a car crash in Amagansett, amid rumors that the driver had been smoking pot, Saul Newton issued a strict order that there would be no illegal drugs— ever. He was convinced that the police or the FBI were looking for some pretext to sweep in and break up the group. When another patient slept with a man who was a police officer, the institute terminated her therapy and forced her to leave her apartment. When a patient who was in graduate school proposed writing a master's thesis on the group, he was kicked out forthwith and accused of being a CIA agent.

In the late 1960s and early '70s, there was a parallel group of therapists and patients, known as "fringe Sullivanians"—therapists who had trained at the Sullivan Institute but practiced on their own. They followed many of the precepts of Sullivanian therapy—encouraging their patients to live in group apartments and experiment sexually— but they were not as doctrinaire and were no longer affiliated with the Sullivan Institute. Their patients sometimes attended Sullivanian parties, but sometime in 1971 or 1972—after a rift with Newton and the Sullivan Institute leadership—they simply disappeared.

7

Strange Interlude

Just when it seemed that Mike Cohen had found the place in life he was looking for, several things happened that briefly threatened it. In 1973, a year after his arrival in New York, his therapist told him that as part of his apprenticeship as a junior therapist, he needed to go live at the Sullivan Institute's headquarters with Saul Newton and Ralph Klein, two of the senior therapists, and a couple of other male group members. When Newton and Jane Pearce divorced, Newton had kept the town house at Seventy-Seventh Street they purchased back in 1950; Pearce retained their house in Amagansett. Pearce had since moved to an all-women's apartment, and the residential part of the institute building was now an all-male apartment for Newton, Klein, Cohen, and three other men.

Cohen had been very happy living in a group apartment with several men his age. His new living situation made him extremely uncomfortable. Ralph Klein was fairly approachable, smart, witty, and intellectually curious. But Cohen found living with Newton to be terrifying. Newton would have been sixty-six or sixty-seven during this period. "He looked like an Upper West Side psychiatrist out of central casting," Cohen said. "A gray beard, glasses, and a severe, forbidding air." For a man his age, he seemed quite fit, with a trim, even taut body whose muscles seemed tense, like a spring ready to pop at any moment. He had a violent and unpredictable temper, and you could never tell what might set him off. "I was terrified and walking on eggshells all the time."

At a certain point during the late spring or early summer of 1973, Sue H. (Penelope Barrett's therapist) asked Cohen if he would help her get pregnant. They had dated occasionally. In the group there were usually a couple of people you dated regularly—people you were really into—and others you saw less frequently. These more casual relationships prevented you from focusing on one person and kept you open to different kinds of relationships. Sue H. was in this second category in Cohen's life. She was more than ten years older and had different friends, but one of the things Cohen liked about the group was that you got to know—and date—people of different ages. He and Sue H. were friends and had a nice rapport. She explained that she intended to be a single mother, that there would be no further obligations on his part. She would ask other men to help as well, so that she would get pregnant more quickly, and no one—not even herself—would know who the child's father was. Cohen agreed without much thought. She was a friend, and they were already sleeping together. Sperm banks were not common at this point, and he was simply helping a friend. "I did it without any hesitation," Cohen said. "I think I would have said yes even if I hadn't been part of the group."

There is a photograph that memorializes their summer romance. They are out at Amagansett at an exhibition of paintings by Janie P., the Bennington artist Richard Elman had brought into the group. Cohen has just come back from the beach. He is a slightly built young man of medium height, with the healthy glow of someone who has just had a swim. He is wearing a shirt open to his navel, exposing a lot of chest hair. He looks handsome and has an amused, somewhat ironic smile on his face. He is standing, and Sue H., in her midthirties with shoulder-length brown hair, is sitting to his right and turning to face the camera with an open, broad, laughing smile. They look very happy.

Not long after this, Cohen's therapist, Joan Harvey, explained that he would need to do a favor for a fellow therapist, her friend and former housemate Helen Moses. Helen had just married Saul Newton and was ready to start having children, and Cohen would need to help her get pregnant. It was not clear why Newton didn't do this himself. Apart from adopting his oldest child, Esther, Newton had produced five children by this point: three with Jane Pearce, two with Joan Harvey. He had now come to regard the idea of biological children as outmoded as the nuclear family. Newton's new wife, Helen Moses, approached the task of conception with a decidedly clinical detachment, referring to it as "the project" and arranging to have sex with four or five men during her ovulation period.

Moses was something of an anomaly in the Sullivanian universe. If many members had a personal or family past in radical politics, she came from a conventional, middle-class Jewish family in the Bronx. A cheerleader and a good student in high school, she had gone to Brandeis University, a school with a strong Jewish identity, while most in the group openly despised religion. She was carefully put together, her clothes never wrinkled, her personal style far more conventional than the somewhat hippieish style of many Sullivanian women. What, Cohen wondered, was this entitled young woman doing in this radical world? But she had doggedly pursued a Ph.D. in psychology, completing her dissertation on time. Her thesis was a field study that aimed to show that young girls who were more independent from their parents were open to a wider range of experience. Armed with a doctorate and married to Saul Newton, Moses had quickly become one of the Sullivan Institute's senior therapists, supervising the younger training therapists such as Cohen. She was quite an attractive woman, with a rather sexy hourglass figure, but this was a situation Cohen wanted no part of. He already found Saul Newton terrifying; the idea of impregnating the man's wife was beyond terrifying. Cohen resisted but agreed to see a doctor that Harvey recommended to check his sperm. When the test showed a healthy sperm count, pressure increased. When Harvey was unable to convince him, Saul Newton got involved and applied the screws. He screamed and threatened. He would throw Cohen out of the training program, throw him out of his apartment, terminate his therapy. He even threatened to have Cohen beaten up if he didn't cooperate.

Cohen thought that in the past year he had found everything he wanted: a community of friends, an interesting profession, a therapist who understood him, a purpose to his life. Suddenly he was faced with the prospect of having all that taken away in an instant. He would be a homeless, penniless, friendless, unemployed twenty-three-year-old with no family and no direction. He reluctantly agreed, but he was so frightened that he was unable to perform sexually. He was sent out to buy some marijuana—normally totally forbidden in the group because of the fear of attracting police attention—in order to calm his nerves. Eventually, he was able to do the deed.

The experience was deeply traumatic for him, but he did his best to put it behind him. It was one night in his life, he told himself. It was over. The polygamous nature of the group meant that sometimes you had sex with people you were not that into. It wasn't such a big deal.

Cohen lived at the Sullivan Institute headquarters with Saul Newton and Ralph Klein for a few unhappy months, and finally Newton told him to move out. He was clearly so anxious and frightened that he was making everyone else nervous. "I was so paranoid, they threw me out," Cohen recalled. He moved down the street to the other Sullivanian town house on West Seventy-Seventh Street, the one owned by the therapist John Cates, where Richard Elman had been living until he left the group a few months earlier. Cohen would, in effect, be taking Elman's place in the house. Although Cohen did not know this, Elman had left because he'd refused to do what Cohen had agreed to do: help father a child against his will.

Cohen was much happier in Cates's town house. The three shrinks living there, Cates, Art Liebeskind, and Dom Antonelli, were kinder and more easygoing. They took two vacations together in the French-speaking Caribbean islands of Martinique and Guadeloupe. They lived almost next door to the jazz legend Miles Davis, the personification of cool, who kept a pet goat. Some mornings Cohen would run into Davis; Cohen would be walking Cates's dog, and Davis would be walking his goat. Cohen was just getting up, and Davis was heading to bed after a long night playing a gig. Davis, who had the reputation of being hostile and distant to white audiences, was friendly to Cohen and clearly enjoyed talking about music.

Settling into this more welcoming environment, Cohen looked back at his terrifying experience of being coerced into having sex with Saul Newton's wife as a speed bump in the progress of his Sullivanian life—or a bad dream that fades in the course of the day. He explained to himself that the personal flaws of the individuals in a movement don't necessarily invalidate the movement itself.

If being pushed to break with his sister and to have sex with Helen Moses didn't force Cohen out of the group, it was partly because those painful experiences were accompanied by a steady rise in his status within the group. As one of the chosen few who were asked to join the institute's training program, he enjoyed a good deal of prestige in a community made up entirely of therapy patients. In the early 1970s, there were about forty Sullivanian patients who either had earned or were pursuing psychology degrees, and none of them were invited to become trainees—a source of some resentment and envy but also admiration. Cohen was among the approximately fifteen chosen for the training program, and most of them had dropped out or were asked to leave. Only a handful, including Cohen, were encouraged to remain as therapists.

In this group there was a clear hierarchy: Saul Newton at the top, accompanied by Joan Harvey, Ralph Klein, and Helen Moses. There were the "second-tier" therapists, the older ones who had been at the institute for years and who also owned houses in Amagansett. Then there were the training therapists, the rising stars of the institute. Of these, Cohen seemed the most prominent and, unlike some of the other younger therapists, had the reputation of being a good, empathic practitioner.

"Mike was likable and had a kind of Bob Dylanesque appeal," said Artie Honan, a group member from 1970 until 1991. Cohen represented a different kind of cool from what Honan had previously encountered. As a high school and college jock, Honan had been used to acquiring status through athletic prowess and macho toughness. Cohen was the opposite of all that, but his slight build, sharp wit, and sensitive personality were evidently admired in Sullivania. Women wanted to sleep with him and men wanted to be his friend. Honan remarks in his memoir of life in the group that he was delighted to be in a house share with Cohen and another training analyst—it conferred a certain prestige on the house and might include invitations to events and parties, including with the top therapists whom everyone (or at least Honan) wanted to be near. Honan, who went into therapy a few years before Cohen entered the group, said that he desperately wanted to join the training program, but when he made his wishes known to a senior therapist, he was suddenly kicked out of a men's group he had been in—which he understood to be punishment for having dared to ask and appearing to question the leadership's decisions.

*　*　*

After a few years of therapy, Penelope Barrett felt profoundly uneasy. She had never experienced the kind of deep identification and conviction that her sister Ellen seemed to feel. Fairly early in her therapy she had thought of quitting. The person to whom she naturally turned to discuss her doubts with was her sister, who was fully absorbed in the Sullivanian principles of her therapy. Ellen rather brilliantly used the logic of a Sullivanian therapist to shoot down the idea of Penelope's leaving. "Oh, that's terrible. That's so sad," Penelope recalled her sister saying. "That's like saying Mom and Dad won. I know how hard it was because I was in the same concentration camp with you. And it's just letting them win." Helen Moses, Ellen's therapist, was fond of the metaphor of the family as concentration camp—something she used with many patients regardless of their family circumstances. "And so I felt like I couldn't drop out," Penelope said. In retrospect, she regretted confiding in someone who was so deeply committed to the group. "Why would I turn myself in to somebody who was part of it? It was a mistake."

When Ellen and her good friend Carol Q. were selected for the

Sullivan Institute's training program, it increased Penelope's sense of alienation. Although she had moved into an apartment with Carol and three or four other Sullivanian women, Penelope was asked to move out in order to make room for another trainee. "They must be better than me," she thought. So she was flattered and pleased when she was invited to participate in a weekend party given by some of the young female therapists, including Ellen. "It was going to be a kind of weekend-long pajama party, just a group of women hanging out together," she recalled. "This was related to the whole Sullivanian idea of chumship, which meant companionship with friends of the same sex. So we were going to have a weekend of chumship. They were mostly a group of young, smart, and attractive young women. We're sitting around talking, and suddenly the phone rings." To her complete surprise, the call was for her, and it was Saul Newton.

Penelope had never met Newton; she knew only that he was the co-author of *The Conditions of Human Growth*. When she got on the phone, Newton asked her whether she would like to have a date with him—that very evening. Penelope was flabbergasted: How did Newton know who she was? How did he know *where* she was? And how did he know that he wanted a "date" with her, which, she knew perfectly well, meant sex. She said no, explaining that she had other plans. After all, she had committed to spending the entire weekend with her new friends. When she got off the phone, the other women at the party crowded around her, insisting that she had made a mistake, and urged her to call back and accept his offer. "He is the kindest man I've ever met," one of them said. Yes, he was much older, another said—Newton would have been about sixty-six at the time and Penelope about twenty-three—but he was "Mr. Natural."

She called back and agreed to see Newton. She walked over to the institute's town house on Seventh-Seventh Street. There weren't many preliminaries or much conversation. He moved quickly to sex, which he clearly expected. "I spent a miserable night," Penelope recalled. "The irony was that he, at age sixty-whatever, couldn't get it up and was determined to keep trying, so he kept me up for hours. I didn't find anything the least attractive about him. With his slightly hooded eyes, he looked like a little rooster." In the years she had been in the group, she had had her share of meaningless sex, but this felt different—and far worse. "In these other relationships, there was something—some mutual attraction, some flirting—this was just degrading. It made me feel like a prostitute."

As she was finishing up at Barnard, Penelope again considered taking her life in another direction. Her writing teacher at Barnard, the celebrated novelist Elizabeth Hardwick, had offered her an exciting but low-paying job at *The New York Review of Books*. Her therapist discouraged her from taking it. "Sue H. told me that if I took the job, I could no longer afford therapy and I would therefore wind up on the street, a drug-addicted prostitute." Since, at the urging of her therapist, she was already sleeping with a lot of people and taking a lot of prescription drugs, the notion that she might actually become a drug-addicted prostitute struck a note of genuine terror in her. This nightmarish vision of her future so frightened Penelope that she dropped the idea without giving it further consideration. "I did tell Elizabeth Hardwick that I couldn't take the job because I needed to be able to afford therapy, and she very gently tried to get me to talk more about it, but I didn't because I sensed that she would disapprove."

Although Ellen Barrett convinced her sister to remain in the group, being a training therapist had its perils for her as well. Sometime around 1973, Ellen was told that she and another young training therapist would be moving into an apartment with her therapist, Helen Moses, and a few other Sullivanian therapists. One of them would be Moses's new husband, Saul Newton, Mr. Natural, who had recently divorced Joan Harvey and married Moses. Ellen knew it was unusual for a patient to be living with her therapist and her therapist's husband, but she never seriously questioned the move. She would live with Moses and Newton for the next eighteen years.

Carol Q., having entered fully into the life of the group, experienced both the good and the not-so-good of it. She made friends with several patients who were musicians and began singing in a band that performed in clubs on weekends out on Long Island. She had a lovely singing voice and a good feel for such slow, bluesy songs as Aretha Franklin's "A Natural Woman" and Marvin Gaye's "Mercy, Mercy Me." At different points she dated the two men in the band. One of her former bandmates, Laura Greenberg, who became a composer and music professor, left a memorable portrait of Carol, whom she referred to by her nickname, Quig:

> The first time I heard Quig's voice was at a Christmas party in the late sixties, when smoking and drinking were still fashionable. I wanted to live in that voice. It was as warm and roomy as a protective cave. Her round Southern accent was soothing; she would tell me anything and I would love to hear it. Her free-flowing laughter, and the relaxed roundness of the body that went with it, told me she indulged and enjoyed herself.

Carol sang in several bands with other Sullivanians. One of them was invited to play at a protest event in Miami at the 1972 Republican National Convention that would renominate President Richard Nixon. Stars of the counterculture Abbie Hoffman and Jerry Rubin— the leaders of the Yippies and defendants in the infamous "Chicago Seven" trial—were there, as was the poet Allen Ginsberg. Carol, though, remembered little of it, as she experienced it in a drunken haze. Her drinking was starting to become a real problem. Sometimes during her sessions with Jane Pearce, when they had run out of things to talk about, they would drink together. For a time, Jane and Carol both tried taking desiccated liver tablets to help them stop drinking; they tasted terrible and didn't work.

As Carol got deeper into the life of the group, she found herself in strange situations she did not fully understand. One evening, probably in 1974, she joined an intervention that three Sullivanian friends were planning in order to rescue (or kidnap) a little boy from his father and restore him to his mother, a Sullivanian patient. The mother was Deedee Agee.

At this point Deedee had been in the group for three years. It had been a wonderful, liberating experience for her, but after three years of therapy, her therapist encouraged her to send her son, Teddy (not his real name), who was five years old, away to boarding school. It was necessary, they explained, to protect him against the toxic effect of the nuclear family. It made sense to her: her roommates had sent their kids away, as had her therapist, Millie Antonelli. And on a practical level, it would be hard, if not impossible, for her to lead the free and creative life she hoped to live if she was looking after a small child. "I was basically being given the choice of sending him away to school or moving out on my own, figuring out how to do that financially, most likely being kicked out of therapy and losing all my friends in the group, giving up the life I'd made there that made me feel some degree of security and community for the first time in my life. I thought I'd be poisonous to him." The boarding school where Deedee sent Teddy (and where several other Sullivanian children were enrolled) normally didn't take children as young as five, but they agreed to make an exception. Things then got complicated: Teddy hadn't wanted to go away, and Deedee's former husband, Bill Bollinger, took the boy out of school and brought him to live with him instead.

"Word came through Millie from on high: I had to get him back at any cost," Deedee later wrote, implying that the order had come from Saul Newton himself. She rented a car and recruited three other group members to go with her to the house in Poughkeepsie where Bollinger now lived. "I was drunk and crazy, and I decided I wanted to go with them," Carol recalled. The plan was for one member of their posse whom the child knew—Mike Veghte, one of the men Deedee was dating—to sneak into the back of the house and fetch the boy. He succeeded, but as Veghte was returning to the car with the child, Bollinger realized what was going on and came running out of the house wielding a baseball bat. "He began smashing in the windows of the car," Carol recalled. Everyone yelled for the driver to get out of there, but for several seconds he seemed paralyzed. Then Deedee yelled, "He's got guns!" Carol thought, "Why the fuck didn't she tell us this before?" Finally, the driver hit the accelerator and the car peeled off, the passengers riding in the open air with two windows smashed in, shards of glass on their laps, and a confused and terrified boy with them. The purpose of the rescue mission was not to reunite the boy with his mother but to send him back to boarding school.

Even when school was not in session, Deedee was told that she should see as little of the child as possible to "save him from a childhood worse than my own," she later wrote. "I was told I was so dangerous to [Teddy] that I shouldn't even spend time with him on vacations, shouldn't visit him. So for two years [Teddy] pretty much stayed at the school living with one of the teachers during vacations. When he did come home, I was told to [keep him] with a babysitter for most of the time."

Carol Q. was one of the people who helped look after the boy, who was clearly extremely unhappy. "He would do things like leave his shoes purposely untied so that when I reached down to tie his laces, he would hit me on the head or run off so that I would have to chase after him. He was very, very angry. He was really messed up."

8

Group Living

It is unlikely that a therapy intent on convincing people that their parents were potential murderers could have won many followers had it not been reinforced by the wider community of patients. Virtually all Sullivanian apartments had weekly house meetings. Although they were primarily meant to work out the practical aspects of communal living—shopping, cooking, cleaning—the meetings often became an extension of therapy. People were expected to share their personal histories, and housemates commented on them as a therapist might, quick to call someone out for "sugarcoating" their past.

Advice to break off ties with your family might as easily come during a house meeting as during a therapy session, so that the message of the single therapist was suddenly amplified multiple times. Everyone was doing the same kind of therapy, so you heard the same things from your friends and roommates, from the people you dated, and in various men's and women's groups you might belong to. For Michael Cohen it was especially intense because he was also training to become a Sullivanian therapist, taking classes, doing therapy three times a week, seeing his own patients about twenty hours a week, discussing his cases in supervision sessions twice a week—all of it laying a theoretical foundation for why parents were bound to resent and feel rage toward their children. "It was systematic and it was relentless and it was everywhere," Cohen said. "And everyone is reinforcing the narrative that your parents were terrible, and it starts to be the narrative you believe . . . I really began to see my family as destructive and evil, and they really were not." With good friends, roommates, and more casual acquaintances all telling you the same thing, it did not seem that it was simply your therapist forcing an interpretation on you. You were hearing the same message, in mono, in stereo, and then in a kind of symphonic chorus.

Moreover, these people were your friends, smart and creative people who genuinely believed what they were saying. The harsh message about family was sweetened by the fun of late-night parties, summers in Amagansett, softball games, dates with pretty girls or cute guys, music and art classes. The theory of *The Conditions of Human Growth* stressed that people needed "alternate validators," people outside the family who affirmed their worth. The community of "alternate validators" that Jane Pearce and Saul Newton wrote about had actually come to pass. It was real, and it was your life. Its existence seemed to confirm the rest of the theory: since the therapists had successfully created this alternative community of peers, surely they were right about the dark, anti-family message as well. This tight-knit community existed in part by excluding family. They were two sides of the same coin.

Arguably, the new community the group offered was more interesting than the family these people had left behind. In Mike Cohen's case, the group had provided him access to a world that was far wider and more compelling than the lower-middle-class neighborhood of Yonkers where he grew up. He learned to play the guitar, attended art shows by his new friends, and watched as his friend Richard Price's first novel grew during the sessions of their writers' group.

Along with providing comfort, community, and the amplification of therapy, the group apartments also provided an extraordinary means of policing and regulating behavior. The therapists had created a set of behavioral codes, after which the community became almost self-governing, allowing the therapists to retreat into the background and intervene only when necessary. "Once we were in that group-living situation, everybody was on the same page," Mike Bray, the former Dominican seminarian, recalled. "So if there was any deviation from the behavior that was expected, you could either be corrected in a group house meeting—and it might not go any farther than that. But someone might bring it to their therapist, and that therapist would instruct the patient to confront the person in the next group meeting to do something. If it was something urgent, the therapist might contact the therapist of the other person."

To some, like Eric Grunin, a musician, the hothouse nature of the group seemed like the warm embrace of a close-knit rural village: "At the end of the day, everybody in every house talks about everything of significance that happened during the day in the village. Everybody knows everything. Similarly, in our group, if I got a job offer in the morning and told my roommates, by evening, everybody was congratulating me."

It also gave life in the community something of a fishbowl quality, with little or no privacy. Because patients predominantly socialized with and dated other patients, news of any problem circulated quickly and could be referred up the line to the lead therapists, who might feel the need to intervene. A small problem could quickly snowball into a big one.

The group apartment operated as an incredible surveillance mechanism in which the patients policed one another. Roommates kept a close eye on how often their friends dated any particular person and wouldn't hesitate to call them out at a house meeting. "Hey, I think you guys are getting into a 'focus'"—the term used by therapists to describe an unhealthy romantic dependency. In order to avoid arousing suspicion, couples who were really close would be careful not to see each other too often. *The Conditions of Human Growth* dedicated an entire chapter to something termed "hostile integration," an infatuation with or intense focus on one person—what most people would call "falling in love."

The house meetings sometimes took on the air of reeducation sessions conducted by the Red Guard during Communist China's Cultural Revolution, in which citizens were scrutinized for their bourgeois tendencies or denounced as "capitalist roaders." At a house meeting, a member of a group apartment could be called out for criticism and, if they didn't respond appropriately, could be kicked out of the apartment and told to find somewhere else to live. This happened not infrequently and might or might not mean being expelled from the group as a whole, which would have to be decided by the leadership.

In some cases, when a roommate attacked someone during a house meeting, it might well be at the instigation of his or her therapist, who felt that someone needed to be pulled into line. The therapist might even dictate a "summary" of a person's character that a patient could use during the house meeting. What appeared at the meeting to be a spontaneous disagreement among roommates might in fact be a carefully orchestrated form of control by the therapists.

Richard Price dreaded the meetings. "I was always nervous about house meetings, which sometimes felt like circular firing squads," he recalled. "I was very careful not to make waves." But one evening he made a serious misstep. "I was a bit nervous, and it was time [for the meeting], and I said something like, 'Okay, let's have this so-called house meeting' or 'Let's get this so-called house meeting going.' And as we sat down, people started talking about washing dishes and the utility bill, and then all of a sudden, somebody goes, 'I'm angry at Richard. Why did you call it a "so-called" house meeting? I find that very hostile.' Then there was a general discussion of my attitude, and these guys who seemed to me kind of semiharmless turned into wolves over such infantile shit. I just remember feeling that with a slip of the lip, you could get in trouble with the Sullivanians."

Thinking about the incident forty years later, Price feels that this readiness of people to pounce on any sign of impurity or deviation from the group norm came from the extreme tension everyone lived with—and the secret doubts they themselves harbored. "If I think back on it, everyone's nerves were at such a high pitch being Sullivanian and suppressing whatever was closing in on them. And I think so many people were afraid to just say, honestly, my life is driving me nuts." The extreme fidelity demanded of the group, Price said, created an intolerable dissonance between your awareness of your own inner doubts and feelings of impurity and the total purity and fidelity that was expected of you and that you imagined others to possess. "You are so wrapped up in your own bad Sullivanian head that you can't see what other people are going through, and because paranoia is grandiose, it's like you're the only bad guy in the world and everybody else is flawless."

Interestingly, the psychiatrist Robert Jay Lifton observed much of the same phenomenon among members of different utopian groups that require total commitment—what he calls "totalist groups." These groups, Lifton wrote, demand levels of purity and commitment that are essentially impossible to meet—everyone has moments of doubt and uncertainty, selfish desires that run counter to the needs of the group—and their members live with the uncomfortable awareness of the gap between the purity the movement demands and the murkier reality inside their heads. In Maoist China, party members were encouraged to engage in self-criticism, confessing their unrevolutionary thoughts and actions while hoping for rehabilitation. But Lifton observed that the "cult of confession" often had the opposite effect. "Rather than eliminating personal secrets, it increases and intensifies them . . . Each person becomes caught up in a continuous conflict over which secrets to preserve and which to surrender, over ways to reveal lesser secrets in order to protect more important ones; over boundaries between the secret and the known, between the public and the private."

A good Sullivanian was expected to be open to the group and not spend too much time alone. If you were spending time by yourself, you were withdrawing, withholding yourself emotionally from others—not growing. Even on nights when you didn't have a date, you were encouraged to have "sleepovers" with people of the same sex. "Guys would have these sleepovers which, if you were a straight man, seemed totally useless to me," Richard Price recalled. "What are we supposed to do, cuddle? I would lie there on the edge of my bed like a plank and get up as early as I could."

Sex in the group was both easy and complicated. The rules of courtship were generally simple and straightforward. If you made a date with someone of the opposite gender, there was a general expectation of sex. It was common for people to say on a first date, "Okay, let's get the sex off the table." Sex was seen as a simple human need, like thirst or hunger, something you should get out of the way so that you could actually get to know the other person. The word "romance" was sometimes used interchangeably with "focus" to describe a dangerous delusion that could lead you down the path to a hostile integration, the Sullivanian definition of marital hell. One way to avoid this was to demystify sex by using the term "fuck date." Some Sullivanian apartments—particularly where roommates shared a bedroom—would have a separate date room that you could sign up to reserve.

At the same time, "dating" was complicated because it took on some of the color of therapy. It was common for each party to tell the other their personal history. If your version of your family history was not horrific enough, you might be accused of "whitewashing." And if things really didn't go well, you might get a "summary," the kind of blistering, often brutal assessment of your character that Sullivanian therapists frequently delivered. Patients scrutinized each other carefully for signs that they were failing to live by the standards set by the therapy. Mike Bray remembers being out on a date with a woman, and he was having difficulty finding a parking space (a classic New York problem). Frustrated, he gunned the car engine, trying to reach a potentially free parking spot. "You're in a rage!" the woman said. "Rage" was a key word in Sullivanian therapy: malevolent mothers who secretly wanted to kill their children were said to be in a rage. Bray realized that he was inching toward a potentially dangerous moment: if this woman deemed him to be in a rage, she might pass that assessment along to others, including her therapist, and it might become a major issue that he would have to contend with in therapy or at an apartment meeting. He made a supreme effort to control his parking frustration and de-escalate the situation in order to avoid censure.

Things could turn bad very quickly. Richard Price enjoyed a remarkable degree of professional success during his first years in the group: he entered therapy in 1972 at age twenty-three and in 1974 published his first novel, which was well received and sold to Hollywood to be made into a movie. He published his second novel in 1976. He was a rising star in a glamorous field and had much more money than most of the other twentysomethings in the group. All the women wanted to date him. At a certain point he was dating no fewer than six of the group's female training therapists. "You have to understand," Price explained, "that in this group the therapists were like God, and these were the demigoddesses." But during a date with him, one of the demigoddesses began questioning him closely about his beliefs and his life in the group. Price did his best to repeat the orthodoxies the group propounded, but evidently he did so with insufficient conviction. "You're full of shit," the woman concluded. "And almost overnight," Price said, "all the other female training therapists dropped me and wouldn't date me anymore."

For some, it was like one long party, sleeping with lots of attractive, smart, and creative people. "I think it was a very different experience being a man," said Sara, a former member who asked me not to use her real name. "I knew guys who said, 'I had the time of my life. I screwed everyone. I would never have had that many dates.' I think for women it was quite different. There was a lot of sexual exploitation. For women, particularly women who were more attractive, you weren't allowed to say no. Or you felt you weren't allowed to say no." At one point an older therapist in the group wanted to date her. She wasn't attracted to him and tried to suggest that they just be friends. "Saul had some choice words to say about that. It was blasphemy to reject [this other therapist] and so I felt I had to sleep with him." (Many women I spoke with felt the same pressure, while some, mostly older women with more life experience and perhaps more self-possession, felt better able to resist it.)

The sex-positive attitude of the group made life relatively easy for its gay members, even if homosexuality was more tolerated than approved of. Members were encouraged to sleep with other members most nights, and same-sex sleepovers could easily end up as sexual encounters. At the same time, gay members were told to at least try heterosexual sex.

Penelope Barrett felt that the group partook of misogynistic and sexist attitudes that were common in the left-wing culture of the period. "Chicks put out" was a phrase she had heard among the radical groups at Columbia when she was a student at Barnard. But the therapy added another layer that made it harder for women to say no. One of the pillars of Sullivanian therapy was the "not-me experience." To grow, they believed, you needed to push yourself into doing things that made you uncomfortable and anxious—override the voice in your head that came from your parents or from society. These were not-me experiences. "The Sullivanians gave it a compassionate spin . . . Of course you feel anxious and uncomfortable with X, Y, or Z, when X might be giving Saul a blow job, Y might be screaming at someone, and Z might be telling your family you never wanted to see them again," Penelope said. This concept of the not-me experience effectively deprived you of any moral compass or independent judgment, as your values were presumed to be the product of your corrupt upbringing. "If I wanted a monogamous relationship—or if I didn't want to have sex with someone because I didn't like him or just wasn't attracted to him—it was because of my bourgeois values."

In one instance Penelope managed to get out of a sexual encounter through an unusual tactic. A guy she didn't like kept bugging her for a date, and she kept making excuses and putting him off, but he wouldn't relent. Finally—almost to her own surprise—she blurted, "Look, my heart's just not in it." As she recalled, "This was such a non-Sullivanian thing to say—no one talked about their heart—that he didn't know what to say. And he gave up."

The group viewed jealousy as a by-product of a capitalist mentality that saw marriage and monogamy as a form of ownership, so you were supposed to cure yourself of any jealous impulses. "My therapist told me that I should learn to enjoy the sounds of the man I was interested in having sex with another woman, that it was a defect of mine that I didn't," Sara recalled.

Eric Grunin insisted that he successfully found ways of coping with this kind of situation. "The moment of truth for me was, I was in my apartment, and my roommate was having a date with someone I liked, and the walls were not really thick, so it was audible, which, okay, was a little weird. I thought, 'Well, you know, you have a date with her tomorrow, so this is no big deal.' It was that simple. If you think of monogamy as property, I didn't actually want to own anybody. I just wanted my needs to get met, and I didn't worry. Now that makes me atypical, an outlier, maybe. There are plenty of people in this world who only want a two-day-a-week boyfriend. They don't care what he does with the other five days."

Not everyone found it so easy. "It was a nightmare," said Amy Siskind, who had been a child of a patient in the sixties and rejoined as a patient herself in the seventies. "Can you imagine? Not only was there jealousy, but a lot of times you had to be directly confronted with it. Your roommate might be dating the person you were in love with, and unless you arranged to be out of the house that night, you might have to be there sleeping when your roommate was in the next room with that person. It was extremely difficult and unpleasant."

Being in a polygamous community could be plenty complicated for men as well. Richard Price recalled a weird encounter he had with Richard Elman, his former writing teacher and mentor. "I went over to his apartment, and he was trying to be one of the boys, talking to me about who's sleeping with whom, and hey, did you ever sleep with this one? And then finally he says, 'You know who is really the best, the best one to have sex with?' And then he mentions my girlfriend, my secret girlfriend, 'cause you weren't supposed to have a real girlfriend, but he knew, he fucking knew. He set me up and then dropped this sadistic bomb on me, and then he looked at me like, 'Why are you freaked out? We're all free as birds here.'"

Of course it happened with some frequency that two people really liked each other and wanted to see each other more than anyone else. But this was seen as an unhealthy dependence that limited your own growth and deprived others of your emotions. "You were not supposed to fall in love, and I fell in love a bunch of times," said Steve Meshnick, the medical researcher. "It's not abnormal for a guy in his twenties to have intense romantic experiences, and you'd have to keep it under the radar. I remember I had this one girlfriend, Stephanie N.—we both had major crushes on each other—but we figured out that we couldn't have two dates a week with one another because people would notice, so we had a date every four days. I tried to navigate the rules as best as I could . . . Once or twice the girl I was dating broke it up because her therapist told her to." This could just as easily happen through a person's roommates. "You could be at a house meeting and someone might say, 'Steve, you are spending a lot of time with Audrey, I think you're in a focus. You need to think about that.'"

Therapists took surprising measures to break up a hostile integration. Sara remembers coming back from a romantic weekend with a man she was intensely interested in and hearing her roommates announce that the man was supposed to father a child with someone else. "I walked back into my apartment and was greeted by one of my roommates telling me, 'Did you hear that X is having a baby with Y?' X was the man I had just spent the weekend with, who'd told me, 'Let's go away next weekend.' These were basically arranged marriages." Often, when a woman in the group wanted to have a child, her therapist would suggest a suitable mate—frequently someone she had little or no connection to—and it might also serve to break up another relationship.

For Michael Bray, who had left a Catholic seminary and a sexless marriage for life in the group, the polygamous lifestyle that had been such a revelation at the beginning gradually grew a bit stale. "It was a transactional kind of thing, and that was easy, but it was the most mechanical thing in the world. The only thing that made it exciting was if one of the beautiful girls asked you for a date. But she quickly became no different from anybody else. Because it was nothing but a sort of unfeeling act, and she'd be fucking somebody else the next day, or maybe a couple of hours later." If you started to actually feel things for the other person, the simple suddenly became complex. "You were conditioned to think that that was actually wrong. You were focusing on somebody rather than circulating . . . In all my time in the group, I never told anybody 'I love you.'"

One reason for that was the total lack of privacy: word would get out and end up in someone's therapy session in no time flat. As one former member put it, "When two Sullivanians had a date, there were four people in the room, the two of you and your therapists."

Ironically, although Bray had joined because of an unhappy marriage and the need for sexual freedom, in the end he found it in many ways easier to have deeper and closer relationships with his male friends. They were less likely to be classified as a "focus" or a "hostile integration." In 1977, Bray and four other men took a trip to Europe together—the first time he had been to Europe—traveling to London, Paris, and Italy. Bray and one of his friends returned early to New York, and three of them went on to Greece. A picture from the trip shows the once clean-cut seminarian with a shaggy mountain-man beard and a tie-dyed T-shirt. After Bray left Europe, one friend, Dick Wasley, a professional clarinet player, got terribly sick. Doctors in Greece couldn't figure out what the problem was, and Wasley was put on a plane to New York, already in a perilous condition. Bray met him at the airport, at which point his friend was barely conscious. Rather than calling an ambulance, Bray decided to pack him into a cab and take him straight to an emergency room. "It was clear he was close to death," Bray said. "For the last ten minutes of the ride, I was having to reach into his mouth and clear his spittle so that he could breathe, and I just kept telling him to hold on."

Wasley survived, but he turned out to have a severe case of Guillain-Barré syndrome, a neurological disorder that virtually paralyzed him for months. For a time, the only body parts he could move were one of his eyes and one of his big toes. Bray and other friends from the group organized a support system for Wasley and gradually helped nurse him back to health. They devised a communication system where they broke up the alphabet into rows and columns, and Dick, by indicating yes and no with his one working eye, formed words one letter at a time. Recounting this more than forty years later, Bray, sitting in a Westchester coffee shop, had to fight back tears and clear his throat. With fondness, he recalled that his friend always insisted—despite the exceptional amount of work involved—on speaking in complete, grammatical sentences. "He would say, 'Could you make a call?' instead of just 'call.'" Later, when he was able to speak again, Dick explained that it was satisfying for him to make full sentences, giving him a sense of capacity and agency.

This was the group at its best: a network of support that helped a friend survive. These were the bonds—as much as or more than the relationship with one's therapist—that kept Bray and so many others remaining in the group.

Not everyone fit into the group lifestyle easily, however. For Carol Q., one of the few Black people in the group, it was often an uncomfortable fit. "Pressure to conform, group pressure," she recalled. She was only seventeen when she entered therapy and sexually inexperienced, and now she was suddenly under pressure not just to have sex, but to have it with multiple partners, and she was told to cool it if she actually started to like someone. The ground rules of life in a Sullivanian apartment were also much more complicated than the usual divvying up of household chores. "There was always an overlay of psychological theory, Sullivanian theory, dos and don'ts according to the Sullivan Institute."

During the house meetings, people could be highly critical if you were not sufficiently scathing in the way you talked about your parents. "I remember this one woman," Carol recalled, "who got furious with me during an apartment meeting because she claimed I wasn't being honest about how horrible my parents were. If you tried to give them a little credit for anything, you were being dishonest." Carol's father— whatever his faults—was a man of considerable substance, a doctor who had made his way through medical school while working as a railroad porter and had built a hospital for Black patients in the 1940s in an area with few if any medical facilities for people of his race.

Carol recalled that at a certain point, when she was considering enrolling at the Manhattan School of Music to pursue a career as a singer, Jane Pearce suggested that she get back in touch with her father and ask him to pay her tuition. She called her parents—with whom she had broken—and arranged to go down and see them. "I insisted absolutely that my mother not be there." She drove down with three friends from the group, including her former roommate and fellow therapist Ellen Barrett, and met her father. When patients saw their parents—generally to ask for money—they were almost always accompanied by other group members. This would prevent them from falling under the sway of their parents again. Seeing his daughter under these awkward circumstances, her father, Dr. Milton Q., said no. The trip left Carol with a bad feeling, especially the way she excluded her mother. "It was just cruel," she said.

Carol also never felt comfortable with the promiscuous Sullivanian lifestyle. She was just starting to get the hang of dating when she was pushed into having multiple sex partners. "You were made to feel like something was wrong with you if you didn't want to have sex with somebody," she recalled. She got close to and was enjoying a relationship with a man named Mark S., but his roommate, Mike Veghte, also wanted to date her. "I think I used alcohol to get out of it," she said. Drinking too much would provide her with an out from having sex—or make it possible to have sex when she didn't really want to. One evening, Veghte was trying to get her to have sex with him, and they wound up in bed together, although they didn't have sex. Sometime during the night, Carol got up—she must have been sleepwalking—and went into Mark S.'s room, waking up to find herself in his bed. Somehow, she concluded, her unconscious had led her to where she actually wanted to be, which was not in compliance with the group's free and easy norms.

The emotional undercurrent of her own therapy and the training she was receiving as a therapist was fear. "There was always the fear, if you leave this group, you are not going to make it, since this is the only world that makes sense. The first words of *The Conditions of Human Growth* were, 'We live in a dangerous world.'"

As a training therapist, she had trouble following the Sullivanian line. "One of the sayings I remember [we were supposed] to tell a client or patient was, 'You're never going to make it on your own without this therapy.' And I never felt right about saying that. I toed the line really well in the beginning, but that just sort of stuck in my throat, because I didn't really believe it. So apparently, I was not convincing." One day, when Carol tried this line on one of her patients, he laughed out loud. And secretly, she found herself agreeing with him.

Carol dealt with the pressures of this new world by drinking, an activity considered by Pearce to be a natural response to anxiety. Before long, her drinking became a bigger and bigger problem. She had trouble doing what she was told to do as a therapist. Finally, it became increasingly clear that Carol, a confused young woman in her early twenties, a college dropout with a serious alcohol problem, should not be treating patients with psychological problems of their own. The leadership decided to remove her from the training program. That meeting was to be a pivotal moment in Carol's life.

"Saul sexually assaulted me," she said. "We were discussing the reassignment of my patients. I was crying, and then he assaulted me. I really don't want to go into detail about it. But just suffice it to say I was in a vulnerable situation, and he, you know, took sexual advantage of me where I was not asking for it. And if it were this—if it had been in this day and time, I'm sure he would be locked up, because I know for a fact that I was not the only one."

A few months after our initial conversation, Carol got back in touch and said that she wanted to talk about it. "It was just such a shock," she said. "I was looking down at this bald head on my breast. I was paralyzed and said nothing. This guy was supposed to be the be-all and end-all of psychology. There was all kinds of revulsion and self-revulsion going on inside of me. And then, all of a sudden, he stopped, and he went back to his chair and he started talking like nothing had happened. And I was still in shock. And then I would see him at parties and he would come up to me and say, 'I want to make it with you.' For a long time, for years, I never told anyone about it. I didn't tell Jane."

After Carol Q. was kicked out of the training program, she was assigned to another therapist. She would no longer be seeing Jane Pearce but would see a young woman a few years older than herself, another training analyst—her friend and former roommate, Ellen Barrett. It was a strange choice of therapist.

In this new role, it seemed as if her friend had turned into someone else. "She was very hard-core. I felt like I was being browbeaten every time I went in there," Carol recalled. At one point, Ellen grabbed Carol's datebook, riffled through it, and then threw it at Carol, berating her for not having enough dates. "I was feeling extremely unhappy and depressed, and I was drinking more, and my new therapist was telling me I had a problem with authority. And when it came to the drink . . . she accused me of mocking Jane, who was an alcoholic. There was no consideration about my alcoholism being connected to my own depression or my own neurosis or problems or anything. She was a mean bitch."

Carol continued: "I didn't feel like there was anything encouraging. So after a while, I started getting angry. I remember one time crying and being angry at the same time, and her dog started barking at me and she was smirking at me. It was just horrible. After that, I would make appointments, but I would not show up. Or cancel them. And finally I left her a message saying I'm not coming back. She had already given me the speech that I'd given other people about how 'You'll never make it outside of this therapy.' But I left."

After leaving the group, Carol tried to stay in touch with some of her friends from the community, but now these "alternate validators" wanted nothing to do with her. "If I tried to call someone in the group, they would say, 'I can't talk to you now. Not ever.' And I would be hung up on. It was very, very painful."

Carol Q. got in touch with her parents and eventually moved back to North Carolina. While considering her time in the group a failed and deeply painful experiment, she had a forgiving attitude toward her first therapist and the institute's founder, Jane Pearce. "I think Jane was blinded by her own theory and lots of hope."

9

The Secret History

When Andy Cates was seven years old, in 1971, his parents began asking him whether he wanted to go away to boarding school. He said no. When they mentioned that the older brother of one of his friends had gone away, he again said no, and no again. Then, at a certain point, they proposed that they would all take a trip together and just look at schools. He wouldn't have to go to one, just look. "That sounds really cool," he thought. "I'm going to get to go on a trip with my parents"— which he had never done before. "I'm going to go on an airplane for the first time . . . That was a pretty big thing for little kids back then." The three of them flew up to Maine and rented a car.

They drove to see a school that seemed quite attractive and well-run; his parents asked him if he'd like to go there. He said no. They drove away and visited a second school. It was much smaller, with fewer facilities, and more disorganized. There were no children Andy's age. The youngest were ten or eleven, three or four years older than Andy. At a certain point Andy was speaking to the principal of the school when he saw his parents walking down the hall, heading toward the exit. "Excuse me, I have to join my parents," he said to the principal. "No, you're not," the man said. His parents walked away without turning around or offering a word of explanation. Andy was left there. "That's how I went to boarding school . . . They duped me. They didn't even say goodbye. They didn't have the guts to say goodbye."

So began a personal odyssey for Andy Cates that involved

five boarding schools—in Maine, New York, Virginia, Arizona, and Massachusetts—during which he experienced and witnessed extraordinary amounts of abuse, from neglect and physical violence to sexual molestation. He did not learn to read until he was eleven. He ran away, got into trouble. One of the schools he attended with several other Sullivanian kids was closed after a government investigation confirmed repeated instances of physical cruelty toward the students.

Andy was one of a few dozen kids from the Sullivanian community who were sent away to boarding school in the 1960s and '70s. People who joined the group who already had children were pressured to send their children away. The select few patients who did have kids after entering therapy were told that their children would be better off in boarding school, away from the toxic influence of their parents.

The story of the children is like a secret parallel history of the Sullivanians. Their absence, in a sense, made the group possible. It would have been difficult for the patients to lead the life they were encouraged to lead—pursuing their careers, having multiple sex partners, taking art classes, performing in plays, hanging out and having sleepover dates with friends, joining women's and men's groups—if they were forced to stay home tucking their kids into bed and reading them stories. Children were another opposite attractive pole that would inevitably pull these parents away from the group. Their exile was the price that needed to be paid for the freedom and self-fulfillment their parents acquired when they entered the Sullivanian community.

Part of the appeal of Sullivanian therapy was that it offered people a kind of extended—potentially infinite—adolescence. The network of group apartments (some in the same building, some just a few blocks away) was almost an extension of the college dormitory. And if you had been too anxious and insecure to fully enjoy the freedom of college life, you could in your twenties and thirties enjoy it in ways you could not as a teenager. ("Youth is wasted on the young," the saying goes.) Children are decidedly out of place in a college dorm. In a way, the Sullivanian community was like the land of the lotus-eaters described by Homer in the *Odyssey*, in which men feast on a fruit that "was so delicious that those who ate of it left off caring about home." And, of course, from the therapists' point of view, children represented a competing set of loyalties that would dilute loyalty to the group as well as the authority of the therapists. Patients were discouraged from having children: "You're not ready, you need to grow," they were told. (One former member had no fewer than seven abortions while in the group.) Of course, the children who existed when someone went into therapy could not be unborn, so they were sent away instead.

The move to separate parents and children was justified by the argument that it was best for the kids. That they almost universally hated boarding school and resented being sent away contradicted this idea and undermined the Sullivan Institute's central claim to have created the optimal conditions for human growth. After all, parents were told that this was being done for the children's good. Adult patients were told that they represented a genuine danger to their children, and so the kids were kept away from New York even during their vacations from school. They were encouraged to cadge invitations from other boarders with whom they might spend their Christmas or spring break. The kids were invariably sent to double sessions of summer camp, and when camp was not in session, many were forced to remain with employees of their shut-down boarding schools.

The parents who sent their children away were not bad people—in most cases they were intelligent, kind, and exceptionally well educated. This was simply a central tenet of the group in which they had chosen to make their lives. Perhaps the most stirring line in Jane Pearce and Saul Newton's "Radical Alternative" essay is "The future belongs to the people who are ready to leave home, both physically and psychologically."

Andy Cates's parents were both therapists in the group that formed the nucleus of the Sullivan Institute in its early years. His father, John Cates, was from a wealthy Southern family, raised in the town of Newnan, Georgia. He went to medical school in Atlanta and served as a doctor in World War II. After the war, he moved to New York and began training to be a psychiatrist. "He was a gay man who met his partner at the end of the war, and they settled in New York," said Eddy Cates,

John's son and Andy's younger brother. A photograph from those days shows John and his longtime partner, Ed Dent, both in uniform, smiling for the camera. John Cates, however, was decidedly in the closet. His sons did not know for sure that he was gay until many years later, but everyone seems to have known intuitively and accepted tacitly that Ed was a fixture in his life for many years. While undergoing his psychoanalytic training in the 1950s, Cates came into contact with Newton and Pearce, and he met Millie Antonelli, who was also training to become a therapist and who would become his wife. Before marrying John Cates, Millie (née Satinoff) was married to another aspiring Sullivanian therapist, Dom Antonelli, whose last name she retained.

Millie was the daughter of Jewish immigrants from Eastern Europe. "My grandfather," Andy explained, "was a peddler who spoke all these languages because he was from Eastern Europe and he catered to the immigrant community, which, because many of them didn't speak English, had a hard time. He would get them whatever they needed—linen, silverware, furniture, watches, everything. He was a walking catalog. And so he would go to the districts in New York where you could get those things. He would get them for people on credit—and then, a couple of days a week, he would walk around collecting his money, up five flights of stairs to get fifty cents from this one and a dollar from that one. That's how he put my mother through college."

Millie was a bright child. Her mother got her a library card before she was even legally allowed to have one and enrolled her in Hebrew school. "My mom was very successful academically, in large part because of her parents," Andy Cates said. "She skipped multiple grades." She attended Brooklyn College and then Radcliffe.

At some point during the 1950s Millie and Dom split up without having had children. Then she and John Cates, with whom she had become good friends, decided to have a family together even though she knew he was predominantly gay—this was rarely discussed, and he never acknowledged it publicly.

John Cates bought a town house on West Seventy-Seventh Street just down the block from Jane Pearce and Saul Newton's home. Like

Jane and Saul, he and Millie lived with other therapists who rented rooms from them, including Millie's ex-husband, Dom. John Cates and Dom Antonelli bought a piece of land near Jane Pearce and Saul Newton's house in Amagansett, where they built a beautiful house together.

"[My mother] and my dad, at some point in the early sixties, decided to form a family in a very nontraditional way," Eddy Cates said. By the standards of that era—or arguably even today—they created a highly unconventional but interesting arrangement: a gay man, his straight wife, her ex-husband, and the therapist Art Liebeskind, each leading nonmonogamous lives, eventually all with children. "Their cohorts were open to really nontraditional structures . . . They were in a nonmonogamous relationship, which was the norm in the group. My father was gay . . . but he really wanted to have kids, and so the group gave him an opportunity to do that." They were all interested in art and ideas. They all took classes at the Art Students League, and John Cates's own paintings show that he took his art seriously. As he had money, Cates also bought paintings by Kenneth Noland and Jules Olitski when they were Sullivanian patients. Curiously, John's longtime partner, Ed Dent—who came from a rather traditional midwestern family—insisted that John and Millie marry so that their children would not be born out of wedlock.

Eddy's older brother, Andy, disagreed with the idea that their father needed the Sullivanian group to lead a free life as a gay man. If anything, Andy saw it as a step backward. John was part of an extremely interesting underground gay community that he turned his back on, Andy Cates argued. John and Ed built a house together in Haddam, Connecticut, where there was a small colony of homosexual men who lived openly but quietly in a don't-ask-don't-tell fashion. They had an interesting circle of friends, including the brilliant and enigmatic writer Frederic Prokosch, whose 1935 novel, *The Asiatics* (an extraordinary imaginary voyage in Asia written by a man who had never set foot in Asia), was praised by writers as different as T. S. Eliot, Albert Camus, and Thomas Mann. There are photographs of the young John

Cates—handsome, blond, with a bit of a cleft chin—and the dashing, somewhat older Prokosch, who, along with his literary production, was a champion squash and tennis player. To Andy Cates's way of thinking, his father gave up this interesting underground life for a place in the Sullivanian world, where, in exchange for acceptance, he took on a fundamentally subservient role. The group allowed John Cates to have a family, but with its anti-family ideology it would force him to send his children away. The group let him be a closeted gay man, but the group's hostility to stable couples and to people outside the group eventually persuaded him to break off his ties with Ed Dent, to whom Andy and Eddy remained very much attached.

Andy may have underestimated the emotional strain imposed by the underground gay life during this period. Frederic Prokosch, without referring openly to his sexuality, hinted at this psychic cost: "I have spent my life alone, utterly alone . . . My real life (if I ever dared to write it!) has transpired in darkness, secrecy, fleeting contacts and incommunicable delights, any number of strange picaresque escapades and even crimes . . . With all the surface 'respectability,' diplomatic and scholarly and illustrious social contacts, my real life has been subversive, anarchic, vicious, lonely, and capricious." It was a courageous but lonely path.

Arguably, John Cates found a kind of compromise that was at least partially successful. In one sense, the unorthodox beliefs of the Sullivan Institute—especially their rejection of monogamous marriage—made it easier for John to have both a family and relationships with men that he pursued separately. And it allowed his wife, Millie, to have a sexual life outside her marriage in addition to the family she built with her husband. At the same time, it made John unusually dependent on the Sullivanian community.

Andy Cates was born in 1964, legally but not biologically the son of John Cates. Eddy came along two years later. At a time when homosexuality was still taboo and gay marriage half a century away, their parents' lives—and the milieu of the Sullivan Institute—appeared quite humane and enlightened. "It felt like it was kind of an interesting way to grow up at that time," Eddy Cates said. "You know, to sort of realize that the way society is structured is not the only way society can be structured. So there was a part of me that thought that was kind of cool, before it all got messed up."

The summers in Amagansett that were so exciting for many Sullivanian patients were also fairly idyllic for the kids, with all the therapists' houses clustered together near Saul Newton and Jane Pearce's place on Barnes Landing. Parents and kids alike were constantly in and out of one another's houses.

"We would wake up at the crack of dawn," Andy Cates said, recalling how he and his brother would go quietly from house to house, waking the children of the other therapists and spending entire days playing. "We played on the beach. We rode our bikes. Sometimes we would just all sleep at Art [Liebeskind's] house night after night. Art was the best."

Millie Antonelli, Andy and Eddy Cates's mother, remembered this time happily. It was a period of sexual freedom, rich socialization, and a close-knit community of peers: "We all had children the same age, and we were dating each other. So you had a close relationship with everybody, and the children were all friends. So that was the best time of my life for me."

Andy found the summers in Amagansett easier than the school year back in New York. In keeping with Sullivanian principles, the children were largely taken care of by babysitters, maybe seeing their parents for an hour or so before bed. When Andy went to school and heard about and saw more of how other kids lived, he felt himself to be different, and he had some difficulty adjusting.

Although his parents' relationship was an innovative compromise, it ultimately didn't work as a marriage. "I remember being curled up on my mother's bed, and we were playing a game of Sorry," Andy recalled. "My father told my mother it was time to stop and for me to go to bed. My mother explained that the game was almost over and to give us a little time. My father was furious and stormed into her room." Things spun out of control. "I remember quite a bit of physical fighting in that period." His parents separated and then divorced. Millie moved out, and Art Liebeskind and his two adopted sons, part of Andy and Eddy's gang, moved in.

*   *   *

All the therapists, along with treating their own patients, were in analysis with one another, and Millie Antonelli was in therapy with Saul Newton. As Andy reached school age, Saul began to convince Millie to send him to boarding school.

"The culture of the group was that mothers were malignant, malevolent," Millie Antonelli said. "One of the reasons I had delayed having children was that I was afraid I'd be like my mother . . . I was actually a very good mother at the beginning, and I always was great with children, and then I fell apart. And at a certain point, maybe when Andy was between four and six, I suddenly found myself acting like her, and nobody helped me. They just said, 'Yes, you're being like your mother.' And it made me very angry. So that's when things started falling apart for me. I got criticized. When I told Jane [Pearce] what was going on, she said, 'Yes, you are being like your mother.' And then Joan [Harvey] and Helen [Moses] came along, and they were super judgmental."

Eventually Millie had a dream that Andy—who didn't like school— got up and was enthusiastic about going to school, but it was a boarding school. She described the dream to Saul, and he began pressing her to send Andy away. The dream would have made it seem to be Millie's idea, when in fact the institute had been pushing all its patients to send their kids away for years. In other words, Millie's dream was likely the result of years of conditioning. Some of her peers, the other therapists in the group, were already sending their kids away. (Saul, Jane, and Joan did not: evidently, they were the only ones who had reached a sufficient level of emotional maturity to live with their own children.) Newton also used dream analysis to convince Millie to send away Eddy, her younger son, two years later when he was seven. "I had a dream in which Eddy was skating in a skating rink," Millie recalled, "and Saul said, 'He's going around in a circle, he's not moving away and becoming more independent.' So that added to my thinking that Eddy wanted to go to boarding school, and that's how it happened."

Eddy said that the notion that he asked to go away to school is a fiction his mother has invented to rationalize a move she still feels deeply guilty about. He has no memory of having asked to go to boarding school, and, in fact, he recalled dreading it: "I think it was pretty terrifying. I remember that I was sick for the first week before I left home, so I left for school a week later than I was supposed to. I think that may have been partially fear. I was not a sickly child." As there were very few boarding schools in the United States that enrolled seven-year-olds, he was taken to a small progressive school in New Hampshire that he later learned was for troubled kids. But Eddy was comparatively lucky in terms of the young couple who presided over the dormitory where he lived. "I survived by latching on to a series of nurturing figures." He was not, however, spared all the dangers of being sent away at such a young age: he was sexually abused by a thirteen-year-old girl. "It often happened with the goading and at the direction of other older students," he said.

The school in Maine where Andy Cates's parents had left him a few years earlier was not set up to deal with a child of seven. The next youngest child there was eleven, and he mostly tagged along with two thirteen-year-old boys. Andy was so young, he lived not in the dormitory but with the director's family. The school was based on the Summerhill progressive model, in which you let the child learn at his or her own pace—or not at all. "There was no school, there were no academics," Andy said. "So I totally forgot all my reading skills."

The kids spent a lot of time outdoors, trapping animals and building tree houses in the woods. After a year and a half, the school was failing economically, and in the middle of the year Andy's parents had to send him to a different progressive school, the Open Community School in Claverack, New York, about two hours north of New York City. Andy was still unable to read. There were other Sullivanian kids at Claverack, but, like most of the boarding schools that took grade school-age children, it was a dumping ground for troubled kids—kids from families that were falling apart, kids with behavioral problems, kids with learning disabilities, or simply kids whose parents didn't want to deal with them. It was chaos. "You could curse, kids could smoke. Kids had sex," Andy said.

You could choose to go to class—or not. Andy frequently chose not to. Instead, he would go to the library and look at picture books.

One kid Andy frequently saw at the Open Community School library was John Putz, another Sullivanian child. While the other kids were off raising hell, John got a series of math exercise books and diligently worked his way through them. "I don't know how he found them," Andy recalled. "Nobody ever looked at them, but John would do them." John's father, Bob Putz, had a Ph.D. in math, and John would go on to get a Ph.D. in physics. "John was going to be brilliant anywhere he went," Andy said.

John Putz was the exception that proved the rule, which was mayhem and neglect. "We basically raised ourselves in those places," Andy recalled. At a certain point, Andy was seriously hurt when he wandered into an unsupervised construction site on the campus. "I almost got killed," he says. He was in the hospital for a week and liked it so much, he didn't want to leave. "I ate the best food I'd had in years; people were waiting on me hand and foot. They actually cleaned me." The hygiene at the school was poor, and the children rarely bathed. "I had athlete's foot that was so bad, the nurses soaked my feet in an alcohol solution for five days straight to get rid of it."

During the year and a half that Andy was in school in Maine, his parents never came to visit, but they did come to a couple of parents' days at Claverack. "They were usually among the last parents to arrive. I was pathetically waiting at the bottom of the driveway for my parents to come." They came up when he was hospitalized, and at a certain point they realized that after four years of ultraprogressive education, Andy, at eleven years old, was unable to read.

Having been tricked into going to boarding school and then abandoned there, Andy found his basic bond with his parents permanently shattered. Yet he was waiting at the end of the school driveway, hoping that the next car to pull in would be theirs.

Andy's disastrous experience ended up benefiting his brother, Eddy. After a couple of years at Eddy's first school in New Hampshire, his parents moved him to a more academically rigorous school, Eaglebrook, in Deerfield, Massachusetts. Two-thirds of his classmates were local children who attended as day students, and only a third were boarders. Rather than being a dumping ground for castaway kids, the school acted as a feeder to Deerfield Academy, one of the top prep schools in the country, which was located in the same town. Though he didn't get much parental care, at least Eddy got a good education.

After Andy's experiences in two progressive schools, John Cates and Millie Antonelli sent him to a much more traditional school in Virginia, for children "with learning and attention issues." Something of a shock for Andy, but a welcome one, it was almost like military school, he recalled. He had to go to chapel, call his teachers "sir," and rather than just walking helter-skelter on the campus, he was expected to march in formation. "You marched to breakfast, you marched to chapel, you marched to class. Everything was orderly. When I first got there, when I tripped over something, I said, 'Oh shit.' The words didn't even leave my mouth when a teacher slapped me hard across the face. But they loved us, and we learned. And it was a caring environment. It was, you know . . . I'm tearing up thinking about it. They were just amazing."

At the same time, with very young children alone and isolated away from home, it was also a place where sexual abuse occurred. Andy witnessed this and was nearly the victim of it. He recalled an incident when he went to find his English teacher, who came to the dorm in the evening to help children with their homework. One evening Andy sought him out with a question and found him in another child's room. "I walked in, and he had his hand in that kid's pants, and I totally blacked that memory out."

At another point Andy was experimenting with a movie camera

his father had sent him as a present. A teacher offered to get the film developed so that they could watch it together. The teacher had a room in one of the school's main buildings, an old Southern mansion. "We started watching the movie, and suddenly I felt his thumb go down the back of my pants. That was weird. And then, when the movie was over, he started showing me pornography. I still remember the book. It was a family, completely naked, not sexual, it was like a nudist book. But on the last page the wife was giving the husband head. And I flipped out and said, 'I want to go, I want to go, I want to go back to my dorm.' I remember getting louder and louder. The guy was like, 'Okay, I'll let you go.' He went to unlock the door. The dead bolt was higher than any kid could ever reach. And this was a teacher. This was a teacher. So I saw stuff like that happen."

Andy does not blame the school, to which he feels an enduring gratitude. "They were innocent. This guy was a jackal. I don't think they could have . . . maybe they could have prevented it. I don't know. But I don't consider myself a victim, because I kind of got out of it. But I feel bad for the other kid. The point of the stories is that our parents put us at risk. That's the reason I'm telling you this—because I can't imagine leaving my kids at a boarding school like that."

After only a year at his Virginia school, Andy, then twelve, was sent to a school in Tucson, Arizona, called Treehaven, where several other Sullivanian kids also wound up. The schools he had been to before would come to seem like paradise compared with Treehaven.

"Treehaven was a prison," said Andy Cates. "Treehaven was hate. They hated us. It was closed down for child abuse. There were individual teachers that were nice and liked us and stuff, but the director of the school hated kids. They just hated us."

(The state of Arizona closed the school in 1980, and its director, Patricia deBoucher, was convicted of being physically abusive to her students.)

Perhaps the quintessential Treehaven story is the "oatmeal story," which was first told to me by John Putz, who overlapped with Andy

Cates both at Claverack and Treehaven. A mother arrived with a very young girl, about three years old, and they decided to have the child spend a day at the school to try it out. She came to breakfast and refused to eat her oatmeal. "So they strapped her to the chair, and she sat there all day basically," John Putz recalled. "We came back for lunch, and she was still there, and at some point during the day they'd taken the bowl of oatmeal and dumped it on her head. So she was sitting there in this chair with the turned-over bowl of oatmeal on her head."

Incredibly, even after this incident, the mother still decided to send the child to Treehaven.

John Putz managed to survive his time at the school by trying to fly beneath the radar, maintaining a low profile, not openly complaining or defying the authorities, and focusing on his studies. Not so fortunate was John's younger brother, Tony, who was sent there at age three, a year or two before John Putz or Andy Cates arrived.

John and Tony Putz's parents had both entered therapy in 1972, but then their mother, Judy Putz, died in a car accident in Amagansett that summer. So Bob Putz became a single father of two small boys overnight. It was not too hard to convince Bob—grief-stricken, in shock, and genuinely overwhelmed by his new responsibilities—that he needed help and was not in the best position to raise his kids. He agreed to send John, who was five, to boarding school that fall. He hired a babysitter to take care of Tony, who was only two. But the following year something happened that ratcheted up the pressure on Bob to send his younger son away as well. Tony and his babysitter had gone to play in Central Park with the child of one of the group's therapists and that child's babysitter. "The story was that Tony pushed this other boy into the pond or something," Bob Putz recalled. "Tony was three. The babysitter said that wasn't quite what happened, but I was told that Tony had tried to kill someone, that I needed to send him away because otherwise he was going to kill someone or kill himself." Bob called around frantically, looking for a boarding school that would take a three-year-old child. There were none, until eventually he heard about Treehaven.

Tony was so young, he didn't live in a dorm but stayed with a couple who taught at the school. The husband and wife who raised Tony "were mean people," said Andy Cates. "They were really angry. I got into a fight with [the husband] once—he kicked my ass good. But I fought back. Tony was maybe four or five when I got there, and he was already a mess. He would be wearing his shoes on the wrong feet and have snot running from his nose. He was totally neglected. He was just a baby . . . And they would yell at him and belittle him. He was not nurtured at all."

One of the many disadvantages of Treehaven was that it was so far from New York that the kids rarely got visits from their parents and were often not brought home during vacations. They were expected to wangle invitations from kids who lived on the West Coast. In many instances they remained at the school even when it was closed.

John Putz and his roommate, Sam Miller (whose mother was a Sullivanian), were forced to stay with the Murphys, a couple who worked as staff at the school. One year, the Murphys didn't have room in their house, so the two boys ended up sleeping in the back of the family's pickup truck. The Murphys were also mean. Mrs. Murphy made them run laps in order to "earn" their meals. "Oh yeah, she said, 'I'm not just going to feed you,'" Sam recalled. "'You've got to earn yours.' So we had to run laps around the track. I mean we were eight or nine. And God knows what our parents were paying them."

At the end of his first year at Treehaven, Sam was in the lucky position of being one of the only Sullivanian children who got to go home during the window between the end of school in early June and the beginning of camp in early July. (All the Sullivanian kids went to camp during the summer.) Sam's father had left the group and had won some limited custody. He got to have Sam one of the three weeks of the June break. They spent the first week together, and at the end of that time his father suggested that he stay another week. Sam was delighted. "The alternative was living in the back of a pickup truck and running laps around a trailer park to eat dinner," Sam said. His mother, Marilyn Miller, had no plans to spend time with him and intended to send him back to Arizona before he started camp. A day or two later he and his father went out to Central Park and got an ice cream from a vendor. Sam remembers distinctly that it was a Bomb Pop—a kind of popsicle with different colors and different flavors. Suddenly he and his father noticed a woman from the group in a jogging outfit stretching. His father, suddenly nervous, started walking quickly in the direction of his apartment. They spotted a second person from the group and then a third. Soon a small crowd of Sullivanians were following them and started screaming, "He's kidnapping this boy!" One of the men managed to get into Sam's father's building and was soon pounding on the door and screaming. Sam's father called the police. "My dad explained what was happening and said, 'His mother's not even here.' The cops are wondering, 'Who are these people? Where's the mother?' And then my mother walked around the corner, and she starts screaming, 'He's got my son.' It's a freaky situation. I think I was nine. And the police officer said, 'Well, who do you want to be with, your mother or your father?' And I said that I wanted to be with my father, but my father said, 'Look, I, you know, I can't.'" Sam's father wasn't sure what to do. Technically, he was in violation of the custody agreement. "She clearly had it down to the minute, probably. And he was probably worried that this was not the way to get custody."

To try to resolve the standoff, Sam's father managed to have his ex-wife phone up to the apartment so that they could work something out. "So she called," Sam said, "and I talked to her, and she said, 'If you want to stay with your father, you can—but I'm never going to see you again for the rest of your life.'" Sam turned to his father, hoping he would say, fine, too bad for her; instead, he hesitated, saying something like, "I'm not going to make that decision. I can't be responsible for your never seeing your mother again." Sam concluded, "So I left with the police officer. My mother picked me up."

Although Marilyn Miller had insisted on enforcing the custody agreement, which gave her the right to the last two weeks of his break, she didn't take Sam back to her apartment. "We got in a cab," Sam said. "We went to the airport, and I went to Arizona. She had the tickets ready. I didn't even go home."

When Sam looks back, it is hard for him not to see this as the pivotal moment of his early life: for a few seconds, the prospect of a family had been dangled before his eyes, only to be withdrawn. "It's a big moment, you know. I mean, my life would have been a lot different if he had said, 'He's my son. See you later, you fucking nut job,' you know. But he didn't, he couldn't do that."

To his surprise and consternation, Sam cannot remember which members of the group formed the posse that began chasing him and his father. "I've definitely blocked things. How could I not remember who these people were? This was a big moment in my life, obviously. I don't remember who they were. And I have weird memories—like I was eating a Bomb Pop . . . I loved those things. I had one in my hand when they surrounded us. That's what I remember. Why do I remember that?"

He remembers the multicolored popsicle beginning to melt in his hand, and not the people surrounding him to take him from his father. It is hard not to think that Sam's Bomb Pop is like Rosebud in Orson Welles's classic movie *Citizen Kane* (1941). The young Kane is riding on a sled in the snow when he is taken away from his parents, and seventy years later he is heard repeating the word "Rosebud" on his deathbed, the name of the sled that evokes for him the simple childhood and the parental love he lost that day.

Andy Cates remembers everyone's surprise when Sam returned to the closed-down school in Arizona. They had all envied the fact that he was the only one of the Sullivanian kids who got to return to New York. "Then he came back early, and we were all saying, 'What the hell are you doing here?' And he told us the story. And that's when we all put our heads together and we knew something was wrong in New York."

How did the therapists convince their patients—who, like most parents, loved their children—to go against one of the most powerful instincts in human nature? The premise of all Sullivanian therapy was that parents damaged and limited their children. After establishing in the first months of therapy that their patients' own parents were violent and murderous people, it was not such a big leap to convince them that they, having been damaged by their parents, would do the same to their children.

"The general construct was, parents were terrible, period," Bob Putz recalled. "I don't remember anything in particular with me, but the whole gestalt of the group was that parents are terrible. So obviously your parents were terrible. Their parents were terrible, you're terrible. Everyone should get away from their parents. The parents should send their kids away as soon as possible. You're doing them a favor. Everyone except for the chosen few. Everyone except for them." This was a bitter reference to the fact that the group's top leaders—Saul Newton, Joan Harvey, and Helen Moses—never sent their children away to school.

Sending away their kids also allowed the parents to lead the ideal life the therapy was trying to promote. "The social environment was great," Bob said. "I knew all these people. I had all these friends, I was dating all these women, and I was like, this was wonderful. I thought it was great. My therapist convinced me sending the kids away was great for them, too. The therapy—I didn't feel like it did much, but you know, what the hell? I thought the social environment was wonderful for a long time."

In 1976, Deedee Agee lost custody of her seven-year-old son, Teddy, whom she had sent away at age five. Fearing that they, too, might lose custody, group parents abruptly stopped sending their children away to boarding school, but the kids who were already away stayed away.

PART III

BUILDING THE FOURTH WALL

10

The Kremlin and
the Gang of Four

In the spring of 1975, Saul Newton and Joan Harvey acquired a sixteen-thousand-square-foot town house at 314 West Ninety-First Street—the equivalent of three large brownstone buildings merged together and large enough to house a small school, which is what it was before they bought it and what it became again later. But starting in 1976, after a year of renovations, it became the new headquarters of the Sullivan Institute for Research in Psychoanalysis. On the ground floor were offices for the therapists and a large conference room for lectures and meetings. On the second, third, and fourth floors were large apartments for the therapists, their children, and various babysitters.

The new headquarters reflected the group's new power structure: Saul Newton and Joan Harvey, his fifth wife, were the two names on the ownership deed. But they were no longer married to each other. While they had two young children from their marriage who were living with them, each had remarried, and they lived on separate floors. Newton was now married to Helen Moses, and, along with the four children they would eventually have together, they occupied the third floor. After divorcing Newton, Joan Harvey had married Ralph Klein, the one-time analyst of Clement Greenberg, Jackson Pollock, Judy Collins, and others. Harvey and Klein, who occupied the second floor, would go on to adopt four children during their years at Ninety-First Street. Ellen

Barrett was one of three other therapists who moved into this building. The group's lead therapists—Newton, Moses, Harvey, and Klein—were the only members of the Sullivanian community who got to live together as intact families with their spouses and children. But, true to the group's principles, the leaders slept in separate bedrooms and continued to have multiple sexual partners. And in keeping with their ideas about the toxic nature of parenthood, they delegated most of the child-rearing to the babysitters, some of whom lived in tiny rooms in the building as well.

Although the numbers fluctuated, there were generally about thirty people living in the house—roughly eighteen kids of various ages and twelve adults, counting therapists and babysitters. It was a large, lively, chaotic household, with multiple dogs and cats, guinea pigs, fish, and birds, with children and pets moving from floor to floor. The kids ate with the babysitters. The adults sometimes ate together and had their own cook—it would eventually be Deedee Agee. Housekeepers—who were sometimes patients who used the work to pay off their therapy bills—cleaned up after them.

The move to Ninety-First Street codified a shift in power further away from Jane Pearce, who moved back into her old town house at Seventy-Seventh Street and became an increasingly marginal member of the group. In the beginning, the Sullivan Institute had been a loose association of like-minded therapists who shared a philosophy and a therapeutic approach and referred patients to one another, but it was an entity without any real structure. Pearce and Newton, as the authors of the group's "bible," enjoyed special prestige, but with the acquisition of the Ninety-First Street town house, it was clear who the real leaders were. All the classes for the institute's training program took place there, and each week all the training analysts received supervision from one of the four lead therapists living there. The leaders were virtually the only people in the entire community who were not in therapy.

Bill Graves, who was in the group from the early 1970s until the mid-1980s, recalled participating in a study group on *The Conditions of Human Growth*, led by a senior therapist, which concluded that "only Saul was capable of love." Graves could not resist remarking sarcastically, "How lonely it must be for him with no one else who could love." Graves saw the absurdity of the statement and found the Saul worship offensive, but he stayed in the group for at least another decade.

When getting the money together to buy the building, Saul Newton did not hesitate to dip into his patients' resources. One patient, R.A., explained that around this time her parents deposited about thirty-five thousand dollars (the equivalent of a couple hundred thousand dollars today) in an account in her name, an education nest egg for her that they were also able to deduct from their taxes. She told her therapist about it, and the next thing she knew, she got a phone call from Saul, asking her to fly to Boston, withdraw the money, and give it to him to help them buy the new Ninety-First Street headquarters. "With a sense of being chosen for a secret and exciting mission, I set off to do this," R.A. wrote many years later. On her way to the airport, she ran into Jane Pearce, who said something like, "This is the best thing you've ever done in your life!" R.A. recalled, "I didn't know how she knew what I was doing, or even knew who I was, which added to the feeling of a CIA mission. So, being a good girl, I carried out the mission, returned with the check, and dutifully handed it over to Saul, who said he would give it back at some point in the future."

When her parents found out about the bank account being emptied, they were extremely upset, but R.A. told them she was using the money for graduate school. Years later, when she actually did want to go to graduate school, she asked for the money back with great trepidation. She got some or most of it back, but in installments. "Part of the sick thing about this episode was that it was framed by my therapist, with Saul's input, as a Robin Hood–type act of righteous theft on my part, taking money from my 'immoral' tax-evading parents—as if creating a gift account for a child isn't a legal and standard part of financing a child's future."

The reconfiguration of power within the group—with its dizzying series of marriages and real estate deals among the leadership—was like European monarchies intermarrying and swapping territories in the making and unmaking of alliances. Newton, Moses, Harvey, and

Klein were two couples but also a unit, sharing spouses, real estate, and power, a quadrumvirate at the head of the Sullivan Institute. (Two of them, Saul Newton and Joan Harvey, as the legal owners of the real estate, had more power than the other two.) The kids in the group—the ones who were off in boarding school—began to refer (quietly, under their breath) to the new headquarters as "the Kremlin," and the four absolute leaders as "the Gang of Four," an ironic reference to the four leaders of China's Cultural Revolution.

Jane Pearce, like a deposed head of state, was able to buy back the town house on West Seventy-Seventh Street, which she had originally bought with Saul in 1950 and which he had obtained in their divorce. She also, at the age of sixty, got remarried, this time to Dom Antonelli, longtime therapist of the group, who was nine years her junior. The marriage, which virtually no one in the group knew about, appears to have existed only on paper, but it served a specific purpose. Two younger female therapists had given birth but had agreed—or been convinced—to give up their newborn babies after being deemed unfit mothers. Both infants were given in custody to senior therapists in the group, one of them to Jane Pearce. Her paper marriage was designed to facilitate the adoption. The bureaucratic paperwork stressed that the child would be better off being raised by a stable married couple than by a young single parent. It is unclear whether this was part of the dynastic reconfiguration. Was it a kind of consolation prize to the cofounder of the Sullivan Institute, who would now become an increasingly peripheral figure in the community she had started?

*　　*　　*

At around the same time, in the mid-1970s, the group underwent a gradual but profound transformation. If some patients who were in therapy in the early seventies might not have thought they were part of any "group," by the end of the decade, that would no longer be the case.

In 1975, a handful of members formed a comedy troupe and started working up skits and putting on small performances. Luba Elman (no relation to Richard Elman), a therapist who had been an actress in Los Angeles along with Joan Harvey, offered to help them. "She came in and kind of directed us and the entire group. Maybe 250 people showed up, and it was a huge success," recalled Elliot K., who was part of the theater's original nucleus. After that, Luba offered an acting class to people in the group. "It filled so fast, she had to do two classes," Elliot said.

During the summer of 1975 out on Long Island, members put on a performance of Thornton Wilder's *The Skin of Our Teeth* (1942), which everyone really enjoyed. That fall, they performed Arthur Miller's *The Crucible* (1953) at a church on the Upper West Side. As the theater company took shape, Luba Elman began seeing it not just as a fun outlet but as a serious project. She had been reading the book *The Fervent Years* (1945), by Harold Clurman, who helped found the Group Theatre in the 1930s to forge a new, socially conscious kind of theater. In contrast to the purely commercial fare of Broadway, the Group Theatre was a collective of writers and directors that included such major talents as Clifford Odets, William Saroyan, and Elia Kazan, who staged such works as Odets's *Waiting for Lefty* (1935), a rousing call to political action.

Elman gave the Sullivanian drama group a name, the Fourth Wall, after the invisible wall that separates the stage from the audience. By 1976, about 110 Sullivanians—nearly a third of the roughly 350 people living in Sullivanian group apartments—had joined the Fourth Wall, so large a group that there was nowhere big enough in Amagansett for them to stay. They took over a dilapidated motel in Southampton and rented an old VFW hall as their theater space. That summer they put on a series of one-act plays, including Ionesco's *The Bald Soprano* (1950), a lighthearted skit called *Midsummer Night's Scream*, and another skit, called *Murphy*, written by the novelist Richard Price, about two grifters (one of them played by Price himself) who pull a con on a bartender. The summer's performances were a big success and a major point of attraction within the group. One group member had written several musical numbers, including a finale in which all 110 members of the Fourth

Wall walked slowly down the aisle to the stage, or from backstage to center stage, singing a rousing anthem. It generally brought the audience to their feet, applauding wildly.

How did the leadership of the Sullivan Institute react to the formation of a highly popular group within the group? There were a couple of telling moments that Artie Honan, then the Fourth Wall's stage manager, recalled in his memoir, *How Did a Smart Guy Like Me . . . : My 21 Years in Sullivanian Therapy and the Fourth Wall Theater Company* (2020). Before the start of one performance, Luba Elman came backstage and told the cast and crew that they needed to wait to begin. "Her good friends Saul and Joan were coming to the show, and they were late," Honan wrote. "I knew from conversations with her that they really weren't her good friends. She was scared of them. She would not have delayed the start of that show for anyone but them. They came forty-five minutes late while the cast and the audience waited in suspension." It seemed like a crude power move by Saul Newton and Joan Harvey. Given that it was a short car ride from Amagansett, the leaders were making a statement.

Honan, who was a close friend of Luba Elman's, knew very well what the power dynamic was between her and Newton and Harvey. Elman had told him once, in a highly distraught condition, that Newton had, in the middle of a dinner, brutally attacked her, humiliating her in front of the assembled company. As a "second-tier" therapist dependent on him for her livelihood, she had taken the abuse and slunk away with her tail between her legs. At another point, Elman had planned to have a child with a French man she had brought to New York. Newton forbade the plan and insisted that the man help another woman close to Newton get pregnant. "Saul was telling Luba that she couldn't have a baby with the man she had planned to have a baby with," Honan writes. "And he was telling that same guy to get another woman pregnant . . . Luba had no choice; she got her therapy referrals from Saul . . . I hated Saul for using his power to force his will on her. But then, I twisted my mind into believing that if Saul wanted it, there must be a good reason."

During the summer of 1977 the Fourth Wall rented a defunct nursing home up in the Berkshires, where they had more rehearsal space than they could afford on Long Island. The leadership, which mostly owned their own houses in Amagansett, decided to follow, renting places in the Berkshires—a curious case of the therapists following the patients rather than the other way around. Parallel to the theater group, dozens of other members formed a kind of musicians' collective, the Music Loft, renting rehearsal space as well. Toward the end of the summer Joan Harvey announced that she was organizing a big concert for all the musicians in the group. It was almost as if she were setting herself—and the musicians—up in competition with the Fourth Wall. Everyone was expected to attend, and Harvey made a point of demanding that everyone hand her their car keys when they entered the performance space. Everyone had to stay until the performance ended. The concert had not been planned. The level of the musicians was highly uneven, and some of the bands were thrown together at the last minute, but the concert dragged on until well after midnight. At around one a.m., a couple of people asked Harvey for their keys. "'You can't leave!' Joan shouted so everyone could hear her. 'People are performing!'" Honan recounts. "I heard later that she punched one of them, a woman, in the stomach for trying to walk out the door."

The creation of the theater group seems to have awakened Harvey's will to power. Elliot K. said that at some point in this period, Harvey, with whom he had virtually no contact, suddenly approached him at a party. "She came up to me," he remembered, "and she basically gave me what they call a summary"—one of those withering psychological dressing-downs that were common in Sullivanian therapy, which was particularly odd given that they barely knew each other. "'I know the sewer that you crawled out of,' she said to me. Literally those words," Elliot recalled. But the summary was followed by an offer of help: "And you need to see a better therapist, so I'm transferring you to Dom." Elliot had been seeing Jane Pearce—whom he rather liked. In other words, Harvey, acting unilaterally, terminated his therapy with Pearce and transferred him to Dom Antonelli. Elliot didn't object. He was a bit surprised, even flattered, by her sudden attention. It was a recognition that, by virtue of his prominent role in the theater company, he had become someone of importance in the group. At the same time, it was also an assertion of Harvey's power, her control over his life, as well as the purposeful marginalization of Pearce.

Starting in 1976, the group rented the Provincetown Playhouse in New York's Greenwich Village, a small theater where Eugene O'Neill had produced some of his work. The next fall they put on an original play, *Don't Stand in the Doorway*, written by the Sullivanian group member Ken Krauss, that was actually reviewed in *The New York Times*. The play, set in 1967 just as a midwestern college is opening its first coed dormitory, features a group of students talking about life, sex, and friends. "For pathos, periodically we shift 10 years ahead—from hopeful past to helpless present," the *Times* critic Mel Gussow wrote. It sounds like an early version of *The Big Chill* (1983), and it fit nicely with the group's ethos: the fraternity and experimentation of the characters' college years—rather like living in a Sullivanian group apartment—in contrast to the dull existence of middle-class life ten years later.

Gussow gave the play a rather mixed review: "'Don't Stand in the Doorway' seems as familiar as 'yesterday's papers,' to borrow the title of one of the show's background songs . . . Mr. Krauss has not managed to individualize all of his characters or to shape an experience into a play." Gussow remarked that most of the performances seemed amateurish, with a couple of exceptions: "Some of the performers seem as green as freshmen, but at least two, Jocko Marcellino and Evie Weitzer, have both personality and acting potential."

Still, it had been reviewed by the *Times*, and this seems to have whetted the appetite of Joan Harvey, who thought that she—after all, she was a former movie star—should take over the company.

Together, Harvey and Saul Newton decided that the theater would become permanent, serving as the principal vehicle and mouthpiece of the group's mission. It would be radical political theater along the lines of the communist playwright Bertolt Brecht's "epic theater." Newton apparently pressured Luba Elman into ceding control of the Fourth Wall, but when the change was presented to the group, it was made to appear voluntary. Elman called for a big public meeting and proposed that the musicians in the Music Loft and the Fourth Wall merge together. This was put to a vote that, like most votes in the group, appeared to be unanimous. Then, after some hesitation, Elman announced that she was stepping down as director of the Fourth Wall.

"I move that Joan Harvey be the new Fourth Wall artistic director," she said, containing her emotions. "I second!" someone shouted. Another show of hands, and Joan Harvey was now the director of the Fourth Wall. Elman sat back down in her seat. Harvey stood and spryly walked onto the stage, smiling. "Her curly black hair had been permed into a pseudo-Afro style which was popular in the mid-1970s," Artie Honan wrote. "She sat on the stage with her legs dangling over the edge and looked directly at the membership, appreciating the applause. 'Isn't it wonderful that the Music Loft and Fourth Wall are now under one roof?' she said, raising her arms. Almost everyone cheered." And then Harvey offered another motion for the group's approval: "I'd also like to propose one more change. I move that my long-time friend and colleague, Saul Newton, be our consultant." Newton had no background or demonstrated interest in theater, but now he was beside Joan Harvey at its head.

The newly expanded Fourth Wall entered into negotiations to lease its own theater as its permanent venue and decided that in order to rehearse and prepare, it would need a summer space that could accommodate the entire roughly 250-person community. The leaders began to get rid of their houses in Amagansett—there would be no more Long Island summer shares—and found a ramshackle, run-down former hotel in the Catskills into which the entire group could be crammed.

Paying to lease a permanent performance space, as well as buying and fixing up "the workshop"—as the former hotel in Accord, New York, was now known—would require money and labor, so everyone would now have to start paying dues. The leadership began creating formal membership lists—the first dates from October 1977, when the Fourth Wall was still performing at the Provincetown Playhouse. By 1978, the lists include a "policy committee." At the top of the list is "Joan Harvey—artistic director"; right below her is "Saul Newton—consultant." Third on the list, as a concession to her role in founding the theater, is "Luba Elman—producer." Soon, though, Luba's name would disappear from the lists, and she would be out of the group, just as Trotsky's picture disappeared from the Soviet photographs of the revolution. She was even accused of stealing a pottery kiln that belonged to the group, necessitating a house-to-house search. (Only in a lefty group would someone be accused of stealing a pottery kiln.)

Not long after, Luba Elman moved back to California, with little explanation. "She'll probably be dead in a year or two," Saul Newton told people. And sure enough, she died of cancer little more than a year later. In all likelihood, Newton knew about Elman's cancer diagnosis, but his prediction served to reinforce his status as an all-knowing shaman. It also confirmed what was an article of faith in the group: there was no future outside of Sullivanian therapy. You either continued to grow or you fell apart.

What began as a spontaneous bubbling-over of the members' creativity—the Fourth Wall—was turned with one decisive move into its opposite, a hierarchical top-down organization. One of the attractive things about the Sullivanians in the 1960s and the early '70s was that they drew in creative people and encouraged creativity. There were writing groups, drawing classes, pottery classes, an improv comedy group, reading groups, at least a few rock bands, and the theater group. Some Sullivanian musicians rented a loft downtown for their rehearsals. Now everyone was expected to be part of the Fourth Wall and to channel most of their creative energies into the theater. Even if you didn't want to act, you were expected to do something: take tickets, build scene decoration, design costumes, run the lighting.

Many of the people who had started the theater group were suddenly demoted from positions of leadership. "[Saul and Joan] called us into their conference room at Ninety-First Street and said, 'We think you need better leadership,'" Elliot K. recalled. "They removed a number of us from the committee." In retrospect, this defining moment in the group's life was, in Elliot K.'s view, not the result of careful planning but an improvisation dictated by opportunity. "I think both Saul and Joan saw this organization as like a gift for them. Here were hundreds of people paying monthly dues, all focused on a task together. Saul couldn't pass it up, he really wanted to be in control of it. And he knew he knew nothing about theater, but Joan did. So, between the two of them, they just decided they were going to take over."

One result of the elevated importance of the Fourth Wall was the elimination of other independent artistic activities. A group of members who were doing comedy sketches together were asked by the NBC network to do a pilot television show. They performed a set of original skits that they had not yet performed for the group, but Joan Harvey threatened to sue them for using Fourth Wall material for their own selfish career goals.

Janie P., although primarily a painter, had joined Lucinda Childs's dance class when she was in the group and continued to dance regularly with several other group members. "We would improvise and choreograph dances, and we did a couple of performances, and it was very, very exciting," she said, recalling specifically the moment in which everyone in the dance group sat on the floor of their rehearsal space and discussed whether they should disband in order to join the Fourth Wall. "I didn't want to do it, and I wanted to keep dancing, but everyone else said they were going to join the Fourth Wall." She saw she had no choice. "It was like communism; we were supposed to give up our own individual artistic endeavors to go into the collective for the greater political good. I just remember being so sad and disappointed."

Janie added that Joan Harvey didn't want her to continue teaching her art class. "It was a drawing and painting class held indoors in the winter, and in the summer in Amagansett. We went outdoors to beautiful places to draw and paint. It was a wonderful experience, and we kept it up for years . . . [Joan] didn't want anyone else having any charisma or influence over people. She didn't tell me directly. She discouraged people from taking the class and gave all of us so much to do with the theater that people didn't have the time." It was presented as the need to focus on a common project. One therapist, explaining it to a patient, said that it was like people in a large boat: it was much easier to "paddle upstream with people who are going the same way."

The shift from Amagansett to the workshop in the Catskills—a direct result of the creation of the theater—also reflected the new power dynamic within the group. In Amagansett everyone was scattered among a dozen or more houses. There was no formal organization. You were encouraged but not required to be part of a summer share. It was loose and unstructured; patients might or might not socialize with the therapists. The older therapists all had their own houses and appeared to be on an equal basis. The patients also rented nice houses, albeit shared with lots of people to save money. At the workshop, the four top leaders—Saul Newton and Helen Moses, Joan Harvey and Ralph Klein—occupied the main building of the camp and had private bedrooms. The rank-and-file members, as well as virtually all the other therapists who were lower on the totem pole, were living pell-mell in what had been the thirty-two moldy hotel rooms, with mattresses strewn on the floor and sometimes eight or nine people sharing a room with a single bathroom. There were five cabins, designated date rooms, where couples could go to have sex, with a sign-up sheet to ration access. Members were assigned jobs that might range from weeding and gardening to taking care of the pool but could also include fixing up the leaders' quarters. The new summer living arrangement reflected a clear reality: there were four people who held the power, and there was everybody else. Even the most embittered former members have some happy memories of summers in Amagansett; not many expressed nostalgia for the workshop.

At the end of September 1978 the group was to take possession of the Truck and Warehouse Theater on East Fourth Street on Manhattan's Lower East Side. Unfortunately, there was a problem. Another theater company occupied the space and was in the middle of a run of a play about a group of closeted gay men who found happiness at the Hot Rocks Hotel, which was also the name of the play.

Evidently, the original tenants were a little behind on their rent, so the owner simply decided to lease it to the Sullivanians. But the first group did not want to leave, insisting that they would make up their back rent—attendance was picking up at the time. Saul Newton decided that the group should take over the theater by force. He planned a three-pronged maneuver, as if he were undertaking the Battle of Guadalajara (a resounding Republican victory during the Spanish Civil War). To lead the charge, he picked Artie Honan, a big, strapping former athlete whom others in the group referred to as a gentle giant. Honan, a social worker, had been a star football and baseball player and a wrestler, and he organized sports activities among Fourth Wall members. In college, he had worked as a bouncer in a bar to make extra money.

Although he was a close friend of Luba Elman's and knew of the cruelties Newton had inflicted on her, Honan was thrilled to be picked for a task of great importance by the group's supreme leader. Disappointed that he'd never been considered for the Sullivan Institute's training program, and as a genuinely enthusiastic member of the group, he craved some sign of recognition from its leadership. He'd had limited contact with Saul Newton and was impressed that Newton knew he'd worked as a bouncer. Honan recruited ten men from among the youngest, biggest, and toughest-seeming in the group. The plan was that they would enter the theater as it was about to close for the night and physically remove the current occupants. A second wave of members carrying power tools would then arrive, take apart the theatrical sets of the current production, and throw them out on the street. Newton called on the entire membership to follow and physically occupy the theater, predicting that when the police came it would be impossible to remove them.

Michael Bray observed the plans for the theater takeover—and, more generally, the formation of the Fourth Wall—with some apprehension. There was no way he was getting onstage and doing anything, he thought. He loved his summers out in Amagansett, spending his weekends biking, sailing, and swimming. His friends in the theater group worked all summer, and at the end of the summer they were as pale as earthworms that had just crawled out from under a rock. "There's something crazy about that," Bray thought. At the beginning, working on the theater was completely voluntary and only a minority of the Sullivanian community in 1976—about a third—were active in it. But throughout 1977, and particularly after Joan Harvey and Saul Newton took over, Bray began to feel increasing pressure to join. "By the fall of 1977 it was very clear to me that my social life was going to be severely restricted if I did not join the Fourth Wall," he said. You were in—or you were out. A membership list from October 1977 counts 206 members, and Bray's name is not on it. "I was one of the last to join," he said.

Bray was aware that with the creation of the theater, something important had changed. "It was clear that this was a takeover, an abrupt kind of power move," he said. "I remember a meeting in which Saul and Joan spoke, and everybody came down to the theater. They said that putting on ordinary plays is something that everybody does. Anybody can put on an *Our Town*. But what's needed in the world are plays and a message that educates people to the dangerousness in the world."

Eventually, Bray gave in, offering to be an usher or a ticket taker but not an actor. "Then I got completely sucked in." The group was putting on a production of *Alice in Wonderland* for children, and they told Bray they needed him for a non-talking part as a playing card. "All you have to do is walk out with this silly costume on," they told him. He reluctantly agreed, but at the last minute they asked him to stand in for the actor playing the White Rabbit, one of the bigger parts in the play. They discovered that Bray, who had an unusually good memory, knew everyone's lines. "I was the first one to learn prayers at the foot of the altar back in fifth grade, so I could memorize shit real fast," he said. He was terrified about going onstage. "But once I did it, I got completely caught up in it. I was putting on this costume and hopping around in this bunny suit, and the kids loved it." To his own and others' surprise, this

quiet, seemingly uptight former seminarian had a sense of comic timing and could be quite funny onstage.

Joan Harvey noticed, and one day when he was backstage at the
Provincetown Playhouse—before they moved into their own theater—
Bray got a phone call summoning him to the Sullivan Institute's head-
quarters and Harvey's residence at Ninety-First Street.

Until this point Bray had barely set foot in the Sullivan Institute's
building and was only dimly aware that there was a leadership and a hierarchy within the Sullivanian community. He still had one foot in and the
other outside the group. Although he was in therapy and lived in a Sullivanian apartment, he had a job as a psychologist at a Brooklyn hospital.
He had never actually met either Saul Newton or Joan Harvey. But after
he completed his Ph.D. in 1976 and began to see private patients (outside
the hospital), he was told that he should be in supervision with one of the
senior therapists at the Sullivan Institute. It is standard for younger
therapists to receive supervision for their caseload, so this seemed
reasonable enough to Bray. He entered supervision with Ralph Klein.

Now he was heading upstairs into the residential part of the institute and was ushered into Joan Harvey's bedroom, where she often received guests and patients. She was in a nightgown, sick in bed. Bray sat
in a rocking chair nearby. He later recalled her telling him: "I wanted
to call you up here because I was thinking about you. Ralph tells me
you are a middling beginner therapist, but that you are not dumb." She
wanted to give him advice on how to make something of himself, and
she proceeded to advise him against continuing to see his therapist, Art
Liebeskind, whom he had been working with for the previous six years.
"Your therapist—" she said. "Now I like him, I don't like him—it doesn't
matter—but he's mediocre. He's a mediocre therapist. And he's going
down the drain . . . There's nothing worse than a mediocre therapist
after twenty years of practicing. They're the most corrupt, stinking,
rotting people. I would recommend—of course you don't have to do
any of this—but I would recommend, if you're really going to get your
life together and not end up like him, that you start therapy with either
Saul, myself, Helen, or Ralph." Bray was stunned by this, his first real

contact with Harvey. He remembers it as "the first glimpse I had of the real power structure."

During Bray's first six years in therapy, he saw a Sullivanian therapist and participated in the life of a loose-knit community. He had no idea that behind the scenes, Newton and Harvey—and to a lesser degree Klein and Moses—were assigning and unassigning patients, favoring or punishing therapists, throwing their weight around. It was now increasingly clear that there was a pecking order among the therapists and that the therapist you saw reflected your standing in the group. Working with the theater, which Joan Harvey now directed, was another means of winning favor and gaining prestige. The older therapists in the group—people like Art Liebeskind, John Cates, and Dom and Millie Antonelli (not to mention Jane Pearce), who had medical degrees or Ph.D.s that Saul Newton did not have—were on the way out. Gradually, their patients would be reassigned, and they would be forced to find work outside the group, which, as medical doctors and trained psychiatrists, they were able to do. Bray felt sorry for his therapist, Art, who was trying in middle age to adapt to the new situation—quite literally dancing to a new tune. "Here was this guy," Bray said, "a five-foot-one psychiatrist tap-dancing across the stage. He didn't want to do this shit. He was resistant to [Harvey's] direction in the theater. He was not a good actor. He was history."

Bray found the situation chilling—as if he were suddenly back in the presence of the Queen of Hearts ("Off with their heads!") from the play of *Alice in Wonderland* he had just been performing in. At the same time, he felt flattered that he was being groomed by the dominant clique in this community and invited to join them in the winners' circle. Faced with the choice of moving up in the world or risking being cast aside like his therapist, he chose the former. "I was in terror. I would do whatever [Harvey] said."

Bray knew that this change of therapist meant much more, that it would require a major reorganization of his whole life. He dropped Art Liebeskind, began therapy with Ralph Klein, went into supervision with Joan Harvey, and ended the most important relationship he had

with anyone outside the group. Early in his therapy he had begun a romance with a colleague at the veterans hospital in Brooklyn where he
worked. After his marriage fizzled, this was the first sustained long-term
relationship he had managed. While most Sullivanians were counseled to
avoid seeing anyone more than once a week, Bray had managed to spend
about three nights a week with the woman in Brooklyn, who had nothing
to do with the group. Somehow their relationship had survived his being
in a polygamous group in which he routinely slept with other women. In
truth, she remained the focus of his emotional life.

Ironically, despite his having other affairs, he in fact experienced
extreme jealousy. Once, when he developed the suspicion that his colleague might be seeing another man, he spent the entire night in a car,
staking out her house. It turned out that she wasn't. Nonetheless, she
didn't much care for his group and its sexual promiscuity. Since he'd
joined the Fourth Wall, the pressure had been building to get him to
break up with her. His old therapist, Art, had done his best to turn Bray
against her, referring to her as "that narrow-minded bitch" and asking
why he bothered to have anything to do with her. "He would not order me
to break up with her, but it was very clear what this was about," Bray said.
Somehow he knew that when he agreed to change therapists, he would
have to fall more strictly in line with Sullivanian orthodoxy. "Within
the same week, I began therapy with Ralph and ditched my girlfriend
of five years. It was like the personal wrenching around of everything."

At the same time (spring 1978), Joan Harvey asked him to try
out for a lead role in her new play, which she had planned as the main
event in the new theater on the Lower East Side the Fourth Wall had
rented for the fall season. The play was a highly autobiographical depiction of Harvey's own experience of breaking away from her parents.
Although she was now forty-five, she cast herself to play her eighteen-
year-old self; Bray, who was twelve years younger, would be reading
the part of her father. He had assumed that the role would go to Scott
Powell, who was a member of Sha Na Na and had already appeared
in a couple of movies. Bray, the reserved former altar boy from Iowa,
was called upon to play a frightening, angry California communist.

"I have always been capable of yelling with a deep, scary voice—not something that has ever been part of my life—but in the audition I kind of reached down and exploded . . . Joan Harvey was weeping and saying, 'Oh, my God, you just had the moment of your life,' and so I was cast as her father."

With the creation of the theater, many people in the group were writing and putting on plays. Elliot K., although a graphic designer by profession, had gone to graduate school in drama, and he asked Bray to act in the play he was putting on for his master's thesis. The part required that Bray shave off his beard, which he did without much consideration. Then he ran into Joan Harvey when they were all up at the group's new summer headquarters in the Catskills, and she looked at his shaved face with what Bray compared to the crazed look of the psychopathic killer in *A Clockwork Orange* (1971). "That's what her eyes were like," he said.

"To think I would shave my beard without checking with her," Bray said. "'Policy meeting!' she yelled. 'We're having a policy meeting!' And she runs and gathers everybody together."

Harvey turned on Elliot K. and began to rain verbal abuse on him, as attested to by Artie Honan, who witnessed the scene. "You son of a bitch," she shouted as the room suddenly got quiet. "What the fuck did you think you were doing? You idiot. You stupid shithead. You're out to ruin my play!" she yelled in his face. "I hope you realize that you've sabotaged the Fourth Wall's fall production." Harvey was less hard on Bray, only suggesting that he put chicken shit on his face to help his beard grow back more quickly.

By late September, Bray's beard had grown back and they had the play ready, but they still could not take possession of the Truck and Warehouse Theater. As a lead actor, Bray was not allowed to participate in the initial takeover of the theater for fear he might be hurt or arrested in the fracas. But he was asked to join the throng of other Fourth Wall people who would occupy the theater after it had been secured, arriving with their sleeping bags and pillows and laying them down in the aisles. Joan Harvey explained to her cast the need for direct action and taking the theater by force. "This scared the shit out of me," Bray said. In Sioux City, Iowa—a very conservative religious community—he had gotten into trouble for throwing a snowball. "I got arrested for hitchhiking. Hitchhiking." So the idea of physically evicting a theater company and risking mass arrest was beyond his ken.

"Everybody's hearts were pounding—to be part of this violent, crazy thing—we were waiting for the police to show up," Bray recalled. And the police did show up, but, totally outnumbered by the presence of about two hundred people, they left shortly afterward. They arrested two group members who used force in kicking out the other theater company, but they didn't challenge the right of the group to occupy the theater. "People were profoundly amazed that it had worked. It seemed to us miraculous," Bray said. Saul had used some muscle, and the theater was theirs. "People in the Fourth Wall were kind of in awe of the powers of the leaders. It was very heady, and I remember feeling 'Well, what else can we do?' And then that fall was the opening of all these new political shows."

The takeover was Artie Honan's night to shine in front of the entire membership. Saul Newton had taken him by the arm and proclaimed to the entire group, "Does anyone here know more about protecting this theater than him?" He had been a big man on campus as a high school jock, and now he was a big man in the group he had chosen to make his life in. That night he slept in the lobby so that he could guard the entrance. One of the women he had dated in the group crawled under his blanket. They had sex on the cold lobby floor, hoping that others sleeping not too far off wouldn't hear.

Most of the two-hundred-plus members took turns camping out in the theater that night and for the better part of a week. Newton, the old communist war veteran, told Michael Cohen that he wanted to toughen up the membership so that they would learn "to stand up to the cops." The theater, after all, was going to be a political group, and revolutionaries needed to be tough. It was the beginning of what many saw as a first step in the gradual "militarization" of the group and the introduction of a certain element of violence. Any uneasiness some may have felt over the use of force was tempered by the fact that it had worked. In an unjust capitalist world, possession was nine-tenths of the law. If the group had gone to court, it might have taken months and hundreds of thousands of dollars in legal fees. In one night, they had a theater. As Ed Boorstein, who taught a course on Marxist-Leninist thought at the institute, liked to say, "If you want to be a revolutionary, you can't be a pantywaist."

Saul Newton began referring to their group as a kind of revolutionary vanguard, a term Vladimir Lenin had used to describe the hard core of full-time revolutionaries who were needed to overturn the old order. Joan Harvey kept a photograph of Lenin in her office. The Fourth Wall was going to do revolutionary theater.

The group's first play, entitled *In the Beginning . . .* , about Harvey's own decision to leave home at age eighteen, is a kind of textbook illustration of Sullivanian therapy. The parents want to limit their daughter because of their own limitations:

> When is the right time—when is it easy to do something you never tried, Dad? Give me a chance, nothing important happens when it's convenient . . .

The mother is manipulative and tries to use guilt to stunt her child's growth. The right response, unsurprisingly, is escape from the family:

> Don't worry, we're not getting married, just making a prison break. Climb the walls to the outside, look around . . . See the sights, it will be fun . . . Oh, Mom, I just need to get away. I need to think on my own and I can't do it here.

There was also a political message about taking a stand, "changing the world," and "making a stink."

In the play, the Sullivanian take on the family intersects with the political: the father refuses to take action politically because, selfishly, he won't be around to enjoy the fruits of change, and he—out of jealousy and hatred—doesn't want his daughter to "have what [he] can't have."

Bray didn't think much of Joan Harvey's play, but his experience of being onstage bore out one of the principles of Sullivanian therapy, which was to encourage people to try new things, especially things that made them anxious. It was the not-me experience, and it could easily be manipulated to force people to do things that they genuinely didn't want to do—such as have sex with people they didn't want to have sex with. But in the case of acting, Bray saw it as positive. "Before long . . . I was out onstage three nights a week, every single week. I thought it was a push toward growth as a person. This is actually enjoyable, and I can fight the anxiety because I've done it. Each night you get anxious in the wings, but then you go out and—you do it."

While privately many people found the plays to be painfully didactic political agitprop, Saul Newton declared that Harvey's work was on the level of that of Bertolt Brecht and that the theater was a vehicle for the group to put its message out in the world and radicalize it. In the group's initial incarnation, its politics had been largely a private affair. The leaders all considered themselves communists, but the therapy was presented as a form of personal liberation and self-actualization. Now it was openly conceived as a collective political enterprise.

Steve Meshnick, a young doctor doing medical research, was away during this period of rapid change and returned to what felt like a very different group. "In 1978, I took a year off and went overseas, and when I came back, the group had sort of completely changed. The Fourth Wall was starting. I had spent a year in Kenya doing research, I had had an amazing experience in Africa. I had been on safaris, done bird-watching. I had all these pictures. Nobody wanted to see them. I had all these stories. Nobody was interested, and they would start telling me, 'The Fourth Wall is doing this. The Fourth Wall is doing that.' It was kind of like people had lost interest in the outside world. They didn't see anything that happened outside the group as being important or interesting."

The group became more insular, but clearly, as Meshnick's story indicates, many people were excited about the theater and the group's new public role.

Being given a major part in Joan Harvey's first play conferred a certain status on Mike Bray. It also placed him in close proximity to Harvey, which was both exciting and nervous-making. He saw her as highly intelligent but extremely mercurial, capable of moving from tears to thunderclaps of rage in a matter of seconds. She had a great deal in common with Saul Newton. They shared a sense of grandiosity, a conviction of their own importance, and a violent temper when someone got in their way. Harvey seemed to genuinely believe that the theater they were starting would change the world, and that it was entirely natural, therefore, to ask everyone to devote their time and money to it. Never mind that the group had great trouble getting people to attend the plays. They gave free tickets to homes for the elderly, halfway houses for recovering drug addicts, programs for disadvantaged youth. Members who taught—and there were many professors and art teachers in the group—were required to bring their classes to each of the group's productions.

Perhaps as a result of his rising status, Harvey asked Bray to give up his job at the Veterans Administration hospital and enter the Sullivan Institute's training program to become a full-time Sullivanian therapist. Unlike most in the training program, Bray already had a Ph.D. in psychology and was earning a living as a psychologist. This invitation was flattering and a bit scary. By committing himself to become a Sullivanian therapist, Bray was placing his whole life—both personal and professional—within the same group. He would now depend on the institute's leadership for almost everything: the apartment where he lived, the community of friends he was a part of, and the income he needed to live. "It felt dangerous," Bray recalled. "I was about to give up any outside employment as a psychologist—I had been running a ward at the Bronx State Hospital. I had worked at the Veterans Administration [hospital]. I could make a living out there as a psychologist. I knew that some therapists had been expelled from being therapists and even kicked out of their apartments. And so it did feel dangerous—this could be life wrecking—but the alarm bell was not loud enough, or I was too deaf to hear it."

He was already in a world almost entirely inhabited and defined by the Fourth Wall: he was living in a group apartment, and virtually all his friends were members. And within the world he had chosen to make his own, being a therapist in the group was unquestionably a promotion that took him into its inner circle. Moreover, refusing their offer could be perceived as a lack of commitment on his part and have negative consequences. It was not an offer he could refuse.

* * *

In the spring of 1978, as the group was preparing Joan Harvey's first play and getting ready to move into the Truck and Warehouse Theater on East Fourth Street, Michael Bray's roommate and good friend Dick Wasley was released from the hospital, where he had been rehabilitating from his near-fatal case of Guillain-Barré syndrome. Finally, Wasley would be able to rejoin his roommates at the brownstone on West Eighty-Seventh Street that he shared with Bray and four others. Wasley was deeply aware that his friends in the group had saved him, forming a powerful network of solidarity around him that helped him recover. While he'd been almost completely paralyzed with Guillain-Barré, he'd fought his way back to health with the constant and unceasing help of his friends. "They set up a schedule so that there would be someone with me every single day during visit hours," Wasley recalled. One of his Fourth Wall friends created a log that monitored the progress of his recovery, added to by the friend who visited him on a given day.

He'd lived on a ventilator in an intensive care unit for three months. When he was able to breathe on his own and was transferred to a rehabilitation center where he relearned to talk, move his limbs, and walk, his friends continued to come every day. On weekends, when there was no rehab, his friends in the group picked him up and brought him back to the brownstone so he could spend the weekend among friends rather than in the institutional confines of a hospital.

The stronger among his friends would lift him, wheelchair and all, up the steps of the brownstone. "They did all this for me," Wasley recalled more than forty years later. It was the fellowship and close friendship he had observed among his friends in the brownstone that had drawn him into the group and had literally saved his life. He owed them so much, he thought, that he could never leave. But around November 1978, a couple of months after the Fourth Wall began its first production in the new theater, something strange and upsetting happened: his roommates asked him to move out. One of his closest friends, Mike F., who had helped him get back from Greece to New York when he was so deathly ill, was also kicked out of the apartment. Wasley doesn't even remember what reasons were given, but he had no choice but to obey.

Michael Bray recalled that the order to have the two men moved out came from the leadership at Ninety-First Street. Despite his close friendship with Wasley, Bray went along with the decision. "Of course, some 'lack of growth' reason was stated at the meeting," Bray said, but he knew that Saul Newton had his own motives. Wasley's place would be taken by Josh Klein, Ralph Klein's son. Josh, at the age of twenty-one, was about to come into a substantial fortune, which he had inherited from his mother, an heiress who died when he was young. This money would help to bankroll many of the Fourth Wall's projects, would pay for the theater on East Fourth Street, and pay for much of the Ninety-First Street headquarters. Sullivanian housing arrangements in the 1970s were usually informal arrangements among friends, based on personal affinity. But sometimes they weren't. As the group morphed into a formal organization, Newton was not shy about intervening when it suited his purposes. Several months after Wasley moved out, Newton arranged for his son Robbie to move into the brownstone as well. It was a way of asserting his power and assuring a nice living arrangement for two of the group's more privileged younger recruits. The friends who had taken such incredibly good care of Dick Wasley in his hour of greatest need acquiesced to his sudden exile without a word of complaint. And he obediently moved to a series of other apartments, where he was never quite as happy.

Saul Newton decided, for some reason, to plant his flag in the Eighty-Seventh Street brownstone, decreeing that he and Marc Rice (one of the other senior therapists living at Ninety-First Street) would become honorary roommates. "Saul and Marc Rice joined the brownstone in absentia," Mike Bray recalled. But no one quite knew what that meant. When the residents of the brownstone failed to invite them to some gathering, Newton was furious. "Saul slapped me across the face, saying, 'You can distribute that to the rest of them.'"

11

Three Mile Island

On the CBS evening news on March 28, 1979, Walter Cronkite, America's most trusted journalist, informed the nation:

> It was the first step in a nuclear nightmare; as far as we know at this hour, no worse than that, but a government official said that a breakdown in an atomic power plant in Pennsylvania today is probably the worst nuclear reactor accident to date. There was no apparent serious contamination of workers, but a nuclear safety group said that radiation inside the plant is at eight times the deadly level, so strong that after passing through a three-foot thick concrete wall, it can be measured a mile away.

Donna Warshaw went to a movie that evening with a friend from the group, seeing—incredibly—*The China Syndrome*, a fictional thriller with Jane Fonda about the cover-up of an out-of-control meltdown at a nuclear power plant. The film came out on March 16, just twelve days before the real accident at Three Mile Island. "We got out of the theater," she said, "and it was, you know, it was probably ten or eleven o'clock at night, and we pass a newsstand and the headlines are 'Three Mile Island.' And the next day we hear that everybody is evacuating. I did, too."

Helen Moses, Saul Newton's sixth wife, was pregnant with her third child. A few other women in the group were pregnant, too, or trying to get pregnant. Every time Helen planned to get pregnant, she encouraged a select few women in the group to have a child at around the same time so their children could be playmates with hers. One of these was her longtime patient and housemate Ellen Barrett, who was thirty-one at the time and had been in therapy for ten years, as well as being a therapist herself for the last eight years. In her effort to conceive, Helen had enlisted the help of Michael Cohen, among others. Joan Harvey and Ralph Klein had recently adopted two small children. Although most New Yorkers did not regard the accident as a matter of direct concern, the group's leaders were convinced that the government was covering up the extent of the accident and the danger it represented, especially for women who were pregnant or trying to conceive. Although New York is two hundred miles from Harrisburg, Pennsylvania, where the Three Mile Island nuclear plant was located, they decided that, for the sake of their children, they must evacuate the city immediately.

Catherine Hemenway, a visual artist, was on a "sleepover date" with another female member when the phone rang. "I had a date with Leslie Freeman at her house, and then in the middle of the night we were woken up by a phone call, telling us about Three Mile Island and that the leadership was sending all their kids to Florida and that everybody should go . . . I went home and found my roommates packing. So I called up someone to take care of my cat and called in sick to work."

Richard Price got back uptown in the early hours of the morning from a date with a woman who was not in the group. He recalled:

I came home at about five o'clock in the morning from seeing someone who lived in the Village. And at 5:15, my phone rings. It was a woman that I had been dating, and it was one of the—one of the longer and more intimate relationships. And she was in a panic. She said, "Saul says everybody has to go down to Florida because there might be a meltdown at a nuclear reactor . . . in Pennsylvania."

Price's initial reaction, having not slept a wink, was to not go anywhere. He lay down in his bed for a few minutes but heard the other phones in his apartment ringing, as well as the sound of his roommates packing, and he got at least three phone calls from friends in the group urging him to go to Florida. At that point, he realized that with the entire group on the move, he had little choice but to go along, for fear he would be ostracized. He soon found himself in a taxi heading to Newark airport and, by the afternoon, on a line for rides at Disney's Magic Kingdom near Orlando.

"I was thinking, 'Orlando, what the fuck?'" Catherine Hemenway said. "We're in Florida, and not even near a beach. I don't have a kid, so why am I at Disney World?" The leadership had chosen proximity to Disney World in order to have an outlet for their kids.

Some people drove, some flew. Some stayed in New York, but within a few days, some 200 to 250 Fourth Wall members had taken over a Howard Johnson's motel near Orlando.

There is debate among former members whether the leadership had ordered the Fourth Wall membership to go to Florida. In fact, the leadership decided to leave town, word traveled through the group like wildfire, and virtually everyone decided to join them. In some ways it was like a flock of birds: as soon as a few members take to the sky after scenting danger, the rest quickly follow and fly in formation. For Richard Price, the Three Mile Island response suddenly gave him the impression that he no longer had control of his life. He canceled two readings he had been looking forward to doing in the Boston area because Ralph Klein—a psychologist, hardly an expert on nuclear energy—insisted that with the "prevailing winds," it would be unsafe.

For Steve Meshnick, who was in his medical residency at the time, Three Mile Island represented a kind of dividing line in his mind. "To me, that was the first time I realized that I had a separate personality from the group. I knew the radiation thing was bullshit and that we were not going to die," he said. He knew that the small doses of radiation involved were not a threat to people living a few miles from Harrisburg, let alone in New York. It was the first time he became aware of a part of his brain that was filtering out things coming from the group's leaders that were exaggerated, wrong, or flat-out crazy. "So even though I stayed in the group, I kept this little space in the back of my head, thinking I've got to live with these fallacies." Meshnick began to experience what is known in psychology as "cognitive dissonance," when your thoughts and actions are out of alignment, or your idea of yourself is at odds with certain facts in your life. He had to reconcile the seeming contradiction between being a rigorous scientist and obeying the dictates of people whose views he had begun to doubt.

But many members had learned to distrust authority because of the Vietnam War, during which the government frequently misled the public. "Hey, they lied to us about Agent Orange, so it wasn't too hard to believe they were lying about this, too," one former member said.

"It all started getting very crazy down there," Mel Zalel recalled. "Part of the reason it was crazy is they were telling us that everybody's going to die, and nobody seemed to die in New York. And then they had one person who said that if there are rays emanating from the current weather patterns, it would direct everything down to Orlando, Florida, and not to New York. And . . . then I remember that Joan Harvey was always crying. She would sit and cry, and people would comfort her, and I guess she was very moved by it all."

For some, the time at the Howard Johnson's was a kind of apocalyptic bacchanalia. People were drinking and taking sedatives. No one knew whether they would be returning to New York or having to start over elsewhere or if the world was coming to an end.

"It felt like we were in the middle of a war and had been evacuated from our homes, possibly not to return again," Amy Siskind recalled. "I seem to remember the whole week through a drunken stupor." At one point Amy found herself in a hotel room with three other group members, and they started having sex. Each couple was on a separate bed, but it was pretty radical for Amy, who had never had sex with someone else in the room. "It wasn't really for pleasure, I don't think—it was almost as if we didn't know what else to do with ourselves," she said. "Maybe it was just a way to forget about the whole thing for a while."

Mike Bray had a similar experience. He, too, found himself on a bed with one woman while two other couples were going at it on two other beds at the same time. He had never had much interest in group sex, but the sudden fear of death seemed to have pushed the members to seek refuge this way. "We were all fucking our brains out." Bray thought that the alarm over the nuclear fallout might be overblown, but he didn't think the evacuation was crazy. "I thought, well, it can't do any harm if we're wrong," he said. "It was like wearing a double condom."

After about ten days, it was decided it was safe to return to New York, and the leadership held sessions to help people come up with convincing cover stories for why they had missed several days of work.

*　　*　　*

On one of the flights back, the airline lost Stuart A.'s luggage. He was already having something of a panic attack imagining his own incineration in a nuclear disaster; then he learned he had lost his job because of leaving town for ten days, and he became even more agitated by the lost suitcase. He started taking some Valium to try to calm down, and later in the evening he appeared to have slipped into an unconscious state from which he couldn't be roused. A couple of friends, worried that he had overdosed—perhaps even tried to commit suicide—took him to a New York hospital to have his stomach pumped and were joined by a few more. Friendships were strong within the group, and people looked after one another. A doctor came out and explained that they would normally release the patient at this point, but he was telling a wild story about having evacuated to Florida with about two hundred other people to escape a nuclear holocaust. Was their friend having delusions, the doctor asked, or was there something to the story? Afraid that the doctor might commit or not release their friend if he seemed crazy, one of them confirmed that the story was true.

Another member, fearing that they had committed an indiscretion—they knew that the leadership prized secrecy and expected all infractions reported—called Joan Harvey to let her know. "I'm going to kill you!" she yelled over the phone. The next day, the leadership directed the entire membership of the Fourth Wall—at this point about 240 people—to attend an obligatory special meeting down at the Truck and Warehouse Theater.

The meeting took place sometime between eleven p.m. and midnight, adding to the anticipation and drama. Michael Cohen, although only twenty-nine, had assumed a position of considerable importance in the group's leadership. He stood up to address the crowd. He read from a prepared speech that began with the ominous words "On Saturday night a viciously antagonistic act to the Fourth Wall and its membership occurred."

Without explaining what had happened, Cohen announced that five people—Stuart A. and the friends who had accompanied him to the hospital—had been expelled from the group and must vacate their apartments within twenty-four hours. The crowd was stunned, wondering what egregious act of betrayal these five had committed. A void quickly formed around the offending members, who shuffled out of the theater looking humiliated. Many people felt bad for them but said nothing.

The purge marked a significant change. "From that night forward, I rarely made any major decisions without considering the Leadership's reaction," Artie Honan wrote. "They were an invisible presence in the back of my mind all the time. The purge created a pervasive fear of banishment, loss of all friends, and group identity. Most of us dreaded general meetings after that."

"I left the next morning, and what happened is that these two or three hundred people completely cut me out of their lives," Mel Zalel, one of the Three Mile Island five, recalled years later to the former group member and sociologist Amy Siskind. His banishment was instant and total. "It was impossible to have anything to do with them, and nobody talked to me. People would avoid me on the street or if I took buses with them. They would stand up if I sat down next to them. I remember getting off a bus with A.P. He was going to my corner, but he pretended to go around the block, and then I met him at my corner. You know, crazy things like that went on."

Richard Price missed the purge because he was in Alabama on a journalistic assignment. After he canceled the two readings he had planned, the leadership okayed his assignment to do a story for *Playboy* on Bear Bryant, the famous Alabama football coach. "They thought it would be funny to send this little Jewish kid from the Bronx south of the Mason-Dixon line, like sending Woody Allen to cover a tough-guy contest. I guess they decided that the prevailing winds weren't going to reach Alabama, so I went. Here I am in this shit-ass hotel in Tuscaloosa, one of these places with the 'magic fingers' mattresses you feed quarters into, and in the middle of the night the phone rings. It was one of the women I was dating in the group, someone I was close to, sobbing so hard into the phone I can barely understand her. Finally, she sobs out the words 'THEY . . . KICKED . . . ME . . . OUT . . . OF . . . THE . . . GROUP!'" As Price sat listening to her weeping, he realized that he envied her. "I'm clutching my head, and I yell back at her, 'Do you know how lucky you are? Count your lucky stars!'" He knew at that point that he needed to leave as well. "And when I came back, the whole group was on a kind of paramilitary footing. One morning I woke up with a splitting headache and went in and told Dom [his therapist] I quit."

If Mike Bray was troubled by the purge, any uneasiness he might have felt was quickly dissipated by a series of new responsibilities that had been thrust on him in Florida. "I became the minister of transportation," he said. No one actually used that term. Joan Harvey and Saul Newton were convinced that in the eventuality—which they considered quite likely—of another nuclear accident, the group needed an elaborate evacuation plan. Bray had spent part of his youth helping out at his father's Ford dealership. He knew cars and had a commercial driver's license. When he was in the Catholic seminary preparing to be a priest, he drove the seminary's bus. He had to come up with a plan for getting 250 people across the George Washington Bridge and then off to some safe distant location in a timely fashion. He went in search of a series of old used school buses that could be put back in good working order and looked for a place to park them on the New Jersey side of the bridge. He found seven buses in junkyards in southern New Jersey. Their gas tanks would allow only about 170 miles of travel before needing to be refilled. In the apocalyptic scenario of a nuclear disaster, with a breakdown of normal life, the leaders wanted buses that could go at least three hundred miles without stopping. Bray enlisted a fellow member, Roger Williams, a sculptor with skills as a welder, to build new gas tanks to double their capacity. "My life started to become almost a throwback to working in my dad's Ford dealership," Bray said.

He also acquired a fleet of motorcycles to drive the group's leaders from their headquarters at Ninety-First Street in the event that leaving the city by car became impossible. He even helped customize a set of backpacks that would allow the women in the leadership to strap a child to their back while riding on the motorcycle. The rank-and-file members would have to walk across the George Washington Bridge. Only Bray and a handful of other people knew where the buses were kept. Meanwhile, the buses could serve to bring outside groups—elderly people from senior centers, recovering drug addicts in rehab facilities—to see the Fourth Wall's dramatic productions. "We also had an ambulance—a licensed Cadillac ambulance—it was kept at a secret location across from where the buses were," Bray recalled. "The plan was that the leaders would get whisked away across the bridge and put in the ambulance, which would have sirens and lights on—it's a licensed ambulance." This would allow the leaders to cut through traffic while the rest of the membership chugged along in the big yellow school buses.

In the weeks after Three Mile Island, the group expanded its activities—and the demands it made on members—in several directions. Convinced that food produced in the northeastern United States was contaminated by radiation, the group created a food co-op, run entirely by members who were required to donate their time organizing deliveries to all the Sullivanian apartments. Everyone would have to participate in "radio watch," in which members took turns listening to two news channels twenty-four hours a day for possible news of a nuclear leak or accident.

The group decided that since it could not trust the government, it should conduct regular monitoring of several nuclear plants scattered across the East Coast. Bray and his sculptor/welder friend carved a hole in the roof of a Volkswagen Rabbit, and two physicists in the group rigged up a generator and a motor that would roll down a customized ramp to take air samples. Monitoring crews would measure radiation levels (gamma rays), set off helium balloons to track wind direction, and record all their findings. About a dozen male members (women were discouraged from doing this because of perceived danger to their reproductive capacity) were recruited for monitoring duty, and they drove hundreds of miles in a single night, monitoring a series of reactors from Indian Point in Westchester to Oyster Creek in New Jersey and Three Mile Island in Pennsylvania. In order to standardize their findings, they placed stakes in the ground so that the group's monitors would always use the same measurement spots.

Although all this added greatly to Bray's duties, he didn't mind. "I liked it because I suddenly rose in the hierarchy." In a group that had become increasingly hierarchical, recognition from those on top became vitally important.

At the same time, the expansion of Bray's role in the group put an end to most of his relationships outside the group. "Up until then, I would say that about a third of my social life was outside the group," he said. Now he had given up his job at the VA hospital, broken up with his longtime girlfriend in Brooklyn, and rarely saw anyone who wasn't in the group. "It was clear that there was no way that I could have outside friends while being the 'minister of transportation,' a therapist, and so fully involved with this weird group," Bray said.

A telling moment that indicated how much the group had reached into his life occurred one morning at about three o'clock, when a group of men sent by leadership arrived at Bray's brownstone to conduct a search. A pair of speakers had disappeared from the theater, and Saul Newton had ordered Artie Honan, who had organized the theater takeover, to put together a team of people to search every closet of every Fourth Wall apartment—so they arrived in the middle of the night and searched. "I remember," Bray said, "because I was in bed with a woman who was not in the group. And all of a sudden, in come five guys at three a.m. going through my closet . . . It was real crazy—imagine the embarrassment and horror." This was a small but significant act of violence directed at the membership itself, indicating that the leadership had the power to reach into their intimate lives at any moment. It also demonstrated the near impossibility of maintaining relationships outside the group.

*   *   *

The sociologist Richard Ofshe has used the metaphor of a crowded bus to describe the way cults or other "high-demand groups" operate. If the driver makes a sudden sharp turn, the passengers who are not holding on to the safety railing will fall off their seats, while those who have a firm hold will grip tighter. This serves the double purpose of getting rid of the less committed members of a group and increasing the commitment of those who remain. Many of the moves the group made starting in 1977—the creation of the Fourth Wall as a formal group with paid membership; the Three Mile Island evacuation in 1979; the purge; and the radio watch, nuclear monitoring, and food restrictions—were all sharp, jarring swerves of the wheel. Some members who had gotten involved for the therapy, the social life, and the fellowship resented all the demands being placed on them, and they dropped out. Less committed members like Richard Price fell off the bus after these latest sharp turns. For those who remained, the group became even more central to their life, and with each new swerve of the bus, their grip grew tighter.

At the institute's height in the mid- to late 1970s, there were some four hundred to six hundred people in Sullivanian therapy, and the boundaries between the Sullivanian world and the outside were fairly porous: people who were patients had friends who were not patients, non-patients might come to Sullivanian parties, and the occasional non-patient might be found living in a Sullivanian group apartment, even if there was always the hope that they would try therapy. Now the boundaries were much clearer. Only about 245 people joined the Fourth Wall, although there was still a small number who continued as patients without joining the theater company. But those who joined increased their level of commitment in terms of money and time. Along with the initial dues of seventy-five dollars a month, which would go up each year, the leadership imposed various "assessments"—onetime payments of several hundred dollars per member for purchasing the theater they'd occupied, another for purchasing the workshop in the Catskills.

Many of those who chose the Fourth Wall compared their commitment to that of a marriage. They were married to the group, to each other. Virtually all members, except for the thirty or so therapists, had regular jobs. With the creation of the theater, their days got much longer. The theater held performances four nights a week (along with children's plays and musical events on the other days), and everyone was expected to do something: act, play music, sew and take care of costumes, run the lighting, provide security, make and move stage sets, print and pass out playbills. After Three Mile Island, members participated in anti-nuclear demonstrations, radio watch, nuclear power plant monitoring, and playing music at public protests. There were frequently committee meetings after the performances, which often began at eleven o'clock at night. And you were expected to keep up your dating life. Michael Cohen said it was common for him to go to bed at three a.m. Many members fueled their eighteen-hour days with coffee and Dexedrine, commonly known as "speed." With all the new demands on their time, there were far fewer opportunities for socializing outside the group, and it became increasingly a world unto itself. The more time the group occupied, the more it became a person's emotional center, their entire world, and as a result, the greater the fear of being kicked out. That threat was always present (spoken or unspoken), preying on people's minds. So when the bus swerved, they held on for dear life.

"We've got a tight little army," Saul Newton confided to Mike Cohen. The old soldier from the Spanish Civil War began speaking increasingly in military terms. Since Cohen had moved into the group's inner circle—one tier down from the four top leaders—as a member of the new policy committee, Newton had taken to explaining in avuncular tones the uses of power and violence he had learned working with the Stalinists in Spain. "Never underestimate the power of purging," Newton told him. Cohen, as the youngest member of the policy committee, was flattered by Saul's Machiavellian confidences on the nature of power and statecraft. "I was the young grasshopper being trained by the wise old Stalinist," Cohen said.

Although Newton was not a sociologist, he understood a lot about the psychology of groups. Before carrying out the purge of the Three Mile Island five, Newton explained to the policy committee, "We had to purge these people. The group is going to have to be more mobilized in the future, because we were under more threat." Showing a similar intuitive understanding of group behavior, Joan Harvey used to say, "We are at our best when we're busy." Keeping people fully occupied—with little time for reflection and grumbling—fostered group cohesion.

Cohen was honored to be given the public role of expelling the hapless victims of the Three Mile Island purge. He knew they had done nothing wrong other than tell a doctor the truth in order to help a friend in trouble. But as a self-styled revolutionary leader, he understood that in order to establish group discipline, it was sometimes necessary to inflict pain and sacrifice. "I took it as a compliment that they wanted me to do something like this [the purge], because it was hard," he said.

It was also a strategic decision to have Cohen be the public face of the purge. "We need someone, other than me or Joan, to make the speech to purge these people," Newton told the committee. "We don't want to make it look as if Joan and I have this much power, and I select Cohen to make the speech." Then there was a vote. It was unanimous, as in any Soviet Politburo meeting of the 1930s.

Cohen was smart and funny and generally well-liked; he was the youngest person in an important leadership role, and some people spoke of him with a mixture of respect and irony as "the heir apparent." In a group that was hyperconscious of its pecking order, Cohen's rise had also caused some to view him with suspicion and fear. Some thought he seemed power hungry, a willing lieutenant ready to do the leadership's dirty work. "That's generous," he said. "I didn't *seem* like a bad guy, I was a bad guy . . . I was all the way in, and I really thought we were making a revolution. There were a couple years there where I was to the left of Mao Tse Tung."

One of Cohen's new responsibilities after Three Mile Island was to create an emergency communications system. His deputy was Michael Bray, as it was important to coordinate getting out the message of potential evacuation with Bray's transportation plans. This work, along with the fact that Bray was now working as a therapist at the Sullivan Institute, began what would become a close and important friendship for both men. They created, among other things, a phone tree that would allow the leadership to reach everyone in the Fourth Wall within fifteen minutes—this, years before the internet and cell phones. Cohen and Bray distributed weekly schedules to all Sullivanian apartments, and members were expected to indicate where they would be day and night over the coming week. People were to fill out their sheets at their weekly apartment meetings, and the sheets were put together in a book kept at the Ninety-First Street headquarters. "People wanted to see this book to see who was dating whom—it became a thing," Bray recalled. "And then it was used as a mode of surveillance, because Harvey realized that she could find anybody at any time."

People in positions of responsibility within the group were required to wear pagers. Rather than seeing this requirement as an invasion of privacy, they viewed it as a status symbol. The important people were suddenly wearing beepers, so others began to lobby to get them. "It became a little like kids in school carrying beepers so people would think they were dealing drugs even though they weren't," remembered Bray. Soon, everyone had a pager.

Cohen, the heir apparent, had moved into the brownstone that Bray, the minister of transportation, shared with a few other men from the Fourth Wall. This brought him into contact with Amy Siskind, who was dating another of his roommates, the physicist Richie Piccioni. One day, after she had spent the night with Piccioni, Amy stepped on a thick, sharp shard of glass, and her foot began bleeding profusely. "Richie had left for work, and I didn't know what to do, so I hopped downstairs and found Mike Cohen and Mike Bray, who were sleeping in the same bed," she said. "I know that sounds a little sexual, but they didn't have a sexual relationship." Cohen had been a Boy Scout as a kid, and he came to her rescue. Something about the intimacy and vulnerability of the moment—his holding her slender, bleeding foot in his hand; the gentleness, competence, and care he demonstrated—lit a spark. And since there was no taboo about sleeping with a woman your roommate was dating, they began a relationship. Amy, a smart, petite dark-haired young woman with a pixieish figure and expressive dark brown eyes, was truly a child of the group; her mother had begun therapy in 1958 as an unhappily married housewife, and twenty-one years later was still a patient, as well as a professor of anthropology. Amy had entered the world of the group at age five, left to join a commune and start a revolution at sixteen, and then returned as an adult patient at twenty.

*   *   *

Jane Pearce did not join the exodus to Orlando at the time of Three Mile Island. Nineteen seventy-nine appears to have been the definitive breaking point for her, after years of gradual marginalization. She would no longer play a role in the psychoanalytic institute she had founded. Saul Newton and Joan Harvey had been quietly reassigning some of her patients to other therapists. It was not publicly discussed, but Michael Cohen had gotten hints of a change when he heard the children of the leaders making fun of Chris Pearce, the child Jane had adopted from Sue H., telling him that he needed to get away from his mother and come live with them. Pearce must have gotten wind of this, as she stopped sending Chris to play with his friends at Ninety-First Street. She continued working as a therapist, rebuilding her practice with a new roster of patients. The rupture with Saul Newton and the Fourth Wall did not appear to have shaken her conviction in the rightness of her approach to therapy. She remained at the old town house that had been the group's original headquarters.

12

The Secret History,
Part 2

By chance, many of the kids who had been sent away to boarding school in the early 1970s happened to be home on spring break when the Three Mile Island accident occurred at the end of March 1979. Some of them had not been allowed home in two or three years. They had been invisible members of the Sullivanian community, now briefly visible, and as always watching and trying to make sense of their parents' world.

"I remember it as a vacation," said Eddy Cates, who together with his brother, Andy, and most of the other kids spent their days at Disney World. The scene back at the Howard Johnson's was less kid-friendly. "I remember coming home to the hotel in the evening, and there were these big parties . . . And that was . . . when some of my peers witnessed sexual abuse. We were teenagers at that time."

One of those witnesses was Andy. "It was an orgy, just a frigging orgy," he recalled. He was especially disturbed by seeing an adult group member having sex with a teenage girl. "I walked past an open hotel room door with my bags on my way to my room, and she was on her back, legs spread and . . . it looked like the full deal . . . We all walked past that same room . . . It was just gross. It was gross on so many levels because her parents let that happen . . . other kids I know have told me about similar things that happened with them."

Another of the boarding school kids explained that he was sexually initiated at age fourteen by a woman in the group who was literally twice his age. "At the age of fourteen I had a sexual relationship with a woman who was twenty-eight, or something like that. A group member. Things that happened to me could be defined as abuse at this stage. But it was the norm. It was acceptable . . . It's funny, I define it as abuse now, but at the time it didn't feel that way. But I know kids who were really abused, preyed on by adults at a very young age."

The Sullivanian/Fourth Wall kids who were away at boarding school were a kind of Greek chorus: seeing everything, knowing everything, but unheard and unseen by the main protagonists of the drama. They had already experienced firsthand the effects of the leaders' child development theories and had concluded that never seeing your parents and spending your vacations sleeping in the back of a pickup truck were not optimal conditions for human growth. As a result, they looked on the changes in the group with jaundiced and cynical eyes.

They were the ones who had begun referring to the group's headquarters at Ninety-First Street as the Kremlin. Ordinary members might have had similar thoughts but would have been loath to voice them. Since the kids were so rarely around and people didn't pay them much mind, they were freer to express their views, at least with one another. Having been away for a couple of years, they noticed more than the adults how drastically the creation of the Fourth Wall and Three Mile Island had changed the life of the group.

"That was a time when we knew it was really pathological," Eddy Cates explained. He remembers how he and his friends found some of the new food restrictions totally bonkers. In theory, members were not allowed to eat anything that was grown or manufactured in the Northeast, but the people in his father's house made an exception for Heineken beer and Häagen-Dazs ice cream. "They said those were okay because they were imported." But looking at the packaging, the kids could see that the Heineken was bottled in Delaware, quite near Three Mile Island, and Häagen-Dazs was a New York City company, founded by Jews from the Bronx. "I think we recognized that there was an irrationality to the conversation at that point . . . They were putting Geiger counters on the microwaves [to measure radiation]," Eddy said.

"That was the beginning of instilling a lot of fear and paranoia that hadn't really existed before," he went on. Growing up, he had regarded his parents' choices—while debatable—as "an extension of the 1960s, an alternative way of conceptualizing and structuring community. Fear and paranoia were not part of the culture." Now, it had gotten dark. "I think we were aware of the pathology before our parents were aware of the pathology."

Andy Cates was able to use his time back in New York to get himself a ticket out of the Treehaven School in Tucson, which he considered a prison. He had a therapy session with Joan Harvey, and he told her how much he hated Treehaven and wanted to change schools. "'I can do that for you,'" Andy recalled Harvey saying. "'I can tell your parents not to send you back, and they won't send you back. I can do that.' She was going to be the hero. It was seductive," he said. On the one hand, Andy was enormously relieved that he would get to leave behind the brutal punishment of Treehaven. On the other hand, Harvey's commanding statement, "I can do that," was also an assertion of her absolute power over his parents, the people who ostensibly should have been making decisions about his schooling. It was a humiliating reminder of the many conversations he'd had with his father that ended with "I'll ask Joan." "Anytime I wanted something or wanted to do something, my dad would say, 'I'll ask Joan.' It got worse." It meant that his father deferred to and depended on Joan Harvey for decisions of any importance.

Not long after this, in 1980, Treehaven was shut down after someone finally denounced the school's principal for hitting one of her students. Most of the Fourth Wall kids who had been out in Arizona came back east and had more opportunity to observe the life of their parents' community. It also meant that they were all required to do therapy again, something most of them had begun at around the age of five or six.

Sam Miller recalled doing therapy as a small boy with Mike Veghte, the only Black therapist (after Carol Q.'s departure) in the group. "Mike was a really nice guy. We would have Chinese food together and play Monopoly, and he would tell me how awful my parents were. That was the sum total of the therapy . . . how it was better for me not to be with them . . . I used to tell my mother: 'Why do I have to go to this therapist? You realize he's telling me what a jerk you are.' 'I don't want to get involved,' she would say, 'That's between you and your therapist.'"

Now that these young people had reached adolescence, the therapy became more intense and more negative. Eddy Cates recalled that when he was very young, he met with a therapist named Trudy Williams for what was almost entirely play. "We got together and we played games. It was a very fun experience. I don't remember any difficult conversations. But then when I hit a certain age, I think when I was twelve or thirteen, it was decided by the group that Trudy wasn't sufficient as a therapist for me. And I ended up in therapy with Ralph Klein. I didn't see him very much, because I was away at school. But whenever I came home, I had to see him. His approach was very humiliating and he would bad-mouth my parents, telling me what awful people they were, to the point where I would just break down in tears. It very much felt like he was trying to destroy me, not really trying to help me navigate the world." Eddy's parents, John Cates and Millie Antonelli, were Ralph Klein's old friends, neighbors, and colleagues from the early years of the Sullivan Institute. The cruelty and humiliation of the therapy was another sign for Eddy that something was very wrong with the group.

His older brother, Andy, recalled a session with Helen Moses in which she suddenly pronounced, "'Andy, your mother is a bitch' . . . It happened out of the blue, it didn't come from anywhere, and it didn't lead anywhere." Andy felt it was almost as if Moses were repeating something she had been trained to say to every child. "As if there were a script and there was a box you had to check off, saying, 'Tell the kid his mother is a bitch' . . . I think every kid in the Fourth Wall will tell you that they were told the same thing." For Andy, having his mother run down by his therapist further weakened the already fragile relationship with his parents that existed after they'd tricked him into going to boarding school.

It was rare for the kids to be in New York for more than a week or two—they were almost always sent to double sessions of summer camp, so there was usually only a short window of time, the gap between the end of school and the start of camp. In the brief periods when they were in New York, they were generally on their own, and they hung out together somewhat apart from the group. Sam Miller and John Putz shared a room in an apartment with John's father. "We stayed up all night watching TV," Sam recalled. "Then we would get up at like noon, go to the movies, maybe go to a Mets game, occasionally watch the Mets game on TV."

Teenage boys who had been packed off to boarding school at a young age were a naturally rebellious lot, their attitude toward the group fundamentally negative. Their hostility came naturally to them, John Putz said. "No one wanted to get sent away—and they had sent us away, and a lot of their practices were insane."

"They were scared of teenagers," said Andy Cates. "We were Kiss and Led Zeppelin fans," said John Putz.

Eddy and Andy Cates, together with another group of boys, stayed in their own apartment that John Cates and Art Liebeskind had rented for them. "I think from the time we were thirteen, we had our own apartment, with our own kitchen," Eddy said. They were upstairs from a group apartment where their parents lived. "We could go down to their apartment to have food if we wanted, or we could prepare it on our own, and being teenage boys, we were mischievous," he recalled. "At one point some of the boys were growing marijuana outside in a window box, and someone who came up to clean the apartment found it, and she told Saul."

This caused a huge crisis. One of the group's strictest rules was no illegal drugs. Saul Newton remained convinced that the FBI or the police were looking for any pretext—such as the presence of controlled substances—to round them up and shut them down. So while people in the group abused prescription drugs, illegal drugs—including pot—

were strictly taboo. Newton decided that Andy Cates and Danny Liebe-skind (one of Art Liebeskind's adopted sons) were the ringleaders of this pot-growing scheme and announced that if there were any more pot incidents, they would be forced to leave and never return.

Not long after, they all went up to the workshop in the Catskills. When it was time to leave, Andy noticed that his friend Danny was late and worried that he might be off scoring some pot. Andy had warned him, "No pot!" That evening, Andy got drunk on some Bacardi rum, and he, his brother Eddy, and a few others played Rambo in the woods near the group's complex. "The next morning, I woke up and I was eat-ing breakfast and me and Danny got called to Saul—which doesn't happen—and Saul said, 'You guys are out. I got reports that there was pot smoking going on.'"

Andy was furious. He hadn't smoked pot, and as he stretched out on a piece of lawn waiting for a taxi that was going to take them to a bus back to New York, Newton came out and began yelling at him. "Saul started ranting at me. He was standing there with a coffee cup while I was sitting down. The coffee was spilling on me, and I thought, 'What the fuck do I have to lose with this guy now?' And I just said, 'If you spill coffee on me one more time, old man, I'm going to kill you.' And . . . he backed up a little bit, and he said, 'If you lay a hand on me, two hundred guys will kill you right now.'"

The boys were put on a bus to New York, with three days to figure out how they were going to spend the rest of their summer. "I was put in a fleabag motel—I'm talking roaches crawling all over the walls. My dad told me, 'You have three days to find a place to go. I'll pay for a one-way plane ticket anywhere at the end of the summer.' But he wasn't going to give me any money, nothing . . . I was seventeen." Andy, in despera-tion, called the director of a summer camp he had attended a couple of years earlier and said that he would do anything—work for free at the camp doing whatever they might need—if he could spend the summer there for room and board. The camp director told him that he could come, that he would meet his plane, and that he didn't even want to know what Andy had done to be sent away. "I ended up having the best summer of my life to date . . . So getting kicked out of New York didn't turn out bad, but the process was bad."

It was another nail in the coffin for his relationship with his parents.

"I hated them," Andy said unequivocally, but without obvious rancor. "I hated them from a very early age. I can't remember not hating my parents, but Treehaven probably was where it was solidified into something that would probably stay, never to be disturbed, because it was just so abusive. And they ignored it and ignored us and ignored us and rejected us."

13

The Security Squad

Alice Gadeloff (later Graves), a twenty-nine-year-old Fourth Wall member, wept when she heard of the senseless killing of the musician John Lennon, shot by a deranged loner who had snagged an autograph from the former Beatle earlier in the day. Like millions of people for whom the Beatles had been the soundtrack of their youth, Alice wanted to attend a candlelight vigil being held the next day (December 9, 1980) in a patch of Central Park (soon to be called Strawberry Fields) near Lennon's home, not far from her own apartment. But she heard that Saul Newton had forbidden it, saying that Lennon's "Give Peace a Chance" politics were not revolutionary enough for the Fourth Wall. She felt bad about not going, but didn't question the right of the group's seventy-four-year-old leader to decide whether she could engage in a personal expression of grief. Then she noticed that one of her roommates, who was also a friend, had quietly snuck off—to attend the vigil, Alice suspected. When her friend returned, they exchanged a curious look that Alice remembered years later: her friend gave her a "I know you know" glance, tacitly acknowledging that she had been at the vigil. Alice regarded her friend with a mixture of envy and anger. She couldn't quite sort out whether she was mad at her for breaking a command or at herself for not doing so. Alice decided not to say anything to anyone about her friend's transgression, which was a small transgression in itself.

A few months later, in late February or early March 1981, Newton convened an emergency meeting of the group's leading therapists at the headquarters on Ninety-First Street. He announced that he had been receiving death threats, and the group needed to adopt new security measures. He asked Michael Cohen to organize a security detail.

Cohen sent a beeper message to Artie Honan, the former athlete and bar bouncer who had organized the theater takeover. Saul had insisted that the group would need forty-two men to provide round-the-clock security at the leaders' residence and at the theater. "We need security here at Ninety-First Street. I've been worried about Joan ever since Lennon's assassination," Newton told him. Honan didn't quite see the analogy between John Lennon and Joan Harvey; Lennon was a global superstar who had been killed by a mentally unstable fan obsessed with celebrities, whereas the group was having trouble getting people to come see Harvey's plays. But Honan was excited that Newton had brought him into the group's inner circle and entrusted him with what Newton considered a vital operation.

A new security desk was created at the ground-floor entrance of the headquarters, with members signing up for three-hour shifts, initially around the clock, later until one a.m. Honan and his crew staked out the apartment buildings of suspect ex-members as well as the buildings where Fourth Wall members were concentrated. Nobody noticed anything out of the ordinary, but it was decided that Harvey and Newton would need to be accompanied by a phalanx of security men when they went down to the theater on East Fourth Street and again when they left. Saul insisted that Artie buy (at his own expense) a one-way mirror so that, in case of a possible attack, security people could watch the audience while the audience watched the show. The theater's electrical system was tricked up so that the security crew could cut all the lights and plunge the place into darkness if they spotted someone pulling out a gun. The group acquired a gun that was loaded with blanks, so it could be fired to scare off potential attackers. Artie decided that he and his crew should get professional training, and he retained an expert in a Filipino martial art called *arnis*, which involved a combination of sticks, kicks, and punches. Two security team members would be seated in the second row on the aisle of either side of the orchestra section, with special *arnis* sticks carefully stored nearby. The security squad did assassination drills in which they would hit the lights, and the lighting team illuminating the stage would follow as the actors onstage dropped to the floor.

Actual threats never materialized, but the security operation heightened the sense of urgency and the importance of the group's mission. This took place in the early months of the Reagan administration, with a new, hawkish government determined to confront the Soviet Union, build sophisticated missile systems, and ignite fears of confrontation with the world's other big nuclear power. Joan Harvey was starting work on a new film about the nuclear arms race. The Fourth Wall, at least by its own reckoning, was now taking on the U.S. military-industrial complex and trying to shut down its nuclear industry. Surely, the leadership thought, our imperialist government would not take that threat lying down and would retaliate sooner or later.

*   *   *

The experiences of Fourth Wall members varied widely, depending on a number of factors: how close they were to the leadership, how much power or money they had, how involved (or uninvolved) they were in the group's main activities, how much contact they had with the world outside the group, whether or not they had a child or wanted to have a child. Being close to the leadership could be a good thing or a bad thing: it could guarantee you a measure of protection and privilege, or it could expose you to extra scrutiny, interference, and sexual predation. Winning an important part in one of Joan Harvey's plays or working on one of her films could grant you enhanced status and visibility in the group. Having a sexual relationship with one of the four top leaders brought you favor and status but also its share of complications. There were people who succeeded in gaining a measure of autonomy and led their lives with a minimum amount of interference. Someone like John M. had a successful career as a graphic designer at a major publication and continued to rise up the paper's masthead during his years in the group. Despite whatever the leaders might say about the "bourgeois" press, this conferred a certain amount of status on him, and though he complied with the basic rules of Sullivania, they did not interfere overmuch in his life. He had a child with another group member, Leslie F., who was Harvey's main assistant on her films, a high-prestige position. Being allowed to have a child—let alone with someone of your own choice—was a rare privilege, reflecting your high standing in the group. As a result, John M. has a positive view of his nearly twenty years in the group: "All things considered, I still wouldn't trade it for another." For him it meant spending his twenties and thirties in a communal setting, exploring an interesting alternative life. When the group folded, he was, as a man in his early forties, in a position to start over and create a second, more conventional family, with a new wife and two more kids.

Although it was in principle an egalitarian communist group, the Sullivanians were remarkably hierarchical, and everyone was aware where they stood at any given moment in the pecking order. Former members speak of themselves and others as being "high status" and "low status," earning "prestige points," being in the group's rank and file or close to the leadership—almost like a caste system, except it wasn't fixed and you could rise and fall with alarming speed.

All the new activities the Fourth Wall came up with—the plays, the film, the emergency communications system, the security detail, the radiation-monitoring team—added considerably to the already long days of most group members. Many Fourth Wall people were working two jobs; some had a day job to make money and an adjunct teaching job in the evening in the field that they loved. Or they were working and putting themselves through law school or medical school. With the formation of the theater company, they'd been required, along with paying monthly dues, to give several hours of their time. Now they were expected to add several more hours of work to their schedule.

"Before that, my life was pretty free," said Bob Putz, the mathematician who joined in the early 1970s and said he loved his time in the group until after Three Mile Island. With two children in boarding school, Putz worked in a corporate job by day and taught at a university by night to pay his bills. "Now I've got to listen to the goddamn radio, I've got to sit at the front door on Ninety-First Street as a guard. I'm in the group that goes out and checks all the nuclear plants to see if they're leaking radiation, starting out at seven in the evening and getting back at seven in the morning." To add insult to injury, a number of the things Putz was being asked to do didn't make a lot of rational sense to him. "They are making all these demands on me, and I don't think a lot of these things. I am basically being a frigging unpaid doorman." Nonetheless, he would remain in the group for several more years.

At the same time, members managed to find little spaces of autonomy and rebellion within an increasingly programmed and controlled life. Artie Honan writes about his annoyance that one of his roommates had volunteered their apartment to do overnight radio watch every other Saturday, presumably to curry favor with the leadership. One Saturday, Honan and a girlfriend were wakened by the alarm going off in the middle of the night, signaling the start of their radio watch duty. They turned on the radio, as well as a cassette recorder, to make sure they didn't miss anything. "As long as we're up, let's make out," Honan told the woman. One thing led to another, and the radio noise vanished into the background. When their radio watch shift was over, they decided to hit rewind to make sure they hadn't missed anything important. The news conveyed nothing of great interest, but they laughed hysterically at the sounds of themselves having sex.

Jon Mack, a member of the nuclear monitoring team, wrote that "there were some 'rewards' for these bizarre all-night expeditions." In defiance of the group's new food restrictions, they enjoyed the guilty pleasure of microwaved burritos at 7-Eleven. "Driving around all night gave me a chance to hear details of my monitoring partners' lives and histories that I would never have known. And the group's pro-sex attitude meant that on occasion, there'd be a woman willing to have an all-inclusive 'breakfast date' before both of us headed off to work."

This exhausting job also conferred status. "The monitoring crew was one of those exclusive teams selected by Saul, and I felt privileged to be on it," Artie Honan wrote. "The members were seen as responsible and dedicated. Joel [a pseudonym for a friend of Honan's] was also on the team, which gave him a boost in esteem because he was not often chosen to be on elite crews. Saul chided him once for using his participation on the crew to get laid more."

Some group members chose to do the minimal amount of required work for the group, but not to get involved in the frantic competition for approval from the leadership. Rachel helped organize a boycott of the Swiss food company Nestlé because of the harmful effects of the infant formula they were selling in the developing world. This was something she did on her own, with others outside the group. Eventually, in 1984, the boycott led to the United Nations adopting a code for the marketing of breast milk substitutes.

Rachel's work on the Nestlé boycott convinced her to enter law school, and for years she juggled work and school. One of her close friends in the group decided to go to graduate school, and they had study dates in the evening as they prepared for exams. She also continued playing in a rock band made up of other Fourth Wall members. "We supported each other, and we all remain friends," she said.

In the end, Rachel may have been lucky that the group's leadership had little interest in her and her political activity. "They didn't respect my politics. I tried to teach about global corporations in the group. No dice." The leadership never arranged a viewing of a documentary she suggested about the Nestlé boycott. "And I thought, fuck this." Nevertheless, she remained with the group until the end, in large part because she had carved out a measure of autonomy, led the life she wanted to lead, had close friends, and had begun dating the man with whom she still lives. Her peripheral position to the leadership—and the fact that she did not have a child—spared her from being interfered with by the Ninety-First Street leaders.

Mike Cohen and Mike Bray had risen up in the hierarchy and were now working very closely with the group's four top therapists. This brought status but also considerable risks.

Mike Cohen, as a longtime patient of Joan Harvey's, was already deeply enmeshed with life at Ninety-First Street. The creation of the Fourth Wall and the group's anti-nuclear focus did little, at the beginning, to diminish his ardor for the cause. Despite Harvey's volatile behavior, he remained devoted to her. His long history with Harvey—he had started therapy with her seven years earlier, in 1973—had had a kind of paradoxical effect on Cohen, simultaneously breaking him down and building him up. She frequently yelled at him, threatened him, demeaned his family as "stupid, fat Jews," called Cohen himself a weak, cowering mama's boy. She had successfully convinced him that if he left therapy with her, he would end up being admitted to an insane asylum, going to prison, or dying by suicide. He had images of himself alone, wasting away in a bleak apartment on the Lower East Side. At the same time, outside of therapy, he was emerging as one of the most powerful therapists in the group after the senior leaders themselves. It was as if—and this was probably the intent of the therapy—he were leaving behind his original identity as a vulnerable Jewish orphan from Yonkers and forging a new Fourth Wall identity as a confident, tough therapist, a fervent revolutionary, and a Fourth Wall leader who could be relied on to rally the troops and bring them into line. "My identity was as a member of this institute, a member of this community—it really made me feel more powerful as a person, really built me up." Along with the sessions in which Harvey screamed at him, there was also a great complicity between them that felt like genuine intimacy. "I could talk to her about what an asshole Saul was or what a fucking prima donna vapid idiot Helen Moses was . . . She would feed it; she would love it; she had the same feelings . . . So I didn't have to hide this with her. Now, if I said it outside of sessions, which I tried to do a couple of times, I got my ass handed to me."

Joan Harvey had assumed a public role in the anti-nuclear movement and was seemingly in danger of assassination, and Cohen began to have fantasies that he would literally give his life for her. "I would come out of a session with Joan and have the fantasy as I walked back to my apartment that if it was needed, I would die for her, I would die for the revolution," Cohen later said. When he conveyed this thought to Harvey, she considered it entirely reasonable, he said, "because her existence in the world politically was more important than mine . . . At that point, psychologically, I was not much different than the guy who would drive a van of dynamite into the American embassy in Beirut." And in many ways his devotion to Harvey served him well: he enjoyed increasing prestige and power within the group.

Cohen and one of his roommates, Danny Pisello, who had a Ph.D. in physics, threw themselves into the task of trying to understand what had gone wrong at Three Mile Island and whether the same dangers were present at other nuclear reactors. "I found an article in German showing that there was a design flaw with the use of zirconium cladding," Cohen said, "and we wrote an article called 'The Zirconium Connection' and I testified in front of the Nuclear Regulatory Commission." Zirconium was used as cladding on the fuel rods in nuclear reactors, and though it functioned well as insulation under normal conditions, in the case of an accident like the one at Three Mile Island, where zirconium is exposed to hot, steamy water, it begins to oxidize and produce hydrogen gas. "So we did some things that were actually contributions and work I am still proud of," Cohen said. He also took time off from his therapy practice to edit a book Pisello wrote (and published) called *Gravitation, Electromagnetism and Quantized Charge: The Einstein Insight* (1979).

At the same time, Danny Pisello wrote a children's play, which the Fourth Wall performed for kids on Saturday and Sunday afternoons. *The King of the Entire World* was a good-natured musical comedy about the king of a tiny kingdom. It also contained whimsical riffs on the nature of light and motion, reflecting Danny's physics background. The play was clever and charming, and many former members consider it the best piece the theater group did in its fifteen years of existence. Among other things, it was a playful spoof on the nature of power that, in retrospect, looks like a gentle parody of Saul Newton:

> *I am the king of the entire world—*
> *I live in the palace and with gold and jewels*

I am the king and make all the rules . . .
I never get tired of people bowing
I can do what I want
'Cause I do the allowing

At the same time, the play had a subtle Sullivanian message tucked inside: the king ultimately decides to give up his little kingdom in order to embrace a wider world of change and growth. The songs were collected on an LP record—designed by a therapist who had been a successful graphic artist before entering the group—and sold. The scientific work on zirconium, the Einstein book, and *The King of the Entire World* fit Mike Cohen's idea of what the group could be: smart, unconventional people doing serious, politically important work while also knowing how to have a good time. The theater's main productions—generally Joan Harvey's plays—were typically performed three nights a week, and the children's plays were performed on weekend days, while a weekly music night (a kind of open talent show) left a channel for some of the group's creative impulses as well as relief from feeling that they were always under Harvey's thumb.

Joan Harvey, as she took on more and more projects and more and more power, became increasingly imperious, temperamental, and unpredictable. Michael Cohen generally had a nine a.m. therapy appointment with her three days a week, and he frequently arrived at Ninety-First Street to find her asleep in bed. He would try to get Ralph Klein to wake her up, which was not always successful. Cohen would have to make her coffee and do their session in her bedroom, with her still in her nightgown, sitting up in bed. She sometimes kept him waiting an hour or two or charged him for sessions that never took place. When he pointed this out, she flew into a rage, kicked him out of her office, and threatened him with expulsion from the group. To keep up her frenetic work pace, she was increasingly dependent on Dexedrine, to power through her days and long nights, and on Seconal, a barbiturate, to be able to sleep at night. She was feeding Dexedrine to those around her as well, to help *them* get through the long days and nights.

Cohen began to worry that he was becoming addicted to the pills, and he was quite sure she was.

Her fits of rage were more frequent and more violent. Cohen saw her strike her babysitters on more than one occasion. Janie P., the visual artist who was drafted to work in the theater's costume department, recalled that Harvey slapped her when she failed to find a pair of Harvey's "special socks" for a performance. The following day, Saul Newton barged into her therapy session and slapped Janie for the same offense.

Cohen watched as Saul Newton exploded into violent fits with his own children or their playmates, creating an atmosphere of terror in the household.

Although it was an official rule at the Sullivan Institute (as in all psychoanalytic institutes) that an analyst was not supposed to sleep with his or her patients, the top analysts in the institute routinely violated this policy. Cohen became increasingly certain that Newton exacted tribute from virtually all his attractive female patients. Harvey was carrying on an affair with Cohen's good friend and roommate Danny Pisello, who was also Harvey's patient, something that put a strain on Mike and Danny's friendship.

Cohen felt jealous and spoke of it to Harvey, so she took Cohen, her patient of eight years, to bed. "I was so terrified that I couldn't perform—she kicked me out in the middle of the night," he said. "Even though she was objectively a good-looking woman, I was never attracted to her sexually. That might have saved me."

Mike Bray, now practicing as an institute therapist, had Harvey supervising his cases. "At one point she said to me, 'You know, you should stop trying to date me during supervision.'" This was the furthest thing from his mind: he was terrified of Harvey and wanted to keep his distance. But he understood that her admonition, "stop trying to date me during supervision," meant just the opposite; it was a subtle but clear invitation to date her outside of supervision. He played dumb and dodged that bullet.

He was not so lucky with Helen Moses, Saul Newton's wife. She approached him and asked him to have sex with her when they were up at the workshop in the Catskills. She was eight months pregnant, which made the request especially terrifying, but he reluctantly complied. When she wanted to continue their liaison, he managed to come up with a convenient case of temporary impotence that put an end to it.

More disturbing in many ways, however, were the things Cohen and Bray were being asked to do in their psychoanalytic practice, in which the patients' needs were entirely subordinated to those of the group.

"After 1978, the shift in therapy—and this was dictated and taught in class—was no longer even ostensibly about creating an autonomous individual," Cohen said. "The job was to create a good member of this community. The goal of the community was to save the world against the threat of nuclear destruction . . . and the individual was completely subordinate to this task. The therapy was to help people become good soldiers in this paramilitary group."

What it meant in practice were things like encouraging patients who had cut off ties with their families to get money out of them for Fourth Wall projects. "How much money is this dinner going to cost me?" Sara, a former member who preferred to use an assumed name, recalled her father saying when they met. "On the one hand," she said, "I was outraged—'How dare you?'—but at the same time, I knew he was absolutely right."

If patients were resistant to following orders or doing the work the leadership demanded, the therapist's job was to make them comply. "So, if they were stepping out of line, or if they were being critical or they had thoughts that something was crazy about the place, your job was to get them back in line," Cohen recalled. "If they were resentful about putting in the amount of work or money that was required to be in the community, your job was to make them good soldiers. Unfortunately, I was very good at making people good soldiers. I was given these kinds of people often . . . I was told, 'Take this person on. We want you to pull them into line.'"

During his work on Three Mile Island and nuclear energy, Cohen had gotten to know a Neapolitan theoretical physicist named Ruggiero de Ritis, with whom he had become good friends. The need to create a kind of research arm for the group's anti-nuclear activity had briefly opened a breach in the ordinarily closed world of the Fourth Wall. Cohen welcomed this, finding a valuable kindred spirit in de Ritis. "He was a veteran of the Italian student movement and been involved in one of its far-left groups in the 1970s. He understood our group perfectly," Cohen said. Having a friend outside the group allowed Cohen to very tentatively express his misgivings about life in the Fourth Wall. "He told me something very interesting. He didn't tell me what to do. He just said, 'Start keeping a diary and write things down.'"

Among the things the training therapists were being told to do was to steer their patients into more lucrative jobs. Saul Newton was increasingly interested in money, and he had asked someone what was the best and most lucrative profession to go into. The answer was computer programming. In the late 1970s and early '80s, most companies were rapidly computerizing, and personal computers were still several years away. In 1982, the group organized a computer class, led by a few members who were capable computer engineers, in order to train others in the basics of programming. They were also trained to make up phony résumés indicating that they had prior experience, and as more of them entered the field, they helped hire other group members.

Michael Bray was instructed to push one of his patients—a graphic artist who wasn't making much money—into programming. "She was literally weeping, saying, 'but I love what I do.'" Rather than discussing how she might change her life in order to keep doing what she loved, Bray continued steering her toward computer programming.

At the same time, he watched the painful drama of his good friend Dick Wasley, the clarinetist who had been paralyzed and nearly killed by Guillain-Barré syndrome. Against all odds, Wasley had regained the use of his hands and fingers and had been able to resume his career as a professional musician, but now he was being forced to give it up for computer programming. Eventually, whether intentionally or subconsciously, Wasley failed at the programming work, allowing him to go back to music.

Bray was also being asked to keep low-ranking group members from having children. Many people who had entered therapy ten years earlier, in their twenties, were now eager to start families. Bray went to consult Helen Moses, his supervisor, about a particular patient who wanted to become a father. "Helen said, 'Oh, well, we'll have to figure out a way to break this to him gently, so I think it's better not to yell at him and tell him that he's an asshole, which is what he is, but we'll say: 'I think you need to grow in these areas.' So I went back and actually told another person that they couldn't have a child. And this started to get to me," Bray said.

At a certain point Cohen's sister contacted him for the first time in years. An elderly uncle had fallen ill, and Cohen was asked to help out. "Saul allowed it because he thought there might be some inheritance money in it for the group," Cohen said. In reality, it allowed him to see his sister for the first time in a decade. He and Bray traveled together to Florida—whenever a group member saw family, they were supposed to have another group member with them. The ostensible reason was that the patient was at risk of regression, of falling under the maleficent spell of his or her parents. Or perhaps the leadership was afraid that if parents met alone with their children, they would convince them to leave the group. To Cohen's astonishment, his sister did not utter a single word of reproach or recrimination for the way he had cut her off—the nasty letters, the hung-up phone calls. "She understood," he said, that his behavior followed a group playbook rather than his own deeper feelings. Her forbearance and enduring affection suddenly looked a lot better than Joan Harvey's histrionics.

Bray also accompanied another group member to see his father, a successful surgeon in the Midwest. He was told to surreptitiously tape-record the encounter. "I was wired with a tape recorder thing down my sleeve." This accompaniment, along with serving as a surveillance system, had another purpose, Bray said. "It helped to infantilize us; it enhanced the perception that our parents were so powerful that we needed to be protected from them."

Bray and Cohen also made a trip out to Iowa, where Bray's parents were still living. His therapist had suggested that getting copies of family photographs would help with his therapy. The trip was something of a revelation. His parents did not express anger for the decade in which they had been shut out of his life. After years of therapy in which they had been portrayed as violent, homicidal people, Mike Bray found it jarring to be sitting in the living room of a harmless-seeming elderly couple, a retired car dealer and his wife, a little dull, a little limited in their life experience, but kindly and well-disposed people, hardly two murderers. "They were just decent people leading regular lives," Bray said. "That started me thinking more about what was real and what was not."

After they returned, Bray showed the photographs to two different therapists. They came up with two different interpretations—both malevolent but decidedly different. Were these people just making it all up as they went along? he wondered.

14

Paternity

One day in December 1981 Mike Bray received a call from Alice D., another training therapist. As Bray recalled, she said, "Listen, I think I'm going to have a baby, and I'd like you to consider being the father." Alice had been brought into the institute's therapist training program while still an undergraduate at Rutgers. Helen Moses had taken her under her wing, and she was one of two female therapists (along with Ellen Barrett) who'd been invited to live with Moses, Newton, Harvey, and Klein at the Ninety-First Street town house, albeit in a little garret room on a newly created fifth-floor annex. Mike and Alice were merely acquaintances. They had never dated and were not even friends. Bray was taken aback, but he knew this was a very important conversation that—either way—could have a major impact on his future. "Gee, I never thought about it," he said, stalling for time. She seemed undeterred: "I want you to think about it. I've talked with Helen, and she thinks you'd be a good father." At this point Bray knew he was in a serious quandary. Given the group's negative views of family, having a child was a big deal, a privilege granted infrequently to a chosen few. He knew that such a decision had been sanctioned at the highest levels.

Being a father in the Sullivanian world was extremely complex business. It didn't necessarily mean being the child's biological father, as biology and paternity in this polygamous group were considered trivial. Conversely, accepting the role of a child's legal father was a major lifetime commitment: you were agreeing to help raise the child and, more important, to pay for the child's care and education. At the same time, Bray had seen the leadership take children away from parents who were deemed not up to snuff.

If Helen Moses had suggested him, it meant that Saul Newton had also approved this particular "baby project." Either path Mike took at this crossroads was fraught with danger: "The leader of the group is now saying, 'I think you'd be a good father,' so if I'm not a good father, I'm fucked." If he said no, he risked the leaders' wrath, with equally unpredictable consequences. He decided to accept.

His next move, however, was not to talk it over with Alice, the prospective mother, but to go see Saul Newton. His therapist at the time was Ralph Klein, but he regularly saw Newton as the supervising therapist for his caseload. Bray felt instinctively that Klein, perhaps the weakest of the big four lead therapists, did not have the power to protect him from the dangers of parenthood. So Bray went to Newton and said, "If I am going to take this on, I'm going to ask if I can be your patient." He explained, "This was ass-kissing at its best, but it was sincere in a way. It was better to tuck myself up under his tutelage and protection."

Bray then asked Saul who was going to help Alice get pregnant. Newton shifted into his more avuncular mode and said, according to Bray, "Listen, I hope you don't get too possessive about this . . . People get all hooked on that, and it's a big source of problems in marriages. It doesn't matter what sperm gets up there first. It's better for this to happen soon. So it's much better if attempts are made with more people to get Alice pregnant . . . Maybe you and Alice can talk about it."

When Bray spoke with Alice, she mentioned a list of four men, including him, as potential contributors to this collective effort. He began to think more about why he, who had virtually no connection with Alice, had been chosen to be the father of her child. She had a serious relationship with Robbie Newton, Saul Newton's oldest son, who was also a group member. You weren't allowed to have an exclusive relationship with anyone, but there were couples who clearly had close and lasting relationships. "Alice and Robbie were a couple," Bray said. Robbie was among the four men who would help get Alice pregnant, but wouldn't it have been simpler to let her have a child with the man she loved without involving Bray and others? And why wasn't Robbie chosen to be the legal father rather than Bray? It was a common (but unarticulated) practice that when the leadership authorized someone to have a child, they tried to pick as the official father someone who was not close to the mother, in order to prevent the development of a traditional nuclear family. Having Bray be the designated dad was clearly in line with that strategy. At the same time, it struck Bray as particularly cruel that Saul Newton would deny his own son the possibility of having a family with the woman in his life. But both Bray and Robbie Newton accepted this arrangement and kept to themselves whatever reservations they may have had.

Bray had one opportunity with Alice, and not long after, he came down with a bad case of herpes, which forced him to abstain for two weeks. By then she was already pregnant—with twins, as it turned out. They never had sex again. They never really clicked as friends, let alone as lovers. But sticking to the program and for the sake of the kids, they became legally married. Sex and love, in the group's eyes, had nothing to do with marriage and parenthood. People in the group were supposed to marry for practical reasons: to save on their taxes, for health or dental insurance, or to establish legal rights as parents. At other times, couples who really wanted to be together invoked these banal pretexts when they secretly married for love.

Nine months after their conception, two adorable but very small twin girls lay quietly in Mike Bray's hands. "When they were born, they were like four and a half pounds," Bray recalled. "I've got one kid in this palm and the other in that palm, and it just transcends everything, and I said, 'Man, I'm going to be there for you girls no matter what. I'm going to be your father.'"

The two girls were fraternal rather than identical twins, and as they grew, they looked surprisingly different. One had dark hair, the other blond. One had brown eyes, the other blue. Looking at them, Bray wondered whether the two children might have different fathers—a rare but not unheard-of phenomenon called "heteropaternal superfecundation."

The dark-haired, brown-eyed one looked a lot like she was Robbie New-ton's biological child; neither Alice nor the other men in the sperm pool had brown eyes. During a doctor's visit, the pediatrician, noting the girls' obvious differences, told Bray that they might well have different fathers. Bray figured that there was roughly a one in three chance that the blue-eyed girl was his biological child. But on an emotional level, it genuinely didn't matter. He loved them both and was committed to raising them as his daughters.

*   *   *

Unbeknownst to Mike Bray, he was not the first person Alice had asked to become the legal father to her children. She had originally approached Mike Cohen, who recalled, "I was close friends with Alice, and she said, 'You're going to be the father.' And somewhere, at an al-most cellular level, I knew I didn't want to do this at that point in my life, and I didn't want to do this with her. I said no, and you can't imag-ine the pressure from Newton and Harvey. I was a really good soldier at this point, and I knew that I might get thrown out of the group. But I just knew at a cellular level I didn't want to do this." He had agreed to help some women get pregnant but had instinctively refused when he'd been asked to act as the legal father.

A number of women in the group—people who had joined in the early 1970s and were now in their late thirties or early forties—were eager to have kids while it was still biologically possible. Children in the Fourth Wall tended to come in waves, in cohorts that generally occurred when Saul Newton and Helen Moses wanted to have another child; she had four children between 1974 and 1982. And whenever Helen got pregnant, she asked a handful of other women, generally other thera-pists, to get pregnant at the same time. This was the case with Alice in 1981, as Helen Moses prepared to have her fourth child. Ralph Klein and Joan Harvey also arranged to adopt another child when the other women had theirs. So there would be five children the same age running up and down the stairs of 314 Ninety-First Street. It fit with Harvey's and the group's ideal of chumship, creating a community of peers. The waves of children that occurred every couple of years became a running joke in the group: "Dues are going up: Helen must be pregnant again!"

Among the chosen few who were encouraged to have children in this period was Ellen Barrett. Like Alice D., she was one of the training therapists selected to live at the Ninety-First Street headquarters. Cohen (along with others) had helped Ellen when she was trying to conceive her first child back in the spring of 1979, and that child was born in early 1980. Although they were not close, Ellen approached Cohen the next year to help her get pregnant again. Partly to mollify the leadership for refusing to be father to Alice D.'s child, Cohen agreed to help both Ellen and Helen Moses in this round of pregnancies. While he'd found it traumatic when he was pressured into helping Helen several years earlier, this time he operated on automatic pilot. It was a couple of evenings out of his life, which seemed like light duty compared with the lifetime commitment of agreeing to raise a child as the designated father.

As a therapist, Cohen was asked or ordered to do something he found much more upsetting. One of his patients, G.T., was dating a woman, R.A., who very much wanted to have a child and was in love with G.T., who wanted to have a child with her as well. "I was told by Moses and Newton to break this up," Cohen recalled. They carried out a kind of pincer maneuver: Cohen would work on G.T. while Alice D., who was given the same order, would work on her patient, R.A. The unsuspecting patients would think this was something that emerged from their own therapy rather than a diktat imposed by Saul Newton and Helen Moses, who, as it happened, was also dating G.T. Cohen was already troubled by many of the things he was doing as a therapist—pushing patients to obey group rules, break off relationships, cut ties with their families, take jobs they didn't like—but looking back, he felt this might have been the single worst thing he did. "To disrupt two people potentially constructing a life together who very well may have been in love with each other and to tell them not to have a child is about as sleazy as you can get."

At a certain point, in the journal his friend Ruggiero suggested he keep, Cohen wrote, "This isn't therapy, it's social control."

At about midnight one evening in the spring of 1982, Cohen got a phone call and was told to go immediately to a hotel on Fifty-Seventh Street to meet Ralph Klein and his longtime therapist, Joan Harvey. Klein said he couldn't explain why over the phone. When Cohen arrived, he found himself in the company of Harvey, Klein, and a gun-toting private detective. Harvey explained that she was now afraid for her safety because of the film she was working on about the American nuclear arms buildup. For the film, she had interviewed top military and intelligence figures as well as political radicals, and she was convinced that the FBI or the CIA was on her trail and likely to try to seize her footage. She needed, she said, to go underground. The detective offered to set her up in a cabin he owned in a remote part of upstate New York. Harvey's departure from Ninety-First Street was a dramatic piece of theater: the group created a kind of motorcade, with about a dozen cars leaving at the same time but then heading in different directions. Harvey would be in disguise, and with many people piling into different cars at the same time, it would be difficult to tell which car the filmmaker was in. "This really had an effect on people. Here one of our leaders has gone underground, and everyone knows it," Cohen recalled. "I was one of the few people who knew the location and was authorized to go visit her."

At the same time, Cohen and Bray were tasked with creating a safe place for Harvey to work at the group's summer residence in the Catskills. They built a bazooka-proof bunker for her editing room. "It had thick steel plates," Cohen recalled. "The room had a trapdoor, so if the CIA were to attack, she could escape through the trapdoor, go through an underground passageway to a place where a car was always kept waiting to whisk her away to safety. There was a man on security duty twenty-four hours a day when she was there."

That summer, while Harvey was busy with her film, Cohen enjoyed a rare stretch of a few months virtually without therapy. During that time he made a trip to Scandinavia with the Fourth Wall's theater group and met a number of people who shared his political ideals but lived very different lives from his, with apartments of their own, love lives, and families. He had an affair with a Dutch woman who was a member of something called Dancers for Disarmament. But when he came back, Joan Harvey pushed Cohen to break off the relationship, insisting that the woman was a Trotskyite. (Were there any of them left in 1982?)

Mike Cohen's frustration with his life in the group was reaching a boiling point: he suggested to Harvey that he might benefit from changing therapists. She flew into an apoplectic rage and threatened him with expulsion from the group. He had explored the idea of pursuing a Ph.D. program in psychology, but again Harvey became angry, insisting that his political work with the group should come first.

At some point in 1982 he realized that he had been in the training program a full decade, and he started to wonder: Would he ever, at some point, graduate and obtain some kind of degree or certificate? When he posed the question to Saul Newton, Saul reacted with fury, as if even asking the question was the height of presumption and insubordination.

One night, at about three in the morning, Mike Cohen was in bed with a woman he was dating named Joyce, someone he felt close enough with to share some of his growing doubts about the direction of the group. She listened and responded sympathetically. Then they went to sleep. The next morning at about eleven o'clock Cohen's phone rang. It was Saul Newton, who said, "I understand you think . . . ," and began repeating some of the things Cohen had told Joyce only eight hours earlier. Cohen knew exactly what had happened. Joyce had had a ten a.m. therapy session with Stephanie N. Why had his girlfriend, who was also a friend, informed on him? She was probably nervous that she'd heard something she shouldn't have—something subversive and dangerous—and felt it was better and safer for her to share it with her therapist. Her therapist, in turn, would have worried that if she didn't report the incident and Joyce told someone else, then *she* would be in trouble. "We had a surveillance system that the Stasi could only have envied. We not only knew what people did and said but what they thought and dreamed about," Cohen said.

"I was literally called a dissident at that point," he recalled. "They said, 'We have a dissident in our midst, this is hurting the group at a time when we really have to be together.'" At a large meeting of high-ranking group members, Cohen was subjected to a long, blistering summary that seemed to last for hours, excoriating him as a dangerous and subversive figure who was in desperate need of reform. The former heir apparent was now viewed as a potential Leon Trotsky.

*   *   *

In 1982, the Fourth Wall—or several dozen members of it—arranged to buy an entire building where about ninety people could live. After more than two decades of white flight, the Upper West Side was being rapidly gentrified, which meant that some people's rents were going way up but also that many longtime tenants with lower rents, including many in the Fourth Wall, had opportunities to buy their apartments at very reasonable prices or were even being offered money to move out. By law, building owners, in order to be able to convert from rental buildings to owner-occupied cooperatives, needed to convince at least half the tenants to buy their places.

One member, Paul Sprecher, and his roommates were positioned to make a handsome profit flipping their apartment. By banding together with a few other group members, they would be able to buy a brownstone together. Sprecher had recently married Deedee Agee, who was one of Mike Cohen's patients. They hoped to have a family, and buying a building might allow them to live together with other group members in a communal setting, combining the best of both worlds: living as a couple yet remaining in the group. Like a good Sullivanian, Sprecher took the idea to his therapist, who happened to be Saul Newton. "I went to Saul, and I said, 'What do you think of this?'" Sprecher would testify in a custody battle that took place in the late 1980s. (All of Sprecher's quotations here come from the extensive testimony and interviews he gave at that time.) Sprecher said, "We could afford it. [Saul] says, yelling, 'You will never live in the same building as that woman! Get that idea out of your head! You'll end up being the same as your stupid father and your stupid mother and your grandfather and your grandmother.'" It was classic Sullivanian therapy: if you live as a couple, you will turn into your parents. Only the leaders were mature enough to handle cohabitation. So Sprecher came up with an alternative solution—buying a much larger building, where they would both live, but on separate floors in all-male and all-female apartments. "So we could go through the same door, but she's on two and I'm on seven," Sprecher said.

Mike Cohen, Mike Bray, and Amy Siskind, along with fifty other group members, put up money to reserve apartments in the new building at 2643 Broadway, at 100th Street. In theory, they were buying shares in the building, although the legal and financial status of the deal remained murky. "There were several co-ops that people had just bought that Newton demanded be sold and the money turned over" to buy shares in the new building, Cohen said.

Still, the group needed to come up with a substantial sum for the down payment as well as a gut renovation of the building's interior to make it serve the group's needs. One of Mike Cohen's patients at that time was John Cates, Andy and Eddy Cates's father, Millie Antonelli's ex-husband. "They extorted one hundred thousand dollars out of John for the creation of the new building," Cohen recalled. "And I was asked to put pressure on him in therapy to give that money. 'You give us the money or you're out—that simple.' Fortunately for me, they got the money out of him even before the next therapy session. But if they hadn't, I would have done that. Here's a guy in his sixties who's been in this group for thirty years, homosexual but trying desperately—and not very successfully—not to be, and he is suddenly faced with the idea of making his life outside the community. I was terrified about making a life outside the community—so the thought of John, at sixty-five, having to leave was almost inconceivable . . . I remember Dom Antonelli, another Ph.D. psychologist who fell from grace . . . they took twenty-five thousand from him."

Scott Powell, one of the founding members of Sha Na Na and now in medical school, had made a lot of money when the band members had been offered their own television show. He agreed to put up some of the money for the building. They did not hire a licensed architect to design the interior, but used a group member, the sculptor Roger Williams. The building was divided into men's and women's floors: the second and third floors, and part of the fourth floor, housed only women, while the fifth, sixth, and seventh floors housed only men. Moreover, in taking over the project, Saul Newton had doubled the number of people going into the new building, drastically decreasing the size of the apartments. Each floor had a kind of rabbit warren of small bedrooms, many of them just big enough for a bed and a dresser. There was a large communal living area and a communal kitchen with a few refrigerators.

"When I saw the plan, I said, this isn't going to work out too well," Cohen said. "Some of the rooms were like closets, but some of them were like mansions." He suspected that the small rooms would go to the rank-and-file members who had little power or status, or to people who were being punished by the leadership, while the bigger rooms would be reserved for people enjoying favor with the leadership. Cohen, who was now on the rehabilitation list after his doubts about the group had leaked out, found himself in a small cubicle, while next door, Roger, who had designed the building, had a palatial room. Cohen found a way of wreaking a little revenge: "At the time, all Sony color TV sets had the same remote-control device, so when Roger had someone over for a date and they were watching something, I would change the channel on his TV—he would get upset and could never figure out what the problem was. So, Roger, if you're out there somewhere listening, it was me."

*   *   *

The AIDS epidemic represented a terrifying prospect for a polygamous group like the Fourth Wall. Early on, in 1981, the disease appeared to be limited to the gay male population—it was initially described as the "gay cancer" and then more technically as GRID: gay-related immune deficiency. But when the disease turned up in heterosexual patients, it was renamed AIDS (acquired immune deficiency syndrome). Although much was still unknown about the disease, it appeared to be transmitted through the exchange of bodily fluids, sexual contact (especially if blood was involved), transfusions, and the sharing of needles among drug users.

In response, the Fourth Wall leadership decided in 1983 that from then on, members could not have sex with anyone outside of the group and must use condoms when having sex. Not all the measures were as logical. Group members had to remove their shoes whenever they entered their apartments. They could no longer eat in restaurants or buy food that had not been prepared by a Fourth Wall member. You could not even buy a cup of coffee you had poured yourself in a deli or coffee shop. At one point, one of the babysitters, perhaps hoping to impress the leaders with her hypervigilance, asked whether she should wash the dog's paws when they returned from a walk.

"That may be going a bit far," Joan Harvey replied. A man raised his hand. "I was brought up by a mother who was phobic of germs, and it's taken me years to undo that," he said, arguing against the paw-cleaning measure. The idea was dropped, but two days later, everyone in the group received a message that dogs' paws must be washed every time they reenter the house. The man with the phobic mother dropped out of the group.

When one member at a meeting—trying to keep track of the dizzying set of commands and prohibitions—suggested that someone write them down and distribute the list, Joan Harvey shot the idea down. "They might think we are some crazy cult if they ever got hold of it," she said.

"One member had lunch with co-workers on a new job, ate a salad, and was fined $500," Artie Honan wrote in his memoir. "Another member ate crudités at a reception with co-workers and was kicked out of the Group. I don't know if someone told the Leadership about their violations. I assumed that they'd told their therapists who, in turn, consulted with Saul about consequences. I was invited to dinner with the director of a college program where I taught, but after I refused to eat her home-made casserole, I wasn't rehired."

The AIDS restrictions were another swerve of the bus; a few fell off, but most held on for dear life.

Though the group's AIDS restrictions were excessive, they were effective. Only one member of the group died of the disease. "I think it certainly saved my life," said Elliot K. "As a gay man in the 1980s, I would have probably gotten sick and died, as so many people I know did."

That spring—of 1983—Eddy Cates received the news that his father would be coming up for parents' day at Deerfield Academy. "I was really excited—he had never come to a parents' day in all my years in boarding school," Eddy recalled. "It was like, wow, an expression of love that he had not demonstrated. But by the end of the trip, it became clear he had an agenda, and the agenda was to tell me that I could no longer come to New York because of AIDS." Eddy, who was fifteen at the time, understood that this made little or no sense. AIDS was in every part of the country, so wasn't a person as likely to contract the disease in Massachusetts as in New York? Eddy was not engaging in risky sex or drug use, so his chances of getting AIDS anywhere were close to zero. Wasn't he more likely to come to harm being unsupervised during vacations, being forced to find places to stay and things to do on his own than being under his parents' care in New York? "Even as a fifteen-year-old kid, I knew that this had nothing to do with AIDS," he said. "I think they used the AIDS crisis to separate people more from the mainstream, to isolate them, stripping away their other emotional connections, make them more vulnerable and easier to manipulate. It was one of two episodes that really solidified my anger toward my parents."

It filled out, for Eddy, a depressing picture of how far his father had fallen during Eddy's own lifetime. He remembered his early life in the town house his father owned on Seventy-Seventh Street. His parents seemed to be part of a rich and interesting alternative community. People like Saul Newton and Joan Harvey had seemed to be his parents' peers, friends, and colleagues. "Growing up in that Seventy-Seventh Street house, there had always been ample space for my father and my mother and each of us kids. Now, seeing my father living in a little cubicle about ten feet by eight feet, just enough to fit a queen-size bed, was very disturbing to me, humiliating. He was a doctor with a substantial income, yet it was clear in a very palpable way that he wasn't in control of his life. I couldn't understand that choice at all."

Eddy ended up staying with his older brother, Andy, who had rented an apartment in Boston for the summer. Andy had just finished high school and was preparing to enter Boston University in the fall.

That same spring, Sam Miller, also fifteen, got a call from his mother telling him that he couldn't come home to New York anymore either. "It's too dangerous for you because of AIDS," Sam recalled her saying. "I said, 'Listen, Mom, I'm not having sex. Unfortunately, I'm not going to have sex with anybody. But it must be really dangerous for you there in New York.' 'Well, I have to be here. I work here. I can't leave, but I'm being careful.' I said, 'This is a little crazy.' So you know what I did? I lived in an apartment in Boston with Andy Cates." Sam was sleeping on a mattress on the floor of a run-down apartment in Roxbury, a high-crime neighborhood, with an unsupervised group of teenagers. "That place was disgusting," he said. "I went to a lot of Red Sox games. I stayed away from New York for a couple of years."

Andy was already a black sheep among the Fourth Wall kids, having been told he could not return to New York, so the new edict did not affect him immediately. After his nightmarish experience at Treehaven, he had been sent to a much better school (Brewster Academy, in New Hampshire) for the last three years of high school. He had been able to make up for some of the time he'd lost at previous schools, graduating only one year later than usual despite not learning to read until age eleven. He won several prizes, and his parents, a bit unexpectedly, attended his graduation. While he was waiting to start at BU, his Boston apartment became a crash pad for several of the Fourth Wall kids who were suddenly at loose ends.

The group's AIDS rules caught up with Andy several months later in a surprising and unexpected way. When he returned to his dorm room late one night during his freshman year, he found his roommate awake, waiting for him. The young man handed Andy a letter and insisted that he read it right away. In it, his roommate explained that he was coming out as gay and felt he needed to inform Andy in case he no longer wanted them to share a room. The university would have allowed Andy to ask for a new room assignment. Andy thought it over and decided to stay. To his surprise, his decision made him a minor celebrity on campus and something of a hero in its gay community. Suddenly, Andy, who was not gay, gained a whole new raft of friends, gay and straight. Eddy visited him and was happy to see his brother, who had suffered so much during his boarding school years, having a good time, partying with friends but also studying hard.

News of Andy's living situation got back to New York, however, and he received a call from his father, who told him that he should not be sharing a room with a gay student. His father said he would pay the extra money for him to move off campus. Andy insisted it wasn't necessary. His father came up to Boston, and they took a short trip together to New Hampshire—the kind of father-son experience Andy had almost never had—but soon it was clear that his father had come to deliver another ultimatum: Andy would have to move out of his dorm or his father would cut him off financially, stop paying for his college. If he moved out, his father would pay for his schooling and his apartment. "I confronted my dad, for maybe the first time," Andy recalled. "I said, 'Dad, you know there are studies that show that you can't get AIDS except through a blood transfusion or unprotected sex.'" Hanging in the air, but left unspoken, was the fact that John Cates was a gay man, and this decree against living with a gay person was both irrational and homophobic, making the situation all the more painful and sad for both. "He looked at me and said, 'I know that's true. You're right'—a rare moment of candor—'but I have to follow the rules because I would be nothing without this group. All my friends are in this group. I can't exist without it.'" Andy moved out and got an apartment off campus. But upon disconnecting from the campus—and feeling demoralized after capitulating to an order he knew to be unjust—something in Andy broke. He began eating and drinking too much, lost interest in his schoolwork, and dropped out of college. "Andy was a mess," Sam Miller recalled. Nonetheless, the Fourth Wall kids who had nowhere else to go continued to stay at his Boston apartment during their years of banishment.

After the promulgation of the group's AIDS rules, Mike Cohen and Mike Bray were asked to travel to a conference in Indiana to raise money for one of Joan Harvey's films. One of the new rules was that members were forbidden to travel except for work. If you traveled, you were required to bring food with you, so Cohen and Bray had brought some salami in a plastic package in their suitcase. When they got to the conference, which was held in a former seminary, they placed the salami by the windowsill of their room, where it would be a bit cooler. It was late November 1983. After a long, frustrating day trying and failing to raise money, they returned to their monk's cell of a room and contemplated the prospect of a dinner consisting of salami that had spent the morning in a suitcase and the afternoon sitting on a windowsill.

"This is crazy, isn't it?" Cohen asked Bray, who agreed. Cohen then turned to Bray and said something like, "I am going take a chance and ask you if I can talk with you about things that people in the group would not want us talking about." "I'll make that vow," Bray said. The first thing they did was go to a local restaurant to eat a normal meal. "I don't think Armageddon is going to happen if we have a cheeseburger," Bray told Cohen, and they sat down and had forbidden food.

This was the "cheeseburger oath," a small act of defiance of the group's increasingly baroque food restrictions. Bray and Cohen were already close friends and had been roommates for a few years, but they had never dared to share their doubts with each other. Over dinner, the two men began to pour their hearts out about their growing unhappiness with life in the group. Above all, they talked about the increasingly unethical things they found themselves doing as therapists: breaking up couples, threatening patients with expulsion, and talking patients out of having children, persuading them to leave the professions they loved, or pressing them to get money from their families. Bray recalled their conversation: "We are perpetrators," he said to Cohen. "We're victims in one sense because we're patients, but now, as therapists, we are perpetrators. We're shoving people into the ovens because somebody told us to. We've got to figure out how to get the fuck out of here."

In their ten-plus years in the group, neither man had ever expressed their negative feelings to anyone so directly, and it all came flooding out. But leaving was not going to be simple. Both had cut off virtually all their ties with relatives and old friends. Their entire web of human connection was in the group. Both depended entirely on the group (and its leadership) for their jobs and their incomes. Neither had worked outside the group for years. Cohen had no training as a therapist except at the Sullivan Institute, which made him uncertified to practice anywhere else. Bray had a Ph.D. and a board-certified license, but leaving for him was perhaps even more complicated now that he had two small children whose mother was very much in the group. He was already afraid that if he angered the leadership, they would take the girls away from him. He and Alice had never really established a relationship. And she and Saul's son Robbie remained extremely close. "They could just decide I didn't make the bottle right or I didn't show up for whatever and say, 'He's a psychopath, we've got to get those babies away from him.' I can't tolerate that possibility." How could he leave the group and remain father to his two daughters?

Although the trip was an important turning point for both men, it was a failure in terms of raising money for Joan Harvey's film. Afterward, Mike Bray recalled Leslie F., Joan's assistant on the film, saying, "This kind of makes one wonder what kind of father you are." Bray took this to be a not-so-veiled threat: if you don't do a better job raising money, we'll take your kids away from you.

It had taken both men about ten years to realize—and to articulate—that they wanted to leave. But wanting to leave and leaving were not the same thing.

15

The Children of the Fourth Wall

By the early 1980s, the Sullivan Institute headquarters where its leaders lived was filled with kids. Pam Newton, the second of Saul Newton's children with Helen Moses, describes an almost idyllic life of noisy, chaotic fun in a household full of children, animals, and toys. Out of the thirty-odd people living in the building, eighteen or nineteen were children. There was a jungle gym in the basement, and at Christmastime there was a huge tree and a high stack of presents. Each family more or less lived on its own floor, but there were no locks and no doors, and children, adults, and pets moved constantly from room to room and floor to floor. "There were kids and pets everywhere," Pam said. A bored child looking for someone to play with had only to run up or down the stairs. "And it was very chaotic, and you couldn't count on anything being where you left it, you know, anything you put down, some other kid would grab it, a dog would eat it or whatever. It was very fluid. There were no boundaries."

The Sullivan Institute stopped urging its patients to send their kids away to boarding school after Deedee Agee lost custody of her son, Teddy, so there was a second generation of Sullivanian kids who grew up inside the Fourth Wall. Given the group's notions about the nuclear family, the presence of children represented a special problem. Although the group was against the traditional family, its leaders would have rejected the idea that they were anti-children. On the contrary, they believed they were creating an ideal world for children, full of contact with other kids and relationships with many different adults, free of the suffocating domination of their own parents. Saul Newton liked to brag that Helen and Joan were model mothers, examples for the whole community.

What was it like to grow up inside the Fourth Wall? The answer depended a lot on who your parents were and where they fit into the group's power dynamic.

In many ways, the children's life was like that of their parents but in miniature. Their care was managed mainly by babysitters who had datebooks for the children, which they were expected to keep very full. "You had to always be playing with other kids, having playdates," Pam Newton recalled. "So I was never alone. I had no privacy."

As in their parents' world, there were few boundaries. Pam's room was on a corridor, with one door opening onto the hallway and the other to another room. Sometimes, people—adults she didn't know—would walk through one of the doors trying to get to somewhere else. At a certain point Pam placed a sign on her door saying, "My room is not Grand Central Station. Please knock!" She recalled staying up late in order to have some time in which she was actually alone. As was the case with the adults, she had sleepover dates almost every night, albeit without sex. "I would say it was both fun and very chaotic, and there was this element of mandatory socialization."

The power hierarchy that existed in the group was very much present in the children's world as well. As the daughter of Saul Newton, Pam was treated "almost like royalty," she said. "But I took it for granted. We always had the nicest rooms when we went up to the workshop in the Catskills. I lived in the main house, and the Klein kids [Joan Harvey and Ralph Klein's adopted children] were in the main house," whereas her good friends "would have to be in these kind of dorm buildings or outbuildings."

Meagan Klein, one of Joan Harvey and Ralph Klein's children, recalled the mountain of presents she and her friends received at Christmas and on their birthdays. "We would receive presents from patients of our parents. Clearly, members felt that in order to stay on our parents' good side, they were compelled to give us a gift, even though they had no relationship with us whatsoever. I remember asking for a video camera and being given, the very next day, a very professional camera. And I remember not liking that, feeling no sense of fulfillment. I felt I should have had to wait. I wanted to have to earn it, the same way I wanted there to be some boundaries."

The children of Saul Newton and Joan Harvey were the only kids who did not have to be in therapy. Pam Newton said jokingly that she supposed her parents didn't want their kids being turned against them, like all the other children had been turned against their parents. "All my friends have stories about being told, 'Oh, that dream means that you hate your mother.' Only the Newton and Klein kids didn't have to do therapy, which is kind of ironic, because I probably needed it. Saul was my dad."

Being around Saul as a child was much like being around him as an adult: you were subject to sudden and unpredictable explosions of anger. "He was very remote and very scary," Pam recalled. "He yelled a lot, and you never knew what was going to set him off." When they were out at restaurants, Saul would dress down waiters, sometimes reducing them to the brink of tears. "For a little kid, he was really scary."

Nonetheless, Pam, as Saul and Helen's child, had a degree of basic security that other children in her orbit lacked. Her best friend growing up was the daughter of a single mother, someone who would have been considered a "lower-status" person in the group. The girl's mother was told in no uncertain terms that her daughter could not be with her more than one night a week. And even then, the child was, in effect, "on call." If one of the leadership kids wanted her to come over for a playdate, she would be summoned from her mother's apartment and expected to appear.

Several non-leadership kids said that they lived in fear of incurring the wrath of Newton and Harvey, who could suddenly turn on them for no obvious reason. There was something especially terrifying about being yelled at by an adult who was not your parent. Moreover, when a Sullivanian therapist screamed at you, they screamed at you the way they might have screamed at one of their adult patients, delivering one of their blistering summaries. "It wasn't just being yelled at, it was . . . a psychological teardown," one of the children said. Rather than being told not to yell or run, the children were bombarded with such terms as "murderer" and "psychopath." The therapists would ask, "Who's the instigator? Who's the ringleader?"

Cohen witnessed one of these painful scenes, in which Joan Harvey dressed down a young patient of his with a vicious tirade. "I was present when I saw Joan scream at her, give a summary about her mother . . . She said to this child, in front of other children, babysitters, 'Your mother is a fucking psychopath. That's why you can't sleep at home. You're better off here. Your mother is a witch.'" From a very young age, his young patient cannily understood the implications of the power dynamic in which she was trapped. At one point she told Cohen, "I don't have to listen to my mother, because I know it's really Saul who is going to make the decisions anyway."

Saul seemed to relish the power he enjoyed over the children. "Well, she thinks of me as her father . . . All the children think and know me as the real father, because I am the one who makes fatherly decisions," he told Cohen. "I'm the real parent, and the kids all know this."

Babysitters, afraid of upsetting the leaders, tended to favor the leaders' kids and, when there were problems, blame the non-leadership kids. The leaders' kids, in turn, were aware of the power their parents exerted and used it to intimidate their babysitters. "They would say such things to their babysitters as 'If you don't watch out, I'll tell my mother and you will be in a lot of trouble,'" Penelope Barrett recalled.

It was painfully clear to the non-leadership kids where they stood in the pecking order. One young woman recalled being asked as a child to accompany Helen Moses and her kids to a Mother's Day lunch. Overcoming her natural timidity, she asked whether her own mother might join them, and she got a decidedly icy "no." "Your mom and I aren't really friends," she recalled Moses replying. "It did not occur to Helen for a second that I might want to be with my mother on Mother's Day," she said.

Despite their countercultural leanings, parents in the group sent their kids to some of the fanciest and most expensive private schools in New York, schools that New York's wealthiest families would kill to send their children to. Pam, who went to the prestigious Dalton School, said that she was instructed in how to talk to outsiders about their unconventional homelife. "We were coached from an early age about how to present it to the outside world: 'My parents bought a building with some friends, and each family has its own floor.'"

Interestingly, one of the Sullivanian kids who had the most positive view of his experience is one who, arguably, suffered a harder fate than many others in the group. Sean Mack was taken from both his parents and raised by a group of ten adult male Fourth Wall members—not his blood relatives—to whom he became very close. While recognizing the extreme injustice of being taken from his parents, he feels he had a richer and more interesting childhood than most people. "I am sad that my mother and father were taken away from me and that I was taken away from them," he said, but added, "I do feel lucky about how I grew up. A lot of people [from the group] have a lot of anger. I don't, partially because that's how I like to approach life. But I also feel that I got the benefit of having ten really brilliant guys take care of me and bring me up. That's amazing, and that's ten times more than some people get."

In explaining his own life story, Sean insists that it's important to understand the different expectations of people committed to an alternative lifestyle. "There was an assumption of communal living, so there wasn't an assumption that there would be a mother and father," he said. His father, Jon Mack, was involved in protest movements at Berkeley in the late 1960s. "Both my parents were interested in psychology and politics and found their way into the group," he said. His mother, Teri Phillips, became a therapist in the group and decided she wanted a child, and Jon was one of the men in her life. "The reality of my conception is more that my mother decided she wanted a baby, which in the group was not looked upon highly. There was certainly a real loathing for family, so her wanting a child was outside the norm of the group at that time. My father was simply someone she was sleeping with. They didn't set out to have a family and be a married couple. She simply wanted to have a family, and he was a sperm donor."

Sean lived with his mother in an all-female group apartment during the first five years of his life, but Jon was a presence in his life from early on and was one of the people who helped take care of him, even though Sean did not know this was his father. "It wasn't until I was maybe four . . . It just became apparent—I look a lot like him—that my father was my father. And he just said, 'You know, I'm your dad.'"

Around that time, he said, the leadership decided that his mother was "unfit," and Sean was moved into a large group apartment where his father lived with about nine other men. "Shortly thereafter, my father and mother went off to Ecuador to adopt another baby, who would become my baby brother. And when they came back, around the time I was six, it was decided that my father really wasn't up to the task either. He was asked to leave that household. And from that point on, I was brought up by this group of guys, whom we affectionately referred to as 'the guys.'"

Artie Honan, the former bouncer and head of the Fourth Wall security squad who was now finishing his Ph.D. in psychology, was one of the ten guys Sean grew up with. When asked about the decision to remove Sean's father from their apartment, Honan said, "It was a miscarriage of justice. And at the time, because it happened in the context of living in the group where those kinds of things happened, I didn't think a lot about what the implications were. But when I looked back at it later, I thought, 'Wow, this was really awful.' I think the saving grace was that he was able to keep some contact with his parents . . . And it was true that we gave him a lot of attention."

Nine out of the ten guys who raised Sean had Ph.D.s, and they took their responsibilities as his caretakers very seriously. He feels he benefited from growing up in an atmosphere that challenged many of the assumptions of mainstream society. "I think there's a validity to questioning our approach to politics, to the planet, our approach to living," he said. "A lot of really awful things happen in families with quote-unquote loving parents, the car in the garage, and a picket fence."

At the same time, Sean clearly felt the impact of being taken from his parents. He initially had trouble adjusting to school, and he got into fights with other kids. "I was a mess," he said. His parents and the guys, however, made sure that he went to some of the best private schools in New York, providing him with the education for a successful career.

Even so, Sean still wonders how they could have allowed their children to be taken from them. His mother died when he was young, so he has only had a chance to have that discussion with his father. "I approached him about this and asked, 'How does a father let that happen?'" Sean said, suddenly overcome with emotion, fighting back tears and pausing awhile before continuing to speak. "He was very upset about it and is still upset about it. The one thing he said that was illuminating is that there was never an assumption that you would bring up your own child. When you have a child in this community, you are accepting that your child will be raised communally."

The communal approach to child-rearing also meant that Sean was raised with a handful of other boys his same age, including Saul Newton's first child with Helen Moses, Keith Newton, and Jesse Rice, another child who was taken from his birth mother and "given" to Marc Rice to adopt. "Keith, Jesse [Rice], and Jesse [L.] are like brothers to me. I grew up with them, and we did everything together. Every spring and winter we went on two-week skiing trips, which were wonderful. And we had so much fun at the [Catskills] workshop, which was like our summer playground."

While he loved hanging out with his best friends, he felt extremely uneasy being at the group's Ninety-First Street headquarters, where two of them lived. "Fear. It is hard to convey . . . even to bring up the level of fear that being around Ninety-First Street held for me as a child." It wasn't just the flashes of Saul Newton's violent temper when the children did something to set him off. "I look back and go, 'What was I afraid of?' But then you have the realization that this is someone who has a power to take your mother away. Like you think you're maybe intimidated by your boss, you think you're intimidated by your superior officer in the army. But this person has like the power of life and death over you."

16

Having Children in the Group

During the 1980s, managing the growing number of children as well as women keen to have children became a major challenge for the therapists. Michael Cohen faced both of these issues with one of his patients, Deedee Agee, who was already a mother of one child and by 1982 was eager to have another.

When Deedee was first assigned to Cohen in 1979, she was thirty-three years old, somewhat overweight, with a bit of a drinking problem, and was regarded by the group leadership as something of a "lost cause," perhaps because she didn't participate much in Fourth Wall activities. She was still recovering from the long, costly legal battles with her ex-husband, who had gained custody of their son, Teddy. She worked as a chef in a restaurant but took on all kinds of extra odd jobs—painting apartments and cooking for people—to pay her legal bills from the lawsuits. On weekends, when everyone else was in Amagansett, she often stayed in the city and walked other members' dogs and fed their cats to make some extra money. Cohen was friends with Deedee's sister, Andrea. The two sisters—both tall and statuesque at nearly six feet—towered over Cohen. Deedee had a pretty, roundish face and an arresting presence, like an opera singer who can dominate a stage. "She often wore long 'hippie elegant' dresses, kaftans," Michael Bray recalled. "There was something majestic about her as she moved."

If Deedee's first years in the group filled her with an exhilarating sense of liberation, the mid-1970s were dominated by the troubles that came after she sent her son to boarding school. This had precipitated the wild rescue (or kidnapping) mission that Carol Q. had participated in as well as a two-year custody battle with Bill Bollinger. Deedee's mother, Mia Agee, had testified against her at trial, arguing that Teddy would be better off with his father than with a mother who sent him to boarding school at age five and rarely ever visited him.

The judge had ruled against Deedee, offering a clear rebuke of her therapy and its child-rearing practices:

> Based on her actions and conduct, the court must conclude that plaintiff is unable to accept the role of a mother and duties of motherhood. She continually defers parental responsibilities to others through schools and camps . . . Plaintiff is still more concerned with herself, her school and her career. Undoubtedly plaintiff loves her son but spends more time with her therapist than she does with her son.

Rather than concluding that her therapist's insistence that she send her child away had cost her custody of her child, Deedee saw the trial in Sullivanian terms: her mother had betrayed her and conspired with her ex-husband to destroy her. At the same time, the court ruling had ratified that she was, in fact, a terrible, unfit mother. The justification for sending Teddy away, after all, was that she wasn't fit to raise him. The fact that the little boy was miserable and didn't want to be sent away only confirmed it: she had failed to make the arrangement work, failed to convince her five-year-old son that going away to school was for his own good. When Cohen began to see Deedee as a patient, she oscillated emotionally between feeling guilty and unworthy as a mother and wanting to regain custody of Teddy. But she wanted custody not to have him come live with her, but to send him away again to boarding school in order to be a good Sullivanian and comply with group policy.

Not having a small child at home, however, allowed her to enroll in a master of fine arts program in creative writing at Columbia. During the time Cohen was seeing her, she stopped drinking, lost weight, looked better, and worked diligently at a novel, which she completed along with her degree. A major publisher was eager to see the manuscript but decided in the end not to publish it.

Part of the therapy, however, was managing her difficult relationship with Teddy. Although the boy lived with his father, she had limited visiting rights during his vacations and the occasional weekend—far more time than her therapists thought she should be spending with him. Despite losing her child, Deedee was a true believer in the Sullivanian philosophy, and she worked incredibly hard to respect its precepts, sometimes twisting herself into knots trying somehow to minimize the time she spent with her son without entirely alienating him. She would arrange for Teddy to stay at another group member's apartment, and she looked for ways he could spend his days on playdates with other group children, when what he desperately wanted was to see his mother. Then she would be deeply hurt when he chose to spend Thanksgiving or some major holiday with his grandmother.

In the summertime Deedee had a month's visitation rights with Teddy—he would have been about eleven at this point—but she was caught in a terrible dilemma. "It was a typical Sullivanian dilemma," Cohen recalled. "The unwritten rule at that point was that kids go to camp in the summer. So here she had Teddy, and she was torn between two things—three things really. One is the group's prerequisite: send him to camp. Teddy wanted to spend the time with her. And her own conflict about wanting to send him to camp—or not. She wanted to spend time with Teddy, but she knew the group would not allow it. Teddy's desire to be with her could get her into a lot of trouble with the group. If he refused to go to camp, she would be criticized severely." Her exhusband also didn't want him to go to camp, and Deedee consulted a lawyer about trying to get a court order to make the boy go.

Teddy decided in 1980 and 1981 to spend the half summer allotted to Deedee with her mother rather than go to camp, a stinging defeat for Deedee: her son had chosen his grandmother—who had testified against her having custody of him—over herself. This would also be regarded within the group as a serious demerit on Deedee's part.

When Teddy was twelve, Deedee opened the boy's diary and found an entry that Cohen later paraphrased in court testimony based on his therapist's notes this way:

> When he was four he said his mother joined a cult, and the cult was called the Sullivanians, and it was the worst thing she could have done. He said in the diary that they believed that parents and children should see as little of each other as possible; that the person who runs this cult is Saul Newton; that Saul makes everybody work 18 hours a day and takes all their money; and everybody has to be on a schedule, and must see a shrink; and everyone in this community—he didn't say community—are basically a bunch of zombies.

Reading Teddy's diary did not change Deedee's commitment to the group, though it saddened her that the boy had such a negative view of her world and her friends. Deedee, with the help of Cohen and his supervisor, Ralph Klein, hatched a plan to get Teddy away from his father and back into boarding school. Because James Agee had attended the prestigious boarding school Phillips Exeter, they were convinced that the school might make a scholarship available to his grandson. The prospect of a scholarship at one of the country's top schools was a strong draw, particularly given that Bill Bollinger's career was floundering and he was sinking deeper into alcoholism.

Even as Deedee's relationship with Teddy seemed irretrievably damaged, in 1982 she was eager for a second chance at motherhood. Starting around the time she had entered therapy with Cohen in 1979, she began dating a man named Paul Sprecher, a highly intelligent, slightly pudgy, bespectacled schoolteacher with a scruffy beard.

Sprecher grew up in rural Wisconsin in a conservative Christian family of Pentecostals who practiced an ecstatic form of evangelical Christianity that included healing and speaking in tongues. He managed to rebel against his background by reading things that went against this belief system. At fifteen, he found a copy of *The Commu-*

nist Manifesto and felt great sympathy with its ideas. He was extremely bright and won a scholarship to Harvard, which was highly unusual for someone of his background. He felt as if he had escaped a cult. After college, he took a job teaching at a New York City private school and happened into a Sullivanian apartment by answering a "roommate wanted" ad. As a lonely newcomer to the city, he had been drawn to the friendship and community the group offered. And when he met Deedee Agee, he fell madly in love.

Deedee continued seeing other people, as the practice in the group required. In fact, for the purpose of obtaining health insurance, Deedee had even married another man in the group, Joe Grossman, whom she also sometimes dated. But when she thought of having a child, it was Paul Sprecher she wanted to have one with. As their relationship deepened, Deedee found herself chafing against the group's rules. She wanted an exclusive relationship with Paul and struggled with jealousy, at the same time being subjected to criticism from her roommates, who complained that she spent too much time with him. "She felt like she was supposed to get more men in her life," Cohen later recalled, "but she didn't want to have sex, make love with anyone but Paul . . . She was really confused."

Respecting the Sullivanian rules, she had one date a week with Paul, but now she found herself not wanting to have sex on her dates with other men, including her legal husband, Joe Grossman. "She said she couldn't stand having Joe touch her," Cohen said. "Joe and she did not see each other that frequently. And she was saying that she didn't want to be making love with anyone but Paul and finally told Joe that she didn't want to be having sex with him on dates, and that got Joe angry. She liked being with Paul as a lover because she didn't feel pressure, that she was not being used as a sex object." Both Deedee and Paul were criticized for being in a focus together.

As Sprecher later explained, "If you focus on just on one person, then you will be so deprived of all the things that other folks have to give that you'll get angry with each other and you'll turn on each other and you'll turn into your parents."

Two other women Sprecher was seeing in that period had given him "feedback"—a Sullivanian term for criticism—namely, that he was too involved with Deedee, that he didn't want to be with anyone but Deedee. It became a topic of criticism at one of Paul's house meetings, with someone asking, "What's up with you and Deedee?"

The criticism became loud and insistent enough that Deedee became angry at Paul and threatened to end their relationship if he didn't make himself more available to others. "She had heard the criticism of Paul, that . . . he wasn't spending enough social time with his roommates," Cohen recalled. "He wasn't dating enough. And she responded by telling him that he had to get his act together or she would end the relationship."

Sprecher recalled that they developed little strategies for carving out time alone together that would evade group radar. "Sometimes," he later testified, "when we were together at the workshop [in the Catskills], we would leave early on Sunday with the excuse that I needed to prepare something for my job—I had just begun a new job in consulting—and we would spend the rest of the day together. So we had those slightly surreptitious getaways."

Occasionally they managed to go away together for the weekend, just the two of them, which was risky because it meant that they were in a focus. On one of those weekends he and Deedee talked about having a child together. They both agreed and were extremely excited about it. Deedee was thirty-five, and if she was going to have another child, this was the time.

Paul was a patient of Saul Newton's, and he brought it up in his next therapy session. Somewhat to Paul's surprise, Saul said, "Why not?"

Having been given Saul's blessing, Paul was keen to have the child exclusively with Deedee, but he soon learned that was not how things were done in the group.

In testimony, Sprecher later explained the method they used: "What Helen directed everybody else to do was to have four or five other people fuck . . . As soon as we had permission, then [Deedee] immediately enlisted four other guys, including Mike Bray, to get [her] pregnant. The notion was that you have a brief fertile period of at most six or seven days . . . and what you wanted was to get the highest possible sperm count . . . So she would sleep with—have sex with—say four guys would be a good rotation. One extra, just in case. Morning and night, morning and night. And then each guy had forty-eight hours before his next performance to build up his sperm count. And this is how we conceived David."

Helen Moses, Alice D., and Ellen Barrett were all already pregnant, and Deedee was told that she needed to get pregnant quickly so that their kids could all play together. "This was presented simply as the way it was done," she later wrote. "As though the whole thing had been thought through thoroughly and tested and was now being handed down to me. This was the way to avoid the pitfalls of the nuclear family, to not fall for the romantic, sentimental notion that your children somehow 'belonged' to you. This was our Brave New World, the progressive and right way of doing things, like having an organic food co-op and not eating too much fat, like demonstrating against nuclear power plants and making sure you had a date every night and sessions twice a week." Paul didn't much like the idea, but he agreed to it.

By the summer of 1982, Deedee was pregnant. When Deedee and Paul learned that she was pregnant, they were ecstatic. They went to an anti-nuclear march the next day in Central Park and told everyone in the group their exciting news. The pair marched arm in arm, stopping occasionally to kiss and hug each other until one group member, Ellen A., confronted them in a rage. It was "sickening" she said, that they were hugging and kissing in public, signs that they were clearly in "a focus." She was also furious that Deedee and Paul hadn't told her of their "project," because she and Deedee, until then, had been good friends and she was one of Paul's weekly dates. She was obviously jealous on multiple levels. "But even that didn't put a damper on my outright joy," Deedee later wrote, "marching along with 100,000 plus other anti-nuke people, the whole city of New York it seemed, under our Fourth Wall banners in our group tee shirts and tight black jeans owning the day, owning the world."

In the three years that Mike Cohen had been treating Deedee, her status within the group had risen. She had gone from lost cause to one of the few non-therapists who had been allowed to have a child within the group. But as Cohen knew, this brought greater risks. He had heard Saul Newton's philosophy of taking away someone's child every year, and if the point was to scare every prospective parent, it had succeeded. Cohen also knew that Deedee did not have a lot of social capital within the group. Because of this, he asked that Saul act as the supervisor in the handling of Deedee's case. He felt it might buy her some protection by giving Saul an investment, along with being Paul Sprecher's analyst, in making sure that their attempt at parenthood worked out. Deedee obtained a divorce from Joe Grossman, and Paul and Deedee became legally married before their son was born.

Deedee gave birth to David on March 28, 1983, and she was thrilled with the birth and the child. Her breast milk came in without a problem, and the child was latching on and feeding well. But within a matter of days, things became more difficult. Like the great majority of newborns, David had some trouble adjusting to life outside the womb. Yet when he began waking up in the night, crying, spitting up his food, or needing to eat again a short time after a feeding, these were seen by the Sullivanian community as signs of Deedee's unfitness and malevolence as a mother. Her roommates began criticizing her for keeping her door closed when she was feeding the child and for being unable to keep him from crying. Deedee was expected to go back to work almost immediately; rather than taking an outside job, she began working as a cook in various Sullivanian apartments so that she could remain close by for breastfeeding. Within just a few weeks David was handed over to a full-time babysitter who assumed principal care of the child. The baby would now spend four or five nights a week with her and only two or three with his mother and for brief periods during the day. Deedee resented these limitations, and the babysitter began reporting back to the leadership that Deedee was an overly possessive and jealous mother—the kiss of death in Sullivania. Rachel, the babysitter, was a patient of Joan Harvey's. Meanwhile, Saul Newton was lecturing Paul Sprecher, his patient, on everything he and Deedee were doing wrong. Mike Cohen, Deedee's therapist, was in supervision with Saul Newton and passing along his instructions and criticism. "He has pains five minutes after eating," Cohen's therapy notes from his sessions with Deedee reveal. "He doesn't take in enough food from the breast, which makes him need to be with her more often, need more breast feedings." This was interpreted in Sullivanian terms as the result of Deedee's manipulating him into needing her.

"They told her that she wasn't happy breastfeeding," Cohen recalled. "They told her that she was miserable. One roommate threatened to have Deedee thrown out of their apartment if she didn't get this situation corrected . . . She had already been kicked out of an apartment, and she knew this was a real threat. She was being watched and scrutinized, and Helen and Saul were in on it . . . and she could be thrown out of this apartment."

Deedee and Cohen knew that the roommates would not be so aggressive in their criticism if they did not have the support of their therapists and the leadership. They knew they were defending the Sullivanian principle that any problem with the child was a direct reflection of the mood of the mother.

"Deedee was getting it from all sides," Cohen recalled. From her roommates, from the babysitter, from Saul Newton, from Joan Harvey, from Helen Moses (who cast herself as the group's premier expert on child-rearing), and from Cohen himself, who was passing along Newton's directives. "She was really in a desperate situation. I actually felt terrible for her at this time. The babysitter is coming in and telling her she is a shit and a violent mother and a psychopath. Rachel had said that Deedee is 'moving in too much.' This is typical Sullivanian language, which is 'You're spending too much time with the baby. You're engulfing the child.'"

The testimony Michael Cohen gave about his therapy with Deedee Agee during a later legal battle between Paul and Deedee over custody of David is based closely on the notes he took during their therapy sessions, and it provides an almost day-to-day account of her ordeal. They show a psychologically fragile woman being worked over, beaten down, and gaslighted into believing that all her maternal instincts were wrong, and even malevolent. The desire to be with him, hold him, comfort him, and feed him were all turned into signs of suffocating possessiveness. Cohen was in the ambiguous position of simultaneously trying to get Deedee to comply with the leadership's wishes and trying to protect her. He observed the gradual evolution in her thinking: "Deedee's reaction at first often was to struggle with the criticism," he recalled. "She would say things like: 'I'm angry with them,' or 'This is crazy, but maybe it's true. It's not true, but maybe it's true.'" Then gradually she would accept and internalize the most negative remarks made about her from her roommates and the community as a whole. Cohen was all too familiar with the syndrome: "Joan Harvey would call me a psychopath, and pretty soon I was calling myself a psychopath. So her reaction first was to struggle with it, and then, within a couple of weeks, I see her in a session where she is saying, 'Yes, [I am] a shitty mother. Yes, I am violent towards David. Yes, I shouldn't be with him.'"

When summer arrived, as Deedee and her family were driving up to the group's Catskill workshop, Rachel the babysitter told Deedee that David had rolled over for the first time earlier that week. Deedee was upset and angry; she realized that she saw so little of her child that she was missing—and being excluded from—important milestones in his life, learning about them only days afterward.

"Then she told me a series of events that happened to her at the workshop," Cohen said, "where roommates of hers were caring for the child on the weekend and didn't allow her to come in, even to spend ten minutes with the child or decide what clothing was appropriate for the kind of weather. She was angry about this, and she was accused by her roommates of being smothering." The morning after arriving at the workshop, Deedee woke up to the sound of David crying outside her window—he had spent the night with Rachel, the babysitter, and was desperately hungry. "I went outside in my nightgown in a fury and told

Rachel to give me the baby, took him inside and put him to my breast and then I didn't give him back to her. All day I held him against me, my roommates glaring and whispering in the distance. I tried talking to some of them, and they all told me I'd had a paranoid, psychotic break, that Rachel was doing what was necessary and that if I wasn't careful, someone else would end up being David's mother."

Her roommates called a special house meeting to discuss "Deedee's bad mood about David." Deedee told Cohen that "she was accused by Rachel in that house meeting of having a mood of horrible paranoia." One roommate of hers was sympathetic to Deedee, arguing that she "was right to want to spend ten minutes with him every once in a while."

Saul Newton, surprisingly, sided with Deedee, saying, "She's the mother, and a baby needs to know who his mother is." At the same time, he decreed that Deedee would be given a strict time limit for feeding her child, seven minutes for each breast. This set Deedee up to fail. The infant, unaware of the time limit imposed on him, would suck away, eager for food and his mother's touch, while Deedee would be looking at her watch, filled with mounting anxiety and then anger as the seven minutes drew near and the baby showed no sign of wanting to stop.

The arrangement almost seemed designed to create the Sullivanian paradigm of parenting, pitting mother against child. The child would inevitably want to prolong the pleasure, nourishment, and comfort of feeding at his mother's breast while the mother, instead of enjoying this moment of intimacy, would begin to become anxious, imagining the attacks and blame that would be directed at her if he did not meet this artificial time limit. She would actually feel all the emotions that *The Conditions of Human Growth* describes as characterizing the malevolent mother: anxiety, impatience, frustration, and anger. "She would report that she's angry at the kid if he doesn't eat in seven minutes, because he's going to get her in trouble because she didn't manage to feed him within seven minutes," Cohen wrote in his notes. She fit the standard profile of the homicidal mother in the Sullivanian worldview: the mother cannot cope with her child's needs and comes to resent and feel anger toward the child. "And David obviously suffered," Cohen noted.

Deedee understood all too well that she was one or two moves from having her child taken from her. Saul had told Cohen that she had to "shape up," get the breastfeeding to work, and submit to the babysitter's authority—or else.

Knowing this, Deedee and Paul actually discussed privately the possibility of leaving the group—a totally radical idea, especially for Deedee, who was a true believer in Sullivanian principles. Both of them had spent almost their entire adult lives in the group. But having lost one child, Deedee could not bear the thought of losing another.

In a therapy session with Cohen, when she raised the possibility of leaving, he pushed back, giving her the standard Sullivanian line that she would be unable to function outside the group. "I told her that she would end up an alcoholic like her father, she would have a premature death like her father," he later testified. "She would be a failed potential genius—her father had at least fulfilled some of his potential—she wouldn't even get that far. She would never be able to exist without the community. She would be depressed, fat, alcoholic, suicidal." (This would have been a few months before Cohen's November 1983 cheeseburger oath, in which he and Mike Bray realized that they needed to leave the group.)

Deedee found her own way out of this terrifying trap, but it took her on a path that led her deeper into the labyrinth. She went to see Saul Newton to inquire about possibly becoming trained as a therapist and to get his advice about life in general. She then went to see Saul's wife, Helen Moses, asking for advice on nursing and motherhood, playing to Moses's vanity over her status as the group's parenting expert. Thirty years later, not long before her death, in 2016, Deedee wrote to friends with remarkable candor about her experience. "I was just beside myself—I had already had my time with David greatly curtailed, and now they were saying I was spending too long nursing and should stop." After this initial meeting with Moses, Deedee asked her if she could switch to her from Michael Cohen for therapy. "Paul and I thought if I saw Helen, it would be a kind of protection for me as David's mother.

[Helen] said she didn't like me, but agreed to see me for six months 'for David's sake.' Then, I had a dream about a rocking chair that I said reminded me of a chair in her office, and my interpretation was that I saw her as my mothering mentor, and she approved of that and said I was good at interpreting dreams. It seemed she liked me better after that." In other words, Deedee did what Mike Bray had done when he went to see Saul Newton before taking on the responsibility of being a father to Alice's children: she sought protection in a powerful leader and engaged in some old-fashioned flattery.

Deedee and Paul hired a new babysitter, and most of the criticism and pressure from her roommates stopped now that she was under Helen's protection. But Deedee discovered that getting close to the leadership had its costs. During the summer of 1983, when most of the Fourth Wall was up at the workshop in the Catskills and Deedee was acting as the group's chief cook, Moses approached her about becoming the regular full-time cook for herself and Newton, as well as the other families living at Ninety-First Street. Deedee instinctively resisted the idea because her therapist would then also be her employer. "I was terrified at the thought and said no at first, that I thought it not a good idea because she was my therapist." Moses was furious at this rejection: "She said I was being contemptuous of her and Saul, that if I were going to turn down such a wonderful growth-enhancing offer of being around such alive and wonderful people, then there was no point in working with me and she'd stop being my therapist." Shaken, and realizing that an angry Helen Moses might have disastrous consequences for her and her child, Deedee took a spoon from the kitchen and drove off and bought half a gallon of Breyers ice cream. "I . . . ate the whole thing, sobbing, in the car before my anger and hurt was cooled down enough to go back and accept the job."

Not long after Deedee began cooking for the families at Ninety-First Street, Saul Newton began coming down and hanging around the kitchen. Before long he asked her for a date. She said she "felt some combination of oh-my-god-I-just-won-the-lottery and sheer terror."

Saul's aura of power and prestige in the group was such that she felt flattered, but this was the man who only recently had been threatening to take away her child. Now she was not only working for her therapist but sleeping with her therapist's husband, who happened also to be her husband's therapist as well as her own employer. Newton, who was seventy-seven at this point, exacted sexual favors from scores of women who passed through his orbit, but Deedee Agee seems to have held a particular interest for him. He soon began telling her that she was one of the three great loves of his life—the other two apparently being Joan Harvey and Helen Moses. And he insisted that she have three dates a week with him. This was highly unusual for Sullivanians, who were generally discouraged from seeing the same person more than once a week. This number was almost certainly not arrived at randomly. Saul knew that Paul Sprecher, Deedee's husband, the father of her child and Saul's patient, had two dates with her a week, and Saul wanted to be top dog. But it was almost certainly more than asserting dominance—it provided Saul with the extra pleasure of watching Paul squirm. When Paul asked Saul why he started dating Deedee, he said, "To make you change." The method for making him change included being physically affectionate with Deedee in Paul's presence.

As painful as this was, leaving the group did not feel like an option to Paul; it was virtually the only life in New York he knew. He'd moved to the city to take a teaching job in the early 1970s at Collegiate, a prestigious private school on the Upper West Side. Knowing few people in the city and suffering from loneliness, he'd rented a room in an apartment with a couple of Sullivanian patients and was delighted to find a community of friends. Not surprisingly, they encouraged him to go into therapy. "I started getting a lot of pressure from people, saying you really don't understand how to live in this scene unless you're in Sullivanian therapy. And the woman I was dating would say, 'You're not treating me very well; you probably don't understand this because you're not in therapy.'" Sprecher joined a house share in Amagansett during the summer of 1974, which solidified his sense of having landed luckily in a special community.

The turning point that got him into therapy came during the Fourth of July weekend that year, when three things happened, which his Sullivanian friends interpreted as "suicide attempts" and cries for help. The first occurred when he was driving with a group of friends and, owing to a momentary distraction, had to slam on the brakes to avoid rear-ending another car. "That was attempt number one," he said. Next, he was swimming in the ocean and got pushed out by a strong undertow. But he was in a cordoned-off part of the water and was pushed against the ropes of the authorized swimming area. "I wasn't at the time that strong a swimmer, and I . . . pulled myself in to shore on the rope. Suicide attempt number two. The third one was, I was playing Frisbee in the backyard of one of the big houses and I backed into a rosebush and lacerated my back. Not serious, but . . . Oh, my God, you're bleeding! That's attempt number three." After that, Sprecher went for a consultation with Ralph Klein, who explained to him that the tension between his Pentecostal background and his current life programmed him for self-destruction.

"Ralph [Klein] said I could be likened to a guided missile which is programmed to self-destruct if it goes off course: 'Now, obviously, you are off course because your parents wouldn't approve of what you're doing. So, of course, you're going to have some danger of destroying yourself, and you need Sullivanian therapy to keep you from destroying yourself.'"

More than most members, Sprecher also wanted the attention and approval of Saul Newton, who impressed him as a leader. While some members preferred to be left alone and avoided taking on positions of leadership in the group's plethora of committees and activities, Sprecher seemed to crave the recognition these things gave him. He fully endorsed and believed in the group's political mission: "Our job was to save the world from nuclear destruction," he later testified. "It gave meaning and purpose to our work."

And yet every time he rose to assume some position of responsibility and prestige in the group, Newton cut him back down to size. When he acted as stage manager of one of their plays, the leadership fired him just days before opening night. A few days after that, Sprecher was expelled from the policy committee—one of the group's most important functions. To his shock and humiliation, Mike Cohen read a ten-minute summary accusing Paul of hating the group's leadership (which was hardly the case). "I was so humiliated," Paul recalled. He had no idea what he did to provoke his sudden ostracism. "It was my first encounter with the practice of chopping off anyone who dared to raise their head and develop their own personal following," he said. But it seemed to have the effect of making him work harder and try to return to the leadership's good graces. After realizing that he and several other members could buy and flip their rental apartments, he had promoted the project of the group buying its own building. But on the eve of the closing, Newton kicked him off the steering committee that had arranged for the purchase. "Saul's pattern of elevating people to positions of prestige and responsibility and then rapidly demoting them was common practice in the group," Artie Honan wrote after having several similar experiences.

By insisting on becoming Deedee Agee's primary lover, Saul was taking this practice of destabilization and demotion to another level. In fact, not long after Deedee began working at Ninety-First Street, she broke off her relationship with Paul entirely. As Paul's therapist, Saul had granted him the privilege of having a child and marrying; now Saul was taking his wife away from him and limiting his access to his own child. Saul enjoyed exercising power and watching people suffer, like a cat who enjoys catching a mouse, then toying with it, letting it escape only to catch it again. "He started dating Deedee to break me . . . to drive me crazy," Sprecher later reflected.

"When David was about seven months old, Helen pushed me to break up with Paul," Deedee wrote. Raising an infant in a polygamous group was proving extremely difficult: Deedee would be nursing the baby while Paul was on a date down the hall with another woman. "[Helen] said my 'jealousy' of Paul's dates . . . showed what a toxic relationship I was in with Paul. I broke up with Paul and weaned David, losing intimate aspects of the two most important relationships I had." Why was Helen Moses doing Saul's bidding by breaking up his lover's marriage? Was she simply following the usual Sullivanian script that all marriages (except those of the leadership) were poisonous and limiting? Certainly, Helen was happy to promote Deedee's relationship with Saul; she herself seems to have had no interest in her husband at this point as a sexual partner, was involved with other men, and was happy that his attention was occupied elsewhere. Years later, Deedee wrote that Helen used her as a babysitter for Saul.

Paul Sprecher now found himself in an unbelievably painful position: he was very much in love with Deedee but had been excluded from her life. He was also greatly limited in the time he could see his son. And he had to live with the reality that his wife was carrying on an affair with his own therapist, right under his nose. In fact, for a time Saul took an empty room at the Fourth Wall building at 100th Street—the building where Paul lived—for his trysts with Deedee. When Paul talked about his jealousy during his therapy sessions with Saul, Saul told him to read Friedrich Engels on the capitalistic nature of family and insisted that Paul treated Deedee like his "broodmare."

Still, Paul did not give up, and six months after their breakup, Deedee and Paul started dating again—a move roundly disapproved of by Deedee's therapist, Helen Moses. "I felt like a relapsed addict," Deedee wrote. Being back with Paul, Deedee was filled with a desire to have another child, something she explained to Saul. "Saul told me (on a date) it was a wonderful idea, but to have it with someone other than Paul . . . I remember sobbing uncontrollably through that night, and I think in the morning he relented—not sure—maybe he just forgot about it." With Saul's blessing—or at least non-opposition—Deedee set out to convince Paul, who, already struggling to make the extra money to support one child, was worried about the financial implications of having two. He had recently left his teaching job at Collegiate and, like many in the group, was beginning work as a computer consultant.

"I pushed him hard, worried that Helen or Saul would suddenly decide I shouldn't have another child, and he agreed," Deedee wrote. They began trying. At the same time, Paul, perhaps because of all the stress he was under, seemed to enter what Deedee described as a "somewhat hypomanic state" (he was later diagnosed as mildly bipolar). At one point he started behaving strangely during a meeting of a "politics committee," a group that met to discuss works of socialist literature. "Paul kind of took over the floor with a long rant about Mao and Saul, pretty incoherent, I worried that he was crazy, as Helen had been telling me for a long time," Deedee wrote. "I talked to her about it, and she urged me to break up with him. I did, and I remember thinking I just have to give up being with someone I love but that was the sacrifice I was willing to make in order to have another child." She seems to have worried that Paul's eccentric behavior might jeopardize her prospects of having another child. Shortly afterward, she found out she was pregnant again.

Helen Moses suggested that she have an abortion. Deedee refused, and Moses didn't push the point, perhaps because of Deedee's relationship with Newton. It had, in effect, provided Deedee with some of the protection she wanted. "I couldn't afford to have the baby by myself, had to find another father, mostly to help with expenses," she wrote.

Deedee's first choice was Mike Cohen, who was a friend as well as her former therapist. She arranged to see Cohen in his office. He recalled the conversation this way:

DEEDEE: Mike, everyone knows you've been in a lot of trouble in the community . . . and you need something to get you back in. And what you need to do is have a child, and I know a woman who is probably pregnant and needs a father for the child, and you would make a great couple.

MIKE COHEN: Who is this woman?

DEEDEE: The woman is me, and you are going to be the father of my child.

MIKE COHEN: Are you pregnant?

DEEDEE: I think so. And I think the baby is Paul's. I haven't told Paul yet, but he's not going to be the father of this next child.

The timing could not have been worse for Cohen: he was finally ready to leave the group. Since summer of 1983, when Deedee had ceased being his patient, a good deal had changed in his life. After the cheeseburger oath he and Mike Bray had taken on that evening in Indiana, he'd slowly been trying to work his way out.

He had finally gotten the courage to leave therapy with Joan Harvey and had switched over to her husband, Ralph Klein. Cohen and Klein had become good friends during the many years when Cohen was a frequent guest at Ninety-First Street. Klein always seemed the most approachable, the least ideological of the Gang of Four. In private conversation, Klein spoke candidly about his frustrations with Newton and Harvey. Cohen took that as an opening for him to share his own growing doubts about the Fourth Wall and even offer proposals for reforming the group by curtailing the power of the leaders. Cohen quickly discovered that despite the appearance of openness, Klein was, at heart, a loyal soldier. Thirty years after treating Jackson Pollock, twenty years after treating Judy Collins and Jules Olitski, Klein was now sixty and not ready to risk turning his life upside down for some quixotic internal revolt. Janie P. recalled the look of terror that came over Klein's face when Newton started screaming at him over something Klein had asked Newton about: "Ralph looked like a frightened rabbit." So when Cohen began articulating his critique of the Fourth Wall, Klein became alarmed and told him he was out of line. In fact, Klein suggested that Cohen needed to change therapists and begin seeing Newton in order to straighten himself out.

Word filtered through the membership that Cohen was entertaining negative, subversive ideas and that he was now on a kind of probation. This was what Deedee Agee was referring to when she said to him, "Everyone knows you've been in a lot of trouble in the community."

In therapy with Newton, Cohen had an even closer look at the way the leadership managed the group. He saw the loose way in which the group's funds were handled, where money ostensibly raised for one purpose would be used for another. As members were working two jobs to pay for therapy, their Fourth Wall dues, and the new building, Newton suddenly bought a farm in Vermont. Everyone else was expected to live as good communists, sacrificing and pooling their resources, while Saul went off and bought a country house for himself and his family. "It was such an outrageous act," Cohen recalled. "People were really pissed off. It was one of the few times I remember dissent coming up in the group."

The leadership responded to the undercurrent of dissent in a remarkably shrewd fashion: encouraging members to perform skits in which they parodied life inside the group, often including specific roasts—sometimes quite harsh—of individual members. One group of members put on a considerably more daring satire on the lack of democracy in the group. In the skit, the leadership proposed that the group move en masse to live on a mountaintop for a year (or something like that). It was put up for a vote, and everyone raised their hand in agreement. One person voted against the motion and was then carried off the stage. Some of these skits—especially those with brutal roasts—were painful to sit through, Cohen recalled, but he saw this encouragement of satire as a brilliant mechanism for allowing the group to relieve the pressure and unhappiness that was building up within the community. It was also a subtle counter to the charge that the Fourth Wall had become a totalitarian cult: What cult would allow its members to make fun of it? Yet in the end, the skits left the leaders firmly in control.

It was clear from listening to Klein and Newton that they saw the membership as a cash cow that could be milked at will. Klein would say, "We need to raise money for Joan's film," and with a thousand-dollar assessment for each member, they could suddenly raise a quarter of a million dollars (in 1984 the equivalent of several million). Newton and the other leaders initiated a system where members would be fined for breaking some rule or other, yet very often no one knew what the rules were until someone was fined. One of Cohen's patients, John Cates, called Helen Moses at ten o'clock on a Sunday morning about a crisis one of his patients was having. He was fined two thousand dollars for calling too early on a Sunday, even though no one had ever heard of such a rule. "Newton . . . would laugh about it with me privately," Cohen said. "He said it was a great way to make income—he wouldn't say for himself personally, but for the organization." Elliot K. was on the funding committee for one of Joan Harvey's films and failed to make a phone call she considered important; he was fined a thousand dollars and kicked off the committee. Elliot, a successful graphic designer with a good income, paid the fine and told Cohen, "It's worth one thousand dollars to not work with Joan Harvey on this committee." Paul Sprecher was fined five hundred dollars for one infraction and five thousand for another. "This kind of stuff was happening all the time," Cohen said.

The punishments seemed to have no rhyme or reason, but that was actually the point, as Newton explained to Cohen in one of those moments when he enjoyed sharing his philosophy of group realpolitik. "You have to be arbitrary," Newton said. Not everyone who called headquarters before ten on a Sunday morning was going to get a two-thousand-dollar fine. "There was a quality of life in the group where you just didn't know when you were going to do the right or wrong thing," Cohen explained, "and Saul understood this very much and told me that he understood the power of his arbitrariness. If you fine one person like this once, you can keep people off base. No one really ever knows what's going to happen." And so one person who violated the food restrictions by eating something at a work reception would be fined five hundred dollars; another would be kicked out of the group; a third might not get fined at all.

In his more unguarded moments Newton was surprisingly candid with Cohen about his own deeply self-interested view of his role. "He would literally sit back with me sometimes and say, 'This is a pretty good job. I control this whole situation. I have X amount of money per patient. I get sex from patients.' He was completely aware of the whole situation."

Cohen had a ten a.m. appointment with Newton three days a week, but he frequently had to wait at least half an hour while Newton finished his nine o'clock appointment with a beautiful former model who had become a therapist and saw Newton for supervision. At a certain point Cohen asked her why their sessions took so long. "You have no idea no idea how difficult it is to get him hard," she said. In other words, Newton—at age seventy-nine, no longer able to do much else—was still demanding sex from his patients and the therapists he supervised. Moreover, *they* continued to pay *him* for his time. "He was a serial rapist," Cohen said.

The more Cohen looked at it, the whole enterprise he had joined thirteen years earlier had gone completely and irredeemably off the rails. "I joined a movement that turned into a business, that became a racket," he said. He had genuinely believed in the promise of a humanist revolution, and it had turned into the cynical and often sadistic use of power, of financial and sexual exploitation.

One of the things that confirmed his decision to leave was his deepening relationship with Amy Siskind, whom he had been dating for a few years. In typical fashion, the group disapproved when their relationship lasted and became closer. At one point Newton overheard Cohen telling Siskind, "I love you," and Newton scolded him in their session the next day. The couple were deemed to be in a focus and told to stop seeing each other. Cohen had had several close relationships with women that were broken up by his therapists over the years—including his relationship with Amy—but he was determined not to let it happen this time. He had a good friend named Linda (one of his only friends from before the group) who sometimes lent him her apartment when she was at work. He would meet Amy there for trysts. Other times, late at night, Cohen went to the office he had in the group building at 2643 Broadway, claiming he had a burst of inspiration and needed to write. He and Amy would meet up and have sex. Conducting a secret relationship—in direct violation of his therapist's orders—made them both realize that if they wanted to keep seeing each other, they would have to leave. A couple was a conspiracy of two, and Amy and Michael offered each other the moral support each needed to make a break with the only life they knew.

They had tentatively set a date about three weeks from the day Deedee Agee came to Mike Cohen and asked him to be the father of her child. He asked for some time to think it over and was hoping to stall in order to give himself the time to make the practical arrangements for leaving. Given his prominence in the group, he knew his departure would be messy and complicated. He could not simply rent a moving van, box up his belongings, and leave. He would have to go with nothing more than the clothes on his back, so he began surreptitiously moving things out of his apartment. Cohen and Mike Bray, in keeping with their cheeseburger oath, had secretly rented a storage space together, into which they began moving their stuff. Newton had said something, echoing the Khmer Rouge, about people needing to get rid of their books, so Cohen used that as a reason for moving out most of his books bit by bit. One day when someone from the group saw him moving things from his room and asked him what he was doing, Cohen suddenly blurted out, "This place is driving me crazy. I'm getting outta here!" He told the truth, but turned it into a joke that served effectively as a cover. The other person laughed and moved on. It worked like the famous "purloined letter" in the Edgar Allan Poe story: the stolen letter was sitting in plain sight on the thief's desk, where no one bothered to look.

Meanwhile, Saul Newton began to apply pressure on Cohen to agree to Deedee's request. "Think of me as the chief rebbe of a European village and this as an arranged marriage," Saul told him, invoking their common Eastern European Jewish roots. When that didn't work, Saul turned threatening. "If you don't have this child, I will take that as a sign that you are not committed to growth, and I'm not going to train any therapist who is not committed to growth, so I'll throw you out of the community." At another point Saul even tried to hit Cohen, but Saul was by now a rather feeble old man, and Mike easily parried the blow. At the same time, Saul declared that Deedee was "the third best mother in the Sullivanian community"—his latest wives, Joan and Helen, were the best two—"and that it would be an honor for me to be the father of this child." Mike demurred, trying to buy a little time.

On the morning of March 17, 1985, Mike Cohen left the group apartment building at 2643 Broadway, never to return. He had arranged to go to the apartment of his friend Linda, who lived several blocks away. She kindly offered him a place to stay for the first days after he left the group. He walked down to her apartment and began to call his patients, explaining that he had left. He also called Deedee and explained that he would not be able to be the father to her child.

Within a couple of hours of his departure, he looked down on the street and noticed a group of guys from the Fourth Wall security detail staking out the apartment, waiting for him. As very few people knew about Linda, who had no connection to the Fourth Wall, someone—obviously a close friend—had volunteered her name or had been persuaded to do so. Now other members, some of them friends, were tracking him down like a wanted fugitive. That was one of the worst things about the Fourth Wall, Cohen thought: it made everyone an accomplice. They induced you to inform on or conduct surveillance of your friends, which served a double function. It provided leadership with a private army and intelligence service, but it also implicated ordinary members in the system of control, giving them a psychological stake in maintaining it. It was harder to criticize the leadership's crueler actions when you yourself had blood on your hands.

Then the phone rang. Startled, he let the call bounce to the answering machine and then heard Saul Newton's voice. Cohen picked up but let the answering machine continue to record. He heard Newton say,

> You cannot do this to me, nobody can do this to me. Not you in your arrogance, not the mayor, Mayor Koch, not Hitler. It cannot be done to me. I will find you. Believe me. If I have to go to the work of mobilizing two hundred people to find you, believe me, I will find you. That will not be fun for anybody.

Cohen then asked Newton, "Are you threatening me?"

> God, am I threatening. I want you here. No, that's a threat [inaudible] son of a bitch. God, this is war and you will do what I tell you or you will have a war on your hands.

Worried that the people downstairs might hassle or threaten his friend Linda, Mike decided to go back to see Saul. Amy was with him.

The surveillance group would go away when he himself went uptown to the group's headquarters, allowing Amy to slip away unnoticed. All her stuff was back at her apartment. Her plan was to wait about ten days after Cohen's departure and then leave with a good friend of hers. She did not want to leave as half of a couple and have her departure trivialized as a romantic drama. She wanted her defection to be understood as a political statement. Meanwhile, Cohen walked to Ninety-First Street and talked to Newton for about two hours. Newton tried to convince him to stay, insisting that he was under a lot of stress and the stress of the group could sometimes get to him. He gave Mike two Seconals and a Valium and urged him to take them and sleep it off. Mike pretended to agree while thinking of another plan. He stayed in a hotel for the next three nights.

Amy Siskind and her friend left about ten days later. When they told their roommates on the fourth floor of 2643 Broadway that they were leaving the group, the other roommates retreated to one of the bedrooms in the apartment to consult in private and then phoned the leaders at Ninety-First Street. When they emerged, they told Amy and her friend that they must leave immediately. The two defectors refused, saying that they had arranged for a moving van to come the next day and they needed the evening to pack up their things and would be gone by morning. When they got ready to leave, one of Amy's roommates called the two women "whores for Mike Cohen." Amy lunged at the woman who had insulted her, and they began to fight. "It's a good thing someone broke it up—she was much stronger than I was!" Amy recalled.

After learning that Mike Cohen would not be available to father her child, Deedee Agee had to find another father. Helen Moses took out her list of Fourth Wall members and came up with an alternative, a man named Bob M., who happened to be gay. After Deedee asked him to be father to her child, he hesitated. He went to see his longtime therapist, Joan Harvey, who evidently didn't know that this whole scenario had been carefully orchestrated by Helen and Saul. She advised him against the idea, so he declined Deedee's offer. "Saul flew into a rage," Deedee

Agee wrote. "He phoned Joan, told her I was pregnant and that she better tell Bob M. to have a child with me or he would throw her film editing machine out on the street and her with it. I was astounded. Later that day, Bob M. came back and said he'd reconsidered."

Initially, Deedee told Bob that she had tried to get pregnant with Paul but wasn't sure she was pregnant. He seemed bothered by the possibility that she might already be pregnant by someone else, so, following Helen's advice, she lied and said she wasn't pregnant. She and Bob then slept together. About ten days later Deedee told someone she was pregnant. Word spread quickly through the village-like community. Paul Sprecher was sitting at the security desk in the lobby of the Ninety-First Street headquarters when someone came along and said, "Hey, did you hear? Deedee's having a baby with Bob M.!" One can only imagine his state of mind. Here he was, providing unpaid guard duty to protect the home of Saul Newton and the other therapists who had taken his wife from him. Now he learns that they have taken his child from him, arranging for his wife to marry someone else who will now become father to Paul's child. As Deedee wrote years later, "Trapped on the desk, in turmoil, he finally called Marc Rice (one of the senior therapists living at Ninety-First Street) to have someone to talk to. Marc instructed him, 'Dissociate, dissociate'" (a psychological term meaning to detach one's feelings from one's thoughts).

17

The Defectors

About a week after his friend Mike Cohen left the group, Michael Bray ran into another therapist, Ellen Barrett. The departure of the former heir apparent was very much on her mind. She stuck out her hand and said, "Well, congratulations, we got rid of the bastard." Bray stood there, paralyzed. He knew the prudent thing was to take her hand and nod in agreement. "I said to myself, 'Put out your fucking hand,' but I couldn't do it." Because of Cohen's former prominence in the group as a close disciple of Saul Newton's, members began to refer to him as Judas. Through his non-gesture, Bray had given himself away.

Bray was more than ready to leave and had remained secretly in touch with Cohen, but he had a wife and two children still in the group and was racking his brains as to how to get out without losing his kids. Over the past couple of years he had lost faith in the group's psychological methods and overall ideology, now seeing its extremely directive form of psychoanalysis as therapists taking over their patients' lives. He saw the training program and its supervision by the Gang of Four as a surveillance system that prevented dissent and enforced conformity, and he now considered the single-sex group apartments, which had at first attracted him deeply, as a means of keeping everyone in a state of extended, permanent adolescence. He viewed the leadership at Ninety-First Street as a kind of feudal monarchy, with Saul Newton as absolute ruler surrounded by vassals, of which, he realized, he was one, and ladies-in-waiting who included Alice D. (the mother of Bray's two children) and Ellen Barrett, both of whom lived at the headquarters in positions that were simultaneously privileged and subservient. His ex-wife, Jeanner, the woman he had been married to when he entered therapy in 1973, was now a member of the royal court as well: the permanent babysitter for most of Joan Harvey's children. She had moved into the headquarters at Ninety-First Street in connection with that position. At one point Harvey had fired Jeanner because one of Harvey's adopted daughters ran to Jeanner rather than to her mother. This dismissal lasted a short while so that Harvey could reassert her primacy, but then she hired Jeanner back, as she was essential to the smooth functioning of Harvey's life.

Mike Bray had had very little contact with his ex-wife during his time in the group. But one day when he was at Ninety-First Street, to his surprise they ended up in bed together. It was something of a revelation, given their fraught, unhappy marital history. "It was a big surprise to me. When we were married, she couldn't deal with sex at all—she was so uncomfortable. But this was easy." It was as if the two of them had wanted to set something right, to part on better terms. It was the one time they slept together. At another point they had arranged to see each other one evening. Mike had been downtown taking an acting class, and he left class with a young woman to whom he had given a ride home. "She asked me up, and we were lying on her rug making out, about to have sex, when I realized that I had a date with Jeanner, so I just got up and left," Bray recalled. Interestingly, when he explained what happened to his ex-wife, she was actually mad at him, not for being late, but for not staying and having sex with the other woman. "That was what you wanted to do, and you should have done it," she said. The woman who had been a strict Catholic and had remained a virgin until marriage had clearly absorbed more of the group's philosophy than he had. "I realized I had a long way to go."

Bray had gone through his own phase of being a true believer. "There was a period of a couple of years where, if they had asked me to drink Kool-Aid, I would have merely wanted to know whether it was lemon, lime, or raspberry." But that time had passed. Bray found himself at Joan Harvey's beck and call doing things that seemed more and more irrational. "We were living in a kind of permanent emergency, but her requests were increasingly personal. I was supposed to track down her date for the night or expropriate someone's Audi to pick up chickens for their dinner."

Perhaps because they sensed some of Bray's ambivalence—and because he had a much milder and less doctrinaire approach than many other Sullivanian therapists—some of his patients felt emboldened to share their own doubts with him. "I felt like I could tell him everything, things I wouldn't have told the other therapists," Alice Gadeloff recalled. "He had a really nice, soothing voice. He didn't scream. He had a great sense of humor." At one point Alice saved up some money to make a trip to Europe—her first—and she asked Mike if she could bring him back anything. "An Alfa Romeo," he responded. When she was traveling, she saw an Alfa Romeo T-shirt and brought it for him.

Alice was a cute, petite Jewish girl with curly dark hair who (like Bray) had joined the group in the early 1970s. It had suited her in the early years to get away from an unhappy family situation, and it helped her develop a healthier and happier sex life. She had been sexually abused by her stepfather, so therapy that saw the family as toxic and dangerous made sense to her. She found a group of friends and fully accepted the idea that life in the Sullivanian community was superior to conventional arrangements. Together with Deedee Agee, she had completed a master's program in creative writing at Columbia, and they produced a group literary magazine for a while. Alice hadn't found the therapy all that helpful and had often clashed with the strictures of the Sullivanian life; she would fall in love with someone and want to spend more time with him than the group's rules permitted or encouraged. She was sometimes jealous that the main man in her life, Bill Graves, seemed to enjoy the sexual freedom of the group more than she did and had three steady girlfriends while she remained primarily focused on him. When her boss at a law firm where she worked as a legal secretary gave her a nice leather briefcase with her initials, A.G., on it, she could not help thinking that if she ever married Bill Graves, she could change her name from Gadeloff to Graves without having to change her briefcase.

Alice's early feelings of euphoria when she joined the group had begun to dissipate by the late 1970s and early '80s. Her therapist, Trudy W., one of the "training therapists," seemed to genuinely dislike Alice and to feel that her role as a therapist was to beat patients into a compliant pulp. "She told me what a terrible person I was," Alice recalled. "'You're just like your mother.' That I hated everybody, was contemptuous of everyone, a terrible teacher. Once, I was assaulted by a crazy person on the street, and she told me this guy assaulted me because he was looking for the angriest person on the street to assault." After the 1978 mass suicide of the Peoples Temple group in Jonestown, Guyana, Alice asked her therapist whether the Fourth Wall was a cult. Her therapist immediately said, "If you ever say that again, I am going to tell Saul, and you will be out of this group."

But with Mike Bray she could actually discuss the possibility of leaving and the practical problems of how she could afford to live in New York if she was not sharing an apartment with several other people, as well as the shock of being on her own after more than a decade with the Sullivanians. Then, suddenly and unexpectedly, her departure happened.

One evening in the spring of 1984, the entire membership was called to a mandatory group meeting at the theater on East Fourth Street. The gathering started at ten or eleven at night because many group members worked evenings. Saul Newton got up and announced a new series of stricter AIDS-related measures: from now on, members who worked as doctors or other medical personnel would have to move out of their apartments and live separately, owing to the possibility that they might come into contact with HIV. This would have an impact on Alice and Bill, as he was doing his medical residency. The measure did not seem in any way necessary: there were virtually no medical professionals in the United States or elsewhere who had contracted AIDS as a result of incidental contact in the workplace. The policy was put up for a vote through a show of hands. There were no secret ballots in the Fourth Wall: open votes made dissent dangerous and virtually non-existent. Alice and Bill were sitting toward the back of the theater. The burly guys in the security squad were walking the aisles. Alice immediately put up her hand along with virtually everyone else in the theater and was alarmed to see that Bill had failed to raise his hand. "It's unanimous," Saul announced. "At that point Bill said, 'You haven't asked if there's anyone opposed.'" Saul was forced to ask about opposing votes, and Bill alone raised his hand, as Alice wrote in her memoir, *Don't Tell Anyone*.

A short while later Alice was expelled from the group. Bill left of his own accord, and they moved into an apartment together. When Alice spoke to Mike Bray about her expulsion, he suspected that the leaders were using her as a way of getting rid of Bill. They did not want to expel him right after his dissenting vote—it would have seemed like obvious retaliation—but they expected that expelling her would achieve the same result: he would leave after she was kicked out. Bill and Alice married not long after, in 1986, had a child, and remained together for the next thirty-four years, until Bill's death in 2020.

The exodus from the group quickened a bit after Bill and Alice's—and especially after Mike Cohen's—departure. Among the new defectors were John O. and Ann W., another couple. They had both bought shares in the building at 2643 Broadway in 1984 and had been bitterly disappointed with the experience. Rather than its being, as they had hoped, a step toward independence and homeownership, it felt like a step backward to something more like a college dorm. Ann had made arrangements to live in an apartment with a group of eight women, only to discover that without consulting them, the leadership had added two other people. "I was hoping that finally control over our lives would be in our hands following the move into the building," she wrote. "Instead, the control and repression in my life increased." And why, at the age of thirty-two, could she not see the man she loved more than once a week?

Moreover, that man—John O., Ann's principal boyfriend—

had learned some disturbing things about the building's finances. A corporate executive with an M.B.A. in finance from Columbia, John was the building corporation's bookkeeper. The management committee, without consulting the shareholders, had loaned one hundred thousand dollars in building funds to help finance one of Joan Harvey's films. Moreover, although the members were told that they had purchased shares in a co-op, the building had never been registered as a cooperative and did not even have an official certificate of occupancy. They had never been issued ownership shares. Legally speaking, they owned nothing. They had been told that they could deduct part of their maintenance from their personal taxes, but the building had, in fact, neglected to pay its taxes. The management of the building was at best grossly negligent, at worst fraudulent.

Ann babysat frequently for a little boy in the group, Danny Mack, Sean Mack's younger brother, who had been adopted by Sean's parents, Teri Phillips and Jon Mack. During the summer of 1984, when Danny was four and a half, the little boy began to show obvious signs of terror whenever he saw Saul Newton, the father of his best friend, Michael Newton. "Danny's reaction seemed to me to be an honest mimicry of the adults around him," Ann wrote in a sworn affidavit for a 1986 lawsuit over the custody of another child. "For an entire summer, Danny was segregated from all other children in the Fourth Wall's country residence." Later that summer Danny was taken away from his mother, who was suspected of being the cause of the little boy's fears, and placed in the care of his father, who had had little to do with him for the previous three and a half years. Danny, like Sean, would be moved to a group apartment and raised by a committee of male group members. A second woman in the group, Carol Buck, had her child taken from her that summer as well. As a woman approaching her thirty-third birthday, Ann could not imagine starting a family in the group.

Ann W. left in late March 1985, and John O. announced that he was leaving not long after. Saul Newton put out the word that John, as bookkeeper, had stolen important financial documents. When he returned to the group building at 100th Street to retrieve his things, he was stopped by four men from the group, pushed up against the wall, and told that he couldn't enter the building. Privately, Saul Newton told Mike Bray, "We know O. . . . didn't take anything."

Just days before Mike Cohen left the group in mid-March 1985, a forty-one-year-old group member named Marice Pappo gave birth to a baby girl named Jessica. She had wanted a child for some time, but the opportunity hadn't presented itself seriously until she began dating Chris H., a dashing young doctor who was five years younger. Tall and athletic, with classic, preppy good looks, Chris was from a well-to-do San Francisco family and had gone to Harvard and the London School of Economics before going to medical school and specializing in nephrology. In a community that had quite a few more women than men and that no longer permitted people to date outside the group, Chris was in high demand, considered quite a catch by the women. Marice was a pretty, petite blonde with a cute snub nose, a slender figure, a sharp intellect, and a heavy Long Island accent. She had written an interesting dissertation on women's fear of success in the early 1970s, when work on the psychological barriers for women was still in its infancy.

Marice had never sought to win a place in the group hierarchy. Rather than becoming a training analyst at the Sullivan Institute, she was pursuing a Ph.D. in psychology at Columbia when she entered therapy with Joan Harvey in 1969. She worked initially as a staff psychologist at a Bronx hospital, although she later shifted into private practice, seeing patients under supervision of the Sullivan Institute. Joan Harvey had brought her into her sphere, using Marice as a frequent babysitter for her children for a number of years. "She wanted me, until she didn't," she recalled. Marice had a long, close romantic relationship with Mike Cohen during the 1970s. Their common therapist, Joan Harvey, felt they were "too exclusive," so Cohen broke it off. "I was devastated," Marice said. "Mike is the one guy in the group, before Chris, I would have married." By the early 1980s she was no longer among Joan Harvey's favored few—Harvey had dropped her as a patient. Then the leadership began to undermine her as a therapist. They made her taperecord her sessions and told her that she was not good at her job. They placed her under the supervision of a younger colleague, Ellen Barrett, who had not finished college, while Pappo had a Ph.D. Then they took away her patients and convinced her, along with nearly half of the Fourth Wall membership, to go into computer programming. This was extremely painful and humiliating. But Marice had begun seeing Chris H., and their relationship kept her tied to the group.

They both dated other people, as was obligatory, but they each considered the other to be the main person in their life. And when they decided to have a child in 1985, they both very much wanted it to be their child together. Marice had enough independence of spirit that as she and Chris went ahead with the pregnancy, she never discussed it with Ralph Klein, her therapist. Saul Newton, who was Chris H.'s therapist, made his own displeasure clear. "We went ahead even though they told us it was a bad idea," Chris said. "I didn't ask [whether we could], but Saul made it clear he thought it was a bad idea." They may have hesitated to interfere with Chris's plans because he had a high standing in the group. Helen Moses used Chris as one of her experts in establishing the group's medical policies, and she also wanted him in the stable of men who graced her bedroom.

Marice gave birth without a hitch, and their daughter, Jessica, began breastfeeding without any difficulty. Marice loved breastfeeding and being at home with her baby, but her roommates began criticizing her almost immediately: she breastfed too much; she preferred to feed the baby in her own room rather than in the common area of the apartment; the baby preferred being with Marice to being with other people. They began pressuring her to go back to work. It was like a repeat of what happened to Deedee Agee. Marice knew that a lot of this was coming from Saul Newton. One of the most vocal critics was Deedee herself, who was Saul's main date in this period. And Marice was also hearing it from Chris, who still saw Saul for therapy three times a week. She reluctantly agreed to go back to work half-time after only four weeks, working from nine in the morning until one in the afternoon. But this created new problems and exposed her to new criticism.

She fed Jessica before going to work and then raced home to see her at two p.m. The leadership selected a babysitter for Jessica—Marice and Chris had no say in the matter—a single man who had never taken care of a newborn and who acknowledged that he felt uncomfortable feeding her. Jessica hardly drank from the bottle and waited to breast-feed when Marice got home, crying often in the meanwhile. "My room-mates and Saul said it was my wish that she not take the bottle, and it was proof of my possessiveness," Marice said. She didn't much like the babysitter, who didn't seem to know what he was doing, and at one point she heard him tell the baby, "It's all right, Jessica, you don't need your mommy; you and I will get through this together." Marice was outraged and told her roommate, Deedee Agee. Deedee immediately called Saul Newton and then returned with his verdict: "Saul said I was driving the babysitter crazy and should not stay on my own floor when I wasn't breastfeeding," Marice recalled.

It is remarkable that Deedee Agee, who had been harassed and bul-lied when she was breastfeeding her son David only three years ear-lier, chose to join the chorus criticizing Marice and trying to limit her time with her daughter. It was a classic case of the victim "identifying with the aggressor," as Sándor Ferenczi put it in his pioneering essay on sexual abuse, "The Confusion of Tongues." Perhaps because Deedee had been allowed to keep her child by submitting to the leadership, she thought this was best for Marice. Or perhaps the only way she could justify the pain she had suffered—to rationalize the cruelty she had tolerated—was to come around to the view that her tormentors had been right all along. Deedee's friend Mike Bray, who had helped her get pregnant with David, was dismayed by her transformation. "She had become a mindless follower, a lieutenant," he said. She served on a new politics committee that strived to introduce members to the classics of the Chinese Revolution of 1949—and to enforce political orthodoxy in the group. The politics committee also undertook a brief campaign to combat "male chauvinism." Because the group now had more women than men, some women were complaining that their sexual needs were not being met. They complained that there had been a kind of unspoken assumption that women were supposed to agree to have sex when asked; now they wanted men to live by the same rule. While Marice was being told by her therapist and others that she was too possessive, Chris was being told far worse things: various women in the group were conducting a kind of whisper campaign against Marice, saying she was drinking alcohol and doing drugs while breastfeeding. "I didn't know what to make of it," Chris said, but he was hearing it from so many directions that he had to assume it must have some basis in fact. Moreover, his analyst, Saul Newton, the great authority figure in his life, appeared convinced that the nasty rumors were true. At the same time, Chris said he didn't dare bring it up with Marice: "It's one of those things where the innuendo is so bad that you would be insulting the person to bring it up and say, 'Are you doing drugs? Why are you drinking when you're breastfeeding?'"

Only two and a half months after Jessica's birth, Marice got a phone call at work; it was Helen Moses, telling her that she was to stop breastfeeding—immediately. In desperation, Marice asked for more time, but Helen told her that it was best if they made Jessica do a "cold turkey" weaning. And if Marice cared about what was best for Jessica, she would comply. She was told that she would be limited to twenty minutes a day in Jessica's company. If Jessica smelled Marice, they said, she would refuse to eat from the bottle.

In a panic, Marice rushed home after work to discover that not only had Jessica's crib been removed from her room, but Marice herself had been moved out of her second-floor apartment—the apartment where mothers and their babies generally lived—and given a room on the fourth floor. Meanwhile, Jessica and her things had been taken up to the large duplex apartment where Chris lived with roughly thirty-five other men on the top two floors of the building. A woman named Helen Kirby, who did a lot of babysitting for the leadership at Ninety-First Street, would now be taking care of Jessica. As it happened, Kirby was the person who had introduced Chris to the group. Chris had become friendly with her brother while studying at the London School of Economics, and when he moved to New York, Kirby's brother suggested that he get in touch with her. "She seduced me immediately," Chris recalled, and soon enough he was in therapy and living in a group apartment. Now, twelve years later, Kirby was his—or rather, Jessica's—babysitter, the gatekeeper charged with limiting Marice's access to her daughter.

In June 1985, only a few weeks after Marice was forced to stop breastfeeding, she was told that her twenty minutes a day with Jessica had been cut to nothing. The baby, she was told, needed more time to adjust to her new circumstances.

In the days that followed, Marice would return home from work, lock herself in her room, and weep. For fear of losing Jessica forever, she was afraid to take any action. The women living on the fourth floor called a meeting and informed Marice that if she continued to stay alone and cry, she would be thrown out of the building.

"My life became a nightmare," Marice later testified in a custody case. "Any indication of my being upset was interpreted by my analyst and the members of the cult as 'dramatic and hateful acting out.' I was told I needed 'pleasure and fun.' Jessica was living two floors away, and I couldn't see her or hold her. If I ran into her by accident, the babysitter, Helen Kirby, would clutch her and turn and run in the other direction."

Initially, Ralph Klein told Marice that she was too possessive and she needed to wait a month or two before resuming motherly duties. "After one month, my husband wouldn't talk to me and simply said that Jessica needed more time away from me. He said if I tried to see her, he would take her and leave the country and I would never see either one of them again." When she went to see Saul Newton, he told her that she should "take pride in giving her time without me, that she would be a better, happier person than I ever was."

Marice had to continue to find a way to hide her emotions and act "normal," as well as continue to "date"—although her husband (Chris H.) would no longer see her—in order to at least appear to accept the group's edicts. The rumor campaign and the fact that her child had suddenly been taken from her made her suspect. Even after Jessica was taken, Marice was shunned, which served to justify the leadership's actions. "I became anathema," she said. "Nobody wants to be with you or talk with you. Except for my friend Mary Siedenstrang—she was very marginal in the group—[who] stuck by me and helped me a great deal. And I had a doctor friend [in the group], Dave Phelps, who was a gay man, and we would walk up from the building at 100th Street to the Columbia University campus." Marice would pour out her heart and cry and then try to recompose herself by the time they got back to the building. "The thing was in the house that if I looked upset or something, then I wasn't happy that my baby was getting a chance at a better life."

After the first couple of months she went to see Joan Harvey to appeal for help. Instead, Harvey recommended that Marice wait till later that summer before seeing Jessica again.

*   *   *

On the evening of July 29, 1985, R.N. and Deedee Agee called a big meeting in the common space on the sixth floor of the group building at 100th Street. With thirty or forty people crowding around, they explained that it would be necessary to carry out a punitive attack on the building next door. The small building was occupied by a few recent college graduates who had been playing around on their roof with balloons filled with paint and in the process had spilled some paint on the side of the Fourth Wall's building. After being asked to remove the paint, the kids refused. They put a doll's head on a lead pipe and displayed it in their window facing the group's building, where it could be seen from one of the women's apartments. Thinking it looked like a voodoo doll, people found this a sinister and threatening gesture. The group decided to teach these kids a lesson—and put an end to this cycle of provocation. They would prevent violence through violence, carrying out a kind of raid, for which they would need about thirty men and women. Everyone would dress in a way that would make them look similar, so they would be harder to identify if someone saw them. They would go in with aluminum baseball bats, hammers, and cans of paint, smashing everything they saw, pouring paint on clothes and furniture.

They were also handing out wooden dowels—the kind of rods that the security service used when practicing *arnis*, the Filipino martial art. Should they encounter people in the building, men should not attack women. The women should attack women, Deedee explained, while demonstrating how to use the sticks to break their ribs. Deedee, who was pregnant with her third child, would not be participating directly in the attack.

When they finished their talk, one of the organizers asked the crowd, "Are you with me?" Bob Putz, who worked as a computer technician at JCPenney, listened to this presentation, muttered "This is crazy," walked out of the living room to his own room, and began to pack his bags. "I took a suitcase and put whatever I could fit into it, because I had to go to work the next day. I called up Mike Cohen [who had already left at this point], and he arranged for me to crash that night. [My wife, Pat Konecky, and I] had talked about leaving, but that was the day I left the group." Two men followed Putz into his room and tried to talk him out of it, but they did not physically try to stop him—perhaps because they were so surprised by his gesture of open dissent. Before leaving, Putz called Pat, who was on another floor in the building babysitting one of Mike Bray's twin daughters, Jackie. Pat had married Bob ostensibly so that she could get dental insurance through his job, but in truth they were very much a couple. They had already talked seriously about leaving the group, but Pat was finishing up architecture school, making money as a babysitter for different Sullivanians.

Pat couldn't join Bob that evening. She had committed to look after Jackie Bray, and she was worried about the impact of her departure on a child she had grown to love. Because babysitters generally spent more time with group children than the children spent with their own parents, the bonds between them were often very close and intense. Nonetheless, Pat knew it was time to make a break, and she began to make arrangements to leave the next day.

Artie Honan was in the group of men who were gearing up to attack the building next door, but he was conflicted, instinctively agreeing with Bob Putz. He knew that what the neighbors had done was nothing more than a harmless prank. And he knew that Saul Newton was almost certainly using this situation to keep the group on high alert, at war with the outside world. Artie had been head of the group's original security squad and had orchestrated the theater takeover, but he had eventually grown tired of being bullied and ordered around by Newton and was relieved when he was dumped as the head of security, accepting a more peripheral role in the life of the group. But he could not say no to his friends who were organizing the attack. "It wasn't right, but I still went along with [the] plan. If I pulled away from the raid . . . I would be defying Saul. I'd be putting a damper on the excitement that Frank [not his real name] had created. I'd be reprimanded, or worse, by Saul the next day."

Two women from the group were keeping watch from a bar across the street, and they phoned when they saw the kids who lived next door leave their building. The squad from the Fourth Wall snuck down the back alley and used a crowbar to open an outside door to the building. Someone handed Artie a sledgehammer, saying, "You can use this better than me." As one of the biggest and strongest men in the group, Artie was among the few who could comfortably wield a sledgehammer. People began smashing dishes, knocking over furniture, taking baseball bats to the television set, the sinks, and the toilets. Artie trained his sledgehammer on a thick butcher-block table in the kitchen, delivering heavy blow after blow. He recalled, "I felt like I was not myself; like a strange rage had taken hold of me." On the one hand, he reveled in his own power: "I'm still king of the hill . . . the only guy who can wield a sledgehammer like this." Yet he realized that he was venting a powerful rage that had nothing to do with the young men who lived in this building.

Mike Bray had listened to the plan of attack, but as the father of two small children, he had taken the role of lookout. The whole thing seemed wildly reckless and dangerous to him: What would happen if police came upon a group of thirty people wielding weapons? Someone might get shot. He and Deedee Agee watched and listened. "We could see them across the street. They went in with baseball bats, fifteen to twenty men, breaking stuff. The noise was huge. They broke their toilet; they broke down walls. It was alarmingly loud. We looked at each other and said, 'This is not good.'"

Years later, in a short fragment Deedee wrote to her sons, she wondered why she had gone along with something that at some level she knew was totally wrong. She wondered why Bob Putz was able to say no and just leave. "Did he have parents to turn to, a place to sleep? Did he believe he would survive outside the group, know that he wouldn't go crazy and kill himself, as the therapists never tired of telling us we would? . . . What made the rest of us unable to do so? . . . I'd not seen my mother in fifteen years, except for her coming to testify against me in a custody case. No money, no job outside the group . . . Still, you must wonder how . . . I, your own mother, ended up in that dark window that night, my mind and heart so not my own."

Deedee's former husband, Paul Sprecher, was in the building, but he begged off participating in the raid. A friend of his was babysitting for his son David, and Paul told him that he couldn't afford to get arrested; there would be no one to take care of his child. He could not help thinking that part of Saul's strategy with this raid was to increase the members' legal vulnerability and bind them more completely to the leadership. They were doing something that risked their getting thrown in jail—or worse.

When the men participating in the raid heard police sirens, they ran back to their own building and set up a security detail to guard the lobby the next day. When one of the young men from next door came over to protest what had happened, one of the men from the group pulled him into the lobby and hit the boy so hard he broke his own wrist. Violence was becoming more and more frequent in the group. The men who beat up the boy were among Bray's patients.

Fortunately for the Fourth Wall, the father of one of the boys who lived next door came over and negotiated a kind of "truce" to this strange feud, agreeing not to press charges in exchange for peace.

Pat Konecky arranged for a mover to take her things from her apartment. Her roommates were alarmed and called her therapist, who happened to be Mike Bray. "He met me in the lobby of the building, and we just went for a walk," Pat said. Bray did not try to talk her out of leaving but instead explained that he was hoping to leave soon and that she would get to see Jackie again. "He knew I was really upset about leaving Jackie—that was very painful for me. But he reassured me that as soon as they could work it out, he was going to be out, and I'd get to see her again."

Bob Putz called his son John, who was still away at boarding school, to tell him that he and Pat had left the group. "It's about time," said John, now seventeen. Bob said, "He was friends with a lot of other kids in the group who had been to boarding school, and they had come to the consensus some time ago that this whole thing was insane."

Not long after the raid, Deedee saw her mother again for only the second time after entering therapy in 1971, the first since her custody trial in 1976. Mia Agee was on her deathbed and had been asking for Deedee. But Deedee wasn't sure her mother recognized her. She died soon afterward, ending any possibility of reconciliation.

*   *   *

Summer came and went, and Marice Pappo was still unable to see her daughter. The timetable for when she might see Jessica again kept changing. "I began to realize that Saul never intended to let me mother my daughter," she later said in a court filing. "I knew they systematically took babies away from the mother."

One day when she ran into Saul Newton, he turned to her and said, "You see, it's possible. It's fine." All Marice could bring herself to say was, "All is possible." She knew she needed to maintain a facade to avoid making her situation worse, but she began to suspect that nothing was going to work. "I realized that I would either kill myself or somehow get her back."

In the fall of 1985, Mike Bray's wife, Alice D., came to him with a new proposal. "Listen, we are paying a lot for private health insurance. Robbie [Newton] has health insurance with his job. If we divorce and

I marry Robbie, I'll get the insurance for me and the girls automatically." When people in the group got married, they usually had to give a totally practical reason for doing so—insurance, taxes, procreation— even when, as in the case of Robbie and Alice, the two people really wanted to be together. Bray thought a minute and said okay, as long as they shared joint custody of their girls. She agreed and in fact filed for an expedited divorce.

Unbeknownst to Alice, she had given Bray exactly what he'd hoped for: a transit visa out of the group. Secretly, he had been to see a lawyer, who advised him to leave the group and sue for divorce. But Bray worried that it might be months or years before he gained any form of custody. Now Alice had granted him joint custody without an argument. The possibility that he might leave the group had never occurred to her. Mike had a lawyer friend in the group draw up the divorce papers. Saul Newton reviewed them and agreed without any fuss. As Bray waited for the divorce to be finalized, he—in close contact with Mike Cohen—began planning his departure, quietly moving some of his stuff out. On December 10, 1985, after receiving the formal notification of his divorce, he slipped out, careful to leave the sleeve of a shirt hanging noticeably out of one of his dresser drawers so that his room still appeared to be occupied. Later that day, he called Alice from his new place to say that he had left. He explained that he intended to see the girls regularly, just as their divorce agreement stipulated. "But that was bogus," she said. Their marriage, she said, was never a real marriage, and the divorce was just a formality. "I have the papers in front of me," he said, "and they look pretty real to me." He knew he was making a kind of declaration of war.

About a week after Bray's departure, Mike Cohen attended the Christmas party of the psychology program at the Graduate Center of the City University of New York (CUNY) and was surprised to see two members of the Fourth Wall there. Along with Cohen, these women were enrolled in the Graduate Center's Ph.D. program in psychology, but they'd avoided him like the plague after he left the group. And because of the group's AIDS and food restrictions, they had scrupulously avoided CUNY social occasions, which made their surprise appearance at the party notable. As the event broke up and he set out for home, he noticed the two women headed for a bank of pay phones.

Cohen didn't think much of it as he got on the subway at Grand Central Station and headed back to the East Village, where he was living with Amy Siskind. When he got off the train at his usual stop at Union Square, he suddenly felt the hands of two men on either side of him grabbing him firmly by each arm and lifting him off the ground. They carried him over to the side of the subway platform and dangled him for a moment over the tracks as a train moved toward the station. "If you keep up what you're doing, the next time, we'll throw you in front of a train," they said. They were both men Cohen knew from the group, one of them a former roommate, people with whom he had been on friendly terms until just a few months earlier. (The organizer of the alleged attack admits the incident happened but that its violence has been exaggerated.)

After they released him, the men ran. Cohen chased after them and then called the police, but by the time they arrived, anyone who might have seen the incident on the platform had gone. According to Cohen, this was both a retaliation and a threat prompted by his helping Mike Bray organize his departure and his legal strategy. Cohen suspected that the two women at the Christmas party had served as lookouts, phoning to let the men know when Cohen was leaving so they would know when to expect him at the Union Square subway station.

Word of the attack circulated among the group apartments on the Upper West Side. Artie Honan, still a loyal group member, felt a combination of panic and relief when he heard the news. Panic that his friend Cohen could have been hurt or killed, but relief that he was not asked to carry out the attack. "I used to be one of Saul's thugs, and I'd done some awful things to people," Honan wrote in his memoir, *How Did a Smart Guy Like Me* . . . "But I had slowly worked myself loose, even though it was at the expense of falling out of favor with him. He certainly didn't call me for those things anymore."

Honan writes that he admired Cohen's courage in leaving the group and deplored the attack against him, but it was not enough to make him want to leave:

> I was close friends with people in the Group. They weren't about to leave, and I couldn't divorce myself from them. Leaving would put an end to all of my relationships in the Group. I was forty-one, and although I had friends outside the Group, they weren't close, not people I could build a life with. And I was still convinced that I was living the best lifestyle. Neither I nor any of my friends questioned whether we'd be happier living outside the Group. We assumed we were in this together. We stayed connected without any critical evaluation of how we lived. But it wasn't just my close friends that kept me. I was attached to the Group. There were people I slept with, played music with, talked to at parties, went backpacking with, traveled with, and discussed politics with. We had an implicit understanding of each other, similar political views, and a willingness to help each other.

Honan explains well the split consciousness of many group members like himself who, at this point, distrusted and even disliked the leadership but still remained solidly in the group. Part of the secret, Honan explained, was carving out spaces of autonomy for himself and doing his best to fly under the radar:

> Like many others I had figured out how to avoid the Leadership. If I stayed, I'd have to put up with the Leadership's bullying, emotional abuse, and restrictive policies. But, like many others I had found ways to get around the Leadership by ignoring their directives. And I kept a low profile by avoiding visits to 91st Street, performing in shows that Joan didn't get too involved in, and not volunteering for any crews that brought me in contact with them.

Honan avoided the nights at the theater that were run by Joan Harvey, and he and his friends went down on Tuesday evenings for the music jam. He and other musicians from the Fourth Wall encouraged people in the audience—mostly kids from youth centers and drug rehab facilities—to write raps that his group would then perform. They played political songs from the Fourth Wall repertory, such as "War Machine" or one about Ronald Reagan called "Hitler with a Hollywood Smile." Most Fourth Wall members were now in their mid- to late thirties, clean-cut professionals working office jobs, and the jam put them in touch with young kids, most of them minority youths, and with the more fun and creative activities that had originally drawn them into the group. Joan Harvey and the other leaders never bothered to come. "I felt like one of those guys in a prison break movie who had discovered a corner of the yard that had no surveillance cameras," Honan wrote.

*   *   *

The Christmas holidays of 1985 were agony for Marice Pappo. She was no longer in touch with her family out on Long Island, and her Fourth Wall family had disintegrated. Her husband, Chris, whom she loved, would no longer see or speak with her, and he evidently considered her a mortal danger to their daughter, whom she was prevented from seeing.

   With the new year, Marice decided to make a final effort to reclaim access to Jessica. Her therapist, Ralph Klein, had seemed sympathetic to her desire to be with her daughter but had continued to push back the time when she was deemed ready, presumably after consulting with Saul Newton. At one point he suggested that she go directly to Saul and tell him what she wanted. On January 12, 1986, she phoned Newton and said she was ready to begin taking care of her daughter again. "You didn't call to ask me—you are telling me, and I won't have that!" Saul told her, screaming into the phone. "He went on to say that just because Jessica came out of my belly, that didn't make me her mother," Marice said. "He said, 'You're not her mother, you're her destroyer.' At that point I hung up the phone." Newton called back ten minutes later to inform her that she was "on probation" in the Fourth Wall because she had hung up on him, and she had three weeks to improve her attitude. "Probation in the parlance of the Fourth Wall meant that I could be thrown out of the company and, subsequently, out of my house, with virtually no notice," Marice explained.

She contacted Chris and insisted that she wanted regular access to Jessica. He again refused, declaring, "The only reason you stayed away from Jessica for the last month was out of disinterest." He again threatened Marice, telling her she better not try to see their daughter. Marice said to him, "We have a problem," to which he replied, "We don't have a problem, you have a problem." That was the end of their conversation.

Three days after her phone call with Newton, Marice went for a session with Ralph Klein. He told her he thought it best if she didn't see Jessica until the child was three years old. Marice was thunderstruck. Klein had always appeared sympathetic to her desire to be with her daughter again, insisting only that she needed some time for "growth and change." "I told him there was no way I could live in the building with Jessica two floors away and not be able to see her or talk to her for two more years," Marice said in a court filing. "He ignored what I said and reasserted himself." Marice left the session convinced she would never see or hold her daughter again.

In a therapy session eleven days later, on January 26, Klein hardened his position considerably. "I was told that he wished I had had my tubes tied rather than have a baby," Marice later testified. "He said I was a murderer, and that if I was going to take my daughter's life by wanting to be her mother, I would do better to kill myself."

At this point she decided she had to take extreme measures. During her crisis, she had gotten back in touch with Mike Cohen, who, in the 1970s, had been her closest friend (and lover) in the group before Chris. "Mike was adorable. He was smart and kind, and I could tell him everything," Marice said. Cohen recalled being initially reluctant to help. "I had spent almost a year trying to extract myself from the group," he said, "and I knew if I helped her, I would get sucked back in and probably spend the next couple of years in the legal battle that would follow." He had already been physically threatened for helping

Mike Bray leave, but given Marice's dire situation, he didn't see how he could say no. Cohen took her to see the lawyer Harold Mayerson, who offered her a piece of highly unorthodox legal advice: the best way for Marice to regain custody of her child was to literally snatch her off the street. As the child's mother, she had a right to her own child, and it would then place the onus on her husband and the group to prove that she did not. Mayerson suggested that she hire two bodyguards and a getaway car. He also arranged for Marice and the baby to stay with people he knew in Philadelphia while they were in hiding.

She confided her plan to one member of the group, her friend Mary Siedenstrang, who offered to help her. Mary agreed to meet up with Marice after she had snatched the baby and go into hiding with her.

On February 5, Marice arranged a date with a friend who was on the Fourth Wall security team. She thought it important to continue behaving like a good Fourth Wall member so as not to arouse any suspicion. She knew her date would be tired after an evening spent doing guard duty at Ninety-First Street and probably wouldn't feel like having sex. She showed him some breathing exercises that were meant to help you sleep and left him sound asleep early in the morning to join the two bodyguards in a car parked not far from the building. She wore a poncho pulled up to her chin so it would be hard for any Fourth Wall members coming out of the building to notice her as they headed off to work.

When she finally saw the babysitter Helen Kirby emerge with Jessica, Marice got out of the car and approached them. "Helen, did Saul tell you I'm going to be able to spend more time with Jessica again?" she asked. Helen looked suspicious and clutched Jessica to her breast. Marice reached for Jessica, and Helen began to call for help. They were right in front of the building. Elsie Chandler, a longtime member, came to Helen's aid. In Chandler's memory, she saw the bodyguard, a hulking man of over six feet, taking the child, and she was convinced she was helping Helen fend off an assault. "He lifted me and Helen into the air," she said. Marice, however, recalled that the bodyguard stood there uselessly until she called on him to help, allowing Marice to pry Jessica free and run to the car with the baby. "Go!" Marice yelled, but the driver sat there. "Go!" she cried. "But my man hasn't come," he replied. Marice insisted, and they sped off, picked up her friend Mary, and fled into hiding.

The taking of Jessica H. immediately created a major crisis in the group. Saul Newton insisted that several surveillance teams be formed in order to find the baby and bring her back. The leadership asked Paul Sprecher to be part of one squad. He was so downtrodden after losing Deedee and their younger son, Jamie (not his real name), that he was actually elated to be asked, seeing it as a sudden sign of favor. He recalled staking out the home of the lawyer Marshall Perlin, who was now part of Marice's legal team. He and another group member sat in a car watching Perlin's residence, as they had seen detectives do in crime movies. But all he managed to achieve in his hours of waiting was to spill coffee on himself.

Another group staked out the downtown apartment to which Mike Cohen and Amy Siskind had moved a few months after leaving the group. Since everyone in the group knew one another and often knew the make of their cars, Amy learned that her mother, Janet Siskind, had been in one of the surveillance squads. Janet had gone into therapy in 1958, when, as a young woman with two small children, she had decided to leave her marriage. In 1986, she was a professor of anthropology at Rutgers. She had been in therapy for nearly thirty years; having fully accepted a therapy that declared that blood ties were meaningless, she now regarded her daughter as a traitor.

Mike Bray had moved to an apartment on Thirtieth Street between Fifth and Madison Avenues. He had also helped Marice with her plans for snatching Jessica and going into hiding. He happened to be away on a trip when she took the child. When he returned, he went to pick up his pet poodle at a kennel, and when he opened the outside door to his building, he was shoved inside the vestibule between the outer and inner door. A second man blocked the outer door, and Bray had no time to get out his key to the inner. In the suddenness of the attack, he lost the grip on the leash, and his dog had remained outside and run off.

"The first thing that freaked me out was that my dog escaped. So I was begging him, please let me get my dog." The two men who staged the attack wore ski masks, but he recognized them both. One had been his roommate, and the other was his former patient. Both of his attackers, together with Bray, were part of the sperm pool that had helped Alice get pregnant and produce Bray's daughters. Now the one inside the vestibule, who was trained in martial arts, was kneeing Bray and knocking his head against the wall. The man outside yelled for them to get out of there, and the pair ran off. Bray got himself up and went in search of his dog. Fortunately, the dog had a leash and collar on. "Thank God somebody came walking down the street with my little poodle and said, 'This dog was running down Fifth Avenue.'"

18

The Unraveling

When hearings began in the lawsuit that Chris H. brought against Marice Pappo to regain custody of their daughter, dozens of Fourth Wall members showed up in cars, carrying walkie-talkies and cruising the courthouse. The idea was to follow Marice back to wherever she was hiding, but it was also a show of force meant to express solidarity with Chris and intimidate Marice and other former members who were her principal witnesses. The move backfired—the courthouse clerks informed the judge—and this paramilitary display of unity undermined Chris H.'s claim of being an ordinary dad trying to regain access to his baby daughter. Instead, it reinforced the perception of a cultish group whose members acted in lockstep at the direction of its leadership.

This was a sign that the group had become so insular that its members—and, above all, its leaders—had lost any feeling for how to manage relations with the outside world. It may have influenced the judge's decision that the group's philosophy and practices were reasonable grounds for assessing what was best for Jessica's well-being. The case would inevitably place the Fourth Wall on trial as Marice and her attorneys argued that it was an unfit environment in which to raise a child.

Just as Marice and Chris's case was starting, Mike Cohen's fiancée, Amy Siskind, learned that her younger brother, Paul—who was only twenty-eight—had died. He had been just a year and a half old when their mother entered therapy, and almost immediately his care was taken over by babysitters. In his early teens Paul had been sent away to an ultraprogressive boarding school, where he built a geodesic dome but got little formal education. He simply left when he was sixteen, hitchhiking across the country and into Latin America, picking up odd jobs when he needed to make money. From a very young age he had almost no contact with his mother. (Though Amy was in the Fourth Wall with their mother, she rarely saw her, except at general group events or social gatherings.) Paul had gone off to live in Israel, and he died under suspicious circumstances that were ruled a suicide. Although the reasons for any individual's suicide are often hard to gauge, Amy saw her brother as a rudderless ship who had run aground without direction or stable parenting. "He was only one and a half, very young to be spending so much time without a parent," Amy said. When she left the group, she wrote to her brother in Israel and tried to reestablish contact. Word of his death was the first news she had of him.

As Marice Pappo's custody battle was heating up, her attorney advised her to take her case to the press, arranging for her to meet with Joe Conason, a highly respected journalist with *The Village Voice*, New York's leading alt-weekly, known for having some of the best local news coverage. The *Voice* began working on a long cover article that told Marice's story, offering an overwhelmingly negative portrait of life inside the Fourth Wall. Marice and a couple of other defectors were the main sources, as people inside the group refused to talk. The story contained a sidebar outlining the group's rules, including the following:

> Do not speak with, write to, or visit your family or old friends, except to ask them for money.
> Do not sleep alone, but do not sleep with the same person more than once a week.
> Do not speak with anyone who left the group.
> Do not sleep more than five hours a night.

> Do not hesitate to give up your own career if you're asked to become a babysitter for group children.

The piece was not one hundred percent accurate. The directives the article laid out described common practices in the group that were not necessarily ironclad rules. People were discouraged from dating the same person more than once a week, but some people got around it. Members were encouraged to sleep with others, even if they weren't having sex, but it didn't mean that no one ever slept alone. There was no rule about sleeping only five hours a night, although group members were so busy, they rarely got a full night's sleep.

Nonetheless, the story blew the lid off what had been a well-kept secret: the existence of a remarkable separate community in the middle of Manhattan, in which a group of therapists regulated the most intimate aspects of their patients' lives, including dating, child-rearing, working, eating, and sleeping.

With the exception of an article published in *New York* magazine in 1975, there had been virtually nothing written about the Sullivan Institute in its twenty-nine-year history—and that earlier article had barely skimmed the surface. Marshall Perlin, who had been the group's lawyer but was now advising its dissidents, told Marice that public exposure would be a powerful weapon against the group. Perlin had become disillusioned with the Sullivanians after his son became a patient, and he had objected to the violent takeover of the theater. He resigned in 1979, when Ralph Klein asked him to represent his son Josh Klein, who was about to turn twenty-one and inherit a great deal of money from the estate of his late mother. Perlin considered it an unethical conflict of interest to represent the institute while also representing Josh, since the leadership might be tempted to dip into the younger Klein's funds (which, in fact, it did). In response to Perlin's advice, Marice gave interviews to a series of local television stations; some of them showed her playing with Jessica as well as talking about her experiences. Suddenly there were camera crews staking out the building at 100th Street as well as the Truck and Warehouse Theater downtown.

The tabloid TV stories tended to run this way:

It started out as an experiment, according to an article in *The Village Voice*, a group of people living in a commune on the Upper West Side of Manhattan were testing out alternative lifestyles. Its former members say it evolved into a bizarre love cult. Alec Roberts has more on the group, including one woman's tale of escape.

Or:

It's been called a love cult. A commune run by a psychotherapist on Manhattan's Upper West Side. Ex-members say they were forced into promiscuous sex and isolated from their families.

Eric Grunin, one of the happiest members of the Fourth Wall, a musician who loved being involved in the theater, regarded Marice's actions as deeply destructive. He recalled seeing her after she lost access to her daughter. "She was very distraught," he said. He understood the urge to kidnap her child but insisted it wasn't necessary. "Any sane lawyer would have told her: Leave and negotiate for custody . . . The more you can be friends with the kid's parent, the better for the kids. Fighting is bad for the kid, no matter what." Even after taking the extreme measure of kidnapping her own child, Grunin said, Marice could have avoided the media frenzy. "Why did there have to be a literally sensational case?" he said. "It was not necessary. The goal was to destroy the group."

Pam Newton, who was ten years old when the Pappo case broke open, recalled the way it was presented at home. "I remember my mom [Helen Moses] saying, 'Wow, Marice Pappo went nuts.' You know, she just went crazy and ran away."

The leaders began referring to the recent defectors—Mike Cohen, Mike Bray, Marice Pappo, and others—as "the contras," after the right-wing militia groups fighting the socialist Sandinista government in Nicaragua with the help of the CIA and the Reagan administration.

Camera crews showed up at the Riverside Church preschool where Karen and Jackie Bray were enrolled. "We had friends who stopped talking to us because their parents told them 'You can no longer play with those children,'" Karen Bray recalled. Their mother, Alice, switched them to another school that fall.

*   *   *

Sam Miller—one of the Sullivanian kids who had been sent away— happened to be doing an internship at *The Village Voice* when the paper was preparing its big story, "Escape from Utopia," on the Marice Pappo case and the Fourth Wall. He was a sophomore at the University of Chicago, on break between terms. Miller was extremely interested in the story and was sure he could tell the reporters a lot they weren't aware of. "They only knew the third of it," he said. But he thought he should speak to his mother first. He rarely saw her, but she was paying his college tuition. "I had a partial scholarship, but she was paying the rest," he said. "She knew that the *Voice* was working on the story, and of course they were all like, 'These are all lies and this is crazy.' And she said, 'Look, Sam, if you talk to them, I'm not paying for college. You're on your own. I'm never talking to you again. That's the end.' I was very upset because I really wanted to speak. So I went to talk to my father, and he said, 'I understand how you are feeling, but do you like where you are going to college? Do you want to go the University of Chicago or CUNY [City University of New York, a public university with much lower tuition]?' 'I like it at Chicago,' I said. And he said, "Cause I can't pay for it. And I believe her. She will stop paying and you will be on your own.'"

Sam held his tongue. "I shut my mouth and thought, I'm just going to get through college."

After that, he thought, he would be an adult, no longer dependent on his mother, and free to speak his mind. But then the next year, his junior year, as he was getting ready to come back to New York for vacation, his mother called him and said she couldn't put him up. Could he find a place to stay with friends? She had also run out of money and couldn't pay his tuition. Ironically, he had lost out both on his opportunity to talk to the *Voice* reporters and on his mother's support. "She didn't tell me. I almost got kicked out. My friend's mother had to pay for my last year of college."

When Paul Sprecher read the *Village Voice* article, it was something of a revelation—even though nothing in the article was news to him. "I really had kind of a dramatic awakening the night that the *Voice* article came out," he later testified. "I woke up the next morning with the thought that I could be free, I could have my time. The article was tilted by maybe ten percent off in exaggerating the strictness and irrationality of the AIDS rules, but clearly there was a lot of truth in it, and so I asked myself, 'Why am I sticking around here?'" After all, he had endured what must have been the worst years of his life: thrown over by the woman he loved; dumped by his therapist, who was now sleeping with his wife; excluded from the life of his own son, who was then handed over to a third man who had been given the task of being father to Paul's child.

Paul's life in the group had become a mix of humiliation and torment. Saul Newton had dropped him as a patient, and his new therapist, the training therapist Ellen Barrett, clearly disliked him and spent their sessions beating him up. When he walked down the hall to her office for their first session, he was feeling glad to have a therapist after spending two weeks in Fourth Wall limbo without one—and then Barrett yelled at him as he entered her office. "She immediately confronted me and told me that I was not to try to control her mind by humming on the way down the hall to her office. I said, 'What are you talking about?' and she said, 'You know perfectly well what you're doing—where did you learn that from? Your mother?'" And it went on from there.

Now that his ex-wife, Deedee, would no longer see him, Paul began dating F., whom he had dated earlier in their time in the group. At one point during the summer of 1985, when the group was up at the workshop in the Catskills, he and F. had taken a walk down the road, holding hands. This was seen as the unpardonable, retrograde behavior of people in a focus. One of his good friends—they'd served together on the group's politics committee—confronted him: "What are you and [F.] doing? That's disgusting, people don't do that in public anymore, who do you think you are, anyway?" In truth, Paul was trying to counter the fact that Saul Newton and Deedee Agee had been ostentatiously walking around arm in arm or holding hands. Paul wanted to respond to this by doing the same thing with another woman. It was a form of rebellion as well as a way of imitating the charismatic leader, a weakness of Paul's. "Imitating Saul was one of the worst possible offenses," he later said. "Pretending you were like Saul. That's stealing God's thunder. Saul can do whatever he damn well pleases, but you better not try to imitate him. I would imagine imitating him. I thought that was the name of the game."

Needless to say, Ellen, his therapist, confronted him: "I understand that you and F. have quite a thing going there."

Although he had agreed to participate in one of the surveillance squads after Marice Pappo seized her daughter, the *Village Voice* article made him realize that he had to find a way out. The evening after reading it, he had dinner with one of his closest friends in the group. In testimony he gave as part of the custody litigation, Paul recounted that when he said that he might have to sue for custody of his son David, his friend got up from the table and didn't speak to him for several years.

He was also concerned that the group was skidding toward increasingly reckless acts of violence. A woman in the group had suggested that she was willing to kill Michael Cohen, Michael Bray, and Marice Pappo. She told him that during her session with Joan Harvey she had said, "Listen, Joan, why don't we just get this over with: my life's not very valuable anyway; let me just kill Cohen and Bray and Marice and have done with it."

In truth, it took another sequence of bizarre events to push Paul over the edge. It began with a stormy house meeting at Paul's apartment in which he was the object of an angry summary by his roommates. His offense was not disloyalty to the group, but having rearranged some of the furniture in their common area without permission. He and a friend wanted to place the chairs to make conversation easier, but they had moved to the side some chairs that were used by the young children who lived in the apartment. An emergency house meeting was called in which Paul was pilloried as "arrogant and grandiose, murderous and psychopathic." The way he lined up the little children's high chairs, one member said, looked like a firing squad.

That this group that had set out to change the world was reduced to fighting over furniture arrangement as if it were a matter of life and death reflects a kind of "narcissism of small differences," a world that had become so insular that every trivial event was magnified into an existential drama. "[One member] was so enraged by my response that he said that if someone didn't restrain him, he would come across the room, beat the shit out of me and throw me out the window," Paul later wrote.

Paul was threatened with being expelled from the Fourth Wall. Ellen Barrett, his therapist, continued to berate him. "She said she didn't care if they threw me out or not. She suggested that I should join our enemies"—by which she meant Cohen, Bray, and Pappo.

Paul decided to prostrate himself before his roommates and beg for forgiveness. "I spoke to my house meeting from my heart and told them I wanted nothing more than to be a good member of the house and a good father. I resigned from every position of responsibility I had ever had in the house and asked never again to be trusted in any position of leadership, however small. I said that my highest hope was to learn to be a good father to my son and a good roommate with my friends. The house was pleased. 'That's what we wanted to hear,' one of them said."

Paul's account of his house meetings (which he wrote as a series of open letters a few days later) seems like a parody of the Stalin show trials of the 1930s, in which, for the greater good of the revolution, loyal Bolsheviks confessed publicly to crimes they hadn't committed. At this particular house meeting, someone noticed that Paul was secretly taping their discussion, and they became enraged. Paul insisted that he was only using the tape recorder to monitor and improve his own behavior. But he was accused of being a spy, and a group of five men took hold of him and insisted that they march over to another apartment a few blocks away, where Paul had an office, to see if he was hiding any more secret tapes. When they were out on the street, on Broadway at Ninety-Ninth Street, Paul managed to break free, taking refuge in a delicatessen. The Korean owners of the shop seemed perplexed by this Upper West Side psychodrama—it was 2:30 in the morning!—but Paul prevailed on one customer to hail him a taxi, and he managed to escape his captors. It was a Sunday night, and he had a major work deadline that week. He was afraid that if he remained in the custody of his Fourth Wall roommates, they might prevent him from going to work the next day and he would be fired from his job.

Paul was fortunate to be able to stay at an apartment his company kept for employees who needed to work around the clock on a deadline. At the end of a frantic week, he began churning out a series of letters to his friends in the Fourth Wall. He insisted that their hyperbolic tone was partly a dramatic pose. "We were a theater company," he later said in self-justification to a court-appointed psychologist. The letters suggest a man in a highly agitated—possibly manic—state of mind. Despite an intense week trying to meet an important deadline for his job, he managed to bang out some 22,115 words—thirty-nine single-spaced pages in three long letters to the Fourth Wall membership. There is a strange grandiosity to many of the passages, with such sentences as "I have the supreme advantage of combining a brilliant tactical and strategic mind which is under excellent control with a body in superb condition."

In one of these letters, he frequently compares Saul Newton to the Wizard of Oz, a small old man who manages to become an absolute ruler by hiding behind a curtain and thundering out his commands through a microphone. (The Fourth Wall had once done its own version of *The Wizard of Oz*, called *The Wizard of Wall Street*, which gave the story a strong anti-capitalist spin.)

> The wizard is a shadow. He has nothing but a very powerful amplifier to frighten children with. When the curtain comes up, you will see a frightened, enraged, impotent old man. He cannot really hurt you, any more than the Wizard of Wall Street or the Wizard of Oz.

In the letters, Paul seems to alternate between a trenchant de-nunciation of the Fourth Wall's having turned into a totalitarian cult and a desperate effort to win his way back, from threats and ex-pressions of implacable hate for Saul Newton to gestures of love and reconciliation:

Do you want to know a secret? Do you promise not to tell the wiz-ard? Do you promise not to tell your mother? I DON'T HATE SAUL. I don't hate him because I am no longer in his power. I am free. I am not in a hostile integration with Saul.

Actually, I love him. I have learned a lot from Saul, and I would love to be his friend. When he first started to drive DD and me apart by deliberately making three dates a week with her in front of me in order to provoke my jealousy, he suggested that perhaps I was jealous because I wanted half of those dates with him, and HE DID NOT LIE. I would love to be able to talk to Saul. I have been wanting to talk to Saul since he stopped seeing me, and the two times I saw him for sessions since were wonderful. He is a brilliant, charming, lively man. He taught me how to be a wizard.

In an open letter to Saul Newton, he wrote:

You know that I go for the jugular in legal fights, and that I have always won. You taught me how to do it, and I would be forced to apply what you have taught me.

You know that I have it in my power to destroy both you and the Fourth Wall, and you know that I have both the guts and the resources ENTIRELY AS A RESULT OF THE WORK OF MY OWN HANDS to do so IF I AM FORCED TO.

But I don't want war, Saul. I want peace. I want security for my-self and my boy, and for all of my friends.

you have been the finest teacher I have ever had.

We will probably lose the custody cases as well, because we ap-pear to be a cult, and we can't conceal that fact forever.

. . . In your terror, you have come to understand nothing but power.

You have been my master, Saul, and I have learned well. You once told me that the greatest pleasure a father or a teacher could have is to teach everything he knows and then to have the student or the child GO BEYOND.

You have done everything in your power to make me hate you, and I have not broken under your vicious assault on me.

Paul adopted an occasionally conciliatory tone partly because he needed to get back into his apartment and his office. At the same time, the letters reflect months of his anguished searching to make sense of what he thinks has gone wrong with the group. He had been secretly reading a book on cults, and he suddenly saw a lot that he recognized: the separation of couples and of parents and children, the insulation from the outside world, the veneration of the charismatic leader, the technique of yelling at people to throw them off-balance.

He started rereading George Orwell. "I went back to look at *Animal Farm* and found some striking parallels to the Fourth Wall—the rules which change all of the time, children (piglets, in that case) taken from their parents, a leader who seeks absolute power and doesn't follow the rules himself (Napoleon the pig as Wizard?), and another leader who was driven out and presented as the source of all evil and a sworn enemy of Animal Farm (Mike Cohen as Snowball?)."

One of Paul's open letters was a program for reform of the Fourth Wall—rather grandly titled "What Is to Be Done," echoing Lenin's famous revolutionary tract of the same name. His program includes the immediate resignation of the leadership, the abolition of the security committee, and the imposition of democratic governance.

Perhaps the most interesting document from Paul's spurt of literary creativity is one he called "Everything You Always Wanted to Know About the Fourth Wall, But Were Afraid to Ask," which includes a pitiless analysis of the group's practices. It is an appeal to the members of the Fourth Wall to take a close look in the mirror, using the format of the bestselling book *Everything You Always Wanted to Know About Sex* (*But Were Afraid to Ask)* (1969), which posed and answered a series of questions. Paul wrote:

> Is there much of anything you can decide without checking with your analyst? Would you change jobs without checking with your analyst? Would you decide which school to send your kid to?
>
> Would you decide to stop dating someone? Would you decide to drop out of a show? Would you go on a vacation? Would you decide to leave the Fourth Wall without checking with your analyst? Of course, you would decide what to eat for breakfast, and what to wear for the day, and what to do (most of the time) at work, BUT NOTICE HOW MUCH OF YOUR LIFE MUST BE CLEARED WITH YOUR ANALYST.
>
> Most likely your analyst has told you in the not too distant past that you are a hateful, psychopathic person, that you are incredibly tied to your mother, that . . . only more intensive work in therapy will help you get better.
>
> Do you want to know a secret? Do you promise not to tell Saul? You will never get better. You are not getting better.
>
> You are not growing up. You will never grow up in the Fourth Wall as constituted, because only THE LEADERSHIP is grown up.
>
> You will never get happier. You will never get less hateful. You will never get less murderous.
>
> You will never get better because you are not free to leave. You are stuck as firmly as you ever were in your home growing up, as firmly as you ever could be in a possessive marriage. You can no more defy THE LEADERSHIP than you could defy your mother.
>
> What's worse, you can't even look forward to growing up, because you should already be grown up! You cannot ever look forward to leaving, can you? EXCEPT you could be thrown out! You could be thrown out for reading this letter!

One question is repeated again and again as a kind of refrain: "Why do Saul and Joan have to yell so much?"

How often have you said, "I can't stand Saul's style?" How often have you thought, "I wish Joan wouldn't yell so much"? Do you know ANYONE who likes their style? Do you know ANYONE who doesn't wish there were less yelling? Do you know anyone who expects it to change?

Yelling is the key to keeping this place functioning the way it does. If there were no yelling, you wouldn't be off balance all of the time. You wouldn't be in a constant state of anxiety for fear of making a terrible, murderous, psychopathic mistake.

I wonder if the theater is really having much of an impact on the world. We don't seem to have very big houses . . . and we often seem to work so hard with very little result.

Why do Saul and Joan have to yell so much?

Why is everything an emergency? Must every mailing be done at the last minute?

Is all food not bought from the Co-op really poisonous?

Why do Saul and Joan have to yell so much?

Why is there so much hatefulness in the company? . . .

Why don't I feel happy?

Why am I angry so much of the time?

Why do Saul and Joan have to yell so much?

Will I be allowed to have a kid? If I have a kid, will I be able to keep him or her, or will I be "taken off" of being a parent like Terry [sic] Phillips and John [sic] Mack, **Sue H, **Carol B, or (dare I say it?) Marice Pappo?

Essentially, this was Paul Sprecher's equivalent to the protagonist in Orwell's *1984* writing "DOWN WITH BIG BROTHER."

Incredibly, after writing the first set of letters, he actually managed to go back to the Fourth Wall—partly to collect things he had left behind—but he left for good a short while later. Paul then filed a custody suit against Deedee Agee and moved into a house in Brooklyn with Mike Bray. There were three Fourth Wall custody cases working their way through the courts—Marice Pappo's, Bray's, and Paul's—all at the same time. Michael Cohen and several other recent defectors also got together to bring a lawsuit to recover the money they had invested in the building at 100th Street and Broadway. They had purchased what they'd been told were ownership shares in the building. Now that they were not living there, they simply wanted their money back.

Reflecting on how long it took him to leave the group, Paul later offered an idea from behavioral economics. "It's like the 'sunk cost fallacy,'" he wrote in a court affidavit. "Every year the cost of leaving got higher and higher because you have invested so much in it. It's like the British and the French governments putting more and more money into the Concorde because they don't want to walk away from all the money they've put into it even though it's just going to keep on losing money. Many of us had been in the group for twelve, fifteen, twenty years, by then you've sunk a lot of your life into it and you feel like what will I have left?"

Facing litigation on four fronts, the Fourth Wall was in something of a financial panic. Saul Newton speculated that the different lawsuits might end up costing a few hundred thousand dollars in legal fees. The cost would have to be borne by a diminishing number of members, as the group had suffered about twenty defections in the past year. There was talk of selling the group's summer workshop in the Catskills.

All the negative publicity generated by the *Village Voice* article and the other interviews Marice Pappo had given began to eat away at Chris H.'s confidence in his legal position. He became increasingly convinced that he was holding a losing hand. Immediately after Marice took their daughter away, he consulted an experienced divorce lawyer, who handled the initial legal work. After she got to know the case, the lawyer leveled with Chris. "If you ever want to see your kid again, you are going to have to leave this group," she told him. "And then Saul said I had to get another lawyer," Chris recalled. For a time, he was represented by Martin Stolar, the longtime lawyer for the Sullivan Institute who had once represented the Black Panthers. "Marty Stolar was clearly not my lawyer. He was the group's lawyer," Chris H. said.

In the first few months after Marice's departure, Chris behaved very much like a loyal Fourth Wall member. In almost every instance it backfired on him. When he was allowed to visit Jessica, he chose to drive down to Philadelphia with Helen Kirby, the babysitter the group had once chosen to take care of Jessica—and the person who had helped keep the baby away from Marice. This was guaranteed to enrage Marice, who would not allow Helen into her house. Chris made matters worse by bringing along a framed photograph of Jessica, Helen, and Chris together and insisted that it hang in the baby's room, as if to remind her who her *real* family was. This visit prompted the judge to issue a restraining order against anyone in the Fourth Wall (except Chris himself) from visiting or contacting the child. The judge ruled out the possibility of Jessica's coming to stay with him at the Fourth Wall building at 100th Street, citing a report by an outside psychologist, who wrote, "In my professional opinion . . . the existence of a climate of coercive persuasion and authoritarianism . . . would [make it] psychologically disastrous for this child . . . to be permitted to reenter or remain in the Sullivan Institute community."

At another point Marice discovered that Chris had brought a tape recorder to gather evidence to use in the custody battle. The judge lost his patience: "This court cannot understand how two seemingly intelligent, educated people can continue to do what they are doing to this child . . . The dispute this past weekend was precipitated by the outrageous behavior of Dr. H. . . . in carrying a tape recorder with him to his visitation."

By July 1986, just six months after the abduction, Chris began to realize that he was losing his case, and that the lawyer who told him he needed to leave the group if he wanted to see his daughter had been right.

Chris H. sent a formal resignation letter to Saul and moved to a small apartment not far from 100th Street. His departure was something of a shock to Steve Meshnick, one of the group's other medical doctors and one of Chris's closest friends. Suddenly Meshnick realized that he envied his friend. "Here was this guy going through something traumatic and heartrending, and I envied him. I realized that I had to leave, so I literally called him up at like eleven o'clock at night and said, 'Can I come stay with you?' and that's how I left the group."

Although formally resigning from the Fourth Wall had initially been a legal tactic, Chris started to see things differently as he began to live on his own and deal with his legal case. Spending more time in Philadelphia with Marice and Jessica, he could see that Marice did not have a drug or alcohol problem and was a good, loving mother.

He also learned that some of his own witnesses were saying things in pretrial hearings that he knew not to be true. Eventually, one member confided to him that she had been lying when she said she'd seen Marice abusing alcohol and using drugs. Chris did not miss being in therapy with Saul Newton, and he began to see how much being in the group had conditioned his way of seeing the world. Although he was still working in a hospital in New York, he began to feel that the center of his life was in Philadelphia, being a father to Jessica. He began to find it strange that he had actually seen Marice—this petite, pretty, and intelligent woman—as a deadly threat to their daughter, and he began to admire the courage she had shown in defying the group and standing up for herself and Jessica. Bit by bit, as they spent most weekends together looking after their daughter, they realized that they did not hate each other, once again recognizing the things that had drawn them to each other in the first place. Eventually Chris moved to Philadelphia, resumed living with Marice and Jessica, and dropped the custody battle.

The publicity generated by the Pappo case stimulated a number of parents and other relatives of group members to reach out to the lawyers involved in the various custody cases, as well as to one another. A group of relatives decided to form an organization called PACT, People

Against Cult Therapy. They gave interviews, appeared on talk shows, and handed out leaflets in front of the theater, warning people about the group. In short, they represented a serious headache for the Fourth Wall. Some had not seen their relatives in more than a decade or had heard from them only when they wanted money. Individual members whose relatives had appeared on television were particularly upset, responding with anger and threats. When Amram Nowak started giving television interviews, his daughter Mara called him and said that if he didn't stop, she would say that the reason she cut off ties with him was that he had sexually abused her as a child. He decided to ignore the threat, continuing to give interviews while adding, "She knows that if she ever wants to get out of this group, this cult, there are people who love her . . . and we would do everything possible to help her."

The parents of another Sullivanian received a phone call late one night telling them that their other daughter, who had become active and vocal in PACT, had been kidnapped. Fortunately, when they called her, they were able to reach her right away and learn that the claim was not true. But the call was intended to frighten them, which it did.

The Sprecher case was the first of the three big Fourth Wall custody cases to make it to trial. Michael Cohen, having been Deedee's therapist, was subpoenaed and served as the star witness. He testified for the better part of a week in April 1989, going through session after session from the four years Deedee was his patient to demonstrate that a parent in the Fourth Wall was not in a position to control the life of her child. Because he was not a licensed therapist, the judge ruled that he was free to speak about the content of Deedee's therapy—a credentialed psychologist would have been bound by confidentiality rules. Portions of his therapy notes were entered into the trial record.

The group was not ready to put Saul Newton on the stand—he was not well—and chose to send Ellen Barrett, hardly a senior therapist, to take his place. "Those were the two worst days of my life so far," Ellen said, "the two days I spent on the stand being grilled by the people in this fucking Sprecher-Agee case. I had no business being on the stand, especially without a lawyer. The only way I got through it was by drinking a quart of vodka in the ladies' room every morning and at lunch. It was a total nightmare."

The trial did not go well for Deedee Agee's side. It came out that she had forged a letter, purportedly written by her ex-husband, in which he recanted much of his testimony and said that he wanted to drop the custody case. She had prepared the letter in collaboration with her therapist, Helen Moses, who provided her with a copy of Paul's signature. (Writing about it years later, Deedee seemed proud of her ability to mimic her ex-husband's writing style and untroubled by her use of deception to try to win her case.)

Deedee had insisted that she and her new husband, Bob M., lived with her two sons in a traditional family setup. A great deal of trial testimony showed that they lived on different floors of the Sullivanian building on Broadway, each in their own single-sex communal apartment, and that Sullivanian parents had limited access to their own children.

In the middle of the trial, Deedee decided to settle the case, afraid that she might lose it—as well as her son David—as had happened in the custody fight for her first child, Teddy. In trying to win custody of David, Paul Sprecher was careful not to attack Deedee personally while making the case that the Fourth Wall was an unfit environment for raising children. This made it easier for them to reach a settlement of joint custody. Deedee agreed to leave the Fourth Wall and share custody of David with Paul, granting her ex-husband what he had been seeking at trial. Secretly, despite everything that happened in the previous three or four years, Paul Sprecher was hoping to win Deedee back.

*　　*　　*

The Sprecher trial, which ended with Deedee Agee agreeing to leave the group, might have seemed to the outside world like a defeat—a long, expensive, exhausting defeat. But Deedee experienced it quite differently.

In the two years before the trial, she had taken a job working with computers—the moneymaking move the group had been pushing many of its members into since the early 1980s—in order to help pay her lawyer (the group paid most of the bills). Deedee—a writer, a cook, and a woman with a strong artistic bent—initially resisted. But then she sprained her ankle and was forced to stay in bed for a week. One of her housemates, who had told her about a job teaching software programs at the United Nations, brought her a bunch of how-to books, a portable computer, and some instructional videos. He would stop by after work and help her begin to master the basics of how to operate a computer. She got the job at the UN, and though she knew little about computers, she knew something about teaching from having taught writing and composition courses. By managing to stay a few steps ahead of her students, she turned the classes into a kind of collaborative learning experience. The students liked her. She got good evaluations and gradually acquired confidence and competence, along with a genuine mastery of the software programs she was teaching. "As time went on and I became proficient . . . I found my sense of myself undergoing a change as well," she later wrote.

She was also in the world outside the group for the first time in years. She had been working around the clock in several Fourth Wall apartments—shopping, cooking, and doing dishes from morning until late in the evening, barely making ends meet. Now she was making considerably more money, working regular hours. She had an office, where she began working on a novella, and she became friendly with students and colleagues who had nothing to do with the group. "In so many ways, my life had opened up," she wrote.

At the same time—to keep legal costs down—she played an active role in preparing the legal briefs and motions for her custody battle with Paul Sprecher. Since she knew the facts much better than her lawyer did, she wrote the first drafts of the briefs and then let the lawyer add the more technical required legal points. "My lawyer, with whom I had become fast friends . . . praised my writing skills highly, not to mention my thinking—he suggested I might want to consider law school myself—and I began to believe in my own mind in a new way."

When her trial began, she took an active part in the litigation as well, furiously taking notes as she sat in the courtroom. "I saw myself as a kind of Joan of Arc figure defending the rights of people in the group to live as they chose, however unconventionally."

After each day in court, Deedee returned to her lawyer's office, pored over Cohen's testimony, and read his handwritten therapy notes recounting her time in the group and her various sexual relations. "Sitting side by side, heads bent to our task, the salacious material, the lack of sleep, all contributed to our shortly afterwards falling into each other's arms, my lawyer and I," she later wrote.

Deedee decided that she might be able to convince Paul to drop the case against her if she agreed to leave the group. This was, in fact, what Paul had been hoping for all along.

Rather than being a deflating experience, the trial—along with her experiences outside the group and falling in love with her own divorce lawyer—had convinced Deedee that she could live on her own, and now she wanted to. "During the five weeks [of the trial]," she later wrote, "I had lost thirty-five pounds and gained a whole new sense of respect for my own thinking, for myself. I had also lost respect for the wisdom of the leadership . . . In truth, the thought of moving out, of living in my own apartment with the boys, of having my life back was too exciting to pass up. Also, my lawyer and I were in love." She figured that the leadership, drained by months of legal bills, would be happy to end the litigation and let her go, as it didn't involve a defeat in court: Paul would be dropping the case.

She arranged to meet Saul Newton, Joan Harvey, Ralph Klein, and Helen Moses in Riverside Park; the leadership was nervous of being overheard or spied upon. It was a beautiful spring day, and Deedee went to the meeting feeling exhilarated. "Walking down a pathway in Riverside Park in my white espadrilles, six foot two and thin and loving it, forged in the transcendence of trouble and handling it, I presented my case to the leadership . . . I said my offer to move out would be my main bargaining chip to get Paul to drop the case. They agreed. I'd found a way to leave the group without retaliation or shunning."

Deedee realized that she had outgrown the group. "Looking back, it seems like a case of mistaken identity—my own mistaking of myself as someone too small." She thought of a science experiment she had done with her children in which you inserted a stalk of celery into a glass of water dyed red. As the dye gradually became drawn into the celery's capillary system, the dye made it possible to see the celery in much greater detail—its veins and arteries, its real nature revealed. In this case, Deedee felt that she had begun to see herself revealed in full. "It was like that, the finding of my voice."

To the chagrin of friends like Michael Bray and the relatives of group members in People Against Cult Therapy, Paul Sprecher dropped his crusade against the group as soon as Deedee agreed to leave. He moved into an apartment near hers, and when her relationship with her divorce lawyer petered out, he won her back.

Paul got back in touch with his Pentecostal family in Wisconsin, and his father greeted him and Deedee with little recrimination and much warmth. His father could not understand the complicated, tortuous journey his son had been on, but he could appreciate that Paul had ended up with an attractive and intelligent wife whom he clearly adored, along with their two children. "I now see why you needed to be in that group all those years," he said, "because it gave you Deedee."

It was not altogether a fairy-tale ending to their trials and tribulations, however. Their reconciliation posed a serious challenge to their younger son, Jamie, who had been raised believing Bob M. to be his father. Faced with evidence that he was not in fact Jamie's biological father, Bob renounced his parental rights, and Paul petitioned to be recognized as Jamie's father and have the boy's surname changed from M. to Sprecher. The child suddenly lost the father he thought he had and was forced to accept as his father a man he barely knew. It was confusing and painful, leaving him with a somewhat strained relationship with both his parents. Meanwhile, Deedee's relationship with her first son, Teddy, was damaged beyond all repair, to the detriment of both.

The Sullivanian leadership, exhausted and frightened by the custody suits and the defections, began to lighten up a bit on the restrictions it imposed on members, in particular keeping most women from having children. With so many people in the group now in their late thirties and early forties, there was a sudden flood of childbearing and adoption. One person who took advantage of this opening was Elliot K., who decided to adopt a child together with a member named Mary, to whom he was close. As critical as he had become of the leadership, he said that the nature of the group—the tolerance of unusual family structures, the fact that everyone took turns babysitting—made it possible for him, as a gay man, to have a child. "I would never have had a child without being in the group—being around other children, babysitting, and feeling like I could be a parent would never have happened for a gay man in the 1980s. Not ever. So, to me, that was incredible. There were negatives and positives to life in the group, but having a community that was there to support you when you had a baby was a big positive. Mary and I didn't live together, but we lived in the same building. There was a community of people who had adopted or had children around the same time. It was nice to have that kind of support."

He also was able to use having a child as a way of dropping out of therapy—a further sign that the leadership was losing its grip. By 1988, Saul Newton, who was Elliot's therapist, was showing clear signs of dementia. It was beginning to rankle Elliot that he was paying for sessions with a therapist who didn't seem to remember what his patient told him from one week to the next. One day, Saul fell sound asleep in the middle of a session, and Elliot just sat there waiting impatiently. Finally, Saul woke up and, with Elliot sitting right in front of him, picked up the phone, dialed Elliot's number, and began speaking into an answering machine: "Elliot, I believe we have a session right now." "He hung up, and I said, 'Saul, I'm right here.' And he got furious, and I said, 'Don't even try to be fucking angry with me. You didn't even know I was in the fucking room, and I paid you eighty dollars for this hour.' And the next session, I decided I was dropping out of therapy. I knew exactly how to manipulate it." He explained that he couldn't afford therapy while supporting a child. Given how seriously Saul took parents' financial responsibility toward their children, Elliot knew that he would agree. And so Elliot K. dropped out of therapy, and no one seemed to notice. He remained in the group, living at 2643 Broadway for the next three years (until the institute dissolved, in 1991) without being in therapy—which never would have been tolerated in an earlier period.

Discipline was clearly breaking down. Penelope Barrett moved into the room of the main man she was dating—in total disregard of the group's usual rules. They talked about having a child together and moving out.

As Saul Newton's mental condition deteriorated, his already pronounced tendency toward sexual predation became even more out of control. He had always demanded sexual favors from his clients and from the female therapists he supervised. But now his demands increased as his sexual and mental powers decreased. "He was a sexual monster, and his preference was not intercourse, it was constant blow jobs all the time," said one female member who suffered frequent abuse at his hands.

Another female group member told the chilling story of how Newton forced her to move out of her apartment when she was six months pregnant. The physical and psychological stress of moving under duress caused her to deliver prematurely and nearly lose the baby, who weighed only 4.5 pounds at birth. Almost as soon as she came home from the hospital, when she returned to therapy—leaving the newborn with a sitter—Newton made her perform oral sex on him. Instead of reaching orgasm, he shat in his pants. After that, she made sure to bring her infant with her to her therapy sessions so that Saul would leave her alone.

His wife, Helen Moses, evidently no longer interested in performing her "conjugal duties," would frequently call various women in the group and get them to come spend the night with Saul. One of them was Janie P., who agreed on several occasions. "Helen was procuring women to sleep with him," Janie recalled. "He was in his eighties at this point. I would go over there and get into bed with him, and he would want to have sex all night, except he couldn't really do it, and I didn't get any sleep. I started saying, 'No, I'm busy,' but I did have a few dates with him, and it was horrible."

In Newton's last years, the age range of women he assaulted grew. One young woman recalled him molesting her when she was only eleven, which would have been in 1986, before his dementia was fully evident. She had always been afraid of Saul, finding him creepy and unsafe. "He would French kiss you when he said good night—I mean he was like a million years old—and he would put his tongue in your mouth and you would just be kind of like frozen. One day, when I was maybe eleven and had just started wearing a bra, he noticed my bra strap. We were in [Pam Newton's] little brother's room, and he was sitting on a bed and pulled me in between his legs and then felt me up for some indeterminate period of time—and it hurt. Then Toni [Klein, one of Joan Harvey and Ralph Klein's children] came in and said, 'Want to play?' And I said, 'Yeah!' And ran off, saying, 'Bye, Saul.'"

At a certain point, when Saul's dementia became more evident and his behavior even more extreme and violent, Helen Moses and Joan Harvey decided that he had to go. What was most striking to Esther Newton, Saul's oldest child, was how, almost from one day to the next, this man who had been revered and feared suddenly became nothing. "[Helen] just dropped him, from what I could see," Esther said. "She kicked him out—she said he was becoming violent with the children, which I can kind of believe—but she dropped him."

A female group member was persuaded to move into an apartment with Saul, and after a while, when his condition continued to worsen, he was moved to a hospital in Brooklyn.

Few people ever visited him there, and when he died, in 1991, someone called Esther and asked, "Do you think we should have a memorial for him?" Esther replied, "I think so." But virtually no one came. Ironically, there were more members from his own nuclear family—his siblings' children, whom he had snubbed—than of the community he had created. His ex-wives Joan Harvey and Helen Moses, whom he had elevated to power at the Sullivan Institute, did not come. "None of the followers were there," Esther said. Other than Esther, only one of his other children, Robbie, his eldest son, came. Saul had perhaps treated Esther, his adopted daughter, better than he treated most of his biological children. He had shown an interest in and helped finance her education, and she had minimal exposure to the Sullivan Institute and the Fourth Wall. She arranged to have an obituary published in *The New York Times* in which she was prominently quoted:

> "He was both hated and loved," said Esther Newton, his eldest daughter, who was not involved in his therapeutic community. "His ideals were lofty—the results are for others to judge," she said. "He was very bright and creative, charismatic and definitely difficult, handsome, attractive to women and tyrannical."

Years after the official obituary, Esther was more candid and ironic when reflecting on her father's legacy, the Sullivan Institute, and the Fourth Wall: "They combined the worst of Marxism, psychoanalysis, and the musical theater."

Esther maintained a relationship with Jane Pearce, the woman who had stolen Saul away from Esther's own mother and had, in turn, been cast off for Joan Harvey and then Helen Moses. Esther recalled visiting Jane when she was quite old and feeling the end was near. Jane shared with Esther a recent dream in which she visited the afterlife. "She said she was floating down the River Styx into Hades on a boat that went aground. She climbed onto the bank and made her way to an old barn that had been converted into a theater. Inside, Saul was bossing everyone around, directing a large cast, rehearsing a musical comedy—a kind of dream parody of the Fourth Wall. She said to herself, 'If he is still in charge, even here in hell, I am not ready to die yet.'" At the same time, Jane insisted on showing Esther a short manuscript. "It was a sheaf of badly written poems of hers from when she and Saul were falling in love. This was when he was still married to my mother and he was cheating on her. Saul obviously was still magical for her, like an evil warlock whose spell she could not break."

PART IV

THE FOURTH WALL CRUMBLES

19

Aftermath

By 1991, with Saul Newton out of the picture, his last two wives—Joan Harvey and Helen Moses, the heirs to the kingdom—were feuding. It was a bit like the end of *King Lear*, when the king's daughters Goneril and Regan, after casting their father out on the heath, turn on each other.

There were still about 170 members of the Fourth Wall at this point, down from a high of about 250, but only about 100 were still paying regular dues. There were a number of empty apartments in the building at 100th Street, making it harder for those left to keep up with the mortgage payments. As they worried about money, members began to inquire more deeply into the finances of the Fourth Wall. Many discovered what John O. had noted years before—that, unknown to the membership, the building at 100th Street had "loaned" one hundred thousand dollars to Parallel Films, the company that produced Joan Harvey's films. It also turned out that the headquarters at Ninety-First Street had been financed in good part by Ralph Klein's oldest child, Josh. In 1979, he had extended a $242,000 mortgage—the equivalent of at least $1 million in 2020 money—to Joan Harvey and Helen Moses. The terms of the mortgage required monthly payments with interest, but no payments had ever been made. The leadership was financing its lifestyle by dipping into the inheritance of one of its members, who was also one of their children. Earlier, Josh Klein had put up the money to buy the Truck and Warehouse Theater as well. It was to avoid this kind of self-dealing and conflict of interest that Marshall Perlin had refused to represent Josh in 1979 and had resigned as the group's attorney.

It also emerged that the leadership at Ninety-First Street had failed to pay its food bill at the Fourth Wall food co-op for years, racking up some thirty thousand dollars in debt, according to one former member who examined the books. The leadership had literally been eating off the backs of the membership for years. They didn't bother paying their own Fourth Wall dues, either, while ordinary members were frequently working two or three jobs to keep up with their therapy bills, monthly dues, and periodic assessments. Many of the members, as they contemplated life after the group, had to come to grips with the fact that despite working for ten, fifteen, or even twenty years, they had little or no savings and often considerable debt.

The financial structure of the Fourth Wall was a kind of pyramid, with all the money flowing upward to the top. One former member showed me her monthly financial accounts from the late 1970s and early '80s, and her therapy bills frequently took up twenty-five or thirty percent of her monthly budget. The therapists—all but the leaders— were required to be in supervision a couple of times of week, so a portion of their earnings moved up the pyramid into the pockets of Saul Newton, Joan Harvey, Ralph Klein, and Helen Moses. It was not that the leaders' lives were all that lavish—although they did have full-time cooks, cleaners, and babysitters working for them, many of whom earned very little, in some cases exchanging their labor for therapy. A great deal of the leaders' money instead went to their children's school tuition. While most of the membership had been prevented or discouraged from having children, the four leaders had some twenty children among them—and all of those children attended New York's finest and most expensive private schools.

As the fight over money got ugly and Joan Harvey and Ralph Klein were facing accusations of financial misappropriation, they moved out of the Ninety-First Street headquarters and into a large house in New Rochelle, a suburb about half an hour north of New York City. A handful of their most devoted patients moved with them. They encouraged their patients to move out of the 100th Street building and to sue the building management in order to get their money back. The group's members were now split between the followers of Joan Harvey and the followers of Helen Moses. The already shaky financial foundation of the group was crumbling, and efforts were underway to sell off the property in the Catskills, the theater, and the headquarters at Ninety-First Street as well as the building at 100th Street and Broadway. The group effectively dissolved.

While the Fourth Wall was crumbling, four of the Sullivan Institute's lead therapists were facing multiple charges of misconduct with the New York State Office of the Professions. The office opened its investigation in the wake of the Marice Pappo case. The investigators focused on Joan Harvey, Ralph Klein, Helen Moses, and Marc Rice, as they all had Ph.D.s and were licensed professionals against whom patients had filed complaints. Saul Newton and the majority of the training analysts were not investigated, as they did not have licenses that could be reviewed or revoked. Anyone is free to offer their services and charge people for therapy, as long as people are willing to pay.

In 1991, Joan Harvey and Ralph Klein agreed to surrender their licenses, although they insisted that they were doing so to avoid the expense of further litigation rather than admitting guilt. In truth, they had fought the investigation for five years, and a decision appeared imminent; voluntarily giving up their licenses offered a face-saving solution when it seemed clear that the licensing board was set to rule against them. The two therapists who fought to the end, Helen Moses and Marc Rice, both lost their cases, with similar kinds of evidence against them.

In Joan Harvey's case—based on the testimony of Michael Cohen and other former patients—the panel heard evidence that Harvey had slept with several of her patients, exploited them for free babysitting services, directed them to cut off ties with their families, ordered them to have sex with people they didn't want to have sex with, yelled and cursed at them, threatened them with expulsion from therapy and the Fourth Wall, and pushed them to change jobs in order to earn more money. What is striking in reading through the charges and findings of the disciplinary panels is the depressing sameness in the therapists' behavior. In all cases, they engaged in multiple conflicts of interest, breaching the normal boundaries of the doctor-patient relationship. Three of the four were found to have had sex with their patients. (Marc Rice appears to have been more careful about this, but one of his patients, Janie P.—whom the disciplinary board did not interview—said that Rice did sleep with her once but apologized afterward.) They all pushed their clients to break with their families, painting their clients' parents as violent and murderous. All of them yelled and cursed at patients and pushed them to abandon their chosen careers to get more lucrative work.

Although Ralph Klein was not known to be as relentless a sexual predator as Saul Newton and Joan Harvey, the panel found that "on numerous occasions, between 1979 and 1985, [he] engaged in physical contact of a sexual nature with his patient . . . to wit, kissing, fondling, sexual intercourse, and cunnilingus during counseling sessions and also during social occasions." Klein denied having had sex with his patients, insisting that his only mistake was to accept as a patient a woman he'd had a relationship with in the past. The panel did not find his explanations credible. Moreover, the members of the panel evidently hadn't heard from the many former patients who subsequently shared their experiences. Marice Pappo said that she maintained a sexual relationship with Klein when she was in therapy with him. She noted a curious detail: "When we would have sex, he would not engage in intercourse." Perhaps this was his way of preserving the notion that he did not have sex with his patients.

Klein seems to have had a particular interest in sex with young girls. Amy Siskind, Michael Cohen's wife, who was a child of five when her mother became a Sullivanian patient, testified that Klein sexually harassed her repeatedly when she was a very young patient: "I entered therapy with Dr. Klein at the age of twelve. He continuously made sexual overtures toward me, and in repelling them, I was told that I was sexually repressed. When I vacationed with him at his summer home in 1968, he secretly watched me taking showers and commented about my genitalia. He also grabbed me and tried to touch me. I was aware at that time that he was having sex with a sixteen-year-old babysitter, and other ex-patients of his have confided in me that he also molested them. As a young adolescent, I spent a considerable amount of time in the community's summer homes in Amagansett. It was common practice for analysts and patients to get drunk and make passes at me. This was considered normal and healthy."

Klein also toed the standard Sullivanian line about parents being violent and murderous, and children needing to break off contact with them, and he pushed patients to have multiple sex partners. He told one patient, whose mother suffered from severe eczema and wore white gloves around the house, that this was an "indication that she hated her kids." He told another patient, a teacher, that she should leave the teaching profession and become a technical writer so that, as the panel wrote, "she could earn enough money to afford the various expenses arising from her affiliation with the Institute."

Like other Sullivanian therapists, Klein discouraged most patients who wanted to have children. "In August 1984, he directed [therapist X] to tell his patient [Z] who wanted to father a child, that he should 'work on other things in his life and think about fatherhood in about ten years.' Klein stated that he thought [Z] was a 'creep' and would never be capable of being a father. [Z] complied." (Names from the disciplinary hearing files have been redacted.)

After giving up his license voluntarily, Klein tried to win it back but was unsuccessful: "The applicant failed to convince the panel that he is aware of the seriousness of his misconduct and that he has taken the restoration process seriously. The panel finds that applicant has not demonstrated remorse or rehabilitation."

Despite losing their licenses, Joan Harvey and Ralph Klein continued seeing patients as unlicensed therapists, retaining a coterie of faithful clients.

Helen Moses and Marc Rice, meanwhile, fought to protect their licenses all the way to final adjudication.

Helen Moses was found to have had sex with numerous patients and training therapists whom she supervised, and also accused of the usual range of offenses in the other Sullivanian cases: directing male patients to participate in sperm pools to help certain women in the group get pregnant, directing women patients to have sex with men they didn't want to have sex with, and directing all patients to break their ties with family. She was also found to have defrauded insurance companies, charging for sessions that never took place.

Perhaps the most interesting thing to emerge from the dry, bureaucratic language and heavily redacted findings of the Office of Professional Discipline is the story of one of Helen Moses's babysitters, Evie W., who lived with Moses and Saul Newton and looked after their daughter Pam. When the group broke up in 1991, Evie went to the licensing board and filed a detailed complaint about her former therapist and former employer, Helen Moses.

Among other things mentioned in the complaint was that Moses used her role as therapist to convince Evie, against her will, to have sex with Moses's husband, Saul Newton, by insisting that "if she wanted to grow and learn she would have to have a sexual relationship" with Newton. The panel noted, "Respondent [Helen Moses] said many things to reinforce her directive to [Evie] to have sex with [Saul] that such a relationship would help [Evie] grow, to change and to open up to more mature relationships . . . [Evie] reluctantly complied with respondent's direction but over a two-year period, complained to respondent many times in their therapy sessions about said sexual relationship."

At a certain point, Helen Moses was dating the same man that her patient Evie was seeing. "When X failed to keep a 'date' with respondent [Moses] in September or October of 1986, respondent directed [Evie] to act in solidarity with [Moses] by refusing to have any further relationship with X. Evie complied with her directive." At another point she discouraged Evie from going back to school and insisted that babysitting for her children was better for Evie than completing her studies.

In 1989, the Fourth Wall leadership had begun to relax some of its AIDS-inspired rules, and the group split into two camps: those who were prepared to have relationships with people outside the group and those who would continue to date only in the Fourth Wall community. Evie began seeing a man outside the group. Helen Moses told her that she was being "cold, reckless and showing that she cared for no one but herself." But a little later, when Evie told Helen during therapy how much she was enjoying her new relationship, Helen encouraged her to recruit the man into the Fourth Wall so that she, Helen, could also date him. The panel then related a further piece of hypocrisy: "In June 1989, respondent told [Evie] not to tell others how much [Evie] enjoyed being with [her boyfriend] because it would tempt them to try relationships outside the Fourth Wall."

When Evie decided to leave the group in 1991, Helen Moses was furious and tried to convince her to at least stay through the summer, at one point threatening Evie with never again being able to see Pam Newton, the little girl she had taken care of for six years, unless she stayed on. Evie refused, left the group, and decided to file the complaint with the Office of Professional Discipline.

After learning that Evie had denounced her, Helen tried to talk her out of pressing charges, insisting that Evie would reduce Helen's family to poverty, including the little girl Evie had helped raise. "Respondent portrayed herself as also being a victim of a 'wild and wacky social experiment' that didn't work and explained that she [Helen] was under peer pressure and maintained that she was also suffering, miserable and exploited."

In the conversation, which Evie recorded, Helen admitted having done many of the things she would later deny when testifying for the disciplinary board. While Helen contested the charges leveled against her, the tape confirmed much of Evie's testimony and shredded Helen's credibility in the eyes of the panel. Using an unusual locution, the licensing board said that it found Moses's testimony "unworthy of belief."

"Respondent tried to minimize her wrongdoing and, in the opinion of this panel, still to this day, does not understand the full extent of the harm done to her patients." Moses was found culpable of numerous counts of "gross incompetence," "gross negligence," and "fraud."

In some ways, the most disturbing of all the ethical violations were detailed in the case of Marc Rice, perhaps because it was the only case that registered the therapists' extreme cruelty not just to patients but also to their children. Rice, who died in 2014, was an ex-marine and former graphic artist who was close friends with Helen Moses. He had a Ph.D. in psychology and was one of the group therapists living in the Ninety-First Street town house with Newton, Harvey, Klein, and Moses, just a rung down from the top on the group's power ladder. (He was also the legal—if not biological—father of Ellen Barrett's two children.)

Most of the charges against Rice are similar to those against the other therapists, but one of the witnesses tells the story of a parent who was induced to send her young children away to boarding school. Jody C. was a young mother when her husband was killed fighting in Vietnam. In the early 1970s she was juggling family and professional obligations, trying to finish a Ph.D. in sociology and raising her children. She entered therapy in 1972, and Rice soon convinced her to send her daughters, then ages eight and ten, away to boarding school. "His explanation was they would greatly benefit by being separated from me, as I was 'an envious, vicious bitch' and an 'unfit mother.'"

In the first years, the girls were in school on the East Coast, and Jody was able to visit them fairly regularly. Then "Dr. Rice advised me to cut my visits down to once every three months or so and to make arrangements to send both children to summer sleepaway camp. He insisted that it was in their best interests, and I complied."

Then Rice convinced Jody to send her younger daughter, Margot, out to the Fenster School in Arizona. When Margot became close friends with the child of another group member, Rice convinced Jody to transfer Margot to another school in order to break up this unhealthy alliance. "In retrospect, I think that they were having a normal close adolescent friendship," Jody said. "The group, however, considers an alliance unhealthy—a conniving, destructive relationship which shuts other people out." So, along with losing her father, being taken from her mother, and then forced to change schools twice, Margot would have to change again, forgo her closest friendship, and start over at a third school.

Margot, quite understandably, desperately missed and wanted her mother, which was reason, in Rice's view, to send her even farther away. "That spring, I was told by Dr. Rice that Margot was 'focused' on me, and that the only cure was to send her to school out of the United States." Margot was sent to a school in England for two years, which she hated. "I was not allowed to have either daughter 'home' for more than two days at a time," Jody C. said. "At Dr. Rice's urging, I told them that they were to spend their vacation time at camp or some other away-from-home activity or as invited guests at friends' homes." The children were responsible for soliciting invitations from other boarders during their vacations. "Since 1975," Jody testified, "my daughters have never spent more than three days' time with me at any given time. By then I had become thoroughly convinced that I was unfit as a mother and would do psychological harm to them if they had too much contact with me."

This situation led to near tragedy when Margot eventually rebelled. She refused to return to England, developed an alcohol and drug problem, tried to commit suicide, was hospitalized twice, and was arrested. Rice convinced Jody to ignore her daughter's increasingly desperate pleas for help. At one point Margot turned up at Jody's apartment, weeping and begging to stay. She had nowhere else to go. Jody called her therapist. "He instructed me to throw [Margot] out of the house, which I did. On a number of other occasions, including two hospitalizations, I was told by Dr. Rice to ignore any and all phone calls from Margot or from authorities calling on her behalf. I complied, believing that to do otherwise was to put Margot's life in danger." Margot ended up at Covenant House, a shelter for homeless or runaway kids.

How was Rice able to convince his patient to ignore all her maternal instincts and be the unwitting agent of so much pain?

Along with Jody C.'s dependency on her therapist, Rice's advice was reinforced by her friends, who were all in the Fourth Wall. "My group friends supported this view, and helped 'protect' my children from me by telling me to disregard any of my feelings to the contrary," she said.

Another part of it was a therapy that stripped Jody of any feeling of self-worth, certainly regarding her abilities as a mother. Since the Sullivanian paradigm was that your parents were motivated by violent, destructive, and murderous intentions, it was easy enough to turn that against the patient. How could a person who was the product of such a toxic family imagine that she could emerge unscathed?

As the disciplinary panel's final report stated, "Between March, 1972, and December, 1982, in numerous counselling sessions, Respondent told his patient that she was a 'bitch,' 'jealous bitch,' 'envious bitch,' 'vicious bitch,' 'cunt,' and a 'psychopath.'" At one point, when Jody, who was very attractive, did not want to sleep with another group member who asked to date her, Rice told her she was a "withholding bitch" and that she should "shut her mouth and open her legs." She complied.

Having manipulated Jody into believing that she was an "envious," "vicious," and "withholding" bitch, Rice had to take only one more step to convince her that she would in turn pass on her share of family poison to her children. "Respondent told [Jody] that her children had to be protected from her envy for their youth and potential."

20

The Reckoning

With the dissolution of the group, the great majority of Fourth Wall members scattered. The eighty or ninety people living at 100th Street and Broadway moved out. The building was sold. The theater and workshop in the Catskills were sold. When the mortgages and debts were paid, most members were lucky to receive a small fraction of what they had invested in the group's properties.

No longer under the thrall of their therapists, many of these people reentered mainstream life. They married, moved to the suburbs, left their jobs as computer programmers, and went back to being teachers, social workers, and artists. Some also had children. Many of the women who had waited too long adopted children. Most reestablished contact with the families they had rejected. A couple of dozen former members—mostly older women—remained in their old group apartments in a building on Ninety-Eighth Street, keeping to the habits of group life but without the leadership. Some continued to see their old Sullivanian therapists, but most did not.

Many Sullivanians—generally those who stayed to the end and had more positive views of their experience—remained closely tied to their friends from the group. Their social lives still revolved around those friendships: they continued to spend Thanksgivings together, attend the same parties, vacation and play music together. For many of these individuals, the Sullivanian community was the only one they had known in their adult life. They had spent the past fifteen, twenty, or even thirty years in therapy and with the same people. The fellowship of the group, the sense of community, and the friendships had always been the best part of this way of life for many, and now they could enjoy that without the interference of the leadership, while also having families and seeing relatives and having friends who had nothing to do with the group. Many of them felt quite lucky: they had more of a community than most Americans, more close and enduring friendships, and now they had their freedom to live as they saw fit.

But emerging from such a highly controlling group was not altogether easy. They were a bit like scuba divers who have been in deep water for a long time and then come up for air too quickly, experiencing decompression sickness (commonly called "the bends"). In deep water, nitrogen gradually builds up in the diver's blood; the deeper the diver goes, the longer he or she remains below, the greater the buildup and the harder the adjustment. Many members had experienced various forms of trauma: some had been sexually abused, forced to do things they didn't want to do, been screamed at and made to feel worthless by their therapists, done things they regretted, and experienced or witnessed acts of extreme cruelty and failed to act.

Despite living in the largest and densest city in the United States, they had been surprisingly isolated and unaware of changes around them. Mike Bray, having lived and worked inside the Sullivan Institute, didn't know how to use an ATM when he first left. When he got in touch with his sister, he discovered that he was now an orphan. His parents had died while he was still in the group. They did not live to meet their two granddaughters or learn that their son did not hate them. His sister had given up being a nun, realized that she was a lesbian, and was living with another woman.

Janie P., the young painter Richard Elman had brought down with him from Bennington, managed a successful transition after nearly twenty years of therapy. She was one of the many people in the group who had been encouraged to take up computer programming in order to make money. "I'm a hopeless technophobe," she said. She didn't have much of a feel for programming but proved to be a good technical writer. "Precisely because I was a non-tech kind of person, I was actually good at writing manuals. I'd ask the kind of dumb question that many ordinary people would want the answer to." Fortunately, even in the 1980s while working as a tech writer, she never lost the thread of her artistic practice. She continued teaching art and always kept a studio, where she painted when she could. In the group's final years she began spending time at artists' colonies, sometimes for several weeks at a time. This helped her focus more on her own work again, and at one of these retreats she met the man who became her husband. Because she had kept working, teaching, and pursuing a Ph.D., she was able to land a job teaching in the art department at the university in the city where her husband lived.

But nineteen years of therapy was not without cost. It was too late for Janie P. to have kids of her own (if she wanted to), and she had lost years she might have been painting—spending time at Fourth Wall rehearsals, babysitting, and writing technical manuals. The requirement of doing therapy two or three times a week meant that despite working constantly for more than two decades, she hadn't been able to save a dime.

Her greatest regret from her time in the group, however, was that she refused to see her mother during the final months when her mother was dying of cancer. She had been estranged from her father and brother, who tried unsuccessfully to get Janie to visit her mother at the end. As it happened, 1991, the year the group broke up, was the year that Janie's father turned eighty. "He asked me to come to his eightieth birthday party, which was held at my brother's house," she recalled. "It was so strange." A whole world and a whole life had happened in her absence. Her brother, whom she hadn't seen in twenty years, had a wife and two children and a raft of friends in a life she knew nothing about. She felt like Rip Van Winkle, who fell asleep in a cave for two decades. "I was the mysterious daughter who had been in a cult," she said. "It was very uncomfortable, but I'm glad that I did it. My father and my brother were both very kind to me. And I attribute that to the fact that they are both social scientists and kind and open-minded people. They knew that I had been brainwashed by a cult. They'd been very upset and angry over the years, but they were not blaming me or angry at me at that time. They were just happy, very happy. And I had a moving conversation with my brother. We went out for a car ride. He said, 'You know, I'm just so glad to see you. I'm very close to my wife, but you're the only person I shared my childhood with.' He started crying, and I was crying. And we've gotten to be close over the years. My father, thankfully, lived to be ninety-four, so I got to spend time with him."

Thirty years later, she still struggled with a certain burden of guilt and shame. She had been hit in the face by Joan Harvey and by Saul Newton, as well as sexually abused by Newton. "I feel terrible shame around that," she said. Shame not so much for what she did, but what she didn't do: "I know a lot of victims of sexual abuse feel shame. I feel like: Why did I continue to see him [as a therapist] when he was making me satisfy him sexually every time? I wasn't able to see it for what it was." But along with these traumas, Janie says that some of the Sullivanian interpersonal skills she learned have stayed with her in the form of enduring close friends and in managing social situations, from faculty meetings to intimate relationships.

After leaving the group in 1991, Elliot K., who had broken with his family even before getting into Sullivanian therapy, got back in touch with his parents and brother. He felt that even though he had needed to take a break from his family in his early twenties, the twenty-year break it turned into was excessive and cruel. His parents were in their forties when he got into therapy—still in the prime of their lives— and when he left the group, they were old. His brother had been a kid of fourteen when he joined the group, and during his twenty-year estrangement Elliot had missed most of his brother's life. He was able to reestablish a relationship with them—even if the bond he had broken never quite healed. "My mother never let me forget it—even, literally, on her deathbed." When his mother was dying, he helped look after her and went to see her every day when she was in hospice. "She looked up at me and said, 'Elliot, you've been so wonderful in all of this—you've worked off at least ten years.' And I looked at her and said, 'Only ten, that means I've got another ten to go—you better stick around!'"

But for Elliot K., the balance of his years in the group was more positive than negative. He formed numerous lasting friendships that carried over into his post-group life. He managed to have an active life as a gay man while also surviving the early and devasting years of the AIDS epidemic, and he adopted a child with another group member— things he felt would have been difficult if not impossible outside the group. After enjoying two decades of uncommitted sex in the group, he got to have the experience of marriage with another man (from outside the group) after the Fourth Wall dissolved. Something of the spirit of the Fourth Wall—its more playful side—lives on in him: when he turned sixty, he put on his own one-man cabaret show for his friends— "Sixty Years in Sixty Minutes," telling of his life in a mix of comic stories and song.

Helen Moses, after moving Saul Newton out of the residence at Ninety-First Street, married another Fourth Wall member and moved to a suburb in Westchester.

Before entering therapy with Saul, Helen had been a rather conventional young woman from a middle-class Jewish family. Many in the group considered her a spoiled, entitled young woman who tasted power as Saul Newton's wife and turned into a Fourth Wall overlord as a result. Even before Saul breathed his last, she had divorced him, found a new man, remarried, and taken her new husband's name. When the group broke up, the couple moved to a prosperous suburb north of New York, and Helen suddenly reverted to form, turning into a suburban wife and mother with a conventional life centered on kids and family. Even though she lost her license to practice as a psychoanalyst, she was able to work as a counselor for troubled youth. In 2014, she succeeded in getting the New York State licensing board to restore her professional accreditation.

After the board's decision, a local Westchester newspaper managed to conduct a brief exchange with a reluctant Moses in the doorway of her home. "This interview can only hurt me," she said, explaining why she would not sit down to speak with the reporter. Although she said she was not embarrassed by her past, she felt it no longer represented her: "It was *then*; I am *now* who I am." She compared herself to the character Don Draper in the television series *Mad Men* (2007–15), a man with a dark secret who leads an apparently conventional life and then partially redeems himself. "I was watching an episode of *Mad Men* the other day, and he says, there is a Japanese saying that says 'a man is the room he's in now.' I don't know if you know that episode? . . . I changed my room, and now . . . basically I'm a good person."

She stressed that she was very young when she got involved with Saul Newton. "I was young. I don't know how mature and rational I was. At the time, it seemed fine. Looking back on it, we were all crossing boundaries in that group. That was a problem."

"I'm much closer to her now actually then I was as a kid. Now we have a more normal mother-daughter relationship," said Pam Newton, Helen's eldest daughter. "My stepdad is more of a real father to me than Saul ever was. My mom and stepdad still kind of talk like they're radicals on the fringes of society, but their life is totally conventional now. They live in the suburbs. They have a dog and two cars. They're not doing anything radical anymore, but they still passionately believe that capitalism doesn't work, our culture is misguided, and our government is corrupt."

Pam continued: "My mom was raised by a housewife mom and an accountant dad in a Jewish neighborhood in the Bronx. She was a straight-A student, a cheerleader. She had a completely normal New York Jewish American childhood. And I think in some part of her, that girl never died." Her time in the group, Pam feels, allowed her mother to explore a wilder and more unconventional life within a highly structured world. "The group made her feel safe somehow. Like we're going to do it in this different way, but Saul's going to tell her how to do it, there are all these structures in place. But as soon as the structure fell apart, I think she snapped back to her original values." She wanted her kids to settle down, choose a career, marry, and have kids of their own. "It's interesting that of her four kids, who are all in their thirties and forties, there's only one grandchild," Pam said. (There are now two.)

When Pam married, in her late thirties, she and her husband went to city hall for a simple civil ceremony followed by a party for friends and family. At the party, Pam asked her stepfather if he was having a good time. "And he said, 'I think your mom is a little disappointed. I think she would have preferred something more traditional.' Are you fucking kidding me?! It was so crazy to me that after my training, my upbringing, my mother would be disappointed that I was not wearing a white dress and getting married in a synagogue." Her mother had not even explained that they were Jewish when Pam and her siblings were kids. "So there's this weird hypocrisy and schizy quality to the adults . . . but it's a good thing that we turned out as functional as we are."

Pam found it much easier to have a relationship with the more conventional mother that Helen Moses turned into after she left the group, but the Fourth Wall remained a point of friction between them. As Pam and her siblings grew up, they began to examine their unusual childhood in a more critical light and to push their mother to talk about the group with greater honesty. "She has these kind of rose-colored glasses on about it and, in my opinion, is in a reality of her own creation," Pam said. "She wants to feel good about her time in the group and doesn't react well to anything critical. She had a good time. She loved raising her kids that way. She loved the friendships. She has eliminated any of the darkness from her narrative. So it can be very, very frustrating to talk to her."

Pam and her husband live on an upper floor of a Brooklyn brownstone, where Pam's husband, a master carpenter, makes furniture in a back-room studio while Pam works as a writer and teacher of writing. Her life does not center around the group, but she maintains close ties with her siblings and with many of the kids who also grew up in the Fourth Wall. "I have pretty mixed feelings about it. I thought parts of it were really fun. You know, I love my friends from the group. I'm not, like, having some big vendetta, but anything that sounds critical to [my mother], she will kind of react to and start self-justifying, so it can be super frustrating talking to her . . . Like I'll say, 'Well, because you and dad were in the leadership,' and she'll be like, 'I wasn't in the leadership,

I don't know what you're talking about. I was just in the group like everybody else.' She doesn't perceive herself as part of the leadership."

Helen Moses insists that Saul Newton was in charge, that she was just another group member, and that the anger former members express toward her is really anger about Saul that gets directed, unfairly, at her. She has evidently forgotten that she was a supervising therapist and that as a therapist, she broke up patients' relationships, prevented weaker group members from having children, kept mothers from their babies, and told child patients that their mother was a bitch. "She is still kind of in the cult in her mind," Pam said. "She still thinks of it as a good thing, a great thing that she did. She sees now that Saul was problematic, and she has apologized to me for not protecting me more from his rages. But she really kind of worshipped Saul. She thought he was brilliant, and he changed her life. She won't admit that there is anything problematic about it. We actually decided six months ago not to ever talk about the group again because for me it's like smashing my head against a wall."

(I made numerous attempts to contact Helen Moses, but she never responded.)

As the Fourth Wall broke up, there was a diaspora out of the Upper West Side, which was rapidly becoming an affluent—and increasingly expensive—neighborhood, especially for those who were now starting families. Many former members moved to Brooklyn, although a sizable contingent crossed the Hudson River, winding up a world away from the radical bohemia of their youth in the nice but decidedly conventional middle-class suburbs of New Jersey.

A number of these ex-Sullivanians ended up in the consulting rooms of Bill and Lorna Goldberg, husband-and-wife psychotherapists who specialize in treating patients who have been in cults. "When I started meeting with people who had come out of the group, I felt these were people who would have been my friends," said Lorna Goldberg, a woman in her early seventies with bright brown eyes and a warm, friendly smile. A contemporary of many of the former Fourth Wall members, she and her husband were both graduate students at New

York University in the late 1960s, very much part of the same demographic and cut from the same cultural cloth as many of the people who ended up in the Sullivanian orbit: they protested against the Vietnam War and were interested in psychoanalysis. "If I was going to join a cult, this would have been the cult for me," she said. "The idea of a radical psychoanalytic group with left-wing ideas was something that would have been very appealing at that time. Combining psychoanalysis with radical left-wing principles was a heady idea that seemed very exciting and very innovative. And you were joining to have a therapist, and you didn't realize the amount of control that would come into being later on. I could have so easily found that group to be perfect, just perfect and fascinating."

Many of the people Goldberg treated were trying to get their lives back on track after fifteen or twenty years in Sullivanian therapy and group living. The former members she saw were dealing with a range of issues, among them that the idealistic and revolutionary promises of the group had, in the end, not added up. "Not only did it add up to nothing, it also set them back because many of their college friends, high school friends, [and] contemporaries [were] all so ahead of them, involved in doing things they would have wanted to do. Many went back to school to do things they wanted to do before the group. A lot of them gave up their dreams and became computer programmers because it was a fast way to make money. They're very smart. Sometimes, they were too old to have children—that happened to many of the women in the group. And that's a very hard thing to grapple with. Sometimes it's easier to tell yourself, 'Well, there were certain good things I got from it,' and they remember the beginning of the group, which was Nirvana, but later on it became more brutal for all of them. That's a painful thing." Confusing as well as painful, for they had to sort out the good from the bad and the real from the unreal. "They're wonderful people. They had crazy beliefs while they were in the group, but friendships were formed, and people often liked each other . . . more than they liked the leaders. So sometimes it's even harder to lose the world of your friends."

For people coming out of a long experience like this, it is very disorienting. On the one hand, in many ways they reverted to their pregroup identity. This is reassuring but also disturbing: Who was I during the years I was in the group? "It shows you the power of the group to change, to put on a whole new cult personality on top of the pre-cult personality," Lorna said. "And then they revert to who they were before, but not quite . . . They've lost those years, and they've lived through the trauma of having something happen to them they never expected to happen. They have to grapple with how much their mind could have changed as a result of that experience, which is quite something in terms of their identity, a sense of the vulnerability of their identity."

*   *   *

While Lorna Goldberg uses the term "cult" to describe the experience of her Fourth Wall patients, many people who were in the group avoid the term.

To them, the word conjures an idea of mindless zombies who essentially lost control of their lives for years—in some cases decades. They continue to think of being part of the group as a choice they made, one that had its good and bad points. After all, many of the members of the Fourth Wall did not renounce the world and all their earthly goods to retire to an ashram somewhere. Some used their time in the group to go to law school or medical school, or work as successful professionals by day, spending their free time in a community with its own rules—but rules they chose to accept. They continue to like and feel close to the friends they made in the group. "Certainly, when I was in the community at age sixteen, I bristled at the term 'cult,'" Sean Mack said. "Less so today, but still today we don't like calling it a cult, even though I recognize that there were a lot of cultlike aspects to it. You can certainly sensationalize it as . . . this horrible sex cult where, you know, children were ripped away from their parents, but that really misses so much, and pigeonholes it in a way . . . I think of it as—as an experiment in . . . alternative ways of living. And I still feel there's value in that."

Others have little hesitation in describing the group as a cult and using terms like "brainwashing." How else, they feel, can they account for having done so many things they didn't want to do: cutting off family members they loved, perceiving their closest former friends to be genuinely dangerous people, agreeing to sleep with people they weren't the least attracted to, giving up professions they loved for computer programming jobs they weren't interested in, putting up with frequent verbal and physical abuse? The therapy effectively rewired their perceptions, so a mother like Jody C. came to believe that her desire to see her own daughters was genuinely selfish and harmful.

"What I did to them was unforgivable in many ways," Jody said. "You have two girls, age eight and ten, who have lost their father, and then their mother disappears on them. I don't know how they got through it . . . I can't say that I was not myself. I can't absolve myself of responsibility. I have to constantly tell myself that, no, I'm not a bad person. In fact, I'm quite a nice person. I may have done some awful things to my kids, but I love them. And I wanted the best for them, and that's really what I thought I was doing."

Jody said that she tries—and somehow manages—to live with a set of deep contradictions, to face honestly the harm she did to her children without tormenting herself while continuing to live her life. "I have to live with both of those things in me . . . In terms of cognitive dissonance, you're not supposed to be able to tolerate that, but I can. I've forgiven myself, and I understand why it happened. But there's nothing I can do about it other than to live my life now. Maybe I compartmentalize and refuse to think about things at times, but I'm not unhappy."

When I first spoke with Jody C. on the phone, I was searching for a word with which to characterize her therapy. "The word is 'evil,'" she said categorically. "Evil."

On reflection, it didn't seem an unreasonable way of characterizing a therapist who called his patient a "withholding bitch" when she was reluctant to sleep with men she wasn't attracted to—a therapist who prevented his patient from seeing her children when they needed her desperately and were in danger of harming themselves. Her therapist, Marc Rice, was dead, and it was hard to assess what drove him to do what he did. In Jody's telling, Rice was "in the thrall of Saul Newton," whom he idolized.

* * *

I thought of this problem of evil and of personal agency and responsibility as I tried to understand the case of Ellen Barrett, another therapist about whom I had heard almost universally terrible things and whose story perplexed me in the extreme. Early on in my research I interviewed a woman named Mary Cherney, who had gotten into therapy while still a teenager in the early 1970s. When Mary was about eighteen, she was babysitting for Amanda Newton, one of the daughters of Joan Harvey and Saul Newton. One Saturday morning out in Amagansett, Mary slept through an alarm and caused Amanda to miss a horseback riding lesson. She woke up to Joan Harvey screaming at her, firing her on the spot, and calling her a jealous psychopath for trying to sabotage her daughter. Mary was then ostracized by the other women in the house she was sharing at the time. Isolated and desperate, she had reached out to her therapist, Ellen Barrett. Rather than empathize with her patient, Ellen called her a "worm" and a "parasite" and "told me that I should kill myself." I found this so shocking that I asked Mary if Ellen had really used those words or if Mary had inferred—and perhaps misunderstood—her meaning. "Those were her words," she said, "that I was a parasite, that the world would be better off without me, that I should kill myself. The whole thing lasted about ten minutes, and I was just shaking and was like 'Oh, my God, now what do I do?'"

It's hard to imagine a worse case of therapeutic abuse than a therapist telling a patient (let alone a teenage patient) to kill herself. Moreover, I kept interviewing others who had Ellen as a therapist, and they also described a hard-core Sullivanian who bullied her patients. "She was a mean bitch," Carol Q. told me. "I felt like every session I was getting beat up." Another former patient said, "She had the reputation of being the ballbuster you got sent to when you messed up." Paul Spre-cher described his year in therapy with her as "a year of browbeating."

Without making Ellen Barrett a particular focus of my research, I stumbled on these stories in the course of my work, but as the tales of therapeutic abuse accumulated, I began to wonder: What kind of per-son would do this to her patients? What had become of her? How did she regard her Sullivanian past? Her real name is somewhat unusual, so I found her on Facebook with considerable ease. Her Facebook page contained a series of warm and fuzzy family photos, an attractive daughter in her thirties, and an adorably cute grandchild. Standard fare for Facebook but somewhat ironic for someone who had been a therapist in a group based on the total rejection of family. The page contained an old black-and-white photograph of her father—a young man in a college jersey throwing a football. That picture of her father, a handsome young man in the 1940s, seemed especially poignant. Knowing what I did about the group, it was virtually certain that she would have broken off all ties with her parents when she went into therapy in the late 1960s. Had her father died while she was in the group—a period that lasted for more than twenty years? Had she broken his heart? And was posting this old black-and-white photo an act of remorse?

Rather than contact her through Facebook, I decided to write to another former therapist to ask for Ellen's email address, a practice I found generally more effective. This other person didn't respond, but when I checked Ellen's Facebook page, it had vanished. Had she learned that I was searching for her and decided to become invisible?

Months later, I received an email from someone who said that El-len Barrett was interested in speaking with me. We met in a Brooklyn diner and ended up talking for four and a half hours—or rather, she ended up talking for four and a half hours as I listened, spellbound. She had the conversational style of an open fire hose. Still attractive in her early seventies, she had shoulder-length hair, a sharp tongue, and a biting sense of humor. In her telling, she was not a bad shrink, but a badly damaged former patient and victim of therapeutic abuse.

Although many people I interviewed did not like to use the word "cult" to describe the Fourth Wall, Ellen Barrett repeated it often.

She described two decades of nearly constant abuse. She was a patient of Helen Moses starting in 1969 and had then been recruited into the training program by her. Moses decided that Ellen and another female training analyst should come and live with her, Saul Newton, and a group of other therapists in the same apartment. For nearly twenty years Barrett lived with her therapist, her therapist's husband, and the other leaders of the group in the headquarters at Ninety-First Street. "Helen Moses ruined my life . . . I became a kind of courtesan," she said, living at the court of the group's royalty. While this appeared to others as a position of privilege, she said it exposed her to years—almost two decades—of financial and sexual exploitation. Not only had Saul Newton sexually abused her, as he did virtually all the women who passed through the residence—babysitters, cooks, cleaners, patients, therapists—but since she was living there 365 days a year, she was abused constantly. "Toward the end of his life I was peeing in a bottle in my room so I didn't have to go down the hall, on the chance that he might see me. That whole house was like a giant blow job factory!" she said.

"I hate to be clinical about this," I said, "but Saul by this point was in his eighties. How could he be having sex several times a day?"

"That's just it," she said. "He couldn't, and that's why it was such hard work. I had to do it so often, I suffered from TMJ."

I had never heard the term "TMJ" and had to look it up afterward: temporomandibular joint dysfunction is extreme pain in the jaw from overuse of the jaw muscles.

At a certain point, to illustrate the reign of terror she lived in, Ellen took a paper napkin from our table and scribbled two numbers on it from memory. "Those were Saul and Joan's numbers," she said. More than thirty years had passed since the group dissolved, but she knew those phone numbers by heart. (I checked the numbers against membership lists, and her memory had not failed her.) "I guarantee you everyone in the group had those numbers etched into their brains, and if you saw those numbers pop up on your pager, you broke into a cold sweat. It meant trouble." At various times during our meeting, when she was trying to make a point with emphasis, she raised her voice in a loud, angry tone before she realized that she was screaming. "I'm sorry," she would say, "it's my PTSD talking. I'm sorry."

Having heard so many similar tales of abuse, I didn't doubt that she had also been a victim, but her take on her experience was at variance with the picture of Ellen I had gotten from others. They described her as an aggressive therapist confidently pushing Sullivanian orthodoxy on her patients. She portrayed herself as a passive victim who was simply carried along by a series of disastrous choices, like a twig in a powerful stream. "You don't seem to understand the importance of transference. It's the whole reason the cult was able to exist," she said.

In her account, her therapist Helen Moses had convinced her to make one disastrous, self-destructive move after another even though she did not want to do any of them: drop out of college; become a Sullivanian therapist when she had no interest in being a therapist; move in with her therapist and her therapist's husband, Saul Newton, even though she hadn't really wanted to; date a man, Marc Rice, whom she had never liked; grant Rice legal standing as her two children's father and give her children Rice's name. "I was in denial," she said.

When I pressed her about having urged her teenage patient to kill herself, Ellen claimed to have no memory of the incident. When I mentioned that several former patients had described her as a brutal therapist, she replied, "I wasn't myself. For twenty years I wasn't myself."

Was it possible to get a person to make a series of terrible decisions over a twenty-year period at the behest of people she claimed to despise? Ellen insisted that I look up the literature on brainwashing, especially a book called *The Rape of the Mind*, published in 1959 by a Dutch psychologist who cited many instances of being bludgeoned psychologically into various forms of compliance. The works on brainwashing are mostly from the 1950s—the period of the novel and movie *The Manchurian Candidate* (1959, 1962)—and the concept is no longer used in scientific literature.

Which version of Ellen was "true"? Was she the mean-spirited bully her former patients described or the fragile young woman who had been manipulated by senior therapists who exploited her financially and sexually? Or both? Is it possible for someone to lose their sense of self so entirely that they can be made into a weak, passive victim as well as an aggressive perpetrator?

There was one moment in Ellen's story that stood out to me for its importance, its undeniable trauma—a moment I didn't doubt, perhaps because it was one of the only times she acknowledged having done something wrong. (In the law, a "statement against interest" has special evidentiary weight.) She told me that in the spring of 1984 Saul Newton induced her to write a letter to her father telling him that she wished he was dead. A week later, her father had a massive heart attack and died. When her mother called to tell her the news, Ellen apparently responded sarcastically: "Do you want me to congratulate you?" Clearly, she felt unspeakable guilt over her actions. I couldn't help thinking of the photo she'd posted on Facebook of her father as a handsome young undergraduate throwing a football. It had been an act of extreme remorse. She believed she had literally broken his heart.

I felt that I began to understand Ellen's story better when I conducted a series of interviews with her younger sister, Penelope, who had been a patient in the group for about nineteen years but was able to leave before the bitter end. Moreover, she had left together with a man she loved, and they had a child and built a successful business together. Ellen, by contrast, left a few years later, a woman in her forties with the sense of having lost twenty years of her life. Her two decades of experience as a Sullivanian therapist were seen in the psychoanalytic community as not only worthless but disqualifying. As she had dropped out of Columbia to become a Sullivanian training analyst, she had to find work without even having a bachelor's degree. As she put it, "I never got my B.A., which is why I am still working and quasidestitute at seventy-two."

Penelope described their parents in more nuanced terms, as highly intelligent and charming people who were caught up in their own interesting lives and had a very relaxed and detached approach to parenting.

They had an active social life, were big drinkers who liked to go to parties, and had extramarital affairs. And they asked a great deal of their eldest daughter, Ellen. Penelope recalled her mother talking to a friend who asked how she managed a busy life with five small children. Her mother replied that she was lucky her two eldest children were girls who took care of the other three. "It's like having two little maids," she said. Ellen's best friend from childhood (Mary Michael Hill) told me a similar story. She recalled that when Ellen was about sixteen, her parents took a trip to England and stayed away for a month. They left Ellen to take care of the family, telling the local supermarket to let her charge whatever she needed until they got back. "My mother was scandalized that Ellen's parents would leave the country for a month and leave a sixteen-year-old in charge alone," Hill said. To manage things, Ellen behaved like a kind of drill sergeant to her younger siblings. "As an older sister, she was a domineering bully," Penelope said. "She was home with the care of her four younger siblings," Mary Michael said. "She told me that she controlled them by what she referred to as 'smacking' them."

This helped make sense of part of Ellen's story and explained why she had been good raw material in the hands of a Sullivanian therapist. She had reasons to resent her parents, even if her family life was hardly a "concentration camp," as her therapist encouraged her to view it. At the same time, her assigned role as family drill sergeant made her a good candidate to become a Sullivanian training therapist, keeping her patients in line as she had done with her siblings.

Penelope believes that her sister has trouble acknowledging the cruel things she did to her patients, because she is not, in fact, a cruel person. "She is funny, smart, and incredibly perceptive," Penelope said. "I feel it's because the kindhearted, compassionate part of herself is so agonizingly guilty that she can't face it. And that makes me very sad. We all did things we shouldn't have in the group. I feel ashamed of stuff I did." Most people committed smaller acts of cruelty and cowardice: informing on friends when they committed some minor infraction, failing to speak up—or joining in—when someone was unfairly attacked or kicked out of their apartment at a house meeting. Ellen, as a therapist, had the power to do more damage, but Penelope isn't sure she might not have done similar things if placed in the same position.

There is another category of former members: those who publicly defend the group but privately acknowledge the abuses that went on. At a certain point, a number of former Fourth Wall members set up a private Facebook forum to discuss their experiences. Even though it was private, a former member shared the contents of the site with me on the promise that I would respect the privacy of the participants and not reveal their identities. It was helpful in terms of understanding the differences between people's public and private attitudes. People who had denied to me that there was anything abusive about the Sullivanian experience were in the discussion group, revealing stories of abuse or responding sympathetically to stories of abuse reported by others. It seemed like a case of not wanting to wash your dirty linen in public. We may speak ill of our own relatives in private, but we'll defend them when an outsider says something critical about them. Former members discussed whether to use the term "cult"; one participant who said he preferred the term "high demand group" went on to describe how Saul Newton had physically attacked him during a meeting and how his therapist had quashed his plan to have a child with another member.

*   *   *

The Fourth Wall certainly had many of the characteristics scholars have associated with cults: a charismatic leader who enjoys exceptional power and privileges within the group, cutting members off from their families, sexual and financial exploitation, interference with married couples by imposing celibacy or polygamy, the promotion of a "fortress mentality" (an us-against-them relationship to the outside world), and a tendency to take up almost all of its members' free time.

But one problem with the term is that it tends to make the Fourth Wall community appear totally foreign and outside the ken of normal experience. In truth, most close communities and religious groups use some of the same strategies for maintaining group solidarity. Ultra-Orthodox Jews, strict evangelical Christians, Salafi Muslims, rule-following Mormons—all impose a demanding lifestyle on their adherents, have a strong sense of the boundary between the community of believers and the impure outside world, and effectively ostracize members who drop out of the faith. The members of the Fourth Wall were not sick or abnormal; they were/are on average exceptionally intelligent, idealistic, and well-educated people.

In many ways, the extreme dependency and abuse in many of the therapeutic relationships in the Fourth Wall were not unlike the dynamic of a bad marriage. As the current partner of one former member told me, "I think I understand what kept Donna in the group," comparing it to her marriage with a controlling husband who wanted her all to himself. "When I married my husband, I had a full life, with lots of friends, and after ten years of marriage, all my friends had dropped away and I was alone with my husband." Millions of people stay in unhappy marriages, convinced that they cannot survive without their spouse.

Moreover, even within a group as controlling as the Fourth Wall, there was a variety of experiences. Some of the people who insist it was a fundamentally positive experience may have genuinely maintained more autonomy and continued to enjoy some of the better aspects of group life with less interference from the leadership. Men generally enjoyed the sexual freedom more than women, who often felt they were pressured to sleep with people they didn't really want to sleep with. Some people managed to get through law or medical school while in the group and were better at not getting pushed around as much by the leadership. People who didn't have children in the group generally had fewer problems than those who did.

"There are people in cultic groups, but it doesn't affect their life that much," said Bill Goldberg, the therapist husband of Lorna Goldberg, who also specializes in treating former cult members. "They might go for a Sunday feast or be weekend participants in workshops. They might go to a church for services and go about their lives as individuals the rest of the week." He stressed that there is no simple definition of a cult. "It's not the ideology, it's the practice."

"There are groups that we would consider benign that a person can enter into in a cultic way, where the group defines their existence, everything they do," Bill said, giving the example of a group that formed around a voice teacher who became the center of her pupils' lives. "They had lessons seven days a week. If they missed a lesson, they had to pay penance in terms of her browbeating. Her child died of muscular dystrophy, and she gave lessons on the day of the funeral. And from then on, she had them by the balls: one of them said, 'I want to miss a lesson because it's Father's Day.' She would say, 'I gave you a lesson on the day of my son's funeral, and you tell me that you're going to miss the lesson because you want to be with your father!' So, a voice class is not a cult, but in this case, it functioned as a cult. The issue is, how does the individual respond to the pressure they're put under? There are some groups where if you're a member, you have to be in whole hog. You can't have been part of the Sullivanians and not be part of the group. This was a group where the boundaries were very strict and the demands were high."

People join cults almost always in the period between their adolescence and early adulthood, in their late teens or twenties. "Their identities are still unformed—they haven't found a partner yet, they might have finished college or have moved to a new city for the first time," Lorna Goldberg explained. "They're in an unfamiliar place, and they're uncertain about their future. They might have suffered the loss of a friendship or a love relationship. They might have suffered a divorce in their family or the death of someone they love. They are moving away from their families, they are very receptive to a new way of life, and they're very idealistic. And they're naïve and a little grandiose. 'We are going to change the world.' And there is an honesty and naïveté. They encounter these therapists with these new ideas—it seems exciting and honest and good—they had no idea that what they saw at the beginning was going to unfold into something quite different for them."

What caused a group that offered an interesting, innovative combination of psychoanalysis and radical politics to make the leap from community to cult? There have been a number of therapy cults over the years, although possibly none as large or as long-lasting as the Sullivan Institute/Fourth Wall community. The one thing they all have in common is the breaching of the normal boundaries between therapist and patient: the patients socialize with (and/or sleep with) the therapists, they do work for and run errands for the therapists, their lives become deeply enmeshed with the lives of their therapists, so that the therapists hold power over the patients in not just one but several ways.

Jane Pearce certainly did not intend to start a cult. She genuinely believed that she had developed an approach to psychoanalysis that would emancipate her patients. But her rigid belief in the scientific truth of her methods convinced her that she had the right, even the obligation, to intervene in her patients' lives—pushing them to break with their families, to take on multiple sexual partners—even if they were reluctant to do so. She also created a set of therapeutic tactics that therapists could easily manipulate if they wished to take over their patients' lives.

The other common element is the abuse of the process of transference. Positive transference—when the patient begins to idealize and develop a dependence on the therapist—is a complex and powerful part of the therapeutic relationship that must be managed with care. It can be an intoxicating experience for therapists to realize that their patients revere them and look to them for guidance in making decisions in their life. It is easy to rationalize, Bill Goldberg said, that you are helping the patient by stepping in and taking control of their life: "We all make mistakes as therapists. I might allow a patient to become dependent on me or to idealize me too much. And then I draw the line. I don't think I could go to that much greater point of really taking over someone's life. But it's a continuum."

"There must have been so much narcissism in these leaders, because the ability to gain control over recruits would make some people uncomfortable with the power and reverence that's coming their way,"

Lorna added. "We're both therapists, and sometimes people are engaged in an idealizing transference with us and we feel uncomfortable about it. We know that's not really who we are. And we begin to try to work things out with our patients so that they'll begin to see us in a more realistic way that's a lot healthier. These people [the Sullivanian therapists] capitalized on the transference that gave them power and control, and they didn't back off from it. They were narcissists."

Daniel Shaw, a psychoanalyst who practices in Manhattan, also specializes in treating patients who have been in cults. He also saw several former Fourth Wall members after they left the group. Shaw came to his specialty because he himself had spent several years in a cult. He agreed that Saul Newton was a particularly toxic kind of narcissist, typical of most cult leaders, who have delusions of grandeur or omnipotence and often embellish or invent parts of their biography. Newton, the only unlicensed psychoanalyst among the original therapists of the Sullivan Institute, was not shy about comparing himself to Freud and Marx; he compensated for his own insecurity about his lack of formal training by embellishing his biography and establishing dominance over his better-trained colleagues. "In order to sustain this delusion of omnipotence," Shaw explained, "there has to be a constant supply of people who can be controlled and subjugated. Saul Newton was certainly a leader along those lines: when he felt his control threatened, he would react with a terrifying rage that would get everybody back in line."

Virtually every cult, Shaw said, regulates and manages the sex lives of its adherents. "Cults are weird about sex," he said. "They either demand that none of the followers have sex or that all the followers have sex with everyone." The Heaven's Gate cult tried to enforce celibacy, whereas David Koresh insisted that his male followers abstain from sex while he took on the "burden" of having sex with their wives. The cult of Bhagwan Shree Rajneesh (the Indian guru who set up a large community in rural Oregon) encouraged a kind of sexual free-for-all. Cults almost always discourage stable marital relationships, where two people's allegiance to each other works at cross-purposes with loyalty to the group.

Newton used sex to satisfy his personal need for dominance and to reinforce his delusions of omnipotence. Daniel Shaw treated several women who were forced to have oral sex with Newton during their therapeutic sessions and who suffered from terrible guilt and shame. "Saul Newton was a phallic narcissistic: he basically wanted his phallus to be worshipped as in Hindu mythology. It's not about his giving love or even fulfilling his desires. It's about power and control."

After I had four or five interviews with Penelope Barrett, she came up with a remarkable insight that clarified for me the centrality of sex—in particular unwanted sex—in the Sullivanian world: "What struck me—just the other day, for the first time," she wrote in an email, "was how huge a part the attack on bodily autonomy played in this." The group's general promiscuity, she said—the feeling that you were not entirely free to decide who could touch or enter your body—undermined your sense of control and autonomy more generally. But the aggressive sexual predation of Saul Newton, she wrote, "took the attack on my bodily autonomy to a whole other level . . . It was incredibly disorienting in a fundamental, almost primitive way. If you don't even have the right to control access to your body, it's pretty hard to maintain a sense of self about anything else."

But Saul Newton—like many cult leaders, Shaw said—took this a step further by getting his followers to violate *other* people's boundaries. According to Shaw, "The cult leader is a person whose need for this omnipotent kind of delusion is so great that it's important that he prove it to himself by being able to violate anyone's boundaries and to further get other people to violate other people's boundaries. This proves his omnipotence."

There was, Shaw noted, a kind of cascade of cruelty and sadism that flowed from the top, starting with Saul Newton, passing through the other therapists he supervised, and trickling down to the patients who, in turn, were encouraged to behave aggressively with other group members.

Thus, Saul Newton would brag to Michael Cohen about pushing

Dom Antonelli, a fellow therapist, into sending his son away to board-ing school and about taking infants away from their mothers. Antonelli, in turn, trained Cohen to believe that his first job as therapist was to convince patients that their parents were evil, and then that they were just like their parents. As Jon Mack, hardly a group dissident—who stayed in the group until it dissolved—wrote in a blog post:

> Therapists in the group were expert at manipulating their patients' self-esteem in such a way that the vast majority remained continu-ally in therapy over the entire life of the group, in some cases as long as twenty-five years . . . Therapists were generally expert at making their patients feel utterly worthless and desperate for their therapists' support. By intermittently boosting and undermining their patients' self-esteem, the Institute therapists maintained enormous control over their patients—and guaranteed an enviable income stream.

The therapists also passed along some of this technique to their patients, who, in turn, did the same thing to one another:

> Throughout the life of the group, the cruelest blows were often struck not directly by the leaders, but by one's friends and peers. Time and time again group members turned against their closest friends when they'd run afoul of the group's leaders. Any individ-ual who began to have some stature in the group was very likely to become the target of such an attack. Suddenly an incident was defined by the leaders as indication that the previously respected friend was not to be trusted, was psychopathic, was a danger to the group. The willingness of friends to jump to this rejection of their most intimate friends testifies to the cultish control [the] group's leaders held over its members.

Often, these attacks were primed and even scripted by the thera-pists, who urged their patients to call out this or that member for their bad behavior. Other times, members with greater status in the group would turn on those who were in a weaker position. Janie P. recalled an incident when she was babysitting for the son of John M. and Leslie F. (she sometimes babysat to supplement her income from painting and teaching). The child had been home sick with chicken pox and, bored by being stuck in bed, amused himself by putting Wite-Out on the pink spots caused by his illness. Janie forgot to have him clean himself off before his mother got home. When Leslie F. saw the Wite-Out on her son, she flew into a rage and fired Janie on the spot. After Janie's roommates heard about the incident, they banded together and kicked her out of their apartment, arguing that she was psychopathic.

It is hard not to fall into line when everyone around you is telling you the same thing. In many ways, the experience of the Sullivan Institute/Fourth Wall is extremely similar to many of the landmark psychological experiments of the 1950s and '60s related to the power of group conformity. In the Asch experiment, a subject is asked to compare a line to three other lines that are placed next to it; one of the three lines is identical in length while one is clearly shorter and the third clearly longer. The subject is asked to pick the line that is closest in length to the first line. But the subject is seated in a row with a group of other people who are confederates, and they answer the same question before the subject gets to make his choice. To the subject's surprise, everyone else picks one of the other lines, clearly a wrong answer. And yet when the psychologist Solomon Asch first ran the experiment, twelve out of the first eighteen subjects went along with the group choice, overriding the evidence of their senses in order to not buck the consensus.

Asch's experiment has been reproduced many times, with similar results: on average, about one-third consistently conform to the majority view, while seventy-five percent conform at least once. Only a distinct minority, twenty-five percent, never conform. However, the rates of conformity drop considerably when one other person picks the correct line before the subject does. In other words, it is easier to buck the majority when you are not alone. This helps explain why it was easier for people to leave Sullivania in its earlier years. Some patients still had friends outside the group who might well tell them, "Hey, this is nuts. You should get out of therapy." But when the group became increasingly monolithic and closed off, it was very hard to leave. This helps explain why Chris H. believed the rumors that his wife, Marice Pappo, was abusing drugs and alcohol even though he had seen no direct evidence of it. "This is what everyone was telling me," he said. Asch proved Orwell's contention that in a totalitarian environment it is possible to convince people that two plus two equals five.

It is not an accident that the Sullivan Institute got its start in the 1950s and '60s, when psychoanalysis was at the height of its prestige and authority and when psychologists frequently felt empowered to try out their pet theories on real people without much regard to the ethical consequences. The Robbers Cave experiment (1954) pitted children against each other in adversarial groups to study the origins of intergroup conflict, with surprisingly explosive results. In 1963, Stanley Milgram had his subjects administer high-voltage electric shocks (or believe they were doing so) to other people in order to test how far they would go in inflicting pain out of deference to authority. In the first of his experiments, two-thirds of the subjects were willing to deliver the highest level of shock. This might explain why, despite signs of obvious pain and trauma, trainees of the Sullivan Institute continued to push their patients to dump their spouses, send their children away, and cut off their families.

In many ways, however, the best analogy is the Stanford Prison Experiment (1971), in which a psychology professor turned the basement of the university's psychology department into a simulated prison and randomly assigned a group of undergraduates to the roles of guards and prisoners. The students adapted so quickly to their assigned roles that they were either inflicting or submitting to rapidly increasing levels of sadistic punishment; the experiment had to be cut short when the lead psychologist seemed to lose sight of the real pain he was causing. Some of the participants showed signs of acute suffering and anguish but still did not simply leave the experiment, which they had every right to do. The student prisoners not only accepted brutal treatment from the guards, but when one prisoner rebelled, the other prisoners ridiculed him. The guards' behavior varied from sadistic to comparatively kind, but this did not alter the general picture. "One or two guards on each shift became progressively meaner over time, others maintained a more even-tempered style, and a few were considered 'good guards' from the prisoners' perspectives," wrote Philip Zimbardo, the Stanford psychologist who ran the experiment. "However, none of the 'good guards' ever intervened to prevent the cruelty of their fellow guards."

That sounds quite a bit like the Sullivanian therapists—who ranged from cruel and sadistic to comparatively sympathetic—none of whom challenged the system that gave therapists such power over their patients. Bill Goldberg thinks that the Stanford Prison Experiment helps explain much about groups like the Fourth Wall. "The experiment was supposed to last two weeks and got called off after six days because the psychologist's girlfriend intervened and said, 'Philip, you've got to stop: this is really hurting people.' And he said, 'No, let's just see how it plays out.' He was getting off on it. He was unconsciously enjoying this terrible, sadistic stuff and not being cognizant of that. Thank God for the girlfriend who pointed it out to him. And you have to give him credit for realizing, once it was pointed out, 'My God, how could I have gone along with it?'" It shows the seductive nature of power—not just for the Stanford students asked to play at being prison guards but for the lead psychologist who got to play God with the people in his experiment. One aspect of the experiment that some have seen as a flaw is that one of the students appeared to be particularly sadistic, having the effect of egging on his peers. (That student later claimed that he was playacting.) But the Goldbergs see this as illustrating something important about the nature of groups: the element of randomness and individual personality in determining the direction things will take.

Without the presence of a dominant and sadistic personality like Saul Newton (and perhaps Joan Harvey), the Sullivan Institute might not have gone to the extremes it ultimately went to. "There is a random element to it. Maybe, without this particular individual, others wouldn't have been so swept up," Lorna Goldberg said. "I think a lot of the people I encountered would have been fine without the group. They might have done a few years of therapy and found their way. They are lovely people."

Some of the Fourth Wall patients the Goldbergs treated ended up becoming therapists themselves. Driven to understand themselves and what kept them in the group for so long, they ended up wanting to work with others. "I was amazed with the number of them that ended up going back to school for a doctorate, then going to a legitimate institute," Lorna Goldberg said. "And they're fine therapists, because their experience has humbled them and they're so aware of the power that a therapist can have. I really have a lot of confidence in these people as therapists."

*   *   *

When I began researching this project, I was curious to know what became of Marice Pappo, whose decision to kidnap her own child was, in effect, the beginning of the end of the group. Others I interviewed had warned me that she would never talk to me. She disappeared after she and Chris H. settled their custody case, and she had never given any more interviews. I located her without much difficulty but waited quite a while before contacting her, fearing that she would not be happy to hear from me. She was living in upstate New York near the Canadian border, working as a psychotherapist. Eventually I summoned my courage and called her; she answered the phone and did not hang up on me. She said she didn't want to be interviewed, but she also didn't appear eager to get off the phone. When I reassured her that she could speak freely, that I would not use her words without her consent, she suggested that we speak again when she had more time.

In searching for her, I'd noticed that Chris H. was listed as a doctor at a hospital in the same town where Marice lived. I wondered whether, as part of settling their legal battle, they had agreed to live near each other in order to share custody of their daughter. But when I asked about him, Marice explained that they had never divorced and remained together as husband and wife. "My aim was to get my daughter back—I was not doing something against Chris. I loved Chris, and wanted to get him out of the group, to get my family back. And once he left, we got back together." I had pored over the voluminous papers of their custody battle and—as often happens in these kinds of cases—it was bitter and vicious. I wondered how these two people could be in the same room together, let alone married and living under the same roof.

After a few more phone conversations, Marice indicated that she was okay with being interviewed for a book, so I decided to drive up to spend an afternoon with her and Chris. They live in a comfortable, pleasant house near Lake George. We spent three or four hours sitting at their kitchen table, talking. She was now a slender, elegant woman in her seventies, looking recognizably like the forty-two-year-old woman I had seen in press photographs from the late 1980s even if her blond hair was now colored and she had shed her Farrah Fawcett haircut. Chris was still tall and handsome, smart and articulate, looking fifteen or twenty years younger than his age. Not only were they still together, but they seemed to genuinely like each other, bonded by their common ordeal. Their daughter had survived her stormy first year of life, become a successful medical doctor, married, and now had a daughter of her own. Pictures of daughter and grandchild were everywhere. And Marice talked about a trip they had made to take care of the baby when her daughter needed some childcare help. It didn't take a Ph.D. in psychology to figure out that Marice and Chris, by focusing so intently on their infant granddaughter, were making up for the catastrophic first year of their own daughter's life. Chris said he could barely remember anything about Jessica's infancy: she had been with a babysitter for most of the time while he was working. Marice, of course, had been prevented from seeing her for six months.

They spoke with thoughtful candor about their time in the group and were gracious and generous in answering all my questions. There was only one moment when the psychological toll of what was perhaps the central episode of their lives showed. After we had been talking for about an hour, I asked Marice if she would recount the story of what had driven her to kidnap her own daughter. Before she could begin, Chris jumped up and said, "Let's go take a look at the garden. I haven't given you the tour!" He was not trying to keep Marice from telling her story or me from hearing it—she would resume as soon as we had finished smelling the roses—but I suspect he had a sudden nervous reaction triggered by the memory of what had to be one of the most traumatic events—possibly *the* most traumatic—of his life. He needed to take a break and clear his head before reliving it.

A few days later Marice asked me what impressions I had of them. I said that I was full of admiration for them both. When I read the proceedings of their court case, their lives had seemed like a human train wreck, with so much hurt and pain it was hard to see how either of them could recover, let alone recover together. I said I was impressed by the strength and generosity they both showed in being able to forgive each other and make a good life for themselves and their daughter.

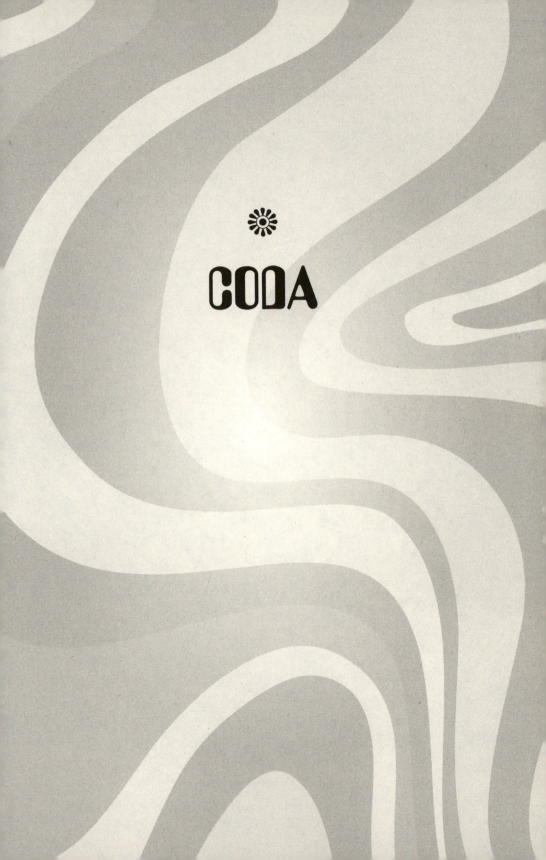

CODA

21

The Kids Are (Mostly) All Right

As the children of the Fourth Wall reached adulthood, established their own careers, and, in some cases, had children of their own, they began increasingly to look back and consider the world in which they were raised. Karen Bray remembers her early years as a kind of battlefield in which her parents fought over the fate of the Fourth Wall. When her father, Mike Bray, left the group in late 1985, he sued for custody of the twin girls he had had with his ex-wife and fellow Sullivanian therapist, Alice D., on the grounds that the Fourth Wall was a harmful cult and not a fit environment in which to raise children. Alice and her new husband, Robbie Newton, moved out of the group's headquarters and into an individual apartment to show that they were not in thrall to the group. They complained bitterly that Bray was waging a war against the Fourth Wall, giving media interviews and allowing their girls to be filmed and photographed, showing that he cared about destroying the group and not about his daughters' well-being. The legal fight was emotionally and financially exhausting, and it went on for years.

"I don't remember a time in my childhood in which fear wasn't a part of my daily existence on some fundamental level," said Karen, who is now a professor of religious studies and philosophy at Wesleyan College, a women's college in Macon, Georgia. Mike Bray's departure had put an end to her living at the Ninety-First Street headquarters with the leadership and playing alongside their children, so it was easy to see her father as a villain. The legal battle he initiated upended her familiar world and raised the levels of tension, blood pressure, and anger in everyone around her. She remembers feeling a sense of dread and terror as her father's car entered the darkness of the Brooklyn-Battery Tunnel on Friday evenings, spiriting her and her sister, Jackie, to the place where he was living in Brooklyn. Then there was the weekend when, instead of staying with him in the city as they usually did, they headed out to the airport, and their father took them off to Iowa to a cousin's wedding. Karen had somehow managed to get to a phone and tell her mother where they were. "I remember being at my uncle's house, and the sheriff coming because my mother had called to say that we'd been kidnapped." Mike Bray had not sought permission to take the girls to this family event—because he was sure their mother would have tried to prevent it. He didn't feel it was her place to decide how he spent his weekends with the kids, but given the Marice Pappo case, it was also understandable that Alice might have thought they'd been kidnapped.

"I remember my mom and my stepdad being angry a lot of the time, and they would openly trash my dad," Karen said. Some of this was standard fare for a bitter divorce/custody battle, but the volume and stakes were raised because it was also a battle over the future and survival of the group. "I blamed him for ruining what I had mistakenly thought was this utopian thing. Like they took me out of this thing because of him." Mike Bray was now sharing a house in Brooklyn with Paul Sprecher, who was waging his own custody battle. The two men were interviewed several times for articles and television news shows about the group, some of which created problems for the girls. "All the children who were supposed to come to my third-grade birthday party canceled because a news report had come out about the case, and my mom had to call their parents and beg them to come," Karen said. "We had friends who stopped talking to us because their parents said, you can no longer play with those children."

By the same token, when she was with her father—and some of his former Fourth Wall friends—Karen was in an opposite, parallel universe, in which her mother's world was evil. She felt scared to speak her mind at Mike Bray's house during the custody battle, and she began thinking that he might be recording their phone calls—which, it turns out, he was. Karen recalled being at a party in Brooklyn with her father and some of the other group defectors when someone telephoned to give the news that Saul Newton had died. Everyone in the room cheered. Karen didn't know what to think or feel. "My sister and I are sitting there like, what are we supposed to do? Saul is one of our best friends. Saul is our stepfather's dad. To my dad's credit, when we were walking home that night, he said, 'Look, are you guys okay? I know that might've been hard,' like he recognized that this constant switching of allegiances might have been hard for us. Because it felt like it was a war. My dad was waging war against the Fourth Wall." Later, she appreciated his determination to extricate his family from the group, but at the time she blamed him.

Karen's twin sister, Jackie, recalled Mike Bray taking them on a holiday trip to San Francisco, the biggest trip they had ever taken. "We were so excited—we rode on cable cars, and it was really cool, and then, a couple of days into the vacation, he said to us, 'Girls, we're going to see a woman, and we're going to talk to her a little bit.' And we spent hours being interviewed about our mom—it was obviously a therapist or an expert witness. And I remember feeling so betrayed . . . 'You said we were going on a vacation.'"

When Mike and Alice settled their custody battle, they agreed to move to the same town in New Jersey so that their kids could easily move between the two households—another disorienting jolt for their kids.

"We went from this communist psychotherapy sex cult in New York City to Ridgewood, New Jersey, the year that George Bush Sr. came there to campaign for president; my sister and I didn't know what we were doing," Karen said. "And no one really helped us figure that out." Even after her mother and stepfather moved out of the Ninety-First Street residence, they continued to see all their friends from the group, and their kids continued to see all their friends. "At any given time, there were half a dozen adults making sure you were warm and fed, and you had all these friends who were like cousins, and from one day to the next—over fucking night—you're living in a suburban home with your one sister and two parents, and you're basically not allowed to see those people again," Jackie Bray said. "That's baggage I carry with me."

Karen and Jackie now moved between these two households, one in which the Fourth Wall was evil incarnate, the other still very much defined by the group, whose members were like members of a secret fraternity, with a tight bond that knit them together but was never discussed—at least not in front of the children. "My two households hate each other," Karen said, "and are exhausted from what they've put each other through, and I'm going back and forth every couple of days between these two houses. One is so angry and resentful and anxious, and the other one is so beaten down and quiet, and I'm, like, chasing after love in both places."

The two households were like fire and ice. Their mother and stepfather's house was more emotionally warm but also full of eruptions of anger and open hostility toward their other parent, Mike. You could go from "Fuck you" to "I love you" in minutes. But they were also always there, even after blowout fights. Mike Bray, by contrast, seemed emotionally shut down. "He put food on the table and a roof over our head," Jackie Bray said. "He wasn't irresponsible or negligent, but he did not remotely make an attempt to connect with us. He has personally described that to us—more to Karen because she asks about it more— that he had to put up this massive wall. He was so full of rage and contempt for our mother that he was scared the only emotion that would come out was anger. But it sucked. He didn't start being an emotionally present father until I was an adult out of college. To be honest, I think as soon as he showed up, I showed up."

When Karen was fourteen, she began suffering from bouts of depression and psychological difficulties. The Bray children never got any therapy after their difficult and tempestuous childhood. Her parents, who with all their faults loved her very much, became extremely concerned, but in Karen's view, they also framed it as "What's wrong with Karen?" She explained, "It became easy for my family to say the problem of this family is Karen's mental health. Karen can be set off by a hair trigger. She's sad . . . Anyone who's studied family system theory knows that if the system is sick, then one person gets designated as the patient, but they're really the symptom of the larger system." Karen felt that focusing on her problems became a substitute for having a frank and honest discussion about life growing up in the Fourth Wall, something her mother and stepfather wanted very much to avoid.

Karen started college, then dropped out, then started again and began working on a long paper about the group. She interviewed her three parents as well as a few other people and began to learn and think more about the impact life in the group had had on her. She had always been intensely aware that there was a pecking order, even among the kids who lived at the group headquarters, and that she was on the bottom of the ladder and had to defer to the children of Saul Newton and Joan Harvey. "She always got to be Barbie, and I had to be Skipper, or we played whatever game she wanted. And if I complained to any of the babysitters, they would yell at me instead of the children of the two leaders." When Karen met up with one of her old babysitters, the woman apologized for not protecting her more, telling Karen that her feeling about a hierarchy among the kids was not just an impression. "She said they were instructed that when they fed the kids, they should be sure to feed the leaders' kids first and if they wanted hot dogs, we ate hot dogs," Karen explained. This helped her understand some things that she carried from her childhood. "I always felt like a lesser person. I was not trained to think of myself as the primary person."

Eventually Karen embarked on what for a child of the Fourth Wall was a highly unusual course: divinity school. The Fourth Wall had been implacably anti-religious. "When I called up my mother and stepfather to tell them that I thought I might believe in God, there was silence on the other end of the phone," Karen said. She was inspired to pursue divinity school and a Ph.D. in theology because her close family friend and neighbor, Paul Sprecher—he and his family also moved to Ridgewood—had himself undertaken a change in career by becoming a Unitarian minister. While Karen was at Harvard Divinity School, she was asked to write a "spiritual autobiography"; it ended up being an in-depth look at the Fourth Wall and the Sullivan Institute. Both sets of her parents gave her all the documentation they had kept from their custody case as well as the notes her father and mother had kept in their time as Sullivanian therapists. The research was a disturbing voyage of discovery. "They broke up couples, took children away from their parents. There are therapists' notes where they tortured members inside the group: 'No, you can't have a child. You can't have a child with this person. You are a bad mother.' Supervising therapists telling junior therapists how to convince a woman she is a bad mother—it was disgusting."

Less dramatic but equally moving to Karen was the correspondence between Mike Bray and his mother back in Iowa, a woman Karen never had the opportunity to meet. The letters start out chatty and newsy—family members catching each other up on their lives. "What's going on up at the lake? Love to dad." But everything changes after Mike Bray enters Sullivanian therapy; he stops writing. At first his mother is puzzled and a little hurt. "There's a note from my grandmother to my dad, saying like, 'We don't understand why you've disappeared from our lives. We don't know what's going on. Like your father says, I must have upset you last time we spoke on the phone. But knowing how I feel about you, I know that just can't be true.' Like, why are you doing this to us? It's cruel. And then there's a postcard typed from my dad that says, 'I've never been happier than I am right now. I am very well. I will no longer be talking to you. If something changes, I'll let you know.' And then there's a last letter from my grandmother that says, 'We don't understand any of this.' They continue to wait for mail that never comes. Finally, his mother writes to him, 'If you ever change your mind, my door will always be open to you.' And that's the last correspondence they ever had. She died while he was still in the cult, and it's heartbreaking." Karen found herself in the library, weeping as she read through these letters. She felt terrible for her grandmother, but she also realized that she, too, had been deprived of grandparents she never had the chance to meet.

Karen Bray interviewed women who had been in the group who described the sexual predation they endured, and she was shocked to discover how prevalent it had been. She found a deposition in which her mother admits that she was not sure who her kids' biological father was, which was an upsetting revelation. Karen now urgently wanted to speak to her mother and stepfather about life in the group and the things she was learning. "I kept trying to get them to talk to me about it. They didn't for many, many years after that. There were times where my mom and my stepdad stopped speaking to me because they were uncomfortable with what I was trying to bring up." At a certain point, her stepfather, Robbie, drove up to Cambridge to try to put their relationship on a better footing, and he agreed to talk about the group. She flung some of her most disturbing discoveries at him. "Like people were raped on a regular basis," she said. He contested that idea, arguing that people were not physically forced into sex. "When someone feels they can't say no to someone who has more power than they do, that's rape," she insisted.

The experience of the children of the group differed, but as they grew up, they began to question things they had taken for granted as kids. Pam Newton, raised as the daughter of two leaders, has gone through a long, complex evolution. "There's been a ton of processing in various forms," she said as we sat at the dining table of her Brooklyn apartment, where she lives with her husband. "I've talked to my friends from the group a ton. I've talked to my old babysitters. For me it's been about, like, first of all trying to understand what the hell that was. What is this thing I was raised in? When you're a kid, you just half understand. It's the only life you know, so you take it as a given. So first it's a process of questioning and wondering exactly what it was. And second, admitting it was a cult. I think I was resistant to that at first because I thought, 'I went to a normal school and normal camp. I wasn't being brainwashed.' At first, when people started calling it a cult when I was younger, I was like, well, it was a commune."

When a lot of the Fourth Wall kids finished college, they returned to New York and began to compare notes about their unusual childhoods. "I was talking to the other kids, and they were really hard on it and they were like, 'We grew up in this sex cult,'" Pam Newton recalled.

"And I was like, 'No, it was kind of fun,' and I was more defensive. I think I had to go through a process in my twenties of really talking to people, finding out what it was, going back and reading the articles and just taking a good, hard look at it."

Pam was ten years old when the Marice Pappo case happened. "I remember my mom saying, 'Marice Pappo went nuts.'" But as Pam got older, she wondered what would drive a woman to steal her own baby. "I began to realize that in many ways it was a textbook cult. I remember watching a documentary about Scientology and hearing all these echoes. There was a charismatic, authoritarian leader. There was a self-actualizing therapy that was going to solve all your problems. People were cut off from other people in their lives and their extended families. I saw my grandparents about once a year, and that was a special privilege granted to my mother. None of my friends ever saw their grandparents."

Karen Bray grew up with Pam just upstairs in the group's Ninety-First Street headquarters and residence. Since Karen is more than six years younger, they didn't play together much as kids but became good friends as adults. "As far as the kids go, there's like a spectrum of anger about it," Pam said. "I'm toward the less angry end of the spectrum. Karen is pissed."

But Karen is careful not to compare herself with others: "There is no Olympics of suffering. We were each traumatized in different ways. And I am very grateful Saul was not my father."

* * *

As the kids of the Fourth Wall came to terms with their past, many of them turned to genetic testing—which became widely available and relatively inexpensive by the 2010s—in order to more clearly establish their paternity.

"Me and another friend from the group found out we were siblings through 23andMe," Pam Newton explained. "That's what started us on this whole journey." Pam and another boy from the group, seven years younger, discovered they were half-siblings. "Neither of us knew who our biological fathers were, and we were like, 'Let's figure it out,' so he was the first sibling I gained."

To her surprise, Pam learned that her biological father was Ralph Klein, their downstairs neighbor on the second floor of the Ninety-First Street compound and also—perhaps more important for Pam—the father of Toni Klein, one of her best friends. The children Ralph Klein had with Joan Harvey were all adopted, so this DNA test now created a link with Pam's friend's father that Toni herself did not have—the source of some tension between them.

Then there was Amanda Newton, who thought she was Saul Newton's daughter (with Joan Harvey). In the end, it turned out that she, like Pam, was actually Ralph Klein's biological child. "So that's a biological sibling I gained," Pam said, "who I already thought was a sibling, but it turns out she is my half sister but from a different dad, if you follow that. We both thought we were Saul's kids, and we both turned out to be Ralph's." (Amanda Newton changed her name to Amanda Klein.)

Kids in the group were gaining and losing parents, gaining half-siblings and losing other siblings, in a confusing merry-go-round of tests. It provided as many twists and turns as the end of a Dickens novel in which mistaken identities are clarified and long-lost foundlings are reunited with their parents.

In some ways, these revelations were less upsetting to the Fourth Wall kids than they might have been for other people. They had grown up together and regarded one another almost as siblings, which, in many cases, they turned out to be. At the same time, these discoveries raised all sorts of questions: What were my parents thinking? It could easily have happened that different children of the group married and had children, only to discover that they were biologically brother and sister.

As it turned out, none of the four children Helen Moses had with Saul Newton were actually his biological children. This revelation was not overly distressing to Pam. "I mean, I'm sort of glad I'm not Saul's child. Even though there were things that people really admired about

Saul, and he was kind of this visionary, he terrorized me as a child and was kind of a monster. I'm glad I'm not related to this person with this crazy temper and dementia and a Messiah complex. Ralph was kinder and gentler . . . He was, according to one of his other kids, the only child who got out of the village in Austria where he was born, who survived the Holocaust. That may be connected to why he was sort of a damaged person. So I'd like to think that I haven't inherited that part of it."

When Pam went to see her mother, Helen Moses, with the discovery about her biological father, her mother seemed to take it in stride. "When I first told my mom, she was like, 'Oh, Ralph, he was always so handsome and intelligent. I always really loved him as a friend.' Like she wanted to spin it as a good thing." But as Pam set about finding out more about Ralph, not all of it was positive. "He was no winner either. I've heard stories from other people about him being like sexually weird, being a flasher, ogling bodies of teenage girls very obviously, being a sexually inappropriate, creepy guy." When she went back to her mother with this information, Helen Moses suddenly changed her tune: "'Oh, yeah, Ralph was totally sexually creepy.' She didn't mention that when I first found out. So, you know, it's like, what? What do I do with this information?"

Pam doesn't feel that it changed her life that much, because it doesn't change her lived experience. She grew up as Saul Newton's daughter, living in fear of him. She never had a single significant one-on-one experience with Ralph Klein. She doesn't regard the siblings she grew up with any differently now that she knows they are half-siblings. Yet it seemed important to know the facts, in part because the children of the group feel their parents were almost never straight with them. "Yes, it matters, but it doesn't ultimately change much, I think, for most of the kids: we want information, we want truth, we want to know who we are and where we come from. But [clarifying paternity] doesn't ultimately change for a lot of us." The one significant exception to this was a good friend of hers who gained a whole new family. "She was raised by a single mom and then found out who her dad was, and now she calls him dad and calls his other kids her brothers and sisters. So she really gained a family."

At some point after Pam got her 23andMe results, Karen Bray went to a birthday party for Sean Mack, another Fourth Wall kid, who was turning forty. (The second generation of kids remain very good friends.) Another girl from the group came up to Karen and said something like, "I always tell people that I know a pair of twins who actually have different fathers." Karen had no idea what she was talking about and just went with the conversation. They were chatting, and Karen said something like, "For years I thought my sister and I might have two different biological fathers because we are so different." But she didn't take the idea seriously. And the people she was talking to at the party said, "'That's what our parents have told us for years.' I thought it was just like a bonkers theory." Karen pretended she had always known but in fact was in something of a state of shock. If she and her sister, Jackie, had different fathers, Karen imagined that it meant that Jackie, who had brown eyes, was Robbie Newton's child and she, Karen, was Mike Bray's—or someone else's.

At the time, Karen was living in New York, and her sister, who works in politics, was in Washington, D.C. But Jackie was coming up to New York, and they arranged to have drinks together. "The first thing out of Karen's mouth was, 'Do you think you could be Robbie's kid?'" Jackie recalled. "And I think I said something like, 'Well, he is my dad.' And Karen said, 'I mean do you think Robbie could be your biological father?' And I remember just as vivid as today in an instant knowing it was absolutely true. And I said, 'Oh, yeah, of course.' And she was like, 'Right, of course.'"

"It was completely obvious that it had been true forever," Jackie Bray said. "It made complete sense that Karen and I were half sisters. We're so different. She's much taller than me. She has had blond hair for most of her life. She's got bright blue eyes." Moreover, the two sisters are temperamentally different. Karen has suffered from depression and has wanted to fully investigate her family's past. Jackie preferred not to look back so much and to get on with her life. She is a successful civil servant and political operative who works at a high level in New York City government. Karen has had a more circuitous path toward a Ph.D. and an academic position.

Jackie had always assumed that they both were Mike Bray's kids. If that were not the case, her mother would have challenged his paternity during their long custody battle. "If it hadn't been, they could have asked for a DNA test, and it would have been game over." But now she realized that if the tests revealed that the two daughters were fathered by different men, it would have opened a Pandora's box during the court case. "That would have opened the floodgates on multiple sexual partners, and so on."

It was Karen who confronted her mother and stepfather about this discovery. "Karen asked them point-blank, and they said 'Jackie is Robbie's biological daughter, but you are not,'" Jackie explained. It took longer for Karen to get them to explain. "It took days to pull the full story out of them," Karen said. During the custody litigation, her mother had had a blood test done; if the results excluded Mike Bray's paternity, he would presumably lose any claim to custody. But the result came back with a strange result: it showed that Jackie and Robbie Newton were a match, but Karen was not. "The test said that your sister is Robbie's and you are not."

After Karen's conversation with Alice and Robbie, Jackie's phone rang. "It was three days before Christmas, and Robbie called and said, 'Hey, Jackaloo'—that's what he calls me. And I said, 'Why are you calling? Does Mom want to know what time we're getting there?' He said, 'I have something to tell you.' I said, 'Okay.' He said, 'I'm your bio-dad.' And I said, 'Oh, yeah. Okay.' He said, 'Do you want to talk more?' And I said, 'No, I get it.' Then I spent the next solid hour staring at my face in the mirror and feeling like it was the first time I'd ever actually seen my face—because I look a lot like him, and I had just never seen him in me."

After this, Jackie went to break the news to Mike Bray, to tell him that he was not in fact her biological father. Alice and Robbie had never told Mike about the blood test. "She said, 'Listen, Dad, there's something very hard that I need to tell you,'" Mike Bray recalled. "I knew this was the moment. And I said, 'You're going to tell me that Robbie's your biological father,' at which point her eyes just grew. I said, 'I've known all along . . . It had to be. You look just like him.' She cried," Mike said, and as he told me the story, he began to tear up. "And then she said, 'But you fought for us anyway.' And I said, 'Of course I fought for you. None of that mattered.'" While it settled Jackie's paternity situation, it unsettled Karen's. "I talked with Karen," Mike said, "and she was troubled because Jackie knew who her dad was but she did not. So she asked me to take a spit test, and I was not a match," he said simply and matter-of-factly, although it must have been a painful discovery.

"So then, the mother had to admit or recall that actually Ralph [Klein] was also, without our knowledge, mixed in there one night . . . or whatever," Mike said. Karen became convinced that Ralph Klein was her biological father. Unfortunately, he died a couple of years before Karen's discovery. "I was furious [with her mother and stepfather]," Karen said. "Why didn't you tell me of this possibility sooner?" Perhaps she might have gotten to know him. She tried, without success, to establish a relationship with some of his kids, but it was tricky. Klein had a couple of (known) biological children and several adopted ones, and not all of them were happy about her sudden claim to his paternity. But one person she spoke with looked at her and said, "You're definitely a Klein!" Karen tried to reimagine herself as Ralph Klein's child and learned what she could about his life. On a trip to Europe, she made a point of stopping in Vienna—Klein was Austrian—and trying to think her way into his past. She looked at the records of Vienna's Jewish community and began developing a new family narrative for herself.

At this point, two other kids from the group—one of them Pam Newton—came to Karen and asked her to do a DNA test. Pam, after all, had learned that she was Ralph Klein's biological child, so if Karen got tested, she could ascertain her paternity and potentially acquire some new siblings. "I said yes," Karen said, "and I am hoping that I am Pam's sister. That would be something interesting to me." Pam also asked Robbie Newton if he would do the test as well. There were kids who were trying to figure out whether they were Saul Newton's biological children, and since Saul was long dead by this point, Robbie's DNA might solve that puzzle. Karen awaited her results, and when she got the email from 23andMe, she was thinking, "The options are either yes, Pam and I are siblings, or we're not." Instead, her genetic profile revealed that her biological father was her stepfather, Robbie Newton. Karen was completely floored. This was the last thing she expected. The blood test done twenty-five years earlier during the custody battle had ruled out this possibility. It had never occurred to her—or to anyone else in the family—that the blood test could be wrong. "It was utterly shocking to me," she said. And surprisingly painful.

One might have thought that this result would have greatly simplified her life. In some ways it had made her family whole again: it turned out that the twin sister she'd grown up with was, in fact, her full sister. And in some ways it was a relief to know she was not the daughter of some dead stranger like Ralph Klein but of one of the two father figures she had grown up with, a man who had always loved her like a daughter. There was a delicious irony in the discovery—they turned out to be what the Fourth Wall had tried so hard to prevent: a perfect, intact nuclear family. Mom, Dad, and two kids. Instead, Karen said, "it set off one of my worst PTSD episodes . . . Not because I don't want to be related to Robbie. I had already found out I wasn't related to Mike. So the pain of that, that we are not blood related, that wasn't it."

What was painful for Karen was the realization that the whole configuration of her early life had been the result of a mistake, a faulty blood test. The central trauma of her childhood had been the vicious custody battle that tore her family apart when she was three and lasted for several years—arguably for her whole life. "It turns out that maybe none of this needed to happen—this intense custody battle that had destroyed both of my households . . . Maybe we were just supposed to be with Alice and Robbie. It's hard for me to say that, because I profoundly love Mike, and now, having lived a whole life with Mike as my father, I would not go back on that. But as a three-year-old, maybe I would have had a calmer life if I'd just been raised by two people who loved each other—and not put through a custody battle." The seven years of litigation had generated so much anger, fear, hate, paranoia, and financial distress, with the children in the middle, trying to make sense of it all. "It set off for me reliving all the most traumatic parts of having to go back and forth between those houses. I was thrown right back into it. And I also thought, 'What more bombshells can I have go off? I've thought three different men were my father in the past three years. I'm exhausted by having to relive the mistakes of my parents.'" At the same time, Karen understood that imagining her life as it *might* have been led her down a maddening, impossible path, with its own share of pain. "Ultimately I would be a different person than I am today. If that path had happened, I wouldn't have Mike in my life. I wouldn't have my stepmom and my stepsisters in my life. I like my life. I like who I am. It's okay."

Surprisingly, the person who understood best why the news of her paternity was so upsetting to Karen was Robbie, her former stepfather and new biological father. Rather than be offended by her reaction to learning that he was her father, he instinctively understood her sense of frustration at fully grasping the extent of the unnecessary pain they had all suffered. "Robbie, to his credit, responded probably best of everyone," Karen said. "He acknowledged why this would be upsetting. He said, 'This feels tragic to me, because I've lost sleep every day of my life for thirty years regretting that I wasn't your father.'" Robbie knew—they all knew—that if the group had not convinced them to play Russian roulette with their children's paternity, all this pain and confusion could have been avoided.

After some discussion, Jackie was picked to break the difficult news to Mike Bray. "I was nominated by the family, at Karen's insistence, to tell Mike," Jackie said. "I remember telling him, and then immediately saying, 'I just want you to know that I'm glad the test was wrong.' Immediately—because I knew where his mind was going to go." He might feel that this nullified what was perhaps the crucial chapter of his life. In order to not lose his daughters, he remained in the group for two years after he knew he wanted to leave. He left only when their mother granted him joint custody. He had spent several years fighting, as he saw it, to free his daughters from the cult and bring the group to an end. She was afraid he would now see it all as a mistake, one that had caused his daughters a lot of pain. "He knows exactly that that was the trauma in his daughters' lives," Jackie said. "And he knows that if the blood test hadn't been wrong, we would have avoided that trauma. Does our love for him and his love for us supersede that trauma? Yes, it turns out that it does. But it's not a given. It was devastating."

Reflecting on the wild paternity roller coaster she and her family have ridden, Jackie said, "If it were a movie, you'd probably say, 'Bullshit. This couldn't happen.' The irony of ironies is that after all [that], we turned out to be a nuclear family."

Jackie and Karen both feel that their story casts a curious light on the life of the group: a community dedicated to breaking up the family was broken up by families. "The deep irony for me is that the Sullivanians put so much emphasis on breaking binary bonds," Karen said, "separating members from their families of origin, torturing members [with] 'You can't have a child, or you can't have a child with this person. You are a bad mother.' And yet custody battles brought this group down." At one point Joan Harvey had tried to get Alice to give up her legal battle and custody of her kids, and she'd refused. It is also an irony that in some ways, biology wasn't always crucial. Mike Bray was somewhat artificially assigned the role of father, but he took it to heart and fought as hard as their biological parents and earned his place in his children's lives by continuing to play that role for them.

After meeting smart, kind, and thoughtful people like Karen, Jackie, Sean, and Pam, who, by virtue of growing up together, have, despite it all, turned into highly functional adults with full lives and strong bonds among them, it is hard not to wonder whether the group in some way succeeded in creating a strong, lasting community. Their parents, too, have a denser network of friends, mostly from the group, than most people.

"I was at a party recently," Pam Newton recalled. "Somebody from the group had his seventieth birthday, and he invited tons of Fourth Wall people, like twenty-five of them. And they all were so psyched to see each other and were dancing and, you know, singing, and it was a big celebration and I thought, 'Oh, that's the good side of the group.' I remember them dancing and playing music and seeming to be having a really good time together, and it was that same vibe, and they all still seem to have a lot of love for each other." At the same time, she said, that sense of nostalgia masks how complicated it was for the kids. "If you asked the kids, do you wish you had grown up in a conventional way, some of them maybe wish they just had lived in an apartment with their parents."

Karen Bray is not so sure how real that sense of community is. "I can't tell what has bound these people together: Is it more the good times they share or the trauma they survived?" she said. "I think probably for the people who were adults, not the kids, they shared some formative times together. You know . . . they shared their twenties and first loves and having kids and playing music. And all those things bind them together. I'm sure a lot of them have those memories. I can also imagine that people who went to fight in Iraq have a close bond with each other, but it's not a justification for going to war. I think they also are bound together because they can't believe what they went through. They survived joining a group and coming out of it and discovering that their parents were dead. They survived someone telling them that they can't have kids and then all of a sudden having to have a kid at forty-two with whoever is willing to have a kid with you."

* * *

Andy Cates had almost no contact with his parents during the final years of the group. His life had gone off the rails a bit after he dropped out of college. One of his friends—another child of the Fourth Wall—told him, "You're a mess," saying that he needed to get his life back together. He ended up joining the marines, which he said saved his life. It was in a sense like joining a cult. "I have been through real brainwashing," he said. "I went to the Marine Corps boot camp and fully submitted myself to that and consciously knowing it at the time." Boot camp is designed to first break you down before building you back up, not as an individual but as a member of a team. Andy, who had such a scattered and messed-up early life, welcomed the structure and discipline of the marines. Unlike Sullivanian therapy, the experience taught him how to take control of his life.

It had been several years since he was banned from New York by Saul Newton, and he had little or nothing to do with his parents. "I didn't talk to my parents for years. When I went into the Marine Corps, I had no intention of ever having a relationship with them. I was thinking of either making a career out of the Marine Corps or finishing school on my own, but I wanted nothing to do with them." But one day he got a letter, a big envelope with multiple pages that contained a long, handwritten letter from his mother, who wanted to reestablish a relationship. Attached to the letter was a yellow sticky note that simply said, "Andy, call. Love, Dad."

It was a small gesture, but Andy understood it was a meaningful one, for his father and for himself. Despite his resolve to have nothing more to do with his parents, despite being toughened up by the marines, he was still, in some ways, a child starved for parental affection, a child waiting at the end of the driveway at his boarding school, hoping his parents would show up for parents' day. "After that, my dad and I rekindled our relationship, and it was great," Andy said. "I went back to New York, and as the Fourth Wall shut down, they came out of their fog and apologized a thousand times for what they had done. They apologized for boarding school. My dad was sorry about making me move out of that dorm room. They were sorry about everything. I mean, they were really, really, really contrite, and my mom probably apologized fifty times for every time my dad apologized. But my dad was not very talkative. So when he apologized, I knew it really meant something."

One curious thing, however, is that Andy's father, John Cates, had fallen in love with acting while performing in the Fourth Wall. Although he was a medical doctor, he wanted desperately to continue to act, and he went to audition after audition. "He waited in those lines, got turned down, and he was persistent," Andy recalled. "Eventually he got a job in Kentucky doing summer stock. He was so excited: 'Andy, they're going to pay me to act! It's going to be room and board and two hundred dollars a week, but they're paying me to act.'" His father did enough professional acting to earn a place in the Screen Actors Guild, which made him enormously proud.

It was not as if everything were suddenly rosy between John Cates and his two sons. When Eddy Cates was an undergraduate at Duke, his father cut him off financially when he refused to reenter Sullivanian therapy. In 1989, when Eddy was finishing up college, he invited his father to his graduation even though they had not spoken in a while. At the graduation, John delivered the news that he had agreed to adopt a child with another woman in the Fourth Wall. "It was arranged through the group," said Eddy Cates. "I think they just wanted to get control over his money." John Cates, who was gay, had no real relationship with the woman who was adopting the little girl, but he would be taking financial responsibility for raising a child whom, in all likelihood, he would not live to see grow up. Eddy was furious. It seemed like the Fourth Wall was sinking its claws into his father, and his father was going along out of a mixture of weakness and blind irresponsibility. Finishing college without his father's support had given Eddy the right to speak his mind, and he let his father have it. "I was like, 'You're a fucking horrible dad, what makes you think that at the age of seventy you should adopt a baby?'" But John did adopt the child, and he left his money in a trust for the mother and child. For Eddy and Andy, both sent away at age seven, it was the Fourth Wall's last revenge.

Eddy, having learned through bitter experience not to count on his parents, succeeded in going to medical school, building a practice in Washington State, marrying, and having three kids. Perhaps in response to growing up in a group that wanted to destroy the family, he set up a family practice. After leaving the marines, Andy finished college and went on to law school, set up a solo law practice, married, and has a family. Given his rocky start, he considers himself extremely fortunate.

For both, achieving a stable, normal life seemed like a semi-miraculous achievement.

Eddy and Andy more or less reconciled with their parents but remained at an ironic distance. When talking about their parents, they are not afraid to speak with total, sometimes brutal honesty or ironic humor. Having fended for themselves from the age of seven, they do not feel the need to sugarcoat their words or be diplomatic.

Sam Miller also made a successful recovery after his miserable years at Treehaven out in Arizona. He graduated from the University of Chicago, is married, has three kids, lives in Brooklyn, and works for a nonprofit health-care provider. He has never fully reconciled with his parents, particularly with his mother, who sent him to boarding school at age seven. He has more of a relationship with his father, but not much. He cannot forget the day when he was back from school, visiting his father, and members of the group began following them, or how his mother had threatened him that if he did not agree to go back to boarding school, he would never see her again. He'd hoped at that moment that his father would say, "Fine, to hell with her, stay with me." But his father waffled, afraid or unwilling to take that responsibility, and his mother whisked him off to the airport, to a school where he would sleep in the back of a pickup truck.

Not surprisingly, Sam's judgment about the Sullivan Institute/ Fourth Wall is one of condemnation without hope of appeal. "I have no sympathy for these people. Everyone talks about how intelligent and educated they were. They were incredibly selfish people who were looking out for themselves. They didn't want anyone impinging on their lifestyle." It wasn't until he was in his forties that Sam confronted his mother about how she had treated him. "I said I need to have this conversation. I asked her why she did it. 'How could you send me away? I told you how horrible it was there. I called. I wrote letters.' I have memories of before I was sent away, pounding on her door, asking to see her, and she just ignored me. And that's a tough memory, you know? But that's what they did. I can't say about other adults. But that's what my mother did. My mother did that to me." His mother sort of apologized, but not really. She continued to believe in the basic philosophy of the group, and she even taught it, he said. "I don't know why these people insisted on having children." (His mother, Marilyn Miller, died in 2021.)

A number of the kids who were sent away proved remarkably resilient and made good lives for themselves despite a very harsh childhood, but Andy Cates, as we were saying goodbye, wanted to emphasize that he, his brother, and Sam Miller were not necessarily typical. "The people you have talked to are people who have done okay, but there were a lot of casualties," he said. Among the Fourth Wall boarding school kids, there was one who committed suicide, another who wound up in prison, and a third who became homeless. More than a few told me that their experiences were too painful to discuss.

Thirty-five years after leaving the group, Michael Cohen and Amy Siskind remain very much married and living in Brooklyn. Cohen completed his Ph.D. in psychology, but after his experience in the group he wanted to focus principally on research. Amy Siskind was beginning graduate school in sociology when they left the group, and she decided to write her dissertation about the Sullivan Institute/Fourth Wall community—not a personal memoir, but a careful, lucid sociological analysis, all the more remarkable because she wrote it while the group was still active, and the only people who would sit for interviews were people like herself who had left. She went on to publish it as a book: *The Sullivan Institute/Fourth Wall Community: The Relationship of Radical Individualism and Authoritarianism* (2003).

The couple's life in the group follows them whether they want it to or not. More than three decades after leaving that building on 100th Street, Cohen and Amy were walking along near their home, and an older woman came up to him and said, "Are you Michael Cohen? I was your patient." "My apologies," Michael said. "No, actually," she said, "you helped me. You were a good therapist." Michael introduced her to Amy, at which point the woman's countenance changed as she remembered that Amy's mother, also a group member, had seduced her boyfriend at the time, helping to break up that relationship. They were amused that the drama of Fourth Wall life would pursue them on the streets of Brooklyn so many years later. It was nice for Cohen to hear that some of his patients feel that he helped them. He makes a point of apologizing when he meets former group members, aware that as a therapist, he caused many people real harm.

At the same time, as a former patient, he still has painful memories. "I left the group in the mid-1980s, and I have nightmares about Joan Harvey about twice a week. Usually I am struggling to get out of the group, and she has some kind of enormous control over my life. Not everyone had that experience, but that was my experience." He considers it part of the particular ethos of the group to have made most of its members simultaneously victims and perpetrators. As a psychologist, and simply as a person, Cohen feels that he learned an enormous amount from a deeply painful experience—albeit at great cost. "I feel that I've been fortunate in some strange way to have had the experience of being brainwashed. I mean, to see the world in a certain way and then come out of it. I really began to see my family as destructive and evil, and they were not. Coming out of it is a difficult process. It's a bitch. But it shows you that the therapeutic relationship is very powerful, [and] if it is abused, it's terrible."

Amy Siskind managed to reconcile with her mother, from whom she had been estranged for many years. Amy's mother, Janet Siskind, while continuing to teach anthropology at Rutgers after the Sullivan Institute's collapse, remained very much in the orbit of Ralph Klein and Joan Harvey as they formed a small community of patients in New Rochelle. After the death of Klein in 2011 and of Harvey in 2014, Amy found it easier to talk with her mother, who seemed happy to reestablish a close mother-daughter relationship. As Janet's health deteriorated in her tenth decade, Amy found herself increasingly taking care of her mother. Her mother was grateful—mindful that her daughter was giving her the kind of care that she as a Sullivanian mother had failed to give Amy. Yet she still steadfastly refused to read Amy's book about the group.

The inescapability of Michael Cohen's unusual past has come home to him with increased intensity in recent years. In 2019, he received an unexpected phone call from someone he hadn't heard from in decades, Ellen Barrett. Because of his closeness to the leadership, when Cohen left the group in 1985, those who stayed behind considered him a traitor. Now Ellen said she needed his help: her two children were desperate to know the identity of their biological father, and Cohen was one of the possible candidates. She and Cohen had not been particularly close and were not regular sexual partners, but when Ellen decided she wanted to have a child in 1979, and again in 1982, and was looking for men to help her conceive, Cohen had agreed. That was what you did in the group. As he was only one of several men involved, he hadn't thought much about it in the years that followed.

But now, decades later, he was faced with his old groupmate, who was now over seventy, and her two children, both in their mid- to late thirties. To reassure him, as well as to encourage him to supply them with a sample of his DNA, they arrived, somewhat to his surprise, with a complex legal document that absolved him of any legal and financial responsibility if he turned out to be the father of Ellen's children. Cohen agreed. It seemed the only decent thing to do. It seemed to matter a great deal to her daughter Chloe (not her real name), now thirty-eight, who was also the mother of a child who might or might not be his grandchild. Chloe described her life growing up in a communal setting as a harrowingly chaotic and destabilizing experience, and she had organized her own life in opposition to the group's principles: she worked in business, made a good living, was married, and had a child in a traditional family. Now she wanted to remove the uncertainty surrounding her biological paternity, something the group had insisted was of no importance.

When the test came back positive—Cohen was Chloe's father—he was not unhappy. She seemed like a lovely young woman, and her sudden appearance felt like an increase of life in his life. But something unexpected happened. Chloe had placed her own DNA profile into the data bank of the genetic testing company, and someone else had suddenly discovered a match. A young man who had also been born in the group had decided to get tested, and he learned that he and Chloe had a parent in common. As they had different mothers, it could only mean that Michael Cohen was their father. When this young man informed Cohen, the shock was much more jarring. He hadn't expected it and hadn't known that his genetic information had been placed in a database. And the young man whom he discovered was now his son was one of the ten children of Saul Newton, a man Cohen had come to loathe.

Disoriented, Cohen consulted a Talmudic scholar to see what his obligations toward these children were according to Jewish tradition and law. "And the Talmud has a very specific answer," he explained. You must guarantee that they can make a living, receive a Jewish education, and marry a Jew. At least the first and most important condition had been met—they were both capable and self-sufficient people. The last two conditions—religious education and choice of spouse—were moot points for adult children in their thirties and forties, each with families of their own.

Even though Cohen had always known that it was a theoretical possibility, it had somehow never penetrated his conscious mind that there might be flesh-and-blood people out there who were his actual children. Or that these people had their own lives, perhaps even living nearby, and that they might have children of their own who were his grandchildren. Accepting the idea was complicated on many levels. It upset the equilibrium of the life Mike had created, which was built around Amy and their daughter, Laura. Now suddenly there were these other children, who, at least chronologically, had come before. To make matters more complicated, he and Amy had adopted Laura. Though it was not easy for them, Amy and Laura reacted with wisdom and generosity. "Maybe this will help you deal with some things that you haven't dealt with," Laura told him. It was a bit like the scene in *The Godfather: Part III* (1990) when Michael Corleone realizes that he can never escape his role in the Mafia: "Just when I thought I was out, they pull me back in!"

In fact, it plunged Cohen back in time, forcing him to think about his life in the group with an intensity he had not felt in many years, especially to think about a chapter of his experience that he realized he had largely buried. When I met with him for a second round of interviews after I had gotten wind of some of the 23andMe revelations, he suddenly stopped and said, "Listen, I want to say something off the record. Please turn off your tape recorder." I did. "You've probably heard by now these stories about the DNA tests," he said. "I just want to be clear: yes, they're true, but I don't want to talk about them. I'd like that to remain off the record." I put that issue aside, but several months later, when we met again, he told me, "My thinking has evolved. I've had a chance to think about it, and I am ready to talk about the whole paternity issue."

The second child Cohen learned that he had fathered was Keith Newton—legally speaking, one of Saul Newton's four children with Helen Moses. To learn that he had served as a surrogate for a man he detested was deeply painful, hammering home the sense that he could not escape Newton's grasp even after his death. Perhaps even harder was that it suddenly brought back to him the horrible circumstances under which this child was conceived. "Rape" was the term Cohen used when discussing it with me. "I have thought a lot about this," he said, explaining why he insists on using such a strong term. "This was not something I wanted to do. Helen Moses was the wife of Saul Newton. I was terrified of this situation, and I didn't want to go anywhere near it." He was ordered to do this and threatened by his therapist, Joan Harvey, and by Newton himself. Since Newton had succeeded in having children in his marriages to Jane Pearce and Joan Harvey, it is not clear why he wanted someone else to inseminate his sixth and final wife. "I was under verbal pressure. I was threatened physically. 'I am going to beat you. You are going to be thrown out of here. You are going to lose your job, be thrown out of your apartment if you don't do this.' I was so terrified, I couldn't perform. They had sent me out to buy some pot and gave me some sedatives to calm me down."

It was one of the worst, most traumatic experiences of Cohen's years in the group. As he began to reflect on it, it felt strange to him that this occurred after he had been in the group for only about a year. Not only had he managed to block it out, but it had in no way prevented him from becoming a true believer in the group's philosophy and form of therapy. Why had he not seen right away that there was something wrong with a group that forced one of its members to have sex and father a child against his will? Cohen had treated it as if it were a kind of nightmare that passes during the waking hours of the next day and is half forgotten. Now, forty-five years later, there was evidence that it was not a bad dream, but something very real. Real enough to have produced Keith, a forty-six-year-old man with a wife and child of his own. Mike had known Keith as a small child, yet he'd never seriously considered that he might be looking at his own son. Someone had once reassured him that Keith was the child of a guy outside of the group whom Helen had been dating at the time. This had helped him put it out of his head. But it was also true that he didn't want to know. "Who was I then?" he wondered. "And who am I now that I could have played with this little boy without realizing that he was my own child?"

While he was absorbing the news that he was Keith Newton's biological father, Cohen got an email from a third child of the group, who was also born in 1974—the child of Sue H., the older therapist whom he had helped conceive shortly before his miserable experience with Helen Moses. It had come about so casually and naturally that he hadn't thought of it often in the intervening forty-five years. Sue had asked for his help in getting pregnant, explained that there would be other men involved and there would be no responsibility on his part. It was a brief romance, and he'd kept a black-and-white photograph of the two of them, taken during the summer of 1973.

The hard part of the story was what happened next. After Sue had her child, Chris, she gave him up for adoption, to be raised by Jane Pearce. Sue H. had been a patient of Saul Newton's, and then he dropped her as a patient, which sent her into a panic. She was assigned to Dom Antonelli. Although she showed no signs of postpartum depression, the leadership decided that she and her child were "too placid," which they interpreted as a disturbing sign of lack of affect, a killing of emotion that would be stultifying to her child. At the time, Cohen hadn't thought too much about it. The senior therapists in the group were major authority figures in his life, and if they decided that she suffered from some form of postpartum depression, he assumed they must be right. Sue H. insisted that the decision to give up her child and give custody to Jane Pearce had been hers alone.

But after seeing the way they gaslighted his patient Deedee Agee and hearing Saul Newton brag about his ability to take children away from their mothers, Cohen now suspected that something of the kind had happened with Sue. They had threatened to take Deedee's son away because he was colicky, and they had taken Chris away from Sue because he was "too placid." In other words, it was a "heads I win, tails you lose" approach, in which the mother could never win: if a child cried, the mother was clearly unfit, and if the child didn't cry, it meant that the mother had transferred her silent depression to the child, squelching its natural vitality. Sue, as a true believer, had never complained to Cohen by saying something like "They took my baby away from me." But in retrospect, he knew it must have been traumatic for her—how could it not have been? After they took the child, the leadership had asked Cohen specifically to take her on a vacation to Cape Cod in order to take her mind off it. Sue later told Chris that after she gave him up to Jane Pearce for adoption, she had not wanted to see him again. Obviously, it was too painful.

Although Jane was the founder of the Sullivan Institute, by the mid-1970s she was already being marginalized. Saul Newton had moved on to Joan Harvey in the 1960s and was now with Helen Moses. They would soon all be living together in the new headquarters at Ninety-First Street. Mike Cohen thought that giving Jane this child might have been a sort of parting gift from Saul, a consolation prize for having been displaced in his affections and pushed out of her leadership role in the group she had cofounded.

In the wake of these revelations, memories long forgotten began coming back to Cohen. He had witnessed a few scenes from the early life of this child, whom he did not know was his. He would see Chris from time to time when he came to the group's headquarters, which were the leaders' residence. When the little boy was about five and Jane

Pearce was out of the group, the other children began to tease and haze him. Cohen heard them say things they had obviously been told by their parents: "The other kids would say, 'I've been told that your mother is a real bitch; that you shouldn't live with your mother, you should be leaving her. It would be better if you lived here.'" At one point Cohen heard Chris say to himself, "I shouldn't be with my mother," having internalized the cruel things he had been told. Eventually, Jane Pearce got wind of this and stopped the boy's Ninety-First Street playdates.

Thinking back to this painful scene, Cohen now realized that he had been watching his own child at two crucial points in his life: being taken from his mother and given up for adoption to someone else, and then hurt and bullied. But Cohen had done nothing, barely even registering what was happening as it was happening.

That child he had helped to conceive—who had been taken from his mother, who had been given to Jane Pearce to raise, and whom he had seen teased, bullied, and then taken from his best friends—was Chris Pearce, the man without a story. The child at the beginning of this book. Discovering his paternity at age forty-six was an important moment in Chris's lifelong quest to reconstruct the story that had been kept from him.

It was not until Chris was fifteen that Jane Pearce finally told him that he was the biological child of Sue H. It was not until he was twenty-five that he actually met her. It was a bittersweet encounter. Chris sensed that it meant something special for Sue to finally meet her own child, now a young adult. At the same time, she was evasive and defensive when he pressed her for details about his origins, insisting that she needed to protect the privacy of others. "I interrogated her for hours on numerous occasions," Chris recalled. "I was trying to figure out who my father was, and she never divulged much more than one inaccurate speculation. So I was left without a story."

Although the group had broken up several years before his first meeting with Sue H. in 1999, it was clear to Chris that his mother had remained a firm believer in the Sullivanian philosophy. She would not entertain the idea that she had been pressured into giving him up.

She chose to regard it as in her and her child's best interest that her therapist convinced her to give him up and assign his custody to Saul Newton's ex-wife. Sue H. had, after all, been a Sullivanian patient and therapist for almost her entire adult life, giving up her only child in order to respect its principles. To have gone against this now would have been, in effect, to admit that her entire life had been an enormous mistake.

As a highly intelligent and sensitive person, Chris understood this and accepted it. On an intellectual level, he found her to be a doctrinaire Sullivanian, but he sensed something unspoken happening simultaneously on an emotional level that felt more important: a sweet feeling of affection, tinged with regret, that she expressed at being reunited with her own and only child. What he felt was the thing that was not supposed to exist in the Sullivanian universe: maternal affection. Even though he was, in effect, a total stranger, there was an electrical current, an emotional bond that belied her rigid position that biology was unimportant, that giving him up for adoption had been the clinically sound thing to do. Yet she would never acknowledge those contradictions. "There must be a concrete wall in her head between her beliefs and her sense of connection to me," Chris said. "The contradiction must be so thick. Can I deal with that contradiction? Absolutely. But surprisingly, so can she."

"I think I've seen her at least once a year for the past twenty or twenty-five years," he said. "I think it's also wonderful and important for her. She might not even say it out loud. I don't even think she would tell me. But she has told me, you know—it's great for her to have this relationship with me."

What was harder for him to accept was Sue's continued reluctance—and the reluctance of others in his life—to explain more about his origins. "That's one of the things that makes me feel very much like an experiment, raised without my biological parents—like I'm the perfect experimental subject." It felt as if Sue and everyone else in a position to know thought that telling him about his birth would somehow throw off the experiment. "So every time I am responded to with silence—every time I am not given an answer—I am immediately brought back to that place where I am a 'control subject' again."

When Chris Pearce talks about not "having a story," he is talking about something much deeper than having a full life narrative. That he endured acts of extreme emotional violence—taken from his mother while still an infant; raised with a group of other children whom he regarded as his brothers and sisters and then being taken from them; being told that his adoptive mother was an unfit mother—which were all deeply scarring and formative events in his life. "Without anyone willing to talk about my story, without reliable memories from early childhood, I have always had to take full responsibility for my own depression, self-hatred, and inability to trust," he wrote to me in an email.

This left him with a series of powerful but fragmentary memories of his early years. He had been an unwitting participant in what turned out to be crucial moments in the life of the group. Conceived collectively as part of a different way of creating family, he was the first child in the group taken from his mother, given to the movement's founder to be raised as a kind of test baby, to demonstrate the correctness of her theories of development. He was raised for about five years in a more or less collective fashion, spending his days at Saul Newton's house, the group's new headquarters, playing with other kids whom he regarded essentially as his siblings. That feeling of closeness—small details like blueberry pancakes in the shape of Mickey Mouse that they used to eat together—are aching reminders of what is his own private paradise lost.

"Why was I removed from my brothers and sisters? Why was I raised alone when I had been part of such a big family? Why was I adopted? I was too young to remember the facts, but the emotional fallout has always been with me, and maybe always will [be]. Jane is implicated in keeping me in the dark as well. The blame for all these things has always been on me." The refusal of the adults in his life to talk to him about his origins, or about the events in his early life, left him to assume that everything that happened was somehow his fault. "No one from the group apologizes or takes ownership for how they treated each other and the children. I've never had anyone to blame, as everyone, aside from Jane, divested themselves of being responsible for me as a child. It has always been the situation that the adults who were responsible for me were blameless for my experiences growing up . . . Everyone is protecting themselves. Even Jane raised me to believe that all my emotional shortcomings and neuroses were solely my own responsibility . . . You can only imagine what I have believed about myself for the last forty years."

Chris also has a distinct memory of Saul Newton threatening to kill him by throwing him out of an upper window of their town house. Chris had messed up a Lego construction that Saul's daughter Pam had built, and Saul became apoplectic. "I have only one memory of Saul, a memory of him screaming at me and threatening to throw me out of a window—I think my first and last direct death threat. I remember this kind of blind fear of a monster of an adult . . . and I believed him, and I imagined what it would be like to be thrown out the window . . . That's my only memory of him."

He did not remember the incident Michael Cohen recalled of his being teased by the other children and told that Jane, whom by then he knew as his mother, was not a good mother and that he should not be living with her. Yet when he read about it in testimony Michael Cohen gave in 1989 (Cohen had forgotten the incident until I showed him his own testimony), it immediately rang an emotional bell. "My tragedy," Chris Pearce wrote in an email, "was in the abuse of my psyche, for instance in convincing me, when I was five, that my mother was incompetent—and then our ultimate rejection from the community . . . It's hard to explain, I don't have anything that I could call a memory. I do, however, have a compulsive fear of rejection by communities of all shapes and sizes, a fantastic fear that groups won't and don't like me and don't want to include me. I idolize and envy others' sense of belonging and sense of community, but I personally can't engage in that way. I am a good collaborator, but it is always frustrated by crippling anxiety in any group of peers or other adults."

Without knowing it, Chris Pearce had witnessed an important

moment in the life of the group: his own exile was because of Jane Pearce's banishment from the institute she had founded. The children of the leadership had mimicked their parents and used their language in turning against their good friend.

A few months after being cut off from his friends at Ninety-First Street, Chris witnessed a strange scene that he couldn't fully understand at the time. He is pretty sure it was shortly after Christmas, most likely in 1979 (according to his babysitter at the time). His adoptive sister, Sarah Newton, the eldest child of Jane Pearce and Saul Newton, who would have been twenty-nine (and was a training therapist in the group), appeared unexpectedly in his room, something he could not recall happening before or since. Equally unusual was the sudden appearance of Jane Pearce who, at sixty-four and not in great health, rarely climbed the stairs to the fourth floor. Suddenly Sarah and Jane began a fierce argument that devolved into a physical fight. A babysitter who was there at the time called Chris out of the room. Sarah left, and Chris remained with Jane, who had broken her wrist in the struggle with her daughter. Although Jane never explained this, Chris feels sure that Sarah had come to take him away. This supposition is supported independently by testimony Michael Cohen gave in 1989, when he related a conversation in which Saul Newton said that he wanted to find a way to get Chris back from Jane Pearce—as if the child were a kind of gift, like an engagement ring that could be reclaimed when the wedding was called off. (Sarah Newton confirmed the encounter but insisted that she knew nothing about any plans to take Chris away from Jane permanently, only that she was concerned that he was no longer allowed to spend time with his Ninety-First Street playmates. She also said that she thought her mother had broken a finger, not her wrist, in the fight they had.)

Jane Pearce, Chris perceived, was afraid of his being kidnapped. At one point she even sent him out of town for a stretch to stay with a former babysitter, a Black woman named Daisy, who had moved to Indiana. "I lived with this Black family in a ranch house in Indiana for what felt like forever but was maybe a week or a month. I was somewhere between six and ten years old. I learned to play Go Fish and drink coffee. Daisy gave me little cups of coffee with cream and sugar. I rarely drink coffee, but when I do, I have this kind of café au lait with sugar, the way she served it to me."

Again, these were fragmentary memories whose importance he felt—"I think about that trip at least once a month"—without fully understanding their meaning or having anyone explain them to him.

Chris has reestablished relationships with his sort-of siblings, Jane Pearce's three biological children—two of whom spent several years in the group—as well as with some of the other people from his early childhood. But on the whole, he has found these attempts frustrating. "No one wants anything to do with me unless I don't ask any questions . . . Everyone is protecting themselves . . . It has always been the situation that the adults who were responsible for me were blameless for my experiences growing up . . . Yet these same parents and therapists would never own or apologize for the interpersonal abuse children lived through under their watch, or even by their own hand. I imagine that owning those mistakes would equalize them with 'normal nuclear family parents.' I have always needed more than that: not only an apology, but I needed my abuse described to me. I needed someone to tell me my story because I was too young to catalog the politics."

Despite his unusual and often traumatic childhood, Chris was an extremely bright student and became an accomplished video animator as well as a college professor of video art. He and his partner have a child together.

When his childhood friend Keith Newton suggested that he do 23andMe along with other kids from the group, Chris jumped at the opportunity, which led to his discovery that Michael Cohen was his biological father.

This turned out to be a happy discovery for Chris Pearce. Cohen and Amy met Chris, his longtime partner, and their child. Like a dutiful grandfather, Cohen brought a present for Chris's son.

"Meeting Mike was wonderful," Chris said. "When I met Sue, I was confronted with how similar we are in appearance and personality, and I had the same experience with Mike. Honestly, I think they are both great people, now that I have gotten to know them more. It seems that all the shitty parts of my personality really do come from early childhood trauma and abuse as a living experiment in that community. It has been nice to see my intelligence and kindness and passions reflected in both of my biological parents. I think it would be a positive experience for anyone who was adopted: to meet your biological parents and have them both be kind and intelligent (despite what they did in their thirties)."

Learning more about his early life from Mike Cohen helped Chris Pearce fill in and rewrite parts of his personal narrative. "The stories have supported my assumptions that I didn't generate emotional memories of abuse from scratch out of my own imagination," he wrote to me. "They support my understanding that my core mistrust of the world, and my mistrust of most people in it, didn't come from my own corrupt soul, but was born validly from experiences of rejection that I was too young to remember . . . This shift in blame from my childhood self to the adults in the group releases me from some terrible feelings of self-blame and self-hatred." At the same time, better understanding of what happened to him during his childhood has filled him with greater anger toward the adults in his life when he was in the group, an understandable reaction that he hopes will not continue indefinitely. "I have been absolved of some self-hatred only to hate others. I see a long, slow path ahead."

After the initial shock of learning of his three biological children, Michael Cohen got used to the idea that these people who had been relative strangers were his children. "Do you have any more surprises?" his daughter Laura said to him at one point. Cohen checked around and began assembling a list of all the group's kids and their biological dads. He is pretty confident that everyone has been accounted for.

Initially, Mike experienced these revelations as a kind of renewed assault from an undead past he thought he had put behind him. Gradually he came to see them as something of an unexpected gift of life. All three of these individuals he helped bring into the world were appealing and interesting people. There was a special bond between him and them, even though it was not like the bond he had with Laura, whom he had raised.

When I first discussed these paternity revelations with him, one of the things that was most striking was that it had taken so long for him to become aware of the children he'd fathered. After all, in each case, he'd had sex with women who were ovulating and trying to conceive, who had become pregnant shortly afterward and given birth roughly nine months later. "Didn't it occur to you at the time, when these babies appeared on the scene, 'These might be my children?'" I asked.

"I know it sounds strange," he said, "but I really didn't."

When we saw each other a couple of weeks later, he said he had been brooding about it, troubled by his apparent blindness. "I was trying to answer your question, and I realized that I was alienated from my potential offspring," he said. These revelations had made him think carefully about the psychological operation that was at work in keeping him from seeing what was right in front of him. What does a person need to kill in himself, he asked, to be able to conceive a child without thinking and without feeling? It was a phenomenon of severe disassociation, a separation from a painful reality in order to cope with it. "Our relationship with family was disrupted at every level: adults from adult parents, adults from their own children, then adults from their own potential children. I had participated in these sperm pools—or whatever you want to call them. We were alienated from sex as part of an act of intimacy and love with another person. If you do that, it's easier to dissociate from the possible offspring of that act."

Finally, we talked about where moral responsibility lies in this whole story. "That's a very personal decision," Cohen said. "I have never forgiven myself for the things I've done. I did things that I think were harmful—I don't think they were evil, but that's just a semantic difference. They were harmful, and I've grappled with that for forty years. I've come to the point of forgiving pretty much everyone else—because they were in a situation not much different from mine. But the four leaders had the real power in the group. I don't know if they were evil, but I hold them responsible. No one was threatening them. I am not sure that there's anyone else . . . that if it weren't for the four of them, things would have gone in the same direction. I don't know if it's a question of power corrupting, whether they were like that before, but I don't care. It doesn't matter who they were before. That's who they became, and there's responsibility there." But even among the four, Cohen sees some differences. "I think Harvey really believed in this stuff. I think she was a zealot. Newton was more cynical about the whole thing. He told me many times, 'Hey, this is a great gig.' He was deeply conscious of the use and management of power." But judgments of others, Cohen said, are extremely difficult. "If there is one thing I've learned in life, it's that 99.9 percent of people attribute other people's flaws to bad character and their own to circumstance."

To the end of her life Deedee Agee struggled with some of the choices she had made. The DNA revelations that rocked former members upset members of her family as well, prompting heated discussions and attempts to understand and explain her early life. In a long unfinished fragment, she tried to make sense of the group's insemination practices that had destabilized her children's lives:

The whole countercultural stance then was that we had to invent new social forms for a new era. Where you came from was of no consequence, established morality was based on some sort of Victorian, anti-pleasure, anti-life world view that made no sense. We had the pill, we had abortion on demand, we had college educations that would enable us to live independently of men, we had control of our reproductive lives, and we had each other. Woodstock nation, instant community that trumped family . . . Women could have children and raise them without men—we had each other, a new community, a new family unencumbered by the ways of the patriarchy, by the old repressive forms we'd all grown up in ourselves and which had made our lives so difficult. We believed that we are all more alike than different, that nurture trumps nature every time, and it wasn't such a big leap to the notion that it was of no account who your biological father was, or whether you even knew who he was.

To those who told her, "Who cares what happened twenty-five years ago? Forget it!" she wrote: "The thing is, I don't believe that works. The past is alive in us always, all the more so when we try to ignore it or forget. It calls for attention like a phantom limb. Sometimes it's more real, more potent than the present."

Sources

Books

The most comprehensive book on the Sullivan Institute is Amy B. Siskind's *The Sullivan Institute/Fourth Wall Community: The Relationship of Radical Individualism and Authoritarianism*. Westport, Conn., 2003.

Valuable firsthand accounts of life inside the group are two self-published memoirs:

Graves, Alice. *Don't Tell Anyone: A Cult Memoir*. Self-pub., 2019.
Honan, Artie. *How Did a Smart Guy Like Me . . . : My 21 Years in Sullivanian Therapy and the Fourth Wall Theater Company*. Self-pub., 2020.

Autobiographical accounts of former members

Collins, Judy. *Sweet Judy Blue Eyes: My Life in Music*. New York, 2011.
Elman, Richard M. *Fredi & Shirl & the Kids: The Autobiography in Fables of Richard M. Elman*. New York, 1972.
Elman, Richard M. *Namedropping: Mostly Literary Memoirs*. Albany, N.Y., 1998.
Elman's unpublished writing about his experience in the group is in the papers of Richard Elman at Syracuse University.
Greenberg, Laura. *Memorizing Time*. New York, 2000.
Excerpts from Saul Newton's unpublished memoir are from Esther Newton's autobiography: Newton, Esther. *My Butch Career: A Memoir*. Durham, N.C., 2018.
A semifictional novel based on her family's experience: Cherney, Kaethe. *Happy as Larry: A New York Story of Cults, Crushes and Quaaludes*. Self-pub., 2018.

Other writings of former members

The unpublished papers of Deedee Agee.

Deedee Agee: A Retrospective. Cohasset, Mass.: South Shore Art Center, 2017. Exhibition catalog.

Agee's essay in *Bill Bollinger: The Retrospective.* New York: SculptureCenter, 2012. Exhibition catalog.

Mack, Jon. "Dreaming of Community: The Fourth Wall." *Reflections in a Cracked Glass* (blog), https://reflectionsinacrackedglass.com/introduction/the-search-for-community/dreaming-of-community/.

The central theoretical text of the Sullivan Institute: Pearce, Jane, and Saul Newton. *The Conditions of Human Growth.* New York, 1963.

Pearce, Jane, and Saul Newton. "Establishment Psychiatry—and a Radical Alternative." Unpublished paper that circulated at the Sullivan Institute, 1970.

Other important texts offering a similar radical critique of the family

Cooper, David. *The Death of the Family.* London, 1971.

Laing, R. D. *The Politics of Experience.* New York, 1967.

On Harry Stack Sullivan

On the history of the William Alanson White Institute: William Alanson White Institute of Psychiatry, Psychoanalysis & Psychology. "Our History." https://www.wawhite.org/about-us/our-history.

On the life of Harry Stack Sullivan: Perry, Helen Swick. *Psychiatrist of America: The Life of Harry Stack Sullivan.* Cambridge, Mass., 1982.

Blechner, Mark J. "The Gay Harry Stack Sullivan: Interactions Between His Life, Clinical Work, and Theory." *Contemporary Psychoanalysis* 41, no. 1 (January 2005).

Evans, F. Barton, III. *Harry Stack Sullivan: Interpersonal Theory and Psychotherapy.* New York, 1996.

Harned, Jon. "Harry Stack Sullivan and the Gay Psychoanalysis." *American Imago* 55, no. 3 (Fall 1998): 299–317.

Hegarty, Peter. "Harry Stack Sullivan and His Chums: Archive Fever in American Psychiatry?" *History of the Human Sciences* 18, no. 3 (2005): 35–53.

On the development and state of psychoanalysis in the United States in the 1950s: Herzog, Dagmar. *Cold War Freud: Psychoanalysis in an Age of Catastrophes.* Cambridge, U.K., 2017.

Rosenzweig, Saul. *The Historic Expedition to America (1909): Freud, Jung and Hall the King-Maker.* Seattle, 1992.

Time magazine cover stories on Sigmund Freud: October 27, 1924; June 26, 1939; April 23, 1956; November 29, 1993; March 29, 1999. Cover story on Carl Jung: February 14, 1955.

On the factionalism of psychoanalytic institutes and the dangers of charlatanism: Thompson, Clara. "A Study of the Emotional Climate of Psychoanalytic Institutes." *Psychiatry* 21, no. 1 (February 1958): 45–41.

On the nature of transference: Ferenczi, Sándor. "Confusion of the Tongues Between the Adults and the Child—(The Language of Tenderness and of Passion)." *International Journal of Psycho-Analysis* 30 (1949): 225–30.

On the involvement of Clement Greenberg with the Sullivan Institute

Gabriel, Mary. *Ninth Street Women: Lee Krasner, Elaine de Kooning, Grace Hartigan, Joan Mitchell, and Helen Frankenthaler: Five Painters and the Movement That Changed Modern Art*. New York, 2018.

Marquis, Alice Goldfarb. *Art Czar: The Rise and Fall of Clement Greenberg*. New York, 2006.

Naifeh, Steven, and Gregory Smith, *Jackson Pollock: An American Saga*. New York, 1998.

Rubenfeld, Florence. *Clement Greenberg: A Life*. New York, 1998.

On cults or high demand groups

Lifton, Robert Jay. *Losing Reality: On Cults, Cultism, and the Mindset of Political and Religious Zealotry*. New York, 2019.

Lifton, Robert Jay. *Thought Reform and the Psychology of Totalism: A Study of "Brainwashing" in China*. New York, 1969.

On psychotherapy cults: Temerlin, Maurice K., and Jane W. Temerlin. "Psychotherapy Cults: An Iatrogenic Perversion." *Psychotherapy: Theory, Research and Practice* 19, no. 2 (Summer 1982).

Court documents

Hoy v. Pappo and Bray v. Dobosh, April 1, 1986, State of New York, index n. 2903/86.

Bray v. Dobosh, April 21, 1986, State of New York, index n. 78613/85.

Sprecher v. Sprecher, State of New York, index n. 75207/85.

Court decision by Justice Frank J. Blangiardo, Bollinger v. Bollinger, May 4, 1976 (contained as an exhibit in Sprecher v. Sprecher).

Richard Ofshe interview with Paul Sprecher, December 30, 1988.

Richard Ofshe interview with Michael Cohen, December 31, 1988.

Richard Ofshe interview with Michael Bray, January 1, 1989.

Richard Ofshe interview with Amy Siskind, March 19, 1989.

On the financing of the group and its real estate: Joshua R. Klein v. Helen Moses, Joan Harvey et al., New York State Supreme Court, County of New York, index n. 18437-91. Mortgages that document the purchase and eventual sale of the Truck and Warehouse theater in the name of Joshua Klein were registered on July 8, 1981, and March 17, 1992.

On the building at 2643 Broadway: Carol Buck, Joshua Klein et al. v. 2643 Real Estate Corp, et al., Supreme Court of the State of New York, County of New York, index n. 31077-91, initial complaint filed November 13, 1991. Affidavits of Marice Pappo, John O., and Ann W., November 21, 1986, in Hoy v. Pappo, as well as in the affidavits of Paul Sprecher in Sprecher v. Sprecher.

On the physical abuse at the Treehaven school: State of Arizona v. Patricia deBoucher, no. 2 CA-CR 2556, Court of Appeals, Division 2, sentence November 24, 1982.

On the assertion of paternity by Paul Sprecher: New York State Supreme Court, County of New York, In the Matter of a Paternity Proceeding, Sprecher v. Miranti, index n. 26569/93.

On the Pearce family in Texas

The Austin-American Statesman: June 27, 1900; May 20, 1904; October 20, 1907; May 23, 1908; July 14, 1920; February 7, 1925; April 5, 1926; January 13, 1932; January 26, 1936; December 16, 1935; October 23, 1938; May 31, 1972; November 4, 1982; October 21, 1995.

On Edwin Pearce's archeological work: Pearce, James Edwin. *Tales That Dead Men Tell*. Austin, 1935.

On the disciplinary cases against Joan Harvey, Ralph Klein, Helen Moses, and Marc Rice

I have relied on:

New York State Education Department Office of Professional Discipline State Board for Psychology.

In the Matter of the Disciplinary Proceeding Against Joan Harvey, n. 10400.

In the Matter of the Disciplinary Proceeding Against Marc Rice, n. 10401.

In the Matter of the Disciplinary Proceeding Against Ralph Klein, Cal. no. 10402, July 17, 1991.

In the Matter of the Disciplinary Proceeding Against Helen Moses Fogarty, n. 12814.

Press accounts of the group

Black, David. "Totalitarian Therapy on the Upper West Side." *New York*, December 15, 1975.

Conason, Joe, with Ellen McGarrahan. "Escape from Utopia." *Village Voice*, April 22, 1986.

Henican, Ellis. "Dads Battle 'Cult' for Children: Lawsuit Penetrating a Shroud of Secrecy at Sullivan Institute." *Newsday*, May 31, 1988; April 8, 11, and 27, 1989; May 9, 1989; October 5, 1989.

Higgins, Lee. "Ex-Psychotherapy Sex Commune Leader Permitted to Practice Again." *Lohud*, September 6, 2014.

Hoban, Phoebe. "Psychodrama." *New York*, June 19, 1989.

Lewin, Tamar. "Custody Case Lifts Veil on a 'Psychotherapy Cult.'" *New York Times*, June 3, 1988.

Offenhartz, Jake. "Inside the Rise & Fall of a 1970s Upper West Side Cult." *Gothamist*, September 21, 2016.

Span, Paula. "Cult of Therapy Parents at War." *Washington Post*, July 27, 1988.

Author interviews

Chris Pearce, Michael Cohen, Carol Q., "Ellen Barrett," "Penelope Barrett," Michael Bray, Karen Bray, Jackie Bray, Andy Cates, Eddy Cates, Alice Elman-Goode, Mary Cherney, Kaethe Cherney, Artie Honan, Barbara Antmann, Donna Warshaw, Dick Wasley, Ellie Bernstein, Amy Siskind, Eric Grunin, "Rachel," Susan Crile, Laura Furman, Sarah Greenberg Morse, Marice Pappo, Chris H., Lauren Olitski Poster, Esther Newton, Paul Newton, Pamela Newton, Elsie Chandler, Elliot K., Sam Miller, Margaret Elman, Jody C., Margot C., John M., Catherine Hemenway, Jackie Gordon, Nathan Stockhamer, Ellen Beener, Mary Siedenstrang, Robert Putz, Pat Konecky, John Putz, Daniel Shaw, Lorna Goldberg, Bill Goldberg, Mildred Antonelli, David Black, "Sara," Janie P., Meghan Klein, Wendy Newton, Sean Mack, Steve Meshnick, Alice Graves, Richard Price, Brin McGee, Mary Michael Hill, Barbara Kane, Barbara Rose, Karen Wilkin, Lynnell Hancock.

Author interviews were supplemented by sworn affidavits, depositions, and court testimony by a wide range of former members, including Donna Warshaw, Amy Weinstein, Chris Hoy, Marice Pappo, Michael Cohen, Amy Siskind, Ann Wormser, John Owens, Jody C., Joan Harvey, Bonnie Bean, Joshua Klein, Michael Bray, Alice Dobosh, Paul Sprecher, Robert Putz, Pat Konecky, and Julia (Deedee) Agee, as well as by the lawyers Marshall Perlin and Martin Stolar.

Acknowledgments

I have never worked on a book in which I needed so much help. My greatest thanks are to the dozens of former Sullivan Institute patients who opened themselves to me with remarkable candor and generosity about parts of their lives that were often quite painful. And they were exceptionally patient when I came back to them repeatedly for more detail and fact-checking. They are listed in the Sources. Many other former members who are not quoted or listed—either for reasons of space or for a desire for anonymity—were equally important to this book. They gave me greater richness of detail and depth to my understanding of the nature of group life. A special thanks to Donna Warshaw and Ellie Bernstein.

My friend and colleague Marty Goldensohn worked closely with me when I began work, thinking it would become a podcast. Thilo Witter helped with early interviews; Maddy Crowell helped transcribe them. Heena Kauser, Isobel Thompson, Vicki Rudnitksy, and Catherine Chermayeff all read early drafts of the book. Rachel Rush, Jay Wickersham, Alice Wohl, and Lucy Stille provided extremely helpful feedback to subsequent drafts. (Rachel and Lucy should get medals for reading it twice.) From start to finish, I received invaluable editorial guidance and feedback at various times from Erika Fry and Livia Manera. Peggy Moorman kept me from making many fatal errors large and small.

Nicholas Patrick Osbourne provided me with an important final reading and external copyediting.

Jonathan Galassi at Farrar, Straus and Giroux deserves special thanks for insisting that I do this story as a book and for being its steadfast champion and reader from initial idea to finished book. Katharine Liptak did superb work in shepherding the book through the many phases of the publication process. Thank you to Maxine Bartow for a thorough and sensitive final copyedit and to Janet Renard for her careful and thoughtful proofreading, which contributed several small but important fixes to the manuscript.

Date Due

Cat. No. 23-233   Printed in U.S.A.

BRODART, C